PREFACE

My purpose in writing this book is grander than those of other "JCL book" authors. I did not set out to write a substitute IBM JCL manual. Instead, my goal was to provide you with the knowledge of MVS JCL that you need to meet your needs as a production applications programmer or end-user computerist and to excel in your career. This focus is something that you cannot readily get from a manual or any other single source. You will find that this book is a self-contained powerhouse unlike any other.

JCL is not an end in itself; it exists simply to make it possible to run programs of different kinds for different purposes. For many years it frustrated me as a programmer that JCL books presented details ad infinitum but never seemed to include the comprehensive examples or the consistent "thread" and practical guidance that you must have when you have actual work to do. I resolved to overcome this limitation of the technical literature, because my programming work and your programming work are too important to allow questions about JCL to stand in the way.

If you are a student or end-user learning programming in the IBM environment, you will find the approach in this book especially valuable. It was my intention to cut through the obsolete trivia that naturally accrue to any technical subject matter more than two decades old. Quite candidly it was a joy to do it. You will also find, as my present students do, that using JCL is a gratifying and rewarding experience when you can do it rapidly with contemporary focus. This is particularly the case when you see how JCL compares with software that you already know how to use on micros or minis and how JCL is now intertwined with TSO/ISPF.

WITH THANKS

I would like to thank Rich Guzik, Pat Heafey, Craig Happel, Jim Dunne, Frank Toth, Tom Vari, Tim Shinnick, Stan Niedzwiecki, Ron Stevens, Linda Meads, Luba Piarowski, Chuck Miller, Melba Smith, Greg Gaskill, John French, Sig Wiener, and the late LaVerne Breen of the Chicago Datacenter, whose work and JCL practices helped shape this book. The experiences of Wayne Bannister, Jerry Wasserman, Bill Cronin, Morris Broker, and Al MacMorries of the Los Angeles County Data Processing Department were also invaluable, as were the insights of Tom Grimes of the Harris Bank.

Dr. Helmut Epp, Steve Samuels, and several members of the staff of DePaul University were of great assistance in the development of this book. The IBM 4381 system provided by DePaul was used to develop many of the examples found here. Several students of DePaul's Computer Career Program, who represented knowledgeable newcomers to the IBM environment, contributed to the content with the questions and issues they raised during several courses in business data processing. Carol Zultner, Mary Murphy, Ivan Siap, and Nancy Blumenthal—four of the DePaul Computer Career Program's many successful graduates—helped in a special way by sharing their perceptions of beneficial topical content, contributing insights and perceptions that helped channel the treatment of many items into contemporary form.

I would also like to note special thanks to Dawne Tortorella, Director of Academic Computing Services of DePaul University, who provided support and assistance in the development of many illustrations. Dawne created a score of the diagrams and illustrations on an Apple MacIntosh and laser printer, and brought to bear not only technical expertise but an artistic hand as well.

Last but not least, I would like to extend my special thanks to Gary D. Brown, whose pioneering *System/360 JCL* of the early 1970s was instrumental in my own introduction to OS JCL.

James G. Janossy

Chicago, Illinois
March 1987

Practical MVS JCL
for Today's Programmers

Practical MVS JCL
for Today's Programmers

James G. Janossy
DePaul University

John Wiley & Sons
New York • Chichester • Brisbane • Toronto • Singapore

Library of Congress Cataloging in Publication Data:

Janossy, James G. (James Gustav), 1947-
  Practical MVS JCL for today's programmers.

  Bibliography: p.
  Includes index.
    1. MVS (Computer system) 2. Job Control Language
(Computer program language) I. Title.
QA76.6.J3623   1987   005.4′422   86-33951
ISBN 0-471-83648-6 (pbk.)

Printed in the United States of America

10 9 8 7 6 5 4 3 2 1

velis et remis

CONTENTS

PART I—ESSENTIAL MVS JCL

APPENDIX

Practical MVS JCL
for Today's Programmers

PART 1

ESSENTIAL MVS JCL

The three operating systems in common use on IBM mainframes are DOS (Disk Operating System), OS/MVS (Operating System/Multiple Virtual Storages), and VM (Virtual Machine). Each of these has its own unique human interface—its own job control language or JCL. This book is about MVS JCL; MVS and MVS/XA JCL are synonomous at the applications programming level. If you are studying or working in a business data processing environment equipped with IBM mainframes, it is likely that you will use MVS JCL, because MVS is IBM's centerpiece business data processing mainframe environment.

Regardless of the level of theoretical knowledge a person may have or the programming language one uses, the initial hurdle to be surmounted in using a machine is simply how to compile and run a program. In Chapter 1 we begin by focusing on how this is accomplished under MVS.

Learning what goes on in a mainframe compile and run, it becomes apparent that a special type of data set plays a significant role in connection with MVS. In Chapter 2 we examine several characteristics of this creation, the partitioned data set, or "PDS." Source code, JCL, and compiled program load modules themselves are stored in this form. We discuss how the PDS provides many of the same capabilities that exist in subdirectory structures under UNIX, DEC VAX VMS, and other minicomputer environments and on micros with MS-DOS. Although MVS does not support subdirectories, we will examine how the PDS accomplishes the same purpose.

What actually happens when a run is made? Chapter 3 illustrates what MVS does and provides in response to a run that invokes the IBM sort utility, then a nontrivial application program—one that produces outputs for a nontechnical user—and then a program that uses an internal sort and does reporting. The material here discusses the run in terms of its JCL "job stream," and provides detailed annotation of the JCL.

By the time you finish Chapters 1, 2, and 3 you will already know and understand quite a bit of MVS JCL. In the discussion that follows these chapters we expand the program executions illustrated in Chapter 3 until they become production MVS JCL. Although the latter chapters of this book each deal with individual aspects of advanced JCL, the examples depict a format, continuity, and consistency that you will find invaluable.

1

Compiling Programs

Regardless of your background, if you are a programmer who uses COBOL, PL/I, FORTRAN, assembler, or even fourth generation languages on a mainframe, you will be deeply involved in JCL to develop and test programs. Unlike the mini and microcomputer environments, MVS is not interactive. JCL provides the means to request MVS to perform program compilations and executions. Compilers, utility programs, and programs you have written are executed via job control language statements. Although it is possible to submit JCL to execute one program at a time, it is more common to compose JCL that specifies several program executions, one after another.

COMPILE, LINKAGE EDIT, AND RUN UNDER MVS

MVS provides no outright means of performing compile, linkage edit, and run processes in an interactive mode.[1] MVS is not "listening" to

3

your terminal at all—or to your keypunch. It is set to receive its work only from the "input queue," a figurative punched card hopper. The ancestors of MVS stem from the early "batch" days of business data processing when there was no such thing as interactive computing. There is no way of dealing with MVS except to compose "batch" files similar to DEC VAX "DCL" command files or IBM PC ".BAT" files. *This is precisely what JCL represents.*

Figure 1.1 is a diagram of the compile, linkage edit, and run processes, labeled for the IBM MVS environment. Figure 1.2 is a listing of the job control language that you might use to submit a file of COBOL source code to the compile, linkage edit, and run processes. This may seem

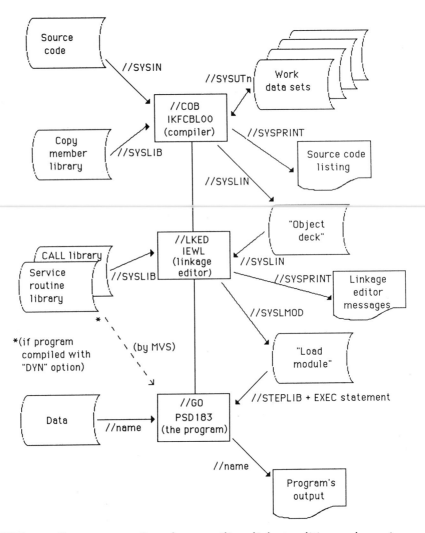

FIGURE 1.1. Program executions for compiling, linkage editing and running on an IBM mainframe under MVS

```
//FSBT686A  JOB AK00COMP,'DP2-JANOSSY',CLASS=E,MSGCLASS=X,           00010000
//  MSGLEVEL=(1,1),NOTIFY=BT05686                                    00020000
//*                                                                  00030000
//*     RAW COMPILE, LINK AND GO              'WHAT JCL DOES         00040000
//*     THIS JCL = BT05686.SOURCE.CNTL(RAWCLG)  'WHERE JCL IS        00050000
//*                                                                  00060000
//*****************************************************************  00070000
//*                                                              *   00080000
//*     EXECUTE COBOL COMPILER                          COB      *   00090000
//*                                                              *   00100000
//*****************************************************************  00110000
//COB       EXEC  PGM=IKFCBL00,PARM=('SXR,DMA,CLI,APOST',           00120000
//  'NOSEQ,NOADV,LIB,DYN')                                          00130000
//SYSLIB    DD  DSN=SYS1.COPYLIB,               '"COPY" SOURCE      00140000
//  DISP=SHR                                                        00150000
//SYSIN     DD  DSN=BT05686.SOURCE.COBOL(PSD183),  'SOURCE CODE     00160000
//  DISP=SHR                                                        00170000
//SYSUT1    DD  UNIT=SYSDA,SPACE=(460,(700,100))   'WORK SPACE      00180000
//SYSUT2    DD  UNIT=SYSDA,SPACE=(460,(700,100))   'WORK SPACE      00190000
//SYSUT3    DD  UNIT=SYSDA,SPACE=(460,(700,100))   'WORK SPACE      00200000
//SYSUT4    DD  UNIT=SYSDA,SPACE=(460,(700,100))   'WORK SPACE      00210000
//SYSPRINT  DD  SYSOUT=*                                            00220000
//SYSUDUMP  DD  SYSOUT=*                                            00230000
//SYSLIN    DD  DSN=&&LOADSET,                  'OBJECT FILE OUT    00240000
//  UNIT=SYSDA,                                                     00250000
//  DISP=(NEW,PASS,DELETE),                                         00260000
//  SPACE=(3200,(500,100))                                          00270000
//*                                                                 00280000
//*****************************************************************  00290000
//*                                                              *   00300000
//*     EXECUTE THE LINKAGE EDITOR                      LKED     *   00310000
//*                                                              *   00320000
//*****************************************************************  00330000
//LKED      EXEC  PGM=IEWL,PARM='LIST,XREF,LET',COND=(5,LT)         00340000
//SYSLIN    DD  DSN=&&LOADSET,                                      00350000
//  DISP=(OLD,DELETE)                           'OBJECT FILE IN     00360000
//SYSLMOD   DD  DSN=&&GOSET(GO),                                    00370000
//  UNIT=SYSDA,                                 'LOAD MODULE OUT    00380000
//  DISP=(NEW,PASS,DELETE),                                         00390000
//  SPACE=(TRK,(2,2,1),RLSE)                                        00400000
//SYSLIB    DD  DSN=SYS1.VSCOBLIB,              'SERVICE ROUTINES   00410000
//  DISP=SHR                                                        00420000
//SYSUT1    DD  UNIT=SYSDA,SPACE=(1024,(50,20))    'WORK FILE       00430000
//SYSPRINT  DD  SYSOUT=*                        'MESSAGES           00440000
//SYSUDUMP  DD  SYSOUT=*                        'ABEND DUMP         00450000
//*                                                                 00460000
//*****************************************************************  00470000
//*                                                              *   00480000
//*     EXECUTE THE NEW PROGRAM (GO RUN IT)             GO       *   00490000
//*                                                              *   00500000
//*****************************************************************  00510000
//GO        EXEC  PGM=GO,COND=(5,LT)                                00520000
//STEPLIB   DD  DSN=&&GOSET,                    'LOAD MODULE LIB    00530000
//  DISP=(OLD,DELETE)                                               00540000
//INDATA1   DD  DSN=BT05686.SOURCE.CNTL(STATEDAT),  'PGM'S INPUT    00550000
//  DISP=SHR                                                        00560000
//OTREPT1   DD  SYSOUT=*                        'PGM'S OUTPUT       00570000
//SYSOUT    DD  SYSOUT=*                        'DISPLAY MESSAGES   00580000
//SYSUDUMP  DD  SYSOUT=*                        'ABEND DUMP         00590000
//                                                                  00600000
```

FIGURE 1.2. MVS JCL for compile, linkage edit, and "go"

intimidating, but let's break it down into its three steps and then analyze each of them separately. Let's start by understanding just what we are looking at: the JCL is a file of lines that could be housed on punched cards or stored as card image, 80-byte records on tape or disk.

A given set of program executions expressed in JCL is called a "job stream." A job stream starts with a JOB statement that carries various identifiers and specifications and is followed by one or more program execution "steps." The job stream is ended with an empty JCL statement that contains only two slashes. In the distant past the punched cards that carried the job streams were actually placed, one job stream after another, into a card hopper and read into the computer. The JOB statements were usually punched on a different color card stock than the other JCL statements, so computer operators could easily separate one job stream from another. Job control language statements are now composed and stored on disk in card image form, but the input queue maintained by MVS still consists of job streams stored one after another, delimited by the JOB statement. The content of a JOB statement is specific to a given installation but its general nature is discussed in Appendix A.

IBM operating systems like DOS and MVS deal with JCL composed of 80-byte card image records. On a DEC VAX minicomputer system or even on an IBM-PC, command files are not fixed length records but are lines in text files, where carriage return/line feed characters delimit the end of one line and the beginning of another. The fact that IBM JCL was originally input on cards, and is still handled as a full 80-byte card image for each line, means that most JCL composition facilities such as TSO, the Time Sharing Option, or punched cards themselves still identify each JCL line by "card number," an optional value placed into positions 73 through 80 of each JCL line. TSO/ISPF can automatically apply these numbers. An executable JCL statement may span more than one card image line. When a JCL statement fits on one card image line, the terms JCL statement and JCL card are synonymous.

JCL to Execute the Compiler

In Figure 1.2, the first step of this IBM compile, linkage edit and run JCL starts at line 7 and ends on line 27. This is 21 lines altogether and seems like quite a lot. All it does is invoke the IBM COBOL compiler and feed it our source code. Why does it require so many statements?

Lines 7, 8, 9, 10, and 11 are all comments. We've made the comments stand out visually with borders of asterisks. Why asterisks? Each line of JCL begins with two slashes //. A comment line begins similarly, with an asterisk as the third character. In other words, //* makes a line of JCL a comment. So we just continue the stars to make a large box and the framed words stand out visually.

Line 12 is an EXECute statement. Its purpose is similar to the single line command entered on a DEC VAX or IBM-PC to invoke a compile or run another program. This line carries the name of the job step. For example, //COB could have been // followed by any eight-character name like //COMPILE, //MYSTEP1, or //DOIT. But for more than 20 years the standard compile JCL provided with MVS has carried a step name of //COB for the compile, //LKED for the linkage edit, and //GO for the run;

it is simply a tradition. After the step name the EXEC statement tells MVS to execute a program named IKFCBL00. Finally, it specifies that the parameter character string "SXR,DMA,CLI,APOST,NOSEQ, NOADV,LIB,DYN" is to be supplied to program IKFCBL00 when it begins execution.

The EXEC statement, except for the step name immediately following the slashes, does much the same thing that a RUN system command does on a smaller computer. It tells MVS to load the named program to memory and to transfer control to it. Assuming that the named program is coded to receive parameter information, like the compiler options indicated here, MVS supplies the parameters or "parms" to the program when it begins execution.

The IBM COBOL compiler is a program named IKFCBL00, a strange name; strange until you understand that IBM labels its system software with names prefixed with three letters that uniquely identify the product for message reporting purposes. IKF just happens to be the prefix chosen for the COBOL compiler error messages. The letters CBL in the name stand for—what else?—COBOL. The last two numbers allow IBM to use similar but unique names for various logic modules associated with the COBOL compiler.

The parameters that the IBM COBOL compiler can receive to "customize" its operation are similar in nature to the options that DEC, Microsoft COBOL, and other compilers may receive. Here is what these commonly chosen parameter options mean:

- SXR indicates that the compiler is to produce a sorted cross reference listing of all data items in the program, just like the one produced with the /CROSS_REFERENCE option on the VAX COBOL compiler.
- DMA requests the compiler to produce a printed "data map" or glossary of working storage in its output.
- CLI stands for "condensed listing" and carries a portion of the machine language generated for the program in summary form. This shows the location in the program of the first machine language instruction that results from each verb.
- APOST indicates that the compiler is to use the apostrophe as the literal framing character, not the quotation mark.[2]
- NOSEQ tells the compiler to forego sequence checking on COBOL line numbers.
- NOADV indicates that we are coding a position for the carriage control byte in our printlines, making them 133 bytes long.[3]
- LIB indicates that the data set designated as the //SYSLIB copy library is to be opened; if we didn't use COBOL COPY compiler directives in a program, we could save a small amount of compile time by coding "NOLIB" instead on the EXEC statement for the compile.

- DYN deals with actions that allow the program to initiate dynamically the loading of routines it CALLs at execution time, including COBOL service routines. This makes the load module smaller; CALLed routines need not be linkage edited into the load module in a static manner, as in most minicomputer and microcomputer environments.

If the EXEC statement at line 12 is analogous to RUN commands such as the VMS and MS-DOS compiler $ COBOL and A> COBOL invocations, what is all the material from line 14 through line 27? These lines equate the names coded after the ASSIGN phrase in SELECT/ASSIGN statements to physical files. In terms of PL/I this is where file names coded in I/O statements are equated to physical files. In terms of FORTRAN on an IBM mainframe "unit" numbers like 5 and 6 are equated here to physical files by association with symbolic names like //FT05F001 and //FT06F001. On a VAX or on a microcomputer you may have coded physical file names in the source code, in COBOL SELECT/ASSIGN statements. This is not done under MVS.

In lines like 14 through 27 requirements for system resources such as disk and tape are indicated to MVS; MVS allocates these resources to job steps based on detailed specifications coded here.

Data Definition (DD) Statements

Data definition or DD statements describe a data set and specify the input and output facilities needed for it. The names indicated at the left side of these statements, such as //SYSLIB on line 14, are symbolic file names that exist within the program being executed.

At the //COB step we are executing a program named IKFCBL00, the COBOL compiler, written by IBM support software personnel. At the DD statements here we see the names that those software authors chose to call the files with which this program, the compiler, deals. //SYSLIB is what the compiler authors associated with the file, or "data set" in MVS parlance, where copylib members are stored. For consistency these software authors chose to label all files read or written by the compiler with symbolic names starting with "SYS." This is a nice convention but it has no bearing on what the compiler does or how it does it; these symbolic names could just as easily have been assigned by the compiler authors as any other name of one to eight characters.

At line 14 we see a DD statement that is commonly referred to as a "DDcard." The name of the statement—//SYSLIB in this case—is a "DDname." This DD statement equates the compiler program's internally coded symbolic file name //SYSLIB with a data set on the computer system called SYS1.COPYLIB. We have to indicate that a data set name is contained on the line; we do so with the word DSNAME, abbreviated

DSN. The equal sign is required between this term and the actual data set name. SYS1.COPYLIB is a typical installation-defined name for the central library where all copylib members used in production programs are stored.[4]

The last two things on this DD statement are a "disposition" indication and a comment:

- DISPosition: Data sets already in existence on the computer system before the step is executed can be accessed by more than one job concurrently. "SHR" means that the data set can be shared with other jobs.

- The comment on line 14, following the apostrophe at the right, is ignored by the JCL interpreter because scanning of a line of JCL stops when a blank position is encountered in the *operative* portion of the statement. We could have started this comment just one space after the "SHR" but same-line comments are usually aligned to make JCL easier to read. There is no requirement to start a same-line comment with an apostrophe; this is simply a convention that helps to make comments stand out visually. *You cannot put blanks into the executable part of a line of JCL because a blank ends the executable part of a JCL statement. You can continue the statement with a comma.*

In line 16 we see another DD statement with a symbolic file name //SYSIN; it is a DDname used by many IBM compilers and utilities to denote the place where user-supplied source code or control statements are input. In this case we see a slightly different type of name after DSN =. We see a data set name, followed by parentheses enclosing another name. We have placed our source code in a special type of data set called a partitioned data set or "PDS," a file segmented into separate members. This statement continues to another line. Commas in prose indicate that "there's more to come after this pause." A comma at the end of the operative portion of a line of JCL says the same thing. Scanning of the line of JCL stops after this comma and we can still place a comment on the same line.

On lines 18 through 21 are four similar DD statements, each with a DDname of //SYSUT and a number 1, 2, 3, or 4. Other strange names? Perhaps it appears so, but another old IBM convention is to abbreviate OUT as UT and to name final or intermediate outputs with SYSUT. In this case these four data sets are work files used by the compiler. In Part 2 we discuss the development of the items on these lines and what they mean. For now it is enough to realize that for each work file required by a program like the compiler we have to supply an interface via JCL to resources on the computer system. For these data sets the resource has to be disk, as opposed to other forms of storage media such as tape, cards, or memory—and we must indicate how much disk space MVS must find and allocate to run the step. "SYSDA" stands for "system direct access" device and is one way to specify these resources, letting MVS choose an available disk to fulfill the request.

Compiler Listing Output

At line 22 we see a DD statement for an output that the compiler program wishes to write to a printer. //SYSPRINT is the IBM COBOL compiler's "output spigot" for the listing of input source code and compile messages. The records emerging at //SYSPRINT are 121-byte printline images. The first character of each record is a carriage control character.

On a VAX or PC the output listing of a program intended for placement on paper is written out as a text file; in other words, a stream of characters in which each line is ended with carriage return and line feed character. This file is readily "TYPEd" on a video screen or printer because these devices obey the carriage return/line feed characters in identical ways to return the cursor or print head leftward and advance to the next line.

On IBM mainframes print output consists of fixed or variable length records, not text file lines. These may be written to a data set with the appropriate specification of file characteristics for new files, or, as in the JCL in Figure 1.2, printlines can be turned directly over to a specialized part of MVS and "spooled" and printed without being written to a data set. We do this by coding SYSOUT-*class* where *class* is a specification that can dictate where and how the print will occur. In this JCL SYSOUT = * is coded to have each print output take the value of the MSGCLASS specification on the JOB statement as a convenience. SYSOUT = A is the customary print class and SYSOUT = X is the usual "held" class for print output to be viewed online via TSO, as described in Chapter 12. At this point you can picture SYSOUT = simply as the term for the system printer.[5] It and many other items have optional entries that are sometimes used for special circumstances, but SYSOUT = is most often used in the form shown here.

//SYSUDUMP, at line 23, is another print output from the step. It is a little unusual, however, in regard to the origin of the DDname. //SYSUDUMP is not a symbolic file name coded within a program. It is a data set written by MVS itself only if the program being run by a job step ends abnormally or "abends"—it blows up.

For example, if a program being executed attempts to divide a number by zero, do arithmetic on a field that does not contain numeric data, or has some other serious logic error, an abend will occur. The normal response of MVS is to issue a "system completion code" that indicates the nature of the problem, dump the program's memory area to paper, and then flush the job from the system.[6] The paper dump may be used for problem analysis and will be printed or stored in a data set as we specify on the //SYSUDUMP DD statement. If we omit this DD statement, MVS will provide the completion code value but not a dump in case of an abend in the step.[7]

Compiler Object File Output

The one remaining DD statement for the compile step of Figure 1.2 occurs on lines 24 through 27 and is the interface between the symbolic name for the compiler's output object file and disk storage resources. Let's examine the four lines of this DD statement and see what they mean:

- //SYSLIN is the symbolic name for the object file coded in the compiler program. Like //SYSLIB, //SYSIN, and //SYSUTn, this is a given; we didn't write the compiler program, and in the JCL to execute the compiler we must use the name coded by the authors of that software.

- The data set name, or DSN, of the newly created object file is &&LOADSET. This is a form different from the DSNs used earlier. Why? We're making use of a handy feature of MVS that allows the creation of "temporary" data sets.

     When we create a data set we can decide whether it will remain on the system after the end of execution of our series of job steps. If we code a name similar to that shown on line 14, the file will be "permanent" and may remain after our job finishes. If we code a name up to eight characters, prefaced by two ampersands &&, we identify the data set as temporary; it is to exist as long as our job is executing and will be eliminated by MVS at job end unless we, ourselves, eliminate it even sooner. Because the only purpose of the object file is to be read by the linkage editor and combined with other items into an executable load module, we want to see it disappear once the job ends. We then continue the DD statement with a comma after this name because we have more to specify.

- For a new data set we can specify a disposition of NEW. We can, however, also specify other aspects of the data set's disposition and we often do. In a format consistent throughout MVS JCL, when additional features of a specification exist, each is separated from the others by a comma. The whole set of specifications is enclosed in parentheses. The commas define positions within the string of specifications and the items are technically known as "positional":

```
DISP=(NEW,PASS,DELETE)
```

The NEW is the status of the data set at the time that the step begins execution. PASS occupies the "subparameter" position that indicates data set disposition at the end of the step. PASS means that we wish to speed access to the data set by a subsequent job step by having MVS retain information about it. Instead of PASS this may be coded as KEEP, the meaning readily apparent, CATLG, for "keep the data set and record information about it in a system catalog," or DELETE.

DELETE, the third DISPositional positional subparameter in this statement, is what we wish to have happen to the data set if the program we are executing abends. Although it is unlikely that the compiler will abend, to MVS the compiler is just a program like any other; MVS treats all programs the same, no matter who wrote them or what task they perform.

- Again, as we did for the compiler's work data sets, we must specify how much disk space is to be allocated to this step by MVS. Disk space specification is discussed in detail in Chapter 8; this is a task imposed on the writer of JCL.

Linkage Editing

The linkage edit step named //LKED executes a program named IEWL. This is another unusual name. Its first three letters relate to its normal and error messages; L, the remaining character in the name, stands for what? "Linkage editor," a standard routine that combines the object data set from the compiler with machine language code for input/output and other tasks to create an executable "load module."

Each jobstep sets a "condition code" value maintained by MVS. A value of zero means successful execution. A step can check the condition code of any or all preceding steps and, based on the outcome of these tests, can be made to execute or not execute. The COND specifications in the //LKED step and the //GO step are tests for these values, to withhold execution of the linkage edit if the compile failed or withhold execution of the new program at the //GO step if the compile or linkage edit failed. We cover COND thoroughly in Chapter 14.

MVS load modules must be housed in partitioned data sets; they cannot be freestanding files. That is why //SYSLMOD, for Load MODule, is written out as a member of a temporary data set defined as a partitioned data set. How is a partitioned data set specified? It's a function of the space allocation that we discuss in Chapters 2 and 8.

//SYSLIB at the linkage editor step is associated with the partitioned data set or "library" in which the machine language input/output logic and other service routines common to COBOL programs are stored. Although this DDname is the same as the copy library DDname for the compiler, it is purely a coincidence and the two libraries have nothing to do with one another.

The //GO Step

//GO is the "run" step of this compile, link, and go JCL. It is here that the program is actually loaded by MVS to memory and given control. Our program is treated exactly the same as the compiler program, the linkage editor program, or any other program; we name it on an EXEC card in order to run it.

//STEPLIB tells MVS from where to load our program; namely, the partitioned data set named &&GOSET that we created earlier housing the load module produced by the linkage editor. &&GOSET is a needlessly strange name; we use clearer temporary and permanent data set names in other examples.[8]

//INDATA1 and OTREPT1: Because our program specified an input file with the symbolic name //INDATA1 and an output file symbolically named //OTREPT1, we code these as DDnames and place appropriate data set interface information on each DD statement.[9] These names match the SELECT/ASSIGN statements in the program:

```
SELECT DATAFILE   ASSIGN TO UT-S-INDATA1.
SELECT REPORT1    ASSIGN TO UT-S-OTREPT1.
```

DDnames of our own making appear in the JCL to connect with physical data sets and MVS system resources. In COBOL programs the trailing portion of the "assign to" name can be eight characters long and becomes the DDname for the matching DD statement. In FORTRAN programs, which do not require statements analogous to SELECT/ASSIGN, the nature of the names is predetermined and only one part of the DDname, which matches the input/output unit number, is subject to change.

//SYSOUT, where any DISPLAYed items are written, is a DDname that the COBOL compiler gives us "free." This DDname should be coded for all COBOL programs.

//SYSUDUMP occurs again in this step, as it did in the linkage edit, if we wish to obtain a memory dump in case of an abend.

If you have developed compiled programs under UNIX, on a VAX, or in the PC environment, you will no doubt see the similarities in this process between such an environment and that of MVS. No terminal session is in effect, however, when your batch compile runs on an IBM mainframe under MVS. Where is the association of symbolic file names to actual data sets going to be established if not in the JCL running the job? JCL navigates a job through a maze of mainframe resources, telling MVS the things it needs to know about each step to allow it to be handled expeditiously and concurrently with the use of system resources by other jobs.

COMPILE AND LINKAGE EDIT, DESTINATION: LOAD MODULE LIBRARY

In the compile, linkage edit, and run job stream of Figures 1.1 and 1.2 our goal was to transform source code into an executable form and then run it. In the mainframe environment programmers may at times compile, linkage edit, and run all in one job stream. But it is more common to compile and linkage edit only and to direct that the load module created by the linkage editor be placed in a permanent load module library. In Chapter 2 we take a close look at the form of data set organization that is used to house load modules. This form of data set, called a partitioned data set, or PDS, also has relevance to the storage of source code and job control statements themselves.

Many different partitioned data sets typically exist on a mainframe. Each programmer usually has a few PDSs to serve as libraries that contain JCL, program source code, and perhaps other items such as text. The installation also provides several other PDS libraries for common use.

A PDS library normally found in a mainframe business data processing installation is a load module library that may be called SYS1.TESTLIB. Another similar library may be called SYS1.PRODLIB. "Testlib" is a partitioned data set that holds the load modules resulting from programmer compiles and linkage edits. "Prodlib" is a PDS in which authorized production program load modules are housed and from which production jobs are run. SYS1.LINKLIB is a "default" load module library in which system support software such as compilers, the assembler, and utilities are housed. It and possibly other PDSs are the load module libraries searched for the program to be executed if no //STEPLIB statement is specified in a step.

Individual students or programmers may at times have their own load module libraries. A partitioned data set may be allocated by using TSO/ISPF function 3.2 or by a simple one-time execution of a job with the appropriate specifications. *Working with Partitioned Data Sets* in Chapter 2 illustrates the job control language for the allocation process. Load modules can be added to an established library with a compile and linkage edit shown in Figure 1.3.

COMPILE AND LINK JCL

Figure 1.3 is a listing of JCL similar to that in Figure 1.2, except that the third step—the run step—has been lopped off. The data set name associated with the //SYSLMOD DDname of the linkage editor has been changed to indicate a permanent load module library as the destination of the load module. In this example BT05686.TEST.LOADMODS is an

```
//FSBT686A  JOB AK00COMP,'DP2-JANOSSY',CLASS=E,MSGCLASS=X,           00010000
//  MSGLEVEL=(1,1),NOTIFY=BT05686                                    00020000
//*                                                                  00030000
//*    RAW COMPILE AND LINK ONLY                    'WHAT JCL DOES   00040000
//*    THIS JCL = BT05686.SOURCE.CNTL(RAWCL)        'WHERE JCL IS    00050000
//*                                                                  00060000
//******************************************************************  00070000
//*                                                            *     00080000
//*      EXECUTE COBOL COMPILER                        COB     *     00090000
//*                                                            *     00100000
//******************************************************************  00110000
//COB     EXEC  PGM=IKFCBL00,PARM=('SXR,DMA,CLI,APOST',              00120000
//  'NOSEQ,NOADV,LIB,DYN')                                           00130000
//SYSLIB     DD  DSN=SYS1.COPYLIB,                   '"COPY" SOURCE  00140000
//  DISP=SHR                                                         00150000
//SYSIN      DD  DSN=BT05686.SOURCE.COBOL(PSD183),   'SOURCE CODE    00160000
//  DISP=SHR                                                         00170000
//SYSUT1     DD  UNIT=SYSDA,SPACE=(460,(700,100))    'WORK SPACE     00180000
//SYSUT2     DD  UNIT=SYSDA,SPACE=(460,(700,100))    'WORK SPACE     00190000
//SYSUT3     DD  UNIT=SYSDA,SPACE=(460,(700,100))    'WORK SPACE     00200000
//SYSUT4     DD  UNIT=SYSDA,SPACE=(460,(700,100))    'WORK SPACE     00210000
//SYSPRINT   DD  SYSOUT=*                                            00220000
//SYSUDUMP   DD  SYSOUT=*                                            00230000
//SYSLIN     DD  DSN=&&LOADSET,                      'OBJECT FILE OUT 00240000
//  UNIT=SYSDA,                                                      00250000
//  DISP=(NEW,PASS,DELETE),                                          00260000
//  SPACE=(3200,(500,100))                                           00270000
//*                                                                  00280000
//******************************************************************  00290000
//*                                                            *     00300000
//*      EXECUTE THE LINKAGE EDITOR                     LKED    *     00310000
//*                                                            *     00320000
//******************************************************************  00330000
//LKED     EXEC  PGM=IEWL,PARM='LIST,XREF,LET',COND=(5,LT)           00340000
//SYSLIN     DD  DSN=&&LOADSET,                                      00350000
//  DISP=(OLD,DELETE)                                'OBJECT FILE IN 00360000
//SYSLMOD    DD  DSN=BT05686.TEST.LOADMODS(PSD183),  'LOAD MODULE OUT 00370000
//  DISP=SHR                                                         00380000
//SYSLIB     DD  DSN=SYS1.VSCOBLIB,                  'SERVICE ROUTINES 00410000
//  DISP=SHR                                                         00420000
//SYSUT1     DD  UNIT=SYSDA,SPACE=(1024,(50,20))     'WORK FILE      00430000
//SYSPRINT   DD  SYSOUT=*                            'MESSAGES       00440000
//SYSUDUMP   DD  SYSOUT=*                            'ABEND DUMP     00450000
//                                                                   00460000
```

FIGURE 1.3. MVS JCL for compile and linkage edit, creating permanent load module

existing cataloged partitioned data set, so we can eliminate some of the parameters associated with this output; we do not have to specify the device or a space figure for an existing data set. Adding a member to an existing partitioned data set does not involve allocating more space because the space for the data set was allocated when the data set was created.

Once a program has been successfully compiled and its load module placed into a permanent load module library the program can be run. Repeated runs of the program do not require compilation and linkage editing unless the source code must be changed. Figure 1.4 is a listing of the JCL that could be used to execute the load module named PSD183 in partitioned data set BT05686.TEST.LOADMODS. This run is a free-standing, one-step job in itself, complete with its own job statement. If other programs were to be executed before and after PSD183, our JCL would contain several steps, each with an EXEC statement, to invoke

```
EDIT --- BT05686.SOURCE.CNTL(RAWGO) - 01.01 ----------------- COLUMNS 007 078
COMMAND ===>  SUB                                        SCROLL ===> HALF
***** *************************** TOP OF DATA ***************************
000100 //FSBT686A  JOB AK00COMP,'DP2-JANOSSY',CLASS=E,MSGCLASS=X,
000200 //  MSGLEVEL=(1,1),NOTIFY=BT05686
000300 //*
000400 //*    PROGRAM EXECUTION                          'WHAT JCL DOES
000500 //*    THIS JCL = BT05686.SOURCE.CNTL(RAWGO)      'WHERE JCL IS
000600 //*
004700 //********************************************************************
004800 //*                                                                 *
004900 //*    EXECUTE THE NEW PROGRAM (GO RUN IT)                    GO    *
005000 //*                                                                 *
005100 //********************************************************************
005200 //GO        EXEC  PGM=PSD183
005300 //STEPLIB   DD  DSN=BT05686.TEST.LOADMODS,        'LOAD MODULE LIB
005400 //  DISP=SHR                                      '<=== NOTE SHR!
005500 //INDATA1   DD  DSN=BT05686.SOURCE.CNTL(STATEDAT), 'PGM'S INPUT
005600 //  DISP=SHR
005700 //OTREPT1   DD  SYSOUT=*                          'PGM'S OUTPUT
005800 //SYSOUT    DD  SYSOUT=*                          'DISPLAY MESSAGES
005900 //SYSUDUMP  DD  SYSOUT=*                          'ABEND DUMP
006000 //
```

FIGURE 1.4.   MVS JCL to execute an already-existing load module

each program load module one after another. This is how production
job streams are structured and the reason that JCL exists.

Figures 1.2, 1.3, and 1.4 illustrate what is referred to as "raw" JCL.
Chapter 16, which deals with cataloged procedures, illustrates how raw
JCL may be "packaged" into a form that can be placed in a special JCL
library. When so packaged without a job card, with no ending null //
statement, and perhaps with symbolic parameters that can be given values externally, the JCL represents a procedure that any programmer can
invoke without having to compose all of the JCL involved.

Most installations provide cataloged procedures for a test compile
without linkage edit, a compile and link edit, and a compile, link edit,
and go. In the contemporary IBM MVS environment these procedures
are named VSCOBC, VSCOBCL, and VSCOBCLG or VSCOBCG.[10] Each
is a different member of a partitioned data set customarily called
SYS1.PROCLIB; IBM provides standard versions of these procedures,
or "procs," but a given installation will often create its own, customized
to specific local conventions, compiler options, libraries, and source code
management practices.

It is important to use the cataloged procedures provided by the installation for program compilation and linkage editing. Often the compilation procs used are intertwined with security software also in use,
with a source code library, with a data dictionary or database, or with
all of these things. Jump ahead to Chapter 16 and browse it if you are
anxious to learn compile and linkage edit cataloged procedures.

REVIEW QUESTIONS AND (*)EXERCISES

1. What primary purpose do DD statements serve?

2. What does a mainframe compiler output in the "object deck" and what does the linkage editor do with it?

3. Describe the differences and similarities between source code, object module, and program load module and indicate which of these is usually retained after a compile, linkage edit, and run.

*4. Obtain a JOB statement valid for your installation and identify the various items of information on it using Appendix A. Tailor the job statement to your own purposes and complete the TSO/ISPF setup areas for hardcopy print found at the bottom of the TSO/ISPF 0.2 and 3.6 screens; take care to specify MSGCLASS = A within the job card on these screens. Enter the job card into a member of your CNTL library for compile, linkage edit, and JCL runs; enter MSGCLASS = X on the job statement for these runs to be able to see your output online using TSO/ISPF.

*5. Enter the JCL for the compile, linkage edit, and go shown in Figure 1.2 into your CNTL data set. Using a job statement valid for your installation, submit this job stream specifying some COBOL program source code at line 16.[9] Examine the results and MVS system outputs.

*6. Use the compile, linkage edit, and go JCL shown in Figure 1.2 to process a set of COBOL source code that contains no errors. Then intentionally introduce an error into the source code to force an abend in the //GO step and run the job stream again. This can be done by leaving a counter unitialized, thus causing an 0C7 "data exception." Change the compiler PARM options to include

```
FLOW=30,COUNT,STATE
```

to activate several COBOL compiler abend debugging aids. Process the intentionally flawed source code and compare the results with the first run.

*7. Use TSO/ISPF function 3.2 or the JCL shown in *Working With Partitioned Data Sets* in Chapter 2 to allocate a load module library for yourself. Then split the RAWCLG JCL of Figure 1.2 into two separate job streams: one that contains the //COB and //LKED steps and one that contains the //GO step. Modify the first of these so that the //LKED step //SYSLMOD DD statement cites your load module library in place of &&GOSET, carries DISP = SHR, and no UNIT or SPACE parameters. Run that job stream to create a load module for a COBOL program. Modify your second job stream, which contains only the //GO step, so that //STEPLIB cites your load module library and DISP = SHR, not DISP = (OLD,DELETE). Run the second job stream after the first and compare the execution of a permanent load module with the compile, linkage edit, and go of a program.

*8. Examine the output produced by the VSCOBOL compiler and find the page that states the compiler PARM options in effect for the run. Match these with the options specified in the EXEC statement for the compiler.

*9. Perform a compile, linkage edit, and run omitting completely the PARM phrase from the EXEC statement in the //COB step. Examine the compiler's output page that states the PARM options in effect and indicate what the defaults are in your installation for SXR, DMA, APOST/QUOTE, SEQ, ADV, LIB, and DYN.

*10. Compile, linkage edit, and run a FORTRAN program with the installation FORTCLG proc or other local standard FORTRAN proc. Examine the steps in the JCL that are drawn in from the procedure library and note the name of the linkage editor program. Describe why the same linkage editor can be used to process the object modules of programs written in different languages.

NOTES

1. Some program development tools and environments, such as TSO, the Time Sharing Option, provide interactive "foreground" compiles but these are a separate development from MVS and JCL. Foreground TSO work is not in the mainstream and is outside the scope of this discussion.

2. An inconsistency exists between the ASCII world and the IBM world concerning the framing of literal strings within programs and in JCL. In plain English a literal string is begun and ended with the double quote mark, shown here in parentheses ("). In IBM mainframe software literal strings are more commonly begun and ended with the single quote mark, more commonly called the apostrophe. The APOST/QUOTE COBOL compiler PARM option allows explicit control over a compile to indicate the framing character used in the source code. Use of APOST is recommended to maintain consistency between source code and JCL.

   The string delimitation anomaly carries over into MVS JCL in the framing of the characters that make up the parameters being input to a program. The apostrophe is used in various other places in JCL in connection with circumstances recognized as analogous to the framing of a literal string. There is no machine-specific basis for the use of the apostrophe by IBM instead of the quote mark. Neither is there an option in the syntax of JCL to allow the use of the quote instead of the apostrophe.

3. VSCOBOL has two different modes of placing the carriage control byte into printlines when AFTER ADVANCING is used. These modes are governed by the compiler "ADV" PARM:

ADV: When ADV is in effect, printlines are coded as 132 bytes in the FD for a print file and the compiler prefixes the 132 bytes with the carriage control byte, writing a 133-byte record. If these printlines are to be stored on disk or tape instead of printed, not understanding how the ADV option works often results in mysterious system abends with the system completion code of 013-20 because the record actually output by the program is one byte bigger than it appears from the coding in the FD.

NOADV: With NOADV as the PARM option, the compiler places the carriage control character into the first byte of the area defined as the print record in the FD, which must be coded as 133 bytes for a full-size printline. With NOADV, stored printlines are the length coded in the FD.

4. SYS1.COPYLIB is a partitioned data set that contains copy library members. The name that appears after a COPY compiler directive in a COBOL program is the member name. This name can be up to eight characters in length. For example, the statement COPY LFWSTDP1 in a program will seek the material at SYS1.COPYLIB(LFWSTDP1), assuming that the installation follows the common convention for naming its copy library PDS in this manner.

5. Because of an unfortunate coincidence in JCL terms, confusion can easily ensue with certain print output. The //SYSOUT DDname to which COBOL programs write DISPLAY output and to which many utilities direct housekeeping output messages is not inherently connected with the SYSOUT= that indicates the system printing facility. //SYSOUT could easily have been named anything else within the COBOL compiler. The fact that the //SYSOUT output of a program or utility is often directed to SYSOUT= may imply some sort of coupling between these items, but it exists only in the eye of the beholder. //SYSOUT can be directed to a disk or tape data set as well.

6. The MVS system completion codes are three-character values expressed in hexadecimal. More than 480 different system completion code values exist; their documentation is spread among several large IBM manuals. Appendix F lists and explains those most commonly encountered.

7. //SYSUDUMP is one way of getting the memory dump. It provides printlines output by MVS, which can be given directly over to the system printer, as illustrated in this JCL. //SYSABEND, if specified, causes a much larger dump to appear for an abend that includes not only the program's memory area but significant portions of the memory used by the MVS "nucleus" itself. The //SYSABEND dump is not normally useful to applications programmers and a DD statement with this DDname should not be coded. If both //SYSUDUMP and //SYSABEND are coded in a job step and it abends, only the last one in the step is used; the first of the two is ignored.

   Unless you actually know how to read a dump, you can omit both //SYSUDUMP and //SYSABEND DD statements. The COBOL compiler STATE, FLOW, and SYMDMP or "symbolic dump" options, the JCL for which is illustrated in items 1 and 2 in Chapter 17, are much more helpful in debugging new or modified programs.

8. The load module in this compile, link, and run JCL is named "GO" and it is housed as a member in the temporary partitioned data set &&GOSET. This is potentially confusing. Adding to the fog is the fact that the name for the run step is //GO. This JCL follows IBM's decades-old example of a compile, link, and run job stream. The JCL shown here could be altered readily to exhibit less cryptic and confusing names, but it purposely matches the original to prevent newcomers from snagging on a cosmetic difference between the example and what they may encounter in a school or installation. The temporary PDS name does not have to be &&GOSET; it can be

any name up to eight characters long, prefaced by two ampersands, such as &&TEMPLMOD. The load module within this PDS can have any name up to eight characters long, such as (ANEWPROG). And the name of the step could be something like //STEPC, //DOIT, or //BLASTOFF. The shortness of the step name //GO provides a minor convenience when the JCL is "canned" as a cataloged procedure. As Chapter 16 illustrates, this step name must preface the regular DDname on DD statements for data sets used by a program that is being processed by a compile, link, and go "proc."

9. The COBOL program used in this example is the focus of Chapter 4 of *Commercial Software Engineering: For Productive Program Design*, James G. Janossy, ISBN 0-471-81576-4, John Wiley and Sons, Inc., 1985. The book provides the complete specifications, design considerations, and source code for this and several other programs executed under MVS. The source code and test data are also available on a diskette you can obtain as indicated in Appendix D.

10. In an earlier version of COBOL the standard procs were named COBUC, COBUCL, and COBUCLG, or COBUCG, for compile, compile and linkage edit, and compile, linkage edit, and go. These and the VSCOBOL procs are very similar. The difference between the two variations of the third proc in each group lies in the fact that IBM supplies a "loader" program that is slightly more efficient for a direct compile, load and go operation. A loader combines the functions of the linkage editor and the EXEC statement. The VSCOBCG proc invokes the compiler, and if the compile is successful the object module is given to the loader. The loader link edits the object module to create a load module, writes it to memory instead of outputting it to a PDS member, and then passes control to the first executable statement in the program. The loader is not often used in the production environment because programs are nearly always stored in load module form and are recompiled only when modifications are made.

2

Information Storage and the Partitioned Data Set

Each character or byte of machine-processed information is made up of a quantity of binary digits, or "bits." Individual bytes of information are grouped into designated "fields" that make up "records," and records are stored in files. When this is done, the storage is said to be record oriented. In many ways record oriented storage resembles the punched card information storage of older times in which one card column represented one byte of information, groups of columns represented fields, and one card alone represented a record. MVS and its predecessors deal with this record oriented view of the world.

On the other hand, information fields may not exist within fixed format records but simply reside in a stream of characters, each line of characters delimited by special bytes such as carriage return and line feed. When data are handled in this form they are said to be in stream or text file format. Data in this form can be fed to a communications terminal or printing device. The delimiting end of line characters will cause the device to return the carriage to the left and move to the next line to place the information properly on a screen or paper.

The interactive minicomputer and microcomputer environments are heavily oriented to stream data transmission and text file information storage. The MVS mainframe environment deals almost exclusively with record oriented information storage. *Many of the features provided by MVS JCL exist primarily to meet the requirements of a record oriented storage approach.* Using these features is easier if you keep in mind the different orientations of the mainframe and other environments.

PROGRAM AND JCL STATEMENTS AS RECORDS

In older times source code, JCL, and even data records were actually prepared with an honest-to-goodness keypunch. In the contemporary world mainframe source code and JCL are prepared on an online programming terminal that communicates with software like TSO/ISPF, the time sharing option; data are often captured online with custom programmed, formatted screens to create records not limited to the 80 bytes of a punched card.

TSO/ISPF is certainly much more capable than a keypunch, but in terms of the storage of program source code and JCL statements the result of preparation is the same. Lines of JCL and source code are stored as 80-byte records. Every statement is a full 80 bytes long, even if it is completely blank; there is no line feed/carriage return to denote the end of a line. There is no such thing as a variable length punched card; a completely unpunched card is 80 bytes of—what else?—spaces. Physical cards, of course, are no longer handled by most installations; instead, the same information, byte for byte, now exists on magnetic storage media such as disk or tape, in "card image" form. All 80 bytes of each card are present without the bulk of card stock.

Understanding the difference between text file and record oriented storage is not difficult, but it should be recognized that *nearly every reference work you are likely to encounter in the IBM mainframe environment will assume record oriented storage for files—the files that contain source code, JCL statements, and data.* On the other hand, *books, compilers, and word processors in the minicomputer or microcomputer environments assume text file storage, as do many non-IBM mainframes.* These assumptions have a bearing on how disk space for files is controlled and allocated in each environment. They have ramifications for the mechanisms developed to optimize file storage and the passage of data between programs and devices. They affect the steps needed to output data and control formatting of print and have a significant bearing on several aspects of mainframe teleprocessing functions.

STORAGE OF FILES

Files are known as "data sets" in the IBM mainframe environment and are collections of records. Files—data sets—exist in great profusion in all environments. How do we house, organize, access, secure from access, and otherwise manage them? This is a central issue addressed by a large portion of any operating system.

The Digital Equipment Corporation VAX is typical of interactive, shared-usage minicomputers that support many active terminal users at one time. Each user may have one or more "accounts" or identifiers capable of creating and owning files. On a system such as the VAX each account has its own directory, which is a file that contains information about other files, similar in function to a table of contents.

On single-user micros that use MS-DOS or CP/M the function of the diskette media physical directory is merged with an "account" function. The micro is a simple subset of a minicomputer; the inventory of files on a given unit of disk media is managed by the diskette or hard disk directory.

MVS does not store files in the same way as the VAX's VMS, UNIX, or MS-DOS. When a mainframe data set is created, it is not "owned" by any account or directory—it has an identity of its own, unrelated to any particular party, physical device, or item of storage media. *MVS data set name does not include device name.* A data set must, of course, exist on specific media mounted on a device, and if that media is disk the identity of the data set will be known to the individual disk's own housekeeping entries, called a "volume table of contents" or VTOC.[1] The VTOC exists for the purpose of managing the available and in-use space on a mainframe disk, and it serves the same purpose as the directory and file allocation table on a floppy diskette under MS-DOS.

Under MVS the identity of a data set and the serial number of the media on which it resides may optionally be recorded in a system-wide "catalog." This catalog makes it possible for jobs to refer to data sets by name alone. When a cataloged data set is to be accessed, MVS searches the catalog for it by name, then generates any necessary instructions to a machine room operator indicating which unit of storage media to mount and the device on which to mount it. MVS manages the equipment configuration and "knows" the nature and availability status of every one of the hundreds or thousands of devices attached to it. If the data set is on permanently mounted disk media, MVS omits any mounting instructions and automatically arranges the resources to give access to the data set.

SUBDIRECTORIES: NOT UNDER MVS!

Under VMS, UNIX, and MS-DOS 2.0 and beyond it is possible to create subdirectories, moving in the downward direction from a "log on" directory. If you have made use of VAX VMS or UNIX, you may be aware of these capabilities, involving $ CREATE/LIB, $ SET DEFAULT, *mknod*, and *chdir* commands. If you have used a microcomputer running MS-DOS 2.0 or beyond, you may also be familiar with these capabilities through use of the *md* and *cd* commands. Directories and subdirectories are one approach to the orderly housing of files.

There is no provision for subdirectories in MVS. Related data sets are associated in two ways, and the system catalog serves as an independent means of informing MVS globally about data sets. These two methods by which data sets are associated and the cataloging capability support all processing that occurs on the mainframe.

File Naming

Data sets on the IBM mainframe may be named by as many as 44 characters. In a data set name letters and numbers and some "national" symbols such as @, $, and #, may occur in groups of up to eight contiguous characters, and must be separated from one another by periods. Thus these are all legitimate data set names:

```
CSCDP.H03.PAYMAST
CSCJGJ.CSC.CNTL
RPL.JJ.MSA27.CEN1990
AK00.C72.GENLMAST.G0796V00
SYS86165.T120914.RA000.FSBT686A.R0000001
```

The groups of characters used to form a data set name, or DSN, are called "qualifiers." The left-most qualifier is sometimes called the "highest level index." Most business data processing installations develop and enforce standards for the formation of one or two qualifiers on the left. Access security systems force the adoption of a naming convention for data sets; this is not only how data sets are named but how security of access is arranged.

This rigorous approach toward data set names in itself provides significant hierarchical file association capabilities because the levels of qualifiers can be regarded in the same vein as the subdirectory capabilities of UNIX, VAX VMS, and MS-DOS. For example, all production data sets for a given department may be named starting with CSCDP. Within this highest level qualifier data sets of payroll accounting applications may be given a second-level qualifier like H03, employee benefits accounting application data sets may be given H09, and data sets of a vehicle inventory system could be identified as V22. Individual data sets within a specific application are distinguished by the unique third portion of the data set name; for example, PAYMAST in CSCDP.H03.PAYMAST. In a VAX environment you might have made CSCDP a directory, H03 a subdirectory within it, and PAYMAST a file within that, resulting in a file name of [CSCDP.H03]PAYMAST. On a PC this might result in a file name like \CSCDP\H03\PAYMAST. The results are really quite similar.

Partitioned Data Sets for Source Code, JCL, and Load Modules

Data set organizational capabilities are provided by MVS in the partitioning of a sequential data set into members. Certain types of information are commonly stored by using this capability.

A partitioned data set is simply a sequential file with two internal parts: its own directory and a data area. The terminology is needlessly confusing; the directory of a partitioned data set resembles the account directory of VAX VMS, UNIX, or MS-DOS only superficially, but it serves a similar purpose. The directory retains housekeeping information about the subfiles or members stored in the data area, most particularly, their names and locations. The directory of the partitioned data set is maintained by MVS and consists of unblocked, 256-byte records in which multiple member entries are stored in a variable format. Although not commonly done, the contents of a directory can be dumped by using IDCAMS or IEHLIST, as illustrated in Chapter 17.

The partitioned data set, commonly referred to as a PDS, has no analog in the VMS, UNIX, or MS-DOS environments; it is purely a creature of IBM MVS. It provides a means to house several types of items:

- Programmer-created and maintained groups of source code and JCL statements
- Libraries of items such as copylib members and utility control statements
- Executable load modules, the MVS equivalent of .EXE files.

Extensive use of PDSs is made by any business data processing installation using MVS. If you work in this environment, you will interact with PDSs from day one. They are used to house the language statements that you create with TSO/ISPF, the most common tool for the development of source code and JCL in this environment.[2]

Partitioned data sets appear to MVS as merely another type of data set. Just as with other types of data sets, they can be created as cataloged or noncataloged files; the cataloging status of a PDS has no impact on its organization as a PDS. In a production environment, however, it is customary to catalog all data sets because the volume of data sets is too great to be readily managed by manual means.

A partitioned data set is named in the same way as any other data set:

```
BTO5686.SOURCE.COBOL
```

or

```
CSCJGJ.CSC.COBOL
```

It is not possible to tell whether the data set is partitioned just by seeing this name, but the system catalog retains information that describes its organization, as does the VTOC for the data set on the disk on which it resides. To deal with a specific member of the partitioned data set we refer to the member within the data set as:

```
BTO5686.SOURCE.COBOL(PSD183)
```

or

```
CSCJGJ.CSC.COBOL(PSD183)
```

The name in parentheses can have up to eight characters in addition to the 44 characters available for the data set name. PSD183 is the name of a member in this PDS—the source code for the program we compiled, linkage edited, and ran in our initial example of JCL.

A partitioned data set is known to MVS as one data set, regardless of the number of members it houses. For this reason, when an access security system is in place, protection applies for the entire PDS. That is, security systems such as RACF from IBM, ACF2 from SKK Inc. and others block access to an entire PDS or permit access to the entire PDS. A PDS as a whole is cataloged, not individual members.

The creation of a PDS and the management of its internal organization is handled by MVS, as is the retrieval of the group of records within it that represent a member. In combination with the naming convention illustrated here partitioned organization allows convenient and efficient use of disk space and the ability to group related information on the mainframe. A programmer in the contemporary MVS environment will typically have at least two PDSs to house the items developed as a part of work activities. To house source code statements this PDS will carry a final name portion of COBOL, FORT, PLI, or ASM, whichever is appropriate for the language in use. To house JCL statements the other PDS would be named something like:

```
BT05686.SOURCE.CNTL
```

or

```
CSCJGJ.CSC.CNTL
```

The specific abbreviations or designations that make up the qualifiers of this name may differ from one installation to another because these are a function of local conventions and standards. The lowest level qualifiers are standard but are used mainly for identification of the contents and have no significant bearing on the treatment of the PDS and its members by MVS.[3]

WORKING WITH PARTITIONED DATA SETS

Creating a PDS and Adding or Deleting Members

Partitioned data sets for source code and JCL statements are normally created by allocating them with TSO/ISPF function 3.2. A new load module data set can also be allocated with this function. A PDS can also be allocated with JCL alone, as discussed below and in Chapter 6.

When a partitioned data set already exists, a member may be added to it or replaced in it by directing the intended contents of the member to a DD statement that specifies the PDS and the member name. This was illustrated in Figure 1.3 in connection with the load module library BT05686.TEST.LOADMODS

```
//SYSLMOD    DD  DSN=BT05686.TEST.LOADMODS(PSD183),
//  DISP=SHR
```

where the new load module for program PSD183 was output as a member of the load module library via this DD statement.

A programmer in a mainframe installation usually does not need to create a load module library because a common load module library will already exist. If you are a student, however, you may need to create a load module library for yourself. This is done by running JCL such as:

```
//******************************************************
//*                                                    *
//*    ALLOCATE A SMALL LOAD MODULE LIBRARY            *
//*    (BLKSIZE CAN BE TRACK SIZE BUT ON 3380 DISKS    *
//*    23476 IS HIGHEST EFFICIENT SIZE)                *
//*                                                    *
//******************************************************
```

```
//LOADALLO   EXEC  PGM=IEFBR14
//ALLO1      DD   DSN=BT05686.TEST.LOADMODS,
//  DISP=(NEW,CATLG,DELETE),
//  UNIT=SYSDA,
//  DCB=(RECFM=U,LRECL=0,BLKSIZE=23476),
//  SPACE=(TRK,(10,2,2))
```

This JCL would be run only once to create the load module PDS. For all subsequent member additions or replacements only the JCL in Figure 1.3 or a compile and linkage edit proc would be specified.

Deleting a member of a PDS is a process much less direct and it is prudent to issue this warning:

WARNING!

Do not attempt to delete a member of a PDS by specifying the disposition of (OLD,DELETE) and naming the PDS and member name. This will delete the *entire* partitioned data set.

A member of a PDS is most often deleted by using TSO/ISPF function 3.1. The IDCAMS or IEHPROGM utility can also be employed for this purpose; IDCAMS is the preferred utility and member deletion using it is illustrated in Chapter 17, item 7.

Viewing a PDS Directory

The directory portion of a PDS may contain information that concerns each member of the data set: creation date, date last modified, current size in records, initial size in records, and the number of lines that have been modified since its creation. When TSO/ISPF has been used to create members in a PDS that contains source code or JCL, the directory entry may also contain the TSO/ISPF logon id of the originator. Figure 2.1 is an illustration of this PDS housekeeping information displayed on a TSO/ISPF screen. It is similar in form to that produced in response to a DIR system command under VAX VMS or MS-DOS, but more informative.

PDS Storage and Reorganization

Partitioned data sets provide source code and JCL storage conveniences and efficiencies but they have certain limitations and upkeep requirements. As members of a PDS are updated by writing them back in the data set they are placed by MVS into the available space that follows the last member of the PDS, and the PDS directory is updated to reflect the new location of the member. The place occupied by the former copy

```
UTILITIES --- BT05686.SOURCE.COBOL ----------------------------------------
COMMAND ===>                                             SCROLL ===> PAGE
   NAME         VER.MOD  CREATED    LAST MODIFIED  SIZE  INIT   MOD   ID
ACCT1401        01.04   84/06/19   86/06/22 10:43  1093  1086    22 BT05686
ACCT1403        01.14   85/02/16   86/11/28 12:17   455   336   191 BT05686
ACCT1408        01.04   83/04/14   86/11/23 10:24   948   838    27 BT05103
ACCT1435        01.00   85/03/04   87/05/01 19:41   457   457    10 BT05686
ACCT1441        01.00   85/04/17   87/04/09 14:42   127   127    22 BT05686
ACCT1442        01.03   85/01/28   87/04/09 13:15    28     9    28 BT05103
FINC1753        01.00   85/02/22   86/12/06 16:47   488   488    19 BT05686
FINC1763        01.03   83/02/09   86/12/07 10:32   455   257     2 BT05686
FINC1810        01.01   84/05/11   86/12/07 12:21   453   453    63 BT05103
FSBT3708        01.04   85/01/19   86/08/07 18:09  1433  1431    14 BT05686
FSBT3719        01.26   85/06/07   86/08/22 10:04  1092   669     7 BT05686
HGRA0227        01.02   83/07/18   86/07/04 09:25   898   897    68 AM16054
HGRA0232        01.14   83/12/13   86/07/05 13:30   419   282    44 AM16054
HGRA0239        01.80   87/01/09   87/07/15 13:16  1405    56    11 BT05686
PSD183          01.07   84/12/08   86/05/06 10:27   233   233     9 BT05686
SRGN5570        01.14   85/01/29   86/05/22 16:41   306   213   156 BT05686
SRGN5573        01.05   82/07/26   86/05/31 18:23  2428  2396    13 BT05686
SRGN5577        01.02   83/10/21   86/06/23 15:13  1161  1184   287 BT05686
SRGN5580        01.00   84/09/29   86/06/18 17:27  1089  1089    92 BT05686
SRGN6222        01.22   84/04/07   86/06/18 17:03    60   669    16 BT05103
**END**
```

FIGURE 2.1.   Source code library directory member list and statistics provided by TSO

or copies of the member is essentially "dead," and is not accessible or reusable until the PDS is reorganized.

Both batch and online means exist to reorganize a PDS. The batch means makes use of—what else?—JCL to invoke the utility program IEBCOPY, which accomplishes the reorganization. Because the net effect appears to be "squeezing" active members to the top of the PDS data area, it is often called compression when initiated online from TSO/ISPF. If not reorganized to reclaim unusable space, the PDS will eventually exhaust its capacity to sustain the addition of more members or the housing of updated members. If this occurs, a system completion or error code of E37 is received when an attempt is made to save another member or modified member in the PDS. Appendix B provides the JCL to perform a batch reorganization on a partitioned data set. As illustrated, a slightly different set of execution JCL is needed to reorganize a source code or JCL library partitioned data set versus a load module library because of the differing record formats.

Different versions of members do not exist in a PDS in an accessible form. Only the most recently updated copy of each member is known to the PDS directory and is accessible. Members of a PDS can be treated as if they were data sets in themselves for nearly all purposes. A member cannot be further subdivided, however; a PDS is not actually as powerful as the subdirectory structure on the VAX, under UNIX, or under MS-DOS.

The minimum space allocation for a data set under MVS is one track of disk space, which is quite a large amount: 19,069 bytes of storage on an IBM 3350 device and 47,476 bytes on an IBM 3380. A data set will always have at least this much space allocated to it even if it contains only one record. If the data set contains only a small amount of information that requires just a miniscule amount of storage media, much space may be wasted by storing it in a simple sequential file. Instead it can be stored with other like items in a partitioned data set as one of many members. Although the PDS must consume one track or more, individual members consume a minimum of only one block of space because each member starts in a new data block.

On a VAX, or on most microcomputers, space is allocated in terms of "granules" or "clusters" composed of a few 512-byte sectors of disk space; therefore there is little space wasted in the storage of small files. Under MVS disk storage is not sectored and granules or clusters are not relevant. Partitioned organization addresses this issue and allows many individual members to exist efficiently in the space allocated to one data set. This space can, of course, be more than one track but for PDSs it cannot spread across multiple disk volumes. Nonpartitioned sequential disk data sets can span more than one disk volume.

The Old Utilities and PDS Member Storage

Partitioned data sets predate TSO/ISPF. At one time, utilities such as IEHPROGM, IEBUPDTE, IEHLIST, IEBPTPCH, and IEBGENER were used by programmers to create, update, and manage source code and JCL PDSs and their members. In the contemporary environment these utilities are used to a much lesser extent; they are typically useful only to a system librarian who installs completed and approved source code and JCL into "production" partitioned data sets. Programmers use the online facilities of TSO/ISPF to work with their PDSs and members, which is the major reason that heavy emphasis on these old OS utilities serves no contemporary purpose.

Member entries are maintained in the PDS directory in alphabetical order even when members are added. Because of the way that a PDS functions, its accessible members are actually stored in the data area without regard to alphabetical order. Each new member or updated copy of a member is placed at the end of the data already in the data area. This has an impact on a full listing of a PDS produced by the utility program IEBPTPCH, which provides it by reading only the data portion of the PDS. For this reason member listings produced by IEBPTPCH do not necessarily present the members in alphabetical order.

IEHPROGM was formerly used to rename members within a PDS. Members can now be renamed by the IDCAMS utility or online by TSO.

When a member is renamed, its name in the PDS directory is simply altered. The entire directory is automatically rearranged by MVS when this is done to maintain the alphabetical order of its entries. The data area of the PDS is not affected by the renaming of a given member.

One or more "aliases" can also be established in a load module PDS directory for a given member to create the capability of referring to the member by different names. This is done occasionally with certain production load modules when an item of system software has a peculiar or cumbersome name; for example, one IBM sort utility called IGHRCO00 is stored under this name in a production load module library. This name, however, is difficult to remember and easy to specify incorrectly because of the contiguous capital letter O and zero and is usually given an alias such as SORT.

Load Module Library: a Special Partitioned Data Set

A load module is not composed of records of data; it represents the groups of working storage and machine instructions that, when loaded to memory, can be run as a program.[4] In the compile, linkage edit, and run JCL of Figure 1.2 the load module output of the linkage editor program IEWL is placed in a temporary data set called &&GOSET. The member created, GO, is specified as a member of that data set; here we allocated the data set as partitioned.[5] *An MVS load module is required to be a member of a partitioned data set.* Unlike the case on a VAX or microcomputer, load modules cannot be freestanding files; under MVS there is no separate file analogous to the .EXE file of the VAX or MS-DOS environments. In the compile, linkage edit, and run jobstream in Figure 1.2 we created a temporary PDS that contains one member to satisfy this requirement. In production work we would customarily output the load module as a new or replacement member of a permanent PDS that existed to serve as the repository of application program load modules. Placement of the load module in a permanent PDS is illustrated in the JCL of the compile and linkage edit shown in Figure 1.3.

When we execute a program under MVS, we at times explicitly specify the library, in other words, the partitioned data set, in which the program load module resides. The load module is obtained from this PDS and loaded into memory and control is turned over to it by MVS when the job step begins execution. How do we tell MVS which PDS contains the load module named in the EXEC statement? The STEPLIB DD statement provides this information—as described in step //GO of the compile, linkage edit, and run JCL in Figure 1.2 and in the run JCL in Figure 1.4. The //COB and //LKED steps of the compile, linkage edit, and go have no //STEPLIB DD statements because the programs executed in each case—the compiler IKFCBL00 and the linkage editor IEWL—are stored in a default load module library reserved for special system-wide support software, named SYS1.LINKLIB. This library is normally assumed to be the one that has the program load module indicated on the EXEC statement if no //STEPLIB DD statement is present.

The execution of many program load modules drawn from a load library PDS, one after another, is the norm in the MVS environment and the mode of operation that JCL was designed to govern. Although program development often proceeds with the creation and testing of one program at a time, these operations are only a tiny subset of possible automated operations. Production application systems do not operate with single programs run manually, one after another; they are made up of several steps that execute load modules in sequence.

DATA SET ORGANIZATION DESIGNATIONS

Under MVS different designations pertain to the various types of data set organization, abbreviated "DSORG:"

Sequential data set	=	physical sequential	=	PS
Partitioned data set	=	partitioned organization	=	PO
VSAM	=	Virtual Storage Access Method	=	VS
ISAM	=	Indexed Sequential Access Method	=	IS
Direct access	=	direct access	=	DA

```
VTOC LISTING FOR VOLUME FSDC03 ----------------------- LINE 000000 COL 001 080
COMMAND INPUT ===>                                            SCROLL ===> PAGE
****************************** TOP OF DATA *****************-CAPS ON-**

   VOLUME: FSDC03
   UNIT:   3380

   VOLUME DATA:          VTOC DATA:              FREE SPACE:  TRACKS CYLINDERS
     TRACKS:    13290      TRACKS:       15        SIZE:      1832      26
     %USED:        86 %    %USED:        28 %      LARGEST:    276      18
     DATA SETS:   223      FREE DSCBS:  579
     TRKS/CYL:     15                            FREE EXTENTS:   54

   DATA SET NAME                         DSORG   TRACKS   %USED   XTENTS
   --------------------------------------------------------------------
   AC90000.E22.GENLPEND.G0552V00          PS     255 TRKS   92 %   3 X
   P.CSCU.MK4CAT                          DA     160 TRKS   56 %   1 X
   P.TRES.DAILYCON                                 0 TRKS    ? %   0 X
   SYS1.VVDS.VFSDC03                      VS       3 TRKS    ? %   1 X
   BT05686.SOURCE.COBOL                  PO     220 TRKS   81 %   4 X
   BT05686.SOURCE.CNTL                   PO      50 TRKS   43 %   1 X
   BT05686.DEVCOPY.COBOL                 PO      70 TRKS   52 %   2 X
   BT05686.SOURCE.SYM                    POU     30 TRKS   22 %   1 X
   BT05772.SOURCE.COBOL                  PO     115 TRKS   60 %   1 X
```

FIGURE 2.2. Disk volume table of contents (VTOC) listing via TSO/ISPF function 3.7

A third letter, U, may be added to this two-letter organization code for PS, PO, and DA data sets to designate an unmovable set. Certain applications that employ relative record locations within the geography of a disk volume are dependent on data set placement or on the continued presence of the data set on a specific type of device. This dependence is limiting and is avoided as much as possible. It is present only on rare occasions; programmers do not ordinarily specify it.

Means are provided to list the names of all data sets on a given disk volume by showing information from the volume table of contents or VTOC of the disk. These listings use the preceding designations to describe the organization of each data set. Figure 2.2 is an illustration produced on a terminal screen during a TSO/ISPF session. Note that the fifth data set shown on disk FSDC03 is BT05686.SOURCE.COBOL—the partitioned data set for which a member list is illustrated in Figure 2.1.

REVIEW QUESTIONS AND (*)EXERCISES

1. Explain where the TSO statistics information is stored in a PDS.

2. Why is it necessary to periodically reorganize a partitioned data set?

3. Explain the relationship between the system catalog and data sets in general.

4. Where are the old, superseded versions of a PDS member and why can't they be accessed?

*5. List all the members of a PDS by using the IEBPTPCH utility illustrated in item 16 of Chapter 17. Explain why this list might not carry the members in alphabetical sequence.

*6. Add three members to an existing partitioned data set using TSO/ISPF, naming one with a name starting with "C," one with a name starting with "B," and one with a name starting with "A," but do so with the "C" name first, then the "B" name, and then the "A" name. Use the TSO 2 edit or TSO 1 browse function to obtain a member list and view the order of the PDS directory after the members are added. Explain why the order of the entries is as you find it.

*7. Obtain a paper listing of a PDS directory, using the IEHLIST utility, as illustrated in item 19 of Chapter 17. Compare it with a screen print of a PDS member list of the same data set taken using the TSO 2 edit or TSO 1 browse function, and explain why both lists are in alphabetical sequence.

*8. Create a member in a PDS, using TSO/ISPF: then delete the member, using the IDCAMS utility as illustrated in item 7 of Chapter 17. Caution: Do not use DISP = (OLD,DELETE) for the PDS.

*9. Reorganize your CNTL PDS, using the JCL illustrated in Appendix B. Your installation may have installed this JCL as a cataloged procedure, in which case you will be able to execute a reorganization by composing and submitting the few lines of run JCL, also illustrated in Appendix B.

*10. Dump the contents of a PDS directory, using the IDCAMS hex dump feature illustrated in item 6 of Chapter 17. Compare it with an IEHLIST listing of the directory and note that the 256-byte directory records begin with two bytes of length data in binary, then several member entries in a variable format. The first 12 bytes of any member entry consist of eight bytes for the member name, three bytes for relative track and block location, and one byte for "user data length" expressed in binary in "halfwords." The value of the user data length field tells how many two-byte units of TSO statistics follow. Compare the user data with the fields shown on a printed copy of a TSO member listing screen for the data set; find and mark the location of each of the items of TSO statistics in the dump for the first member.

NOTES

1. It is easy to confuse the VTOC acronym with a form of program logic design tool known as a visual table of contents. IBM coined the acronym for its introduction of mainframe hard disk drives in the 1960s, but anyone is free to create strings of words that produce an identical acronym—which is exactly what happened with VTOC some years later.

2. TSO can create and modify normal sequential files as well as members of partitioned data sets. By far the most prevalent practice, however, is for a programmer to house the source code for individual programs as members of a PDS.

3. Because TSO is the primary vehicle used to create and update PDSs that house program and JCL statements, a few naming conventions are more or less enforced. TSO in the ISPF/PDF mode—Integrated System Productivity Facility/Program Development Facility—defaults to the display of the most significant columns of the card image for various source code languages, depending on the final qualifier of the PDS name. For example, COBOL source code may be line-numbered in columns 1 through 6. When full screen editing is done on a COBOL-numbered member of a data set such as BT0586.SOURCE.COBOL, columns 7 through 78 are shown on the screen. However, if you are editing a member of a data set named BT05686.SOURCE.CNTL, normally used to house JCL statements, the display is initiated showing columns 1 through 72; JCL carries TSO-applied line numbers in columns 73 through 80.

   Do not confuse these data set name components with the COB, PAS, PLI, BAS, OBJ, LIB, and other suffix identifiers of the VAX or PC environments. The PDS name conventions have no meaning outside the program development environment of TSO/ISPF. Mainframe compilers have no default expectations concerning the names of the data sets that house source code input to them and no defaults concerning the physical data set names of their outputs.

4.   The length of the records that make up the members of a PDS can be anywhere in the range of 1 to 32,760 characters, the same range as that of other types of records under MVS. However, all records in all members of a PDS defined to house *fixed* length records must be the same length. The record length is established at the time the PDS is allocated. PDSs can also be defined to house variable length records or "undefined" data. A PDS created to house load modules, such as &&GOSET in the JCL of Figure 1.2, is of undefined format. Undefined does not carry the common language connotation of unknown; it means that no MVS deblocking services are desired. PDSs created to house TSO command lists, or CLISTS, and certain types of data are typically of format VB containing variable length blocked records.

5.   The single difference between allocating disk space for a simple sequential file and allocating space for a partitioned data set is that zero directory blocks are requested for a sequential data set. Some quantity of directory blocks is requested in the SPACE parameter to create a PDS. We discuss the SPACE parameter in Chapter 8.

3

MVS Job Execution

In this chapter we examine a job stream that invokes a series of job executions involving programs for which load modules have already been prepared and placed in a permanent load module library. We start by looking at a graphic representation of what the job stream does and then examine the job control language that defines this series of steps to MVS and MVS/XA.

Figure 3.1 describes the execution of three programs, one after another, and the data sets that enter each program or are produced by it. A job stream diagram shows the individual processes or job steps, the serial order of their execution, and the "information commodity," data sets, input and output by each step.

The job stream in Figure 3.1 is typical of a test job stream that might be designed to accept transactions destined for a sequential update pro-

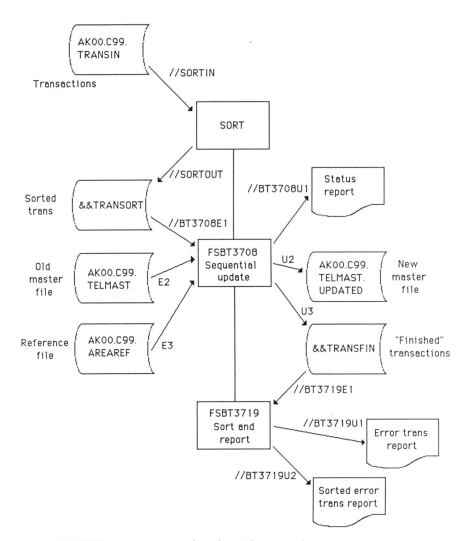

FIGURE 3.1.   Sequential update job stream for testing purposes

gram.[1] After sorting, the transactions are fed to the update routine, which applies them to an existing master file to create an updated master file and certain report outputs. Finally, outputs from the update are reduced to printed form by a third program.

OVERVIEW OF AN EXAMPLE JOB STREAM

In the first step in Figure 3.1 the IBM sort program is executed. This program is a general purpose sorting utility that carries a name like IGHRCO00, given an alias of SORT for ease of reference. It can be directed by control statements to sort any file or collection of files into the desired order. For this job stream we have a data set named AK00.C99.TRANSIN which consists of update transactions that were keyed into machine readable form in a data entry operation. The sequential update requires these transactions to be in order of their key field.

In the second step we execute a sequential update program named FSBT3708. The sorted update transactions are fed into FSBT3708, which also reads two other data sets—an existing master file and a reference file used to load a lookup table. Program FSBT3708 creates three outputs, two of which are data sets and the third, a report. In the third step another program of our own making, designated FSBT3719, is executed. This program reads one of the data sets output by the second step and processes it to generate two additional reports.

Sequential updating of master files is a common operation in business data processing even when the master file is also updated online during business hours. Bulk update with voluminous keyed transactions occurs in off hours when the master file is removed from online access. In this operation transactions that have been batched and keyed are made to interact with a master file and a new master file is created. Records on the master file for which valid change transactions were present are written to the new master file in updated form. Master file records for which no valid transactions were present exist on the new master file as they did on the old one.[2]

The sequential matching process relies on the fact that master file records are stored in sequential order by the unique key field value of each record. Although transactions are not typically prepared in this sequence, they must be in such a sort sequence to permit a sequential update program to process them. Program FSBT3708 arranges for the interaction of a data set that contains sorted transactions with the master file and creates an updated version of it. Program FSBT3708 also outputs a file of finished transactions, each of which is a copy of an original 71-byte update transaction to which has been appended an extra 31 bytes. The extra data tacked onto each transaction include the error codes, if any, that the transaction generated in the course of the update. This data, plus the identity of the transaction preparer and the identity of the data entry operator who keyed the item—already contained within the transaction—allow a range of reporting to be done that provides user feedback concerning error transactions. Figure 3.2 shows the format of the transactions and is provided here to help you to visualize the scenario.[3]

The last program in the job stream, FSBT3719, reads the data set of finished transactions output by the update routine, the 102-byte records in Figure 3.2. The program processes these transactions to produce two reports: a list of error transactions in key sequence and a list of error

TRANSFIN

ORIGINAL TRANSACTION

Employee id	Call date			Area code	Rate code	Call length	Filler	Preparer id	Preparation date		
	mo	da	yr						mo	da	yr
x(4)	x(2)	x(2)	x(2)	x(3)	x(1)	99v99	x(18)	x(4)	x(2)	x(2)	x(2)
1 4	5 6	7 8	9 10	11 13	14	15 18	19 36	37 40	41 42	43 44	45 46

ADDED BY TRANSACTION KEYER

Keying date			Keyer id	Batch id	Sequence number within batch	Keyer terminal id
mo	da	yr				
x(2)	x(2)	x(2)	x(4)	x(3)	9(4)	x(8)
47 48	49 50	51 52	53 56	57 59	60 63	64 71

ADDED BY UPDATE JOB

Filler	Update run date			Update error codes	Error count	Cycle number	Filler
	mo	da	yr				
x(6)	x(2)	x(2)	x(2)	x(5)	9(2)	9(7)	x(5)
72 77	78 79	80 81	82 83	84 88	89 90	91 97	98 102

TRANSIN

FIGURE 3.2. Update transaction format for example job stream

transactions sorted in transaction preparer and transaction batch order. To generate the second of these reports the program performs an internal sort and then a control break report on the sorted error records, "breaking" to a new page for the error transactions of each transaction preparer. The reports provide easily segregated feedback for each transaction preparer, and the failed transactions for which each preparer is responsible can be located, corrected, and resubmitted. The fact that FSBT3719 uses internal sorting gives us the opportunity to see the similarities in JCL for an external and an internal sort.

To complete the illustration of the major role of DD statements as interfaces between symbolic filenames and physical data sets see Figure 3.3. This is a reproduction of the first several lines of the COBOL source code for FSBT3708 and includes the SELECT/ASSIGN statements. The DD statements in the JCL do not need to appear in the same order as the SELECT/ASSIGNs in the program.

MVS and MVS/XA JCL for the Job Stream

The JCL shown in Figure 3.4 implements the program executions in our three-step sequential update. A general similarity in its appearance to

```
IDENTIFICATION DIVISION.
PROGRAM-ID.     FSBT3708.
AUTHOR.         S CHANAWAN AND J JANOSSY.
INSTALLATION.   FARNON STANDARD.
DATE-WRITTEN.   MAY, 1986.
DATE-COMPILED.
*REMARKS.       LAST UPDATE 03-22-87  JJ    ORIG 04-12-84  SC
*
*               THIS PROGRAM UPDATES A SEQUENTIAL MASTER FILE
*               WITH TRANSACTION DATA. A REFERENCE FILE IS
*               LOADED DYNAMICALLY AT RUN TIME, PROVIDING THE
*               INFORMATION FOR ONE OF THE TRANSACTION EDITS
*               AND THE APPLICABLE TRANSACTION RATE.
*
*               DESIGNED BY S. CHANAWAN AND J. JANOSSY.
*               ADAPTED FOR TRAINING. IDENTICAL TO "PSD186"
*               ON PAGES 395-405 OF COMMERCIAL SOFTWARE
*               ENGINEERING, ISBN 0-471-81576-4, JOHN WILEY
*               AND SONS, 1985, EXCEPT FOR ADDITION OF THE
*               OUTPUT OF FINISHED-TRANS (BT3708U3). NOTE
*               CHANGE IN TRANSACTION RECORD SIZE AND CONTENT.
*
*
ENVIRONMENT DIVISION.
CONFIGURATION SECTION.
SOURCE-COMPUTER.  IBM-4381.
OBJECT-COMPUTER.  IBM-4381.
SPECIAL-NAMES.    C01 IS PAGE-EJECT.
*
INPUT-OUTPUT SECTION.
FILE-CONTROL.
    SELECT SORTED-CALLS-FILE   ASSIGN TO UT-S-BT3708E1.
    SELECT MASTER-FILE-IN      ASSIGN TO UT-S-BT3708E2.
    SELECT REFERENCE-FILE      ASSIGN TO UT-S-BT3708E3.
    SELECT MASTER-FILE-OUT     ASSIGN TO UT-S-BT3708U2.
    SELECT REPORT1             ASSIGN TO UT-S-BT3708U1.
    SELECT FINISHED-TRANS      ASSIGN TO UT-S-BT3708U3.
*
```

FIGURE 3.3. SELECT/ASSIGN statements of example COBOL program

the compile, link, and run JCL is apparent. Many years ago a ragged, unaligned JCL style prevailed and comments were often omitted. TSO has made a great difference in JCL; TSO is a source code and JCL "word processor" that makes it easy to compose clear material, unlike the card punch.

Note that among the first comments at the top of the JCL is a line that identifies the member name of the JCL and the PDS in which it resides. Without a comment line like this, it's impossible to determine where the JCL is stored. *This is a set of testing JCL, not production JCL.* Production JCL is normally documented and identifiable in its own right. Testing JCL needs an identifying comment to indicate where it is stored simply as a matter of practicality.

Sort JCL

In //STEPA we execute the IBM sort utility. There is no //STEPLIB DD statement because the sort utility is usually housed in the default load module library, SYS1.LINKLIB, or in another of the "automatic call" load module libraries.[4] There is, however, a special library named at a DD statement that carries the DDname //SORTLIB. A number of modules of the IBM sort utility are housed in SYS1.SORTLIB and it functions as a load module library for the sort only.

The input to the sort is fed to it at the DDname //SORTIN. Like the DDnames associated with the compiler and other "already provided" software, we have no latitude in the choice of this DDname; its name was chosen by the authors of the sort utility program and it is a "given." The output from the sort emerges at the DDname //SORTOUT.

The input to the sort is a data set named AK00.C99.TRANSIN, to which we give nonexclusive "share" access. This data set is known to the system—it was cataloged when created or shortly thereafter—and we need not specify the volume serial number of the media on which it resides or the device on which the media is mounted. We have not specified the type of unit that this device is; MVS will obtain that information from the system catalog.

The output from the sort is a temporary file named &&TRANSORT. Because we are creating this data set, we must specify the unit or the type of unit, the disposition, and the characteristics of the data set in terms of record type, length, and blocking. Since the unit is disk, we must indicate the quantity of disk space to be allocated. Chapters 7 and 8, which deal with the DCB and SPACE parameters, cover these items in depth.

We see in //STEPA's DD statements the familiar //SYSOUT and //SYSUDUMP. The sort utility outputs a few messages concerning its operation to //SYSOUT; some IBM utilities, on the other hand, write

```
//FSBT686A  JOB AK00TEST,'DP2-JANOSSY',CLASS=E,MSGCLASS=X,
//  MSGLEVEL=(1,1),NOTIFY=BT05686
//*
//*    TEST RUN OF SEQUENTIAL UPDATE FSBT3708 -- VER 1
//*    THIS JCL = BT05686.SOURCE.CNTL(BT3708V1)
//*
//************************************************************
//*                                                          *
//*    SORT TRANS FILE                              A        *
//*                                                          *
//************************************************************
//STEPA     EXEC  PGM=SORT
//SORTLIB   DD   DSN=SYS1.SORTLIB,
//  DISP=SHR
//SORTIN    DD   DSN=AK00.C99.TRANSIN,
//  DISP=SHR
//SORTOUT   DD   DSN=&&TRANSORT,
//  UNIT=SYSDA,
//  DISP=(NEW,PASS,DELETE),
//  DCB=(RECFM=FB,LRECL=71,BLKSIZE=6177),
//  SPACE=(6177,(32,7),RLSE)                '2800 TRANS
//SYSOUT    DD   SYSOUT=*
//SYSUDUMP  DD   SYSOUT=*
//SORTWK01  DD   UNIT=SYSDA,SPACE=(CYL,2,,CONTIG)
//SORTWK02  DD   UNIT=SYSDA,SPACE=(CYL,2,,CONTIG)
//SYSIN     DD   *
    SORT FIELDS=(1,4,CH,A,9,2,CH,A,5,4,CH,A,14,1,CH,D)
/*
//*
//************************************************************
//*                                                          *
//*    UPDATE MASTER FILE                          B         *
//*                                                          *
//************************************************************
//STEPB     EXEC  PGM=FSBT3708
//STEPLIB   DD   DSN=BT05686.TEST.LOADMODS,
//  DISP=SHR
//BT3708E1  DD   DSN=&&TRANSORT,
//  DISP=(OLD,DELETE)
//BT3708E2  DD   DSN=AK00.C99.TELMAST,
//  DISP=(OLD,KEEP)
//BT3708E3  DD   DSN=AK00.C99.AREAREF,
//  DISP=SHR
//BT3708U1  DD   SYSOUT=*
//BT3708U2  DD   DSN=AK00.C99.TELMAST.UPDATED,
//  UNIT=SYSDA,
//  DISP=(NEW,CATLG,DELETE),
//  DCB=(RECFM=FB,LRECL=314,BLKSIZE=5966),
//  SPACE=(5966,(4210,850),RLSE)            '80000 RECS
//BT3708U3  DD   DSN=&&TRANSFIN,
//  UNIT=SYSDA,
//  DISP=(NEW,PASS,DELETE),
//  DCB=(RECFM=FB,LRECL=102,BLKSIZE=6222),  '2800 TRANS
//  SPACE=(6222,(46,9),RLSE)
//SYSOUT    DD   SYSOUT=*
//SYSUDUMP  DD   SYSOUT=*
//************************************************************
//*                                                          *
//*    PRODUCE TRAN REPORT (INTERNAL SORT)         C         *
//*                                                          *
//************************************************************
//STEPC     EXEC  PGM=FSBT3719
//STEPLIB   DD   DSN=BT05686.TEST.LOADMODS,
//  DISP=SHR
//SORTLIB   DD   DSN=SYS1.SORTLIB,
//  DISP=SHR
//BT3719E1  DD   DSN=&&TRANSFIN,
//  DISP=(OLD,DELETE)
//BT3719U1  DD   SYSOUT=*
//BT3719U2  DD   SYSOUT=*
//SORTWK01  DD   UNIT=SYSDA,SPACE=(CYL,2,,CONTIG)
//SORTWK02  DD   UNIT=SYSDA,SPACE=(CYL,2,,CONTIG)
//BT3719SM  DD   SYSOUT=*
//SYSOUT    DD   SYSOUT=*
//SYSUDUMP  DD   SYSOUT=*
//
```

FIGURE 3.4. MVS JCL for sequential update testing job stream

similar messages to a DDname of //SYSPRINT.[5] Abnormal ending of the sort utility resulting in a memory dump is rare, but the //SYSUDUMP DD statement provides a means of receiving a dump if an abend does occur. The remaining DD statements for //STEPA provide sort work space for the utility and give it the control information that tells it what record positions to sort on, the nature of the fields, and whether ascending or descending sort order of the field is desired.

//SORTWKnn, where nn is 01 through 32, provides the disk space needed by the utility to do its work. At least two such allocations are required to sort fixed length record data sets and at least three are needed for variable length record data sets; more are specified when large data sets are sorted. The amount of space provided across the work space allocations has to be sufficient to house the entire file, which includes certain housekeeping data appended to records by the sort.

//SYSIN is the DD name at which the sort utility seeks control statements. Although many types and formats of control statements exist to cause special processing to occur, the basic format, shown here, is rather simple; this one specifies four sort keys. The primary sort key starts in position 1 for a length of 4 bytes, it is character in format, and we want the sort order to be ascending on this field.[6] Starting in position 9 of each record for a length of 2 bytes is a character field that is the secondary sort key. We also want sort order to be ascending on this key—it will "break a tie" when the primary sort keys of two records are the same. A third sort key starts in position 5. A fourth sort key is found in position 14 and this one sorts in descending sequence.

Of interest to us in connection with //SYSIN is the fact that this job stream illustrates how "immediate" or "instream" data can be specified. Control statements are card image information, as is all of JCL. Much more in the old days than at present it was common to include items like the sort control statements right in the JCL. It is possible, more or less, to interrupt the JCL statements with a statement such as this; the asterisk means in this case "data follows immediately."

All the card images following the "DD *" statement will be regarded as data fed to the DDname of the statement. When does MVS start regarding the card images as JCL statements again? Once it has encountered a card image that begins with /* in the first two columns.[7] Instream data have significant limitations and no place in production job streams because they cannot be specified within cataloged procedures, as discussed in Chapter 16. Here we are looking at a test job stream, where instream data and control statements are a convenience to a programmer.

We could have housed the control statements for the sort as a member of a PDS. For example, we could have housed them in a member called SORTCTL1 in the PDS that contains the JCL, BT05686.SOURCE.CNTL.

Then, instead of specifying that instream data follow by using DD * on the //SYSIN DD statement, we would have coded it this way:

```
//SYSIN   DD  DSN=BT05686.SOURCE.CNTL(SORTCTL1),
//  DISP=SHR
```

Program Execution JCL

In //STEPB of the sequential update job stream JCL we see again the now familiar groups of DD statements for the execution of an application program. This step carries the //STEPLIB DD statement, naming the partitioned data set in which the program load module resides. The load module is a member named FSBT3708; it was placed in BT05686.TEST.LOADMODS by the linkage edit of a compile and link edit job stream. The only parameter necessary to specify for this DD statement is the DISP, which we indicate as share, SHR.

We next see six DD statements that carry names associated with SELECT/ASSIGN statements in the COBOL program illustrated in Figure 3.3. There is one DD statement for each data set with which the program deals, including the file of printlines that constitute REPORT1. Notice that the DD statements in the JCL for this step do not have to follow the order of the corresponding SELECT/ASSIGN statements in citing the data sets. It is necessary only that a DD statement be present for each data set.

The DD statement with the name //BT3708U2 deals with the new master file data set created by the program. The DD statement //BT3708U3 deals with another data set created by the program, the "finished" transactions, which are 31 bytes longer than the original transactions. Both DD statements must specify many more parameters than "read" access DD statements. When we are creating a data set, information needed by MVS to write its data set label and handle the data set is normally supplied in the DCB parameter, as discussed in Chapter 7.

As done in the compile, link, and run JCL, where we created a temporary data set to house the object and load modules, and as in //STEPA of this job stream, in //BT3708U2 and //BT3708U3 we must indicate the unit or type of unit, the disposition of the data set, the DCB, and the values for disk space allocation. Some of these, however, are different for the two new data sets.

In //BT3708U2 we are arranging for the new master file to be housed. We must specify a data set name different from the original because only one data set of a given name can be cataloged under that name. The generation data group or GDG capability of MVS, which we discuss in Chapter 13, provides a means of using the same data set name to create successive "generations" of a file; GDGs are often used for production master files. GDGs, however, require special setup. Unlike the case with the VAX's VMS, which creates file versions automatically, the capability to create generations does not come free under MVS. In this case we vary the new master file data set name simply by appending more characters to the original. We used .UPDATED here, but anything would have been satisfactory; these characters have no bearing on the status or treatment of the data set.[8]

For the new master file data set emerging at DD name //BT3708U2 we have indicated a DISPosition of (NEW,CATLG,DELETE). The NEW indicates the status of the data set as the step starts execution. CATLG is coded in the second subparameter, where we indicate the status of the data set as we wish it to be after the step concludes. If we had specified KEEP here, the data set would have been created, but no information about it would have been placed in the system catalog. The next time we had to access the uncataloged data set we would have had to specify the volume serial number of the disk or tape device on which it was written. CATLG is a convenience of MVS and is used in nearly all contemporary work when permanent data sets on disk or tape are created.

The DELETE in the third position of the DISP parameter specifies what we want done with the data set if the *step* fails to execute properly. It means, quite obviously, that we wish the data set to be eliminated.

At the bottom of //STEPB we again see the //SYSOUT DD statement, to which any DISPLAY output from the program is directed, and the //SYSUDUMP DD statement, where a memory dump is written if the program terminates abnormally.

Internal Sort JCL

//STEPC of the sequential update is rather anticlimactic after //STEPB; it is the execution of another COBOL program, one that appears to deal with three data sets: the temporary data set of finished transactions output by //STEPB and the two sets of report printlines generated here. Program FSBT3719, however, needs an internal sort. *A program that makes use an internal sort actually requires the same sort utility used by the external sort;* COBOL and PL/I do not in themselves contain sorting logic, although each provides a SORT verb. When an internal sort is invoked in a COBOL or PL/I program that uses a SORT verb, the compiler arranges for the linkage editor to bring together the program load module and the sort program load module.

Because some of the sort utility routines are loaded by it only when needed and are housed in their own library, we see the same DD statement that carries the name //SORTLIB in this step that we saw in //STEPA. Although it is our responsibility to provide a sort control statement for the sort utility as a control card at //SYSIN in //STEPA, *in an internal sort the compiler formats a control statement and passes it to the sort.*

Figure 3.5 illustrates the top portion of the source code for program FSBT3719, which is executed in //STEPC. There are four SELECT/AS-SIGN statements: one for the finished transaction file, two for the two sets of report printlines, and one for the "sort work space" or "SD" file. On some other lines of computers the work space required by the sort utility is actually provided at the file named in this SELECT/ASSIGN. Under MVS the SELECT/ASSIGN statement for an SD file is a dummy statement, which exists only to meet the grammatical requirements of COBOL. No matching DD statement is coded for it in the JCL; if one is coded, it will not be used. For a program that features an internal sort under MVS the sort work space for the sort utility comes from exactly the same place that it would for an external invocation of the sort; that is, from explicit DD statements carrying names //SORTWKnn.[9]

At //STEPA a //SYSOUT DD statement is provided for the external sort. Messages generated by the sort program, such as statements of records read, written, and options and parameters in effect for it, are output here. When the sort utility is invoked by a program that uses the SORT verb, any DISPLAY messages generated by that program are also directed to such a DD name. If no provision were made to separate these print outputs and we coded DISPLAY statements in a COBOL program, the print from the sort and the program would be jumbled together. COBOL provides the ability to replace the DDname to which the sort utility

```
          IDENTIFICATION DIVISION.
          PROGRAM-ID.     FSBT3719.
          AUTHOR.         J JANOSSY.
          INSTALLATION.   FARNON STANDARD.
          DATE-WRITTEN.   MAY, 1986.
          DATE-COMPILED.
         *REMARKS.        LAST UPDATE 05-22-86  JJ   ORIG 05-20-86  JJ
         *
         *                THIS PROGRAM READS THE FSBT3708 FINISHED TRANS
         *                FILE AND PRINTS TWO REPORTS FOR END USER. ONE
         *                REPORT SHOWS ERROR TRANSACTIONS IN ORDER OF KEY,
         *                OTHER REPORT SHOWS ERROR TRANS SORTED BY THE
         *                ID OF TRANS PREPARER WITH CONTROL BREAKS.
         *
          ENVIRONMENT DIVISION.
          CONFIGURATION SECTION.
          SOURCE-COMPUTER.  IBM-4381.
          OBJECT-COMPUTER.  IBM-4381.
          SPECIAL-NAMES.    C01 IS PAGE-EJECT.
         *
          INPUT-OUTPUT SECTION.
          FILE-CONTROL.
              SELECT FIN-TRANS-FILE     ASSIGN TO UT-S-BT3719E1.
              SELECT TRANS-SORT-FILE    ASSIGN TO UT-S-BT3719W1.
              SELECT REPORT1            ASSIGN TO UT-S-BT3719U1.
              SELECT REPORT2            ASSIGN TO UT-S-BT3719U2.
         *
```

FIGURE 3.5. SELECT/ASSIGN statements for COBOL program with internal sort

writes its messages. The following statement has been coded in program FSBT3719:

```
MOVE 'BT3719SM' TO SORT-MESSAGE
```

SORT-MESSAGE, however, is not coded in working storage; it comes free with the SORT verb. The sort utility will now send its housekeeping message print to //BT3719SM; therefore we see a DD statement in //STEPC that carries this name.

Naming Conventions and Their Importance

Conventions are often institutionalized within business data processing organizations for the naming of programs and the formation of DDnames within programs. In this job stream we see an illustration of common conventions. A firm named Farnon Standard Corporation owns the installation in which this job stream has been prepared.[10] Farnon Standard is composed of several divisions, all of which use the centralized data processing facility. Each of these divisions is responsible for costs incurred for computer time and related resources. It is necessary for job names and data set names to reflect, in part, the organizational breakdown in order that appropriate accounting may be done. The programs shown here are related to Farnon Standard's Belvidere Tool Division; hence the nature of the naming convention is evident: "FS" denotes Farnon Standard and "BT" stands for Belvidere Tool.

Each division of Farnon Standard has a few to several mainframe applications, that is, "systems." We see that the programs in this job stream deal with application 37 of Farnon Standard's Belvidere Tool division. We would expect all the other programs within this series to begin with FSBT37.

The naming convention for DDnames falls directly out of the program names. It is apparent that DDname //BT3708E1 is associated with program FSBT3708. What does the "E1" stand for? Its simply something to make the DDname unique; the E indicates "entry." An I for "input" might be plainer, but an I and the number 1 are so hard to distinguish on output that the I has been avoided. Similarly, //BT3708U1 is an output. This naming convention avoids use of the "O" and uses IBM's own penchant for UT for "OUT," because the letter O and the number zero are also easy to confuse on printed output and video terminals.

These naming conventions are not dictated by anything in MVS, and significant variations on this theme can be found among installations. Every installation, however, will have some naming convention, because of the nature of large, shared-usage mainframes and the realities of data set security, work place organization, and business cost accounting. All of the examples in this book follow the standard naming convention described for a simple reason. The sooner you become accustomed to using multilevel name qualification, standard naming conventions, and contemporary JCL formatting, the sooner you will become more productive in business data processing.

MVS OUTPUTS FROM A RUN

Figure 3.6 is an extended illustration that gives in full the output generated by MVS when it performs the program executions we have directed. This output is not from our programs; it is from MVS itself. The level of detail MVS provides is often more minute than we care to see, but these are helpful if trouble is encountered during the run.

```
              J E S 2   J O B   L O G  --  S Y S T E M   M 5 F S  --  N O D E   F S D C L A 0 1


12.27.43 JOB 1415  $HASP373 FSBT686A STARTED - INIT 15 - CLASS E - SYS M5FS
12.27.43 JOB 1415  SMF103I JOB FSBT686A  STEP 001 OF 003  STARTED  12:27
12.27.43 JOB 1415  IEF403I - FSBT686A - STARTED
12.28.03 JOB 1415  SMF103I JOB FSBT686A  STEP 002 OF 003  STARTED  12:28
12.28.35 JOB 1415  SMF103I JOB FSBT686A  STEP 003 OF 003  STARTED  12:28
12.28.39 JOB 1415  IEF404I - FSBT686A - ENDED
12.28.39 JOB 1415  $HASP373 FSBT686A ENDED

------ JES2 JOB STATISTICS ------

 14 FEB 87 JOB EXECUTION DATE

      75 CARDS READ

     334 SYSOUT PRINT RECORDS              System part 1

       0 SYSPUNCH RECORDS

    1.04 MINUTES EXECUTION TIME

1     //FSBT686A  JOB AK00TEST,'DP2-JANOSSY',CLASS=E,MSGCLASS=X,        JOB 1415
      //  MSGLEVEL=(1,1),NOTIFY=BT05686
      ***
      ***      TEST RUN OF SEQUENTIAL UPDATE FSBT3708 -- VER 1
      ***      THIS JCL = BT05686.SOURCE.CNTL(BT3708JJ)
      ***
      *********************************************************
      ***                                                    *
      ***      SORT TRANS FILE                       A        *
      ***                                                    *
      *********************************************************
2     //STEPA     EXEC  PGM=SORT
3     //SORTLIB   DD    DSN=SYS1.SORTLIB,
      //  DISP=SHR
4     //SORTIN    DD    DSN=AK00.C99.TRANSIN,
      //  DISP=SHR
5     //SORTOUT   DD    DSN=&&TRANSORT,
      //  UNIT=SYSDA,
      //  DISP=(NEW,PASS,DELETE),
      //  DCB=(RECFM=FB,LRECL=71,BLKSIZE=6177),
      //  SPACE=(6177,(32,7),RLSE)             '2800 TRANS
6     //SYSOUT    DD    SYSOUT=*
```

```
7       //SYSUDUMP   DD  SYSOUT=*
8       //SORTWK01   DD  UNIT=SYSDA,SPACE=(CYL,2,,CONTIG)
9       //SORTWK02   DD  UNIT=SYSDA,SPACE=(CYL,2,,CONTIG)
10      //SYSIN      DD  *
        ***
        ************************************************************
        ***                                                      *
        ***    UPDATE MASTER FILE                          B     *
        ***                                                      *
        ************************************************************
11      //STEPB    EXEC  PGM=FSBT3708
12      //STEPLIB    DD  DSN=BT05686.TEST.LOADMODS,
        //  DISP=SHR
13      //BT3708E1   DD  DSN=&&TRANSORT,
        //  DISP=(OLD,DELETE)
14      //BT3708E2   DD  DSN=AK00.C99.TELMAST,            ┌──────────────────┐
        //  DISP=(OLD,KEEP)                               │  System part 2   │
15      //BT3708E3   DD  DSN=AK00.C99.AREAREF,            └──────────────────┘
        //  DISP=SHR
16      //BT3708U1   DD  SYSOUT=*
17      //BT3708U2   DD  DSN=AK00.C99.TELMAST.UPDATED,
        //  UNIT=SYSDA,
        //  DISP=(NEW,CATLG,DELETE),
        //  DCB=(RECFM=FB,LRECL=314,BLKSIZE=5966),
        //  SPACE=(5966,(4210,850),RLSE)                 '80000 RECS
18      //BT3708U3   DD  DSN=&&TRANSFIN,
        //  UNIT=SYSDA,
        //  DISP=(NEW,PASS,DELETE),
        //  DCB=(RECFM=FB,LRECL=102,BLKSIZE=6222),       '2800 TRANS
        //  SPACE=(6222,(46,9),RLSE)
19      //SYSOUT     DD  SYSOUT=*
20      //SYSUDUMP   DD  SYSOUT=*
        ************************************************************
        ***                                                      *
        ***      PRODUCE TRAN REPORT (INTERNAL SORT)       C     *
        ***                                                      *
        ************************************************************
21      //STEPC    EXEC  PGM=FSBT3719
22      //STEPLIB    DD  DSN=BT05686.TEST.LOADMODS,
        //  DISP=SHR
23      //SORTLIB    DD  DSN=SYS1.SORTLIB,
        //  DISP=SHR
24      //BT3719E1   DD  DSN=&&TRANSFIN,
        //  DISP=(OLD,DELETE)
25      //BT3719U1   DD  SYSOUT=*
26      //BT3719U2   DD  SYSOUT=*
27      //SORTWK01   DD  UNIT=SYSDA,SPACE=(CYL,2,,CONTIG)
28      //SORTWK02   DD  UNIT=SYSDA,SPACE=(CYL,2,,CONTIG)
29      //BT3719SM   DD  SYSOUT=*
30      //SYSOUT     DD  SYSOUT=*
31      //SYSUDUMP   DD  SYSOUT=*


IEF236I ALLOC. FOR FSBT686A STEPA
IEF237I 925  ALLOCATED TO SORTLIB
IEF237I 72C  ALLOCATED TO SORTIN
IEF237I 54B  ALLOCATED TO SORTOUT             ┌──────────────────┐
IEF237I JES2 ALLOCATED TO SYSOUT              │  System part 3   │
IEF237I JES2 ALLOCATED TO SYSUDUMP            └──────────────────┘
IEF237I 92D  ALLOCATED TO SORTWK01
IEF237I 929  ALLOCATED TO SORTWK02
IEF237I JES2 ALLOCATED TO SYSIN
IEF142I FSBT686A STEPA - STEP WAS EXECUTED - COND CODE 0000
IEF285I   SYS1.SORTLIB                                KEPT
IEF285I   VOL SER NOS= FSDC82.
IEF285I   AK00.C99.TRANSIN                           KEPT
IEF285I   VOL SER NOS= DPU259.
IEF285I   SYS87045.T122743.RA000.FSBT686A.TRANSORT   PASSED
IEF285I   VOL SER NOS= BT0188.
IEF285I   JES2.JOB01415.S00102                       SYSOUT
IEF285I   JES2.JOB01415.S00103                       SYSOUT
IEF285I   SYS87045.T122743.RA000.FSBT686A.R0000001   DELETED
IEF285I   SYS87045.T122743.RA000.FSBT686A.R0000002   DELETED
IEF285I   JES2.JOB01415.S00101                       SYSIN
IEF373I STEP /STEPA  / START 87045.1227
IEF374I STEP /STEPA  / STOP 87045.1228 CPU   0MIN 00.88SEC SRB   0MIN 00.09SEC VIRT   56K SYS   256K
```

50

```
IEF236I ALLOC. FOR FSBT686A STEPB
IEF237I 92C  ALLOCATED TO STEPLIB
IEF237I 540  ALLOCATED TO SYS00006
IEF237I 54B  ALLOCATED TO BT3708E1
IEF237I 714  ALLOCATED TO BT3708E2
IEF237I 714  ALLOCATED TO BT3708E3
IEF237I JES2 ALLOCATED TO BT3708U1
IEF237I 92A  ALLOCATED TO BT3708U2
IEF237I 54B  ALLOCATED TO BT3708U3
IEF237I JES2 ALLOCATED TO SYSOUT
IEF237I JES2 ALLOCATED TO SYSUDUMP
IEF142I FSBT686A STEPB - STEP WAS EXECUTED - COND CODE 0000
IEF285I   BT05686.TEST.LOADMODS                     KEPT
IEF285I   VOL SER NOS= FSDC53.
IEF285I   SYS6.PRODCAT.FSDC62                        KEPT
IEF285I   VOL SER NOS= FSDC62.
IEF285I   SYS87045.T122743.RA000.FSBT686A.TRANSORT   DELETED
IEF285I   VOL SER NOS= BT0188.
IEF285I   AK00.C99.TELMAST                           KEPT
IEF285I   VOL SER NOS= FSDC03.
IEF285I   AK00.C99.TELMAST.UPDATED                   CATALOGED
IEF285I   VOL SER NOS= FSDC22.
IEF285I   SYS87045.T122743.RA000.FSBT686A.TRANSFIN   PASSED
IEF285I   VOL SER NOS= BT0188.
IEF285I   JES2.JOB01415.S00105                       SYSOUT
IEF285I   JES2.JOB01415.S00106                       SYSOUT
IEF373I STEP /STEPB   / START 87045.1728
IEF374I STEP /STEPB   / STOP  87045.1728 CPU    0MIN 00.52SEC SRB    0MIN 00.11SEC VIRT    36K SYS    264K


IEF236I ALLOC. FOR FSBT686A STEPC
IEF237I 92C  ALLOCATED TO STEPLIB
IEF237I 925  ALLOCATED TO SORTLIB
IEF237I 54B  ALLOCATED TO BT3719E1
IEF237I JES2 ALLOCATED TO BT3719U1
IEF237I JES2 ALLOCATED TO BT3719U2
IEF237I 92D  ALLOCATED TO SORTWK01
IEF237I 929  ALLOCATED TO SORTWK02
IEF237I JES2 ALLOCATED TO BT3719SM
IEF237I JES2 ALLOCATED TO SYSOUT
IEF237I JES2 ALLOCATED TO SYSUDUMP
IEF142I FSBT686A STEPC - STEP WAS EXECUTED - COND CODE 0000
IEF285I   BT05686.TEST.LOADMODS                     KEPT
IEF285I   VOL SER NOS= FSDC53.
IEF285I   SYS1.SORTLIB                              KEPT
IEF285I   VOL SER NOS= FSDC82.
IEF285I   SYS87045.T122743.RA000.FSBT686A.TRANSFIN   DELETED
IEF285I   VOL SER NOS= BT0188.
IEF285I   JES2.JOB01415.S00107                       SYSOUT
IEF285I   JES2.JOB01415.S00108                       SYSOUT
IEF285I   SYS87045.T122815.RA000.FSBT686A.R0000001   DELETED
IEF285I   SYS87045.T122815.RA000.FSBT686A.R0000002   DELETED
IEF285I   JES2.JOB01415.S00109                       SYSOUT
IEF285I   JES2.JOB01415.S00110                       SYSOUT
IEF285I   JES2.JOB01415.S00111                       SYSOUT
IEF373I STEP /STEPC   / START 87045.1728
IEF374I STEP /STEPC   / STOP  87045.1728 CPU    0MIN 00.75SEC SRB    0MIN 00.08SEC VIRT    68K SYS    288K


IEF237I 54B  ALLOCATED TO SYS00001
IEF285I   SYS87045.T122844.RA000.FSBT686A.R0000001   KEPT
IEF285I   VOL SER NOS= PUBL99.
IEF375I JOB /FSBT686A/ START 87045.1727
IEF376I JOB /FSBT686A/ STOP  87045.1728 CPU    0MIN 02.15SEC SRB    0MIN 00.28SEC
```

FIGURE 3.6. MVS/XA system outputs: job log, allocation/deallocation reports

A separator page carries the job name in large block letters. This page is not shown here. It carries the job name; that is, the FSBT686A that follows the slashes on the JOB card. It also carries the job number assigned when the job is submitted. This is a number issued by MVS; the numbers increment upward by one as each job is received in the MVS input queue. The starting job number is usually reset to zero at the beginning of the business day. The MVS run outputs are divided into three "system" parts, followed by whatever print output has been directed to the same SYSOUT class as MSGCLASS.

The first of the system parts is a high level summary that includes some of the messages written by MVS to the computer operator's console during the run. Messages indicate when the job started, when it ended, and if it ended normally or abnormally. This part is labeled "system Part 1" on Figure 3.6. It is officially called the "JES Job Log"; JES is the job entry subsystem, the component of MVS that accepts, manages, and reports on jobs.

The second of the system parts, labeled "system part 2" on Figure 3.6, consists of a listing of the JCL submitted.[11] This listing reformats the JCL slightly by replacing the slashes in comment lines with asterisks; thus a line starting with //* now begins with ***. In addition, complete JCL statements are numbered at the left side. Because a statement may span more than one line or card image, fewer statement numbers than lines are found. *Error messages that indicate JCL errors specify the statement number, not the line or card image number on which the error occurred.* In this part of the system output, instream data, that is, data within the job stream after a DD * indication, does not appear. It isn't JCL, and this listing shows only JCL. Instream data will appear as program output at the end of system reports if the program receiving it writes it out; most utilities do so.

The third of the system parts of the output from the run—system part 3—may or may not begin with "substitution JCL." This part is called the "allocation/deallocation report" because it shows the devices and data sets allocated to the run and their subsequent deallocation and disposition. It does not start with substitutions in this case because we have submitted the JCL itself as a whole. Substitution refers to the replacement of symbolic place holders in the JCL with specific values and is related to the use of JCL that has been "canned" as a cataloged procedure.

Cataloged procedures, or "procs," are simply JCL like this, stripped of a JOB card and // null ending card, and placed in a common procedure library or "proclib." Procs have a great deal of relevance to production JCL; that is, JCL packaged for repeated submission by other than the originator. Aside from a compile and link proc that programmers typically use, JCL testing usually follows the pattern of raw JCL submission, then testing as an instream or noninstalled proc, and placement as a real proc into SYS1.PROCLIB or another designated production library. We convert a production version of this JCL into a proc in Chapter 16.

Explanation of Allocation/Deallocation Report

The third part of the system output for this job is the most voluminous and detailed. It begins with a line prefaced by a message identifier,

IEF236I. On this line is listed the job and step name for which additional information follows.

The information that follows, prefaced by message identifier IEF237I, lists the devices, by hardware device address, that MVS has allocated to each data set. The data sets are listed by the DDname of the DD statement in which they are mentioned, in DD statement order. Interspersed on occasion between them are device allocations made for MVS's own purposes.

The end of the allocation messages for a job step is marked by a line that carries identifier IEF142I, which is an important line: it tells whether or not the step was executed and whether it executed successfully. The COND CODE on this line shows the value, if any, that we moved to RETURN-CODE in a COBOL program, coded after STOP in a FORTRAN program, or posted with PL/I. If we did not take this action in the program and it encountered no problem that forced an abnormal ending, the COND CODE value is printed as four zeros. IBM utilities place values like 0004, 0008, 0012, 0016, and 0020 in the return code if error conditions are experienced. The meaning of these code values for the utilities is summarized in Appendix E. If a step ended abnormally, the system completion code generated by MVS for the event prints on this line.

Following the IEF142I line for the job step, we see messages beginning with the preface IEF285I. These lines show the disposition of each physical data set after the step has ended. Each data set is accorded at least two lines, the first of which names the data set and, to the far right, indicates the status in which it has been left after the step. The second of the lines gives the volume serial number of the media on which the data set resides. For certain manipulations, such as the deletion of a cataloged data set, four lines are printed. The first two indicate that the data set was uncataloged; the second pair is almost identical, but indicate that the data set has been deleted.

If, for some reason, we are creating a data set but not cataloging it, the system output lines identified with the preface IEF285I are vital to us. They carry the identity of the media on which the data set has been written. Most often, when data sets are created, we allow MVS to find available media on which to write the data set. If the JCL does not call for cataloging the data set, the IEF285I lines are the only indicators that can tell us where the data set has been placed.

The final two lines for a step are labeled with the identifiers IEF373I and IEF374I. The first of these lines indicates the step name, the date it started to execute, expressed in Julian format, and the hour and minute, expressed in military 24-hour time. The second line gives the date and time the step finished and may also indicate, with hard-to-read spacing, how much CPU or central processor time the step used, and some other information including real and virtual memory.

The display of information, starting with a line labeled IEF236I and ending with a line labeled IEF374I, states all that the system normally tells us about the execution of a given job step. If there are more steps in the job stream, the cycle of messages repeats for each step in this pattern.

Finally, at the end of the entire job, there may be tasks remaining for the system to complete before the housekeeping for the job stream is complete. For example, if temporary data sets have been used in the run, and the last step using them doesn't indicate a DISP = (OLD,DELETE) to delete them, MVS takes care of the deletion at the end of the run. Since MVS "uses itself" for this type of action, the deletion of the passed temporary data set receives IEF285I messages. Other data sets created and used by the system for its own purposes also are deleted in this way and receive similar messages.

When all is finished, MVS writes two final detail lines, labeled IEF375I and IEF376I. These lines indicate the starting date and time of the entire job, its ending date and time, and the total CPU time that was used.

Customized MVS System Output

The information output by MVS, illustrated in Figure 3.6, is that which a "plain vanilla" version of MVS generates. This print results from a large stream of information recorded by MVS in the "system management facility" or "SMF" file. The selected parts of this information normally reduced to paper by MVS are just that: selected parts.

It is possible for installations to modify the routine that prints the JES job log and system reports to display additional information. Certain software packages for job resource accounting are also available to intercept the SMF data flow and pick off information useful for billing and accounting; some of this software may also add to or change the information presentation in the system parts of the job stream output.

Although the plain-vanilla MVS printed job-stream information includes quite a bit, it leaves out some data that installations often want to see. This involves the amount of data read or written to each device and data set. I/O makes use of "channel programs," via the execute channel command macro instruction, "EXCP." Counts of EXCPs for each data set are included in the SMF data flow but are not printed by the plain vanilla MVS system reporting component.

If system output from the machine you use appears slightly different from that shown here, most likely your installation has enhanced the system reports to carry EXCP count information. One channel command execution occurs for each block of data read or written, not for each record. The EXCP count for a given data set indicates how much I/O occurred for it, including data set label reading or writing. This allows a close approximation of the number of records read or written to a data set, useful to know when a job fails and problems must be resolved.

ERRORS AND SYSTEM COMPLETION CODES

There are potentially several different points at which a job stream may fail, all the way from incorrect JCL syntax to program logic failures, data set or I/O problems, or illogical JCL. The simplest job errors relate to incorrect syntax or the coding of a parameter in an invalid manner. This type of error becomes immediately apparent because the JCL scanner, MVS software that initially processes the JCL, "bounces" the syntax it finds to be improper. The following message is typical:

```
STMT NO. MESSAGE
   6     IEF642I EXCESSIVE PARAMETER LENGTH IN THE DSNAME FIELD
```

This is the result when a data set name with too many characters in one of its levels is coded. Many other examples produce the same result: incorrectly placed commas, missing commas, a missing parenthesis, and incorrect statement format.

It is possible to catch syntax errors without actually attempting a run of a job stream by coding the TYPRUN = SCAN option on the job card:

```
//FSBT686B  JOB AK00TEST,'DP2-JANOSSY',CLASS=E,MSGCLASS=A,
//  MSGLEVEL=1,NOTIFY=BT05686,TYPRUN=SCAN
```

This invokes *only* the JCL scanner, which is handy when JCL is being composed and the actual programs or data sets are not yet in place, as a means of cleaning up minor errors in advance of real testing. A minor annoyance develops when actual runs are initiated and one has forgotten to remove the TYPRUN = SCAN; nothing happens except the scan.

JCL Errors Other than Syntax

A second class of errors may be confused with simple syntax errors due to the type of message that is received. The basis is ostensibly a "JCL ERROR." This message is misleading, however; the cause may not be JCL at all but the lack of a data set or disk space.

If a job stream attempts to access a data set that is not on the system, or is present but not cataloged and the job assumes that it is, MVS presumes that the JCL is wrong; that perhaps the data set name has been mispelled. To track down the cause of such an error we must examine not only the job log but the allocation/deallocation report as well. The job log for a failed job is illustrated in Figure 3.7; the corresponding detailed messages located within the allocation/deallocation report appear as

```
IEF212I FSBT686B STEPB BT3708E2 - DATA SET NOT FOUND
```

and identify the step and DDname involved. The data set name, as well
as the presence of the data set on the system, should be checked. It is
possible that the name is incorrect or that the data set was inadverdently
deleted by some earlier action. JCL ERROR can also occur when a data
set is requested and found but resides on a device different from the
type coded in the JCL. This is one compelling argument in favor of cataloging all data sets; the system catalog records the device type needed
by a data set, making it unnecessary to code the UNIT parameter to access
the data set after creation.

JCL ERROR can be caused by insufficient disk space on the system
to allocate to the step. Note that this situation differs from running out
of disk space after a step has started to execute. Running out of disk
space after a step has started execution is covered by a definite system
completion code, as we discuss below.

The consequences of a JCL ERROR are not the same as those of syntax
errors. For a syntax error, the job stream never actually starts running
at all. For a JCL ERROR, the job does start running, but MVS kills it at
the step that encounters the error and all subsequent steps are *ignored
completely*. Although JCL ERRORS are relatively easy to diagnose, they
present special problems in the recovery of failed production jobs, as
discussed in Chapter 14.

A related type of error for which MVS also provides clear and con-
spicuous reporting lies in the area of missing DD statements. Figure 3.8
illustrates messages received when no DDname is found that matches
one coded in a SELECT/ASSIGN statement. In fact, multiple errors are
shown in this four step job stream. The first step of the job stream was
executed successfully. No DDname appears in JCL matching one used

```
              J E S 2   J O B   L O G   --   S Y S T E M   M 5 F S   --   N O D E   F S D C L A 0 1


20.51.53 JOB 1922  $HASP373 FSBT686A STARTED - INIT 11 - CLASS E - SYS M5FS
20.51.53 JOB 1922  SMF103I JOB FSBT686A  STEP 001 OF 004  STARTED  20:51
20.51.54 JOB 1922  IEF403I - FSBT686A - STARTED
20.51.55 JOB 1922  SMF103I JOB FSBT686A  STEP 002 OF 004  STARTED  20:51
20.51.55 JOB 1922  IEF453I FSBT686A - JOB FAILED - JCL ERROR
20.51.55 JOB 1922  $HASP395 FSBT686A ENDED

------ JES2 JOB STATISTICS ------

 14 FEB 87 JOB EXECUTION DATE

       83 CARDS READ

      131 SYSOUT PRINT RECORDS

        0 SYSPUNCH RECORDS

     0.03 MINUTES EXECUTION TIME
```

FIGURE 3.7. MVS/XA job log from a failed run: JCL error

```
          J E S 2   J O B   L O G  --  S Y S T E M   M 5 F S  --  N O D E   F S D C L A 0 1


08.19.20 JOB  323  $HASP373 FSBT686A STARTED - INIT 19 - CLASS E - SYS M5FS
08.19.20 JOB  323  SMF103I JOB FSBT686A  STEP 001 OF 004  STARTED  08:19
08.19.20 JOB  323  IEF403I - FSBT686A - STARTED
08.19.27 JOB  323  SMF103I JOB FSBT686A  STEP 002 OF 004  STARTED  08:19
08.19.33 JOB  323  IEC130I BT3716U1  DD STATEMENT MISSING
08.19.33 JOB  323  + IKF115I- QSAM ERROR - AT DISPLACEMENT 000C1C IN PROGRAM FSBT3716   FILE STATUS IS 90
08.19.35 JOB  323  SMF103I JOB FSBT686A  STEP 003 OF 004  STARTED  08:19
08.19.42 JOB  323  IEC141I 013-18,IGG0191B,FSBT686A,STEPC,BT3723E2,714,FSDC03
08.19.42 JOB  323  IEC141I BT05686.SOURCE.DATA
08.19.42 JOB  323  IEA995I SYMPTOM DUMP OUTPUT
                     ABEND CODE SYSTEM=013  TIME=08.19.42 SEQ=01339 CPU=0000 ASID=0027
                     PSW AT TIME OF ERROR  075C1000   00DEA396  ILC 2  INTC 0D
                       NO ACTIVE MODULE FOUND
                       DATA AT PSW  00DEA390 - 41003786  0A0D45E0  372A5820
                       GPR  0-3  00DEA4F8  A0013000  00007134  40DE9D72
                       GPR  4-7  007C8BE8  027C8F24  007C8ED4  027C8F24
                       GPR  8-11 007C8EF4  00FBB590  58FD0178  007C86DC
                       GPR 12-15 00FDCA8F  00000052  80DE9E62  00000018
                     END OF SYMPTOM DUMP
08.20.06 JOB  323  IEF450I FSBT686A STEPC - ABEND=S013 U0000 REASON=00000000
08.20.06 JOB  323  SMF103I JOB FSBT686A  STEP 004 OF 004  STARTED  08:20
08.20.06 JOB  323  IEF404I FSBT686A - ENDED
08.20.07 JOB  323  $HASP395 FSBT686A ENDED

------ JES2 JOB STATISTICS ------

 14 FEB 87 JOB EXECUTION DATE

        83 CARDS READ

       143 SYSOUT PRINT RECORDS

         0 SYSPUNCH RECORDS

      0.23 MINUTES EXECUTION TIME
```

FIGURE 3.8. MVS/XA job log from a failed run: DD statement error and unrelated missing PDS member

in the program in its second step; the system clearly complains of this fact with a message labeled IEC130I.

Figure 3.8 also indicates how some types of errors do not cause abandonment of the job stream. This job continues to be processed even though its second step had a missing DD statement and an access method error. Its third step, named //STEPC, sought a member it could not locate in the stated PDS, and received a system completion code of 013-18. This type of failure does cause the job stream to be abandoned; the fourth step is shown starting but is merely passed through by MVS without execution.

Job Abends and System Completion Codes

As discussed in Chapter 14, both MVS and the program itself have the capability of communicating with the outside world via a coded value. The code with which a program does this is the user return code. The code by which the system communicates is the system completion code. The system uses the latter code to indicate why a run failed when it happened during the actual execution of a step.

System completion codes are three position values expressed in hexadecimal. The value of zero—000—is posted by MVS when a step executes and ends normally. When a system completion code other than 000 is present, the job log carries a message that starts with an identifier like IEF450I. This message line contains the system completion code and the user return code, but in fact when a system completion code is posted no user return code will ever be shown by MVS; its system code preempts the message line.[12] An error message, citing the job name, step name, and DDname appears as:

```
IEF450I FSBT686A STEPA SORTIN - ABEND S013 U0000
```

Several hundred circumstances can cause a nonzero system completion code to be posted. Some of the code values are complete indications of the problem; others are broken down further by reason codes that follow the main code. Appendix F lists the commonly encountered system completion codes and reason codes, and suggested actions to resolve the situations that provoke their issuance.

The job log format of the completion code for a failure differs between MVS and MVS/XA. Figure 3.9 illustrates the format of an 806 error under MVS; the code and its reason code breakdown are printed in the format 806- 4 on a single line. Figure 3.10 shows how this same type of error is reported by MVS/XA. The XA rendition is more comprehensive but also slightly more difficult to interpret.

MVS/XA provides a symptom dump that includes the contents of all

```
         J E S 2   J O B   L O G  --  S Y S T E M   M 5 F S  --  N O D E   F S D C L A 0 1


10.33.42 JOB 516 &$HASP373 FSBT686A STARTED - INIT 8 - CLASS E - SYS M5FS
10.33.42 JOB 516 SMF103I JOB FSBT686A  STEP 01 OF 04  STARTED  10:33
10.33.43 JOB 516 IEF403I - FSBT686A - STARTED
10.33.51 JOB 516 IEA703I 806 -4 FSBT686A STEPA    MODULE ACCESSED FSDATECV    <-------
10.33.51 JOB 516 IEF450I FSBT686A STEPA - ABEND S806 U0000
10.33.51 JOB 516 SMF103I JOB FSBT686A  STEP 02 OF 04  STARTED  10:33
10.33.51 JOB 516 SMF103I JOB FSBT686A  STEP 03 OF 04  STARTED  10:33
10.33.51 JOB 516 SMF103I JOB FSBT686A  STEP 04 OF 04  STARTED  10:33
10.33.51 JOB 516 IEF404I FSBT686A - ENDED
10.33.51 JOB 516 &$HASP395 FSBT686A ENDED

------ JES2 JOB STATISTICS ------

14 FEB 87 JOB EXECUTION DATE

     83 CARDS READ

    161 SYSOUT PRINT RECORDS

      0 SYSPUNCH RECORDS

   0.61 MINUTES EXECUTION TIME
```

FIGURE 3.9. MVS/SP job log from a failed run: missing load module

J E S 2   J O B   L O G   --   S Y S T E M   M 5 F S   --   N O D E   F S D C L A 0 1

```
10.35.14 JOB  518  $HASP373 FSBT686A STARTED - INIT 17 - CLASS E - SYS M5FS
10.35.14 JOB  518  SMF103I JOB FSBT686A  STEP 001 OF 004  STARTED  10:35
10.35.15 JOB  518  IEF403I - FSBT686A - STARTED
10.35.19 JOB  518  CSV003I REQUESTED MODULE FSDATECV NOT FOUND
10.35.19 JOB  518  IEA995I SYMPTOM DUMP OUTPUT
          ────────▶   ABEND CODE SYSTEM=806  TIME=10.35.18 SEQ=01234 CPU=0000 ASID=0032
                      PSW AT TIME OF ERROR  070C1000   80FFFE44  ILC 2  INTC 0D
                      NO ACTIVE MODULE FOUND
                      DATA AT PSW  00FFFE3E - 5610A4DA  0A0D186D  58D002FC
                      GPR  0-3  00806000  80806000  00000D20  00FBB590
                      GPR  4-7  00000010  007FF0F8  007D8850  00F84A00
                      GPR  8-11 00000026  007D8850  80FFFA5A  00000C00
                      GPR 12-15 00000000  007D8850  80FFFDDE  00000004   ◀────────
                   END OF SYMPTOM DUMP
10.35.19 JOB  518  IEA450I FSBT686A STEPA - ABEND S806 U0000 REASON=00000000
10.35.19 JOB  518  SMF103I JOB FSBT686A  STEP 002 OF 004  STARTED  10:35
10.35.19 JOB  518  SMF103I JOB FSBT686A  STEP 003 OF 004  STARTED  10:35
10.35.19 JOB  518  SMF103I JOB FSBT686A  STEP 004 OF 004  STARTED  10:35
10.35.19 JOB  518  IEF404I FSBT686A - ENDED
10.35.19 JOB  518  $HASP395 FSBT686A ENDED

------ JES2 JOB STATISTICS ------

  14 FEB 87 JOB EXECUTION DATE

      83 CARDS READ

     189 SYSOUT PRINT RECORDS

       0 SYSPUNCH RECORDS

    0.55 MINUTES EXECUTION TIME
```

FIGURE 3.10. MVS/XA job log from a failed run: missing load module

16 general purpose CPU registers at the time of the abend, something for which one has to hunt in a dump under MVS. But to see the reason code breakdown under MVS/XA you need to realize that this code, abbreviated "rc" in manuals, is really a return code from lower level system assembler modules. Return codes, including those from system software modules, are conveyed in register 15. Hence for the 806 abend as reported by MVS/XA, the "- 4" reason code is present on the line labeled GPR 12-15 that displays the contents of general-purpose registers 12 through 15; it appears as 00000004 in the last column.

In both renditions a system completion code of 806 indicates that a load module a step had attempted to access could not be located in the partitioned data set named at //STEPLIB or regarded by default as the load module library. Confirm this interpretation in Appendix F. For this type of error subsequent job steps are abandoned by MVS, for it merely acknowledges them without giving them control.[13]

The special program exception codes such as 0C4 and 0C7 which result from logical errors within programs are really just a subset of system completion codes. Appendix F provides extended coverage of the circumstances in which program exception codes can be received beginning on page 412.

REVIEW QUESTIONS AND (*)EXERCISES

1. What major elements are usually shown in a graphic presentation of a job stream?

2. A programmer developed a new program named FSBT0533 and compiled and linkage edited it placing the load module in a PDS named BT05712.TEST.LOADMODS. In an attempt to execute the program, however, she omitted a //STEPLIB DD statement. What is likely to be the result?

3. A programmer spelled a data set name as AK00.C99.SORTTRANS instead of AK00.C99.SORTTRAN. What is likely to be the result when the JCL is submitted for a run?

4. Under MVS, where is the sort work space for an internal sort provided?

5. What happens to a five step job stream if a DDname is mispelled in the third step?

6. Why is the MVS-generated print that documents a job's processing called an allocation/deallocation report?

*7. Add TYPRUN = SCAN to the job card for any JCL you have already composed and used successfully to execute a program. Submit the JCL and explain what happens and why.

*8. Develop a job stream that sorts a test data set into ascending sequence on a numeric field and then lists the sorted data with a simple IEBPTPCH illustrated in item 14 of Chapter 17. Code the sort control statement as instream data and indicate why it appears where it does in the printed outputs.

*9. Code an IEBGENER step as illustrated in item 12 of Chapter 17 to copy 80-byte card image data to a temporary sequential disk data set. Code //SYSIN DD * for the input to IEBGENER, and physically copy in the source code for a program at this point, following it with /* and any other necessary DD statements. Code a second step, invoking IEBPTPCH, to read the temporary data set and list on paper the records in their entirety without concern for individual fields. Use the job stream to copy the source code to print. Then delete the imbedded source code, replace it with some JCL statements from some other assignment, and attempt to reuse the job stream to list the JCL. Explain why this second attempt fails and code an appropriate means of making it succeed.[7]

*10. Write, compile, and linkage edit a program in COBOL, PL/I, or assembler that adds two variables and prints the result on a report;

the variables within the program should be properly initialized. House the load module for this program in an appropriate load module library. Take a copy of the program source code and remove initialization for one of the variables to be added, creating a program that will fail with an 0C7 system completion code. Build JCL to execute the correct program seven times in sequence, once in each of seven steps, and run it. Then replace the execution of the correct program at the third step with the execution of the program that will incur the 0C7. Run this job stream and explain how and why MVS treats the steps following the third step.

NOTES

1. The example job stream is sufficient to perform a run of the update program and could test the group of programs. This test is often called a string test and it follows individual program testing. This is not representative of a full scale production job stream that would execute these programs in a production mode because of several factors that are beyond the scope of discussion here. We consider these additional factors, such as providing the capability to recreate report outputs, generation data group handling of files, job stream restart and recovery, and cataloged procedure use in Chapters 4 through 16. A programmer's test job stream is used initially for discussion purposes to focus attention on basic issues common to all job streams.

2. The example job stream invokes an update run with only one type of transaction— a change transaction. The run does not perform master file adds or deletes. For a complete discussion of sequential update and add/change/delete processing, which includes the generic logic model that defines this process, see Chapters 14 and 15 of *Commercial Software Engineering: For Productive Program Design*, James G. Janossy, ISBN 0-471-81576-4, John Wiley and Sons, Inc., 1985.

3. Except for the finished-transaction output associated with DDname //BT3708U3, program FSBT3708 is identical to program PSD186, which is the focus of Appendix B of *Commercial Software Engineering*, cited in Note 2 above. In that appendix the full background scenario and specification for this master file update routine are provided. This background is not essential to an understanding of the JCL discussed here, but depending on your own exposure to software design and business data processing, you may find it helpful.

4. A //STEPLIB DD statement is needed when the program named in the EXEC statement is not stored as a member of the partitioned data set named SYS1.LINKLIB or another automatic call library. Generally speaking, only standard software like compilers, utilities, and production programs are placed in SYS1.LINKLIB and automatic call libraries.

5. Despite its imposing stature in automation, IBM is composed of people, too. A vast army of programming personnel created OS and its utility programs in the early 1960s. Given the size and scope of the undertaking, it is to be expected that variation occurred in things like the DDnames that utilities use for message outputs and inputs. Inconsistencies in the format of control card statements for the sort and other utilities sometimes make the composition of control statements an error-prone process. Learning these subtleties becomes less frustrating when one realizes

that MVS is not a monolithic, omnipotent entity but rather an assemblage of different software elements evolved from the efforts of thousands of skilled people over a number of decades.

6. Common sort format codes are CH for character PIC X data, ZD for zoned decimal PIC S9 fields, PD for COMP-3 packed decimal data, and BI for binary COMP fields. Additional specialized format codes exist and are documented in programmer's manuals for sort utilities, but those other formats are so much less commonly applicable that they do not warrant emphasis.

7. The beginning of instream data is denoted by the DD * statement. The end of the data thus imbedded in JCL is denoted by the card image starting with /* or by the next executable JCL statement. This is nearly always workable. When, however, it is JCL statements themselves are housed instream as data, a different delimiter is needed. This situation often developed in the transition period between punched card usage and TSO, when decks of JCL statements were prefaced by JCL to copy the JCL statements to disk libraries. The JCL statements to be copied were to be treated as instream data and manipulated by simple JCL that invoked a copy program such as IBM's IEBGENER utility.

To allow for these rare occurrences MVS has two means besides DD * of using instream data. To handle JCL as data the statement can be coded as DD DATA, for example:

```
//SYSIN   DD DATA
```

This allows the instream data that follows to begin with two slashes and still be regarded simply as data. The end of the instream data is marked by the /* card image.

If the instream data contains the /* symbols in columns 1 and 2, it is possible to define some other delimiter for the end of data. This can be done by coding:

```
//SYSIN   DD *,DLM='xx'
```

The xx in this statement can be any two characters that do not occur in the first two columns of the data. For example, if these two characters were specified as 'QT' a card image that contains QT in columns 1 and 2 must be placed after the last card of instream data to signal the end of the data.

As a carryover from the earliest days, MVS will generate a DD card with the DD name of SYSIN if it encounters card images that do not begin with // or /* and are not preceded by an indication of instream data. This has little utility in the contemporary environment but may occasionally raise a question when it occurs because of the incorrect entry of the first or second character of a JCL statement. The //SYSIN statement generated carries the comment GENERATED DD STATE-MENT. *DD statements appearing in JCL but not used by a program do not constitute an error to MVS.* The generation of a //SYSIN statement by MVS for what might be an incorrectly keyed DD statement can actually be troublesome, because it masks the real syntax error that must be corrected.

8. The JCL in this chapter causes a new master file named AK00.C99.TELMAST.UPDATED to be output and cataloged. Once cataloged this data set must be uncataloged or deleted before the JCL is resubmitted to make another run. In Chapter 6 we discuss how the IEFBR14 utility and the DISP parameter of the DD statement make it easy to do this automatically.

9. Sort work space can also be allocated by MVS dynamically, even when the sort utility is being accessed from within a program that uses the SORT verb. This involves use of a DD statement that carries the name //SORTCNTL. See item 3 in Chapter 17 for additional information on this capability.

10. Farnon Standard Corporation is a fictitious entity. Any similarity between this name and the name of a real business organization is purely coincidental.

11. The restatement of the JCL shown in Figure 3.6 as system part 2 is actually simpler than it would have been if this job stream had been executed as a cataloged procedure. As illustrated, the JCL itself is simply listed by the system. When executed as a cataloged procedure, the JCL is listed and the symbolic parameter substitution JCL follows immediately. Chapter 16 provides in-depth information on instream and cataloged procedures.

12. Third party, non-IBM software, such as a tape management system, is sometimes spliced into MVS by an installation. It is possible for this software to intercept normal MVS completion code posting routines and to cause a nonzero system completion code and a nonzero user return code to be printed at the same time. MVS itself never uses both codes at the same time.

13. See Chapter 14 for information on the EVEN and ONLY specifications of the COND parameter, which can direct MVS to do more than merely acknowledge the presence of a step following one that abended.

—————— PART 2 ——————

WORKADAY JCL

In the chapters that follow we concentrate on the parameters that may be present in various combinations in any given DD statement. Because the use of real-life examples is critical to demonstration of these JCL details, the next chapters continue to build on the example sort and sequential update job stream illustrated in Figure 3.4. We take that test job stream and develop it into professional caliber JCL, then develop it further into a fully recoverable, production grade cataloged procedure.

It is easy to become frustrated with JCL because of the terminology used to discuss it. The format of JCL syntax illustrated earlier began the process of bringing order to your JCL without lumbering through verbiage concerning parameters and subparameters. You have seen JCL in which DD statements have been coded in this format:

```
//BT3708U2   DD   DSN=AK00.C99.TELMAST.UPDATED,
//    UNIT=SYSDA,
//    DISP=(NEW,CATLG,DELETE),
//    DCB=(RECFM=FB,LRECL=312,BLKSIZE=5928),
//    SPACE=(5928,(4250,30),RLSE)
```

In formal terminology these five lines constitute one JCL DD statement.
Each item such as UNIT, DISP, DCB, and SPACE is a *keyword parameter*
of the DD statement. Breakdowns within a parameter, such as NEW,
CATLG, and DELETE of the DISP parameter, are *subparameters*. Although different types of JCL statements have parameters, it is the keyword parameters of the DD statement that are by far the most essential
to learn well.

There are 32 parameters such as DSN, UNIT, and DISP defined for
the DD statement. When a major new device or feature becomes available,
IBM may add one or more parameters to the DD statement to deal with
it, as was done with the AMP parameter for VSAM. The present 32 parameters are technically known as keyword parameters because the word
such as UNIT or DISP is important, not its position in the DD statement.
Among the 32 DD keyword parameters only eight are used in nearly all
JCL; many DD statement will require only one or two of them, and some
are used only for disk, some for tape, and some for print. It makes a
great deal of sense to leave a purely alphabetical recitation of DD parameters to reference manuals and concentrate on the heavily used parameters first. These eight DD parameters are:

DSN	(Chapter 4)
UNIT	(Chapter 5)
DISP	(Chapter 6)
DCB	(Chapter 7)
SPACE	(Chapter 8)
VOL	(Chapter 9)
LABEL	(Chapter 10)
AMP	(Chapter 11)

Although these keyword parameters can be coded in any order within
a DD statement, there is a reason to address them in the order shown.
This order places at the top the main parameters that almost always
appear on a DD statement. Those at the bottom of this short list will
appear less commonly or only in specialized cases. In the next chapters
each of these eight parameters is discussed individually.

Chapter 12, the last in this section, is dedicated to printed output and
provides information on nine additional specialized DD keyword parameters: BURST, CHARS, COPIES, DEST, FCB, FLASH, OUTLIM,
OUTPUT, and UCS. These parameters apply only to printed output.

4

DSN: Data Set Name

Data set name is coded DSNAME or more commonly DSN. It is one of the most prominent of all DD statement keyword parameters. When specified, it is usually placed first in the series of parameters on a DD statement.

Under MVS and MVS/XA a data set name can be up to 44 characters in length. This is not an arbitrarily specified figure; it results from the fact that the originators of OS JCL envisioned that a DSN would have as many as four levels of full length name "qualifiers" in addition to the eight character name itself:

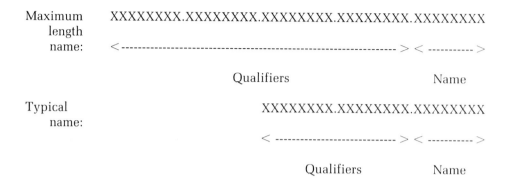

Maximum
length
name:

Typical
name:

Because a qualifier or name can have up to eight characters and the periods separating the qualifiers and name really do exist in the overall data set name, a total of 44 characters is supported. The portions of the data set name between periods are sometimes referred to as "simple" names. When only one group of eight or fewer characters makes up the entire data set name, the data set is said to have a simple name.[1]

Data set name qualifiers need not be a full eight characters long. If these portions of the overall data set name are shorter, the 44 characters can conceivably have more individual portions, separated by a greater number of periods. In practice, data set names are customarily formed with three parts, such as BT05686.SOURCE.CNTL. VSAM data sets usually have one or two additional parts that identify particular components such as data, index, or "path," something quite different from the MS-DOS "path." It would be highly unusual for a data set name to require as many as the 44 allowable characters.

The highest level qualifiers of data set names are regarded as special; they are made known to the system catalog and are tied into the operation of access control or security software. This provides the ability to associate data sets with major groups of users and within a user community to associate data sets with different application systems. This also makes it possible to confine access to data sets to specific parties. The highest level qualifier is sometimes called the "high level index," a term that stems from its identification in the system catalog. TSO data sets are customarily named with the TSO logon identifier as the highest level qualifier. For this reason a TSO user identified as BT05686 would have a COBOL or PL/I and a CNTL data set named similarly to:

```
BT05686.SOURCE.COBOL
BT05686.SOURCE.PLI
BT05686.SOURCE.CNTL
```

DATA SET NAME FORMATION

The characters used to form a data set name can include upper case letters, numbers, other alphanumeric symbols such as the hyphen, a "plus zero" and the few "national symbols" such as @, #, and $.[2] Use of the last five symbols, however, is usually frowned on because they are unusual, they detract from legibility, and because letters and numbers provide thoroughly satisfactory data set naming capabilities. Each qualifier—each portion of the data set name preceding the portion of the name after the last period—must start with a letter or a national symbol; numbers cannot be used to start a qualifier or name.

Data Set Names and Their Meanings

Absolutely every data set on an IBM mainframe has a data set name even though in some DD statements no DSN is stated. When DSN is omitted, it does not mean that the data set involved has no name. It simply means that the system by default constructs a name for the data set; the JCL has declined to specify a name; therefore MVS itself must do it.

There are two classes of data set: permanent and temporary. Data set name distinguishes these two classes. There is one type of name for a permanent data set, also known as a "nontemporary" data set, and two types of name for a temporary data set:

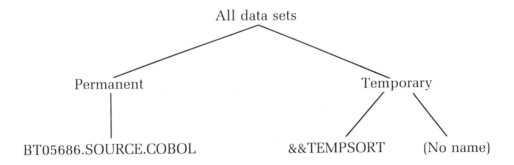

Permanent Data Sets

At the time the data set is created a permanent data set name is supplied by the DSN parameter in JCL in a format in which the name is not prefaced by two ampersands. This data set is usually intended to remain on the system after the job ends and carries a disposition, or DISP, of (NEW,KEEP) or (NEW,CATLG). The data set need not remain on the system after the job stream ends. It can be deleted in a subsequent job step that carries a reference of (OLD,DELETE), but if created with a permanent name with a DISP as above, and not explicitly deleted, it will remain in existence. An example is AK00.C99.TELMAST.

If the same permanent data set name is inadvertently coded in two output DD statements in JCL, resulting in an attempt to create duplicate data set names, a JCL error may result and the job may be terminated. If MVS happens to assign a different disk unit for the second identically named data set, it will be written. But MVS takes no precaution to find a different disk unit for the same-named data set; it can assign the same unit that it chose for the first occurrence of the permanent data set name, causing a job failure. An attempt to catalog a duplicate data set name is not fatal; it simply generates an inconspicuous message on the allocation/deallocation report:

```
IEF285I   AK00.C99.TELMAST                        NOT CATLG 2
IEF285I   VOL SER NOS= FSDC03
```

Temporary Data Sets

Named Temporary Data Set.   At the time a named temporary data set is created an unqualified name is supplied that follows the conventional character usage for a name; it is one to eight characters in length and prefaced by two ampersands.[3] The data set is usually given a disposition of (NEW,PASS) in the step that creates it and can exist only until the system automatically deletes it at *job end.* The data set can be read and passed again by a job step that references it by name and carries a disposition of (OLD,PASS) or it can be read and deleted by a job step that carries a disposition of (OLD,DELETE). An example is &&TRANSORT. Each step can open a temporary data set once; a given step cannot open it, close it, and open it again.

No DSN Temporary Data Set (Work File).   At the time the unnamed temporary data set is created no name is supplied in JCL; the DSN parameter is omitted from the DD statement. By leaving out the DSN parameter MVS is told to create the data set name itself, which it does by using the literals "SYS" and the Julian date, time, job name, and other items. *The name generated is always unique.* This handling is appropriate for work files such as those used by the compiler and sort utility. This data set can be given a disposition of (NEW,PASS), in which case referencing the data set requires the use of a "referback," a technique discussed later in this chapter. Most commonly, an unnamed data set is intended to be used in and exist only for the duration of the job step and no disposition is coded, a fact that implies a DISP of (NEW,DELETE). The system will automatically delete this data set at the end of the *job step*.

PARTITIONED DATA SET MEMBER NAMES

To refer to a member of a partitioned data set the member name is stated in parentheses after the data set name:

```
BT05686.SOURCE.COBOL(FSBT3708)
```

When so referenced, MVS provides all the support necessary to extract the member from the partitioned data set and provide it to the DD statement accessing it. It appears to the program accessing the member that the records are coming from a freestanding sequential data set.

The member name of a partitioned data set can be one to eight characters in length. The same restrictions apply for a member name as apply for any qualifier of the data set name: the name can be formed with letters, numbers, or the national symbols @, #, or $. The name cannot start with a number; the leading position must be a letter or national symbol. Because a data set name can be as long as 44 characters, accessing a member within a PDS at this maximum length could conceivably result in JCL spanning 54 positions, including the parentheses surrounding the member name.

A whole partitioned data set is referenced simply by its name, such as BT05686.SOURCE.COBOL. Aside from knowing that this name appears to be the type one installation uses for a TSO library data set, it is not possible to know just by looking at the name whether it is a partitioned data set. Some utilities that work with PDSs require that reference to the data set name be coded in this way, without any specification of members. If this reference is inadvertently made to a PDS when a member within it is really desired, a JCL error will result.

GENERATION DATA GROUP NAMES

Aside from the requirements specified for the characters used in naming a data set and the size and nature of the qualifiers, only one additional restriction exists for data set naming. This restriction deals with the nature of the final part of the data set name and the fact that it should not be coded in the unusual form "GnnnnVnn" where "nnnn" and "nn" represent numbers. In other words, a data set should not be given a name like this unless special arrangements have been made:

```
AK00.C99.TELMAST.G0342V00
```

The stipulation exists because the final part of a data set name is sometimes written in this way by MVS itself. When the generation data group or "GDG" facility is used, arrangements are made to have the name preceding the "GnnnnVnn" known to the system catalog as a GDG "base." These arrangements make it possible for different generations and versions of the data set to be created without actually having to specify the last part of the name. It becomes possible to reference different generations of the data set by relative generation number. The current generation of the data set is specified by a zero in parentheses after the established data set name:

```
AK00.C99.TELMAST(0)
```

The preceding generation of the data set is referenced with a minus 1 in parentheses

```
AK00.C99.TELMAST(-1)
```

and the next generation is created with a positive 1:

```
AK00.C99.TELMAST(+1)
```

Older generations and successive generations can make use of other integer specifiers.

The system regards a data set with GnnnnVnn as the last part of the name as a member of a generation data group. It is inappropriate for a data set to carry this type of name if no arrangements have been made to support it as a member of a GDG. Although it is not often useful, it is possible to reference a real member of a GDG with its "absolute" name, the full name including the GnnnnVnn, instead of the generation number. We discuss GDGs in depth in Chapter 13.

MISUSE OF QUOTES (APOSTROPHES) IN CODING DSN

Confusion easily ensues in connection with the use of the IBM quote, the apostrophe, surrounding a data set name. This element of confusion usually appears when personnel become familiar with the TSO mode of specifying the data set name and then erroneously transfer the same technique to JCL.

Using TSO/ISPF, access to the members of COBOL, PLI, and CNTL libraries is made by filling in fields at the top of a screen, like the function 2 edit and function 3 utility screens. The labels on these fields identify the qualifiers of the data set name from the highest level down to the member name:

```
PROJECT  ===>   BT05686
LIBRARY  ===>   SOURCE
TYPE     ===>   COBOL
MEMBER   ===>   FSBT3708
```

When an item other than a TSO library data set is referenced, the name is entered at the bottom of the TSO screen in a horizontal format. Member names for PDSs then need to be entered using parenthesis around the member name. TSO by default appends whatever is entered in this location as a data set name to the TSO user's account identifier. Thus if a person logged on as BT05686 enters the name of the installation copylib on the TSO 3.3 utility screen, to copy member LFWTSDP1 into his or her own library, this would be entered

```
OTHER SEQUENTIAL DATA SET  ===>   SYS1.COPYLIB(LFWSTDP1)
                                                    wrong
```

but TSO actually sees the name as

```
BT05686.SYS1.COPYLIB(LFWSTDP1)
```

which is not correct. The means of preventing TSO from prefacing the data set name with the TSO account identifier is to surround the data set name with apostrophes and to enter it as

```
OTHER SEQUENTIAL DATA SET  ===>   'SYS1.COPYLIB(LFWSTDP1)'
                                                      right
```

which makes it explicit that we have provided the entire data set name.

Confusion arises when the same practice is carried over to JCL. *In JCL the data set name should almost never be surrounded with apostrophes;* there is actually a good deal of danger in coding DSN with surrounding apostrophes. It is necessary to code the data set name in JCL with surrounding apostrophes only when the name contains special characters like the hyphen and the apostrophe. Use of these symbols within a data set name is widely regarded as unusual, error prone, and unnecessary, even more unnecessary than use of the national symbols @, #, and $. Surrounding apostrophes are needed only for the symbolic parameter that supplies a data set name outside the raw JCL on the "run decks" that submit canned cataloged procedures, as discussed in Chapter 16.

The danger in using apostrophes to surround a data set name in JCL is that certain special symbols found in data set names actually communicate needed information to MVS. If these symbols are obscured by enclosing the data set name in apostrophes, the name will not be perceived by the system as intended. A JCL error may result, or even worse, a data set may actually be written with the parentheses around a PDS member name or generation data set reference *as part of the name itself.* There are several instances in which a data set name *must not* be surrounded by apostrophes: for partitioned data sets, for generation data group data sets, for temporary "&&" data sets, and for "referback" data set references.

The safest course of action concerning DSN specification in JCL is to not use special symbols, including the national symbols @, #, and $, in data set names. Plenty of inherently more legible and readable characters can be used—namely ordinary letters and numbers. If you follow this advice, you will never need to code DSN in JCL surrounded by apostrophes.

DSN REFERBACKS

It is possible to indicate DSN as a "referback" instead of coding a specific data set name. This makes it possible to have MVS "copy" the data set name from a prior job step. The occasions on which this is useful are limited, but much older JCL may rely on this feature and a programmer must be able to recognize it.

Figure 3.4 illustrates the JCL for a programmer's test of the FSBT3708 sequential update routine and the FSBT3719 reporting program. In //STEPA the sort utility is reading a data set of transactions at its //SORTIN DD statement and is outputting a temporary data set at //SORTOUT

```
//STEPA     EXEC  PGM=SORT
//SORTLIB    DD   DSN=SYS1.SORTLIB,
//  DISP=SHR
//SORTIN     DD   DSN=AK00.C99.TRANSIN,
//  DISP=SHR
//SORTOUT    DD   DSN=&&TRANSORT,
//  UNIT=SYSDA,
//  DISP=(NEW,PASS,DELETE),
//  DCB=(RECFM=FB,LRECL=71,BLKSIZE=6177),
 -
 -
//STEPB     EXEC  PGM=FSBT3708
//STEPLIB    DD   DSN=SYS1.TESTLIB,
//  DISP=SHR
//BT3708E1   DD   DSN=&&TRANSORT,
//  DISP=(OLD,DELETE)
 -
 -
```

which is being read in //STEPB at the DDname //BT3708E1. It is possible
to code the //BT3708E1 DD statement as

```
//BT3708E1   DD   DSN=*.STEPA.SORTOUT,
//   DISP=(OLD,DELETE)
```

by using a DSN referback. In a convention somewhat uniform throughout
all of JCL the asterisk signifies that the parameter is to come from somewhere else; in this case from //STEPA's DD statement named //SORTOUT.

Use of DSN referbacks tends to make JCL more difficult to maintain
because close attention, scrutiny, and manual examination of preceding
steps is needed to comprehend what a given job stream is doing. Use
of referbacks also seriously complicates the restart of a job if a failure
or interruption has occurred. The original developers of JCL envisioned
DSN referbacks as a convenience that would allow the DSN in early
steps to be modified without requiring modification of later steps that
use the same data sets. In actual practice production JCL itself is not
modified for each run. JCL is canned in cataloged procedures, as discussed in Chapter 16, and symbolic parameters are used to allow
changeable items to be specified for each run.

A referback capability also exists for the VOL parameter. VOL referbacks are especially useful when more than one data set is to be written
on the same scratch tape, as discussed in Chapter 9. A referback capability similar to that of the DSN referback is provided for the DCB parameter and is most often used in connection with the writing of generation data group data sets, as discussed in Chapter 13. The direction
of print to SYSOUT = * is in effect another form of referback, as discussed
in Chapters 1 and 12. A little-used referback capability also exists for
the PGM name parameter of the EXEC statement. The //GO step in Figure
1.2 could have been coded in this manner

```
//GO    EXEC  PGM=*.LKED.SYSLMOD,COND=(5,LT)
```

but this is of so little contemporary utility it is regarded as an item of
JCL trivia.

NULLFILE AND DUMMY

In addition to the requirement to avoid coding a data set name using
the characters GnnnnVnn for the last part of the name, it is necessary to avoid the unintentional use of a data set name of NULLFILE
or DUMMY. MVS regards these names as dummy names. NULLFILE
and DUMMY can be used to cause output directed to a DDname to be
discarded.

NULLFILE is sometimes coded as the default DSN on the PROC statement in a cataloged procedure. Full DD statement parameters, such as DISP, DCB, SPACE, VOL, and/or LABEL follow the procedure's DSN symbolic parameter within the proc. When an output data set name is supplied by a symbolic parameter on the EXEC statement that invokes the procedure, it is used to replace the symbolic parameter at the DSN. When, however, the run deck EXEC statement does not supply a symbolic parameter for the DSN, the default DSN of NULLFILE applies and the DISP, DCB, SPACE, VOL, and LABEL parameters are checked for correct syntax but are otherwise ignored. A definite data set name of NULLFILE is a requirement for JCL in this case, because if a DSN symbolic parameter is given no value for an output data set, the system will generate a data set name.

If NULLFILE or DUMMY is to be coded in testing JCL to discard the output from a DD statement, it is usually necessary to code it with at least the block size of the output. This is because the program still requires at least one record length of buffer into which each record being written is parked but never picked up by MVS. Most programs do not specify block size but pass up the opportunity and expect JCL to do it. If we were testing the sequential update job stream in Figure 3.4 and wanted temporarily to discard the new master file output, we could code the //STEPB DD statement //BT3708U2 in this way:

```
//BT3708U2   DD DUMMY,DCB=BLKSIZE=314
```

or

```
//BT3708U2   DD DSN=NULLFILE,DCB=BLKSIZE=314
```

Coding DUMMY on an input DD statement causes an end-of-file condition to be encountered at the first attempt to read from the DDname. This has relevance in program testing to verify the action of a program when it encounters an empty input data set. It also applies when IBM utilities like IEBGENER, the copy utility, are executed without control cards and //SYSIN is coded as //SYSIN DD DUMMY.

DATA SET NAME RETENTION BY MVS

The system catalog stores entire data set names. The name stored by the catalog can be up to 44 characters in length and includes the periods separating portions of the name.

A tape label does not store the entire data set name; it stores only the rightmost 17 characters. The origin of this economy lies in decisions made decades ago when portions of MVS software dealing with tape handling were developed. The data set label on tapes was intended to provide for the storage of a full length eight-character name and one prefacing qualifier, in accordance with the ANSI standards for tape labeling. IBM tape labels, which differ internally from ANSI standard labels, share the same DSN field size. The less-than-complete DSN recorded in the tape data set label usually presents no problem of ambiguous access to data because nearly all tape data sets are cataloged, and the catalog stores the full data set name.

The data set name for disk data sets is stored in the volume table of contents, or VTOC, for the disk volume and all 44 positions of a data set name are stored. The name is recorded in the "format 1" DSCB, or "data set control block" record, created in the VTOC for the data set by MVS I/O software.

REVIEW QUESTIONS AND (*)EXERCISES

1. Must all MVS data sets have names? Discuss this in terms of the use or omission of the DSN parameter on a DD statement at which a new data set is created.

2. Identify the "national" symbols and discuss why their use in data set names is not common.

3. In what ways is a temporary data set different from a permanent data set?

4. What happens if a DD statement at which a new data set is created specifies an existing data set name and the DISP parameter is coded DISP = (NEW,CATLG,DELETE)?

5. What is the maximum length of a PDS member name?

6. How is a generation data group data set name similar to a the DSN for a DD statement that accesses a member of a PDS?

7. When should the data set name specified in JCL be enclosed in parentheses?

8. Code 12 legitimate and typical data set names, making three sequential data set names, three partitioned data set names, three temporary data set names, and three maximum length data set names of any data set organization.

*9. Alter the compile, linkage edit, and run JCL in Figure 1.2, dummying out the compiler's //SYSPRINT output. Run the job stream and identify in the system allocation/deallocation report how MVS tells what it did with this output. Note: To do this you need to know that the compiler writes its printlines as 121-byte records, including the carriage control character.

*10.   Enter the JCL for the compile, linkage edit, and run of a program shown in Figure 1.2, duplicating the //GO step to name the last two steps //GO1 and //GO2; the program load module will be executed twice. To do this you must change the DISP = (OLD,DELETE) on the first //GO1 step //STEPLIB to DISP = (OLD,PASS). Alter the //INDATA1 DD statement of the //GO2 step so that instead of specifying the actual data set name it will now use a DSN referback to access the same data set as input into //INDATA1 in the //GO1 step. Run the job stream and examine the system allocation/deallocation report; explain how MVS reports the actions it took in regard to this referback. See Note 9 in Chapter 1 if you wish to use the specific source code cited in this JCL or use any COBOL, PL/I, or FORTRAN source code you wish, adjusting the //GO step DD statement names and compiler name as dictated by your installation. The JCL cited here is one of several items available on the diskette you can obtain by following the instructions in Appendix D.

NOTES

1. A permanent data set named with one simple name cannot be cataloged and is of no use in the contemporary environment. Examples with such unrealistic data set names are avoided in this book.

2. The "plus zero" that may be used in a data set name is a carryover from punched card days and is the overpunched number zero, a card column punched with the "12" row and the "0" row. It equates to a hexadecimal value of C0 and today carries the printable representation in EBCDIC of "{" which is the left brace. Its utility in data set names is now nil; the abandonment of the card punch rendered the plus zero a historical curiosity.

3. It is possible to code a temporary data set name with only one leading ampersand, as in &TRANSORT. The name then serves a dual purpose. If the JCL is canned as a cataloged procedure as discussed in Chapter 16, the DSN can be treated as a symbolic parameter and assigned a different value; if no value is assigned, the name is treated as if it were coded a temporary data set such as &&TRANSORT. For JCL not used as a cataloged procedure it is customary to use the double ampersands.

5

Unit: Device Specification

Every item of equipment offered by IBM for attachment to a mainframe carries a distinct type and model number. Disk units in contemporary MVS use include the 3330, 3350, and 3380 units. Tape drives in use include the 3420, the standard 10-½ inch, 9-track reel-to-reel tape drive, and the newer 3480, an 18-track cartridge tape drive. Printers include the impact 1403 and 32xx family and the laser technology 3800; card readers and punches are still in limited use in some installations and carry identifiers like 3505, 3525, and the 3780 remote job entry (RJE) station. Control units, terminals, optical character readers, and other devices have unique type identifiers. Different data set and I/O requirements demand the association of a program input or output with the correct device. Under MVS, up to 1,400 devices may be attached to the mainframe; under MVS/XA, the upper limit is more than 4,000 devices.

I/O devices are attached to the mainframe by hardware interfaces of various kinds that deal through "channels." The attachment points for devices, regardless of the specific hardware, are referenced as "hardware addresses." Thus a given 3420 tape drive may be attached at hardware address A58, another at 959, and still another at D5A. Each disk unit is attached at a specific address and every other device is attached at some unique installation-determined address.

The UNIT parameter of the DD statement exists to provide the means of associating the statement with an appropriate device. In some cases it is not necessary to code the UNIT parameter on a DD statement for an existing data set because the unit needed for it is already known to the system via the system catalog. When a data set is to be created or it exists but is not cataloged, there are three ways of making the required association:

- Via a device hardware address
- Via a device type
- Via a symbolic device list name

The UNIT parameter also provides the means of specifying a count of devices to be used for a data set and to delay the mounting of demountable media on the device or devices.

WHEN UNIT CAN BE OMITTED

The UNIT parameter can be omitted from a DD statement when the data set referenced by the statement already exists and is cataloged. When a data set is cataloged, at its creation or at a subsequent time, it is known to the system. One of the items that MVS records in the catalog is the device type on which the data set must be mounted to be accessed.

UNIT can be omitted when a data set is received by a job step as a result of a PASS. When a data set is passed to a subsequent job step using the DISP subparameter PASS, MVS records and retains certain information about the data set. One such item is the unit type required by it.

UNIT can be omitted when the data set being referenced is a VSAM data set even when data are being written to the VSAM data set for the first time. A VSAM data set, unlike a sequential, partitioned, or ISAM data set, cannot be created by JCL and a program outputting data. A VSAM data set must first be defined by using control statements acted on by IDCAMS, the "IDC" Access Method Services utility. The definition process specifies the UNIT and volume serial number of the media that is to house the VSAM file. When a job step accesses a VSAM file, MVS already knows the UNIT on which the data set resides.[1]

UNIT is not coded for data sets that are printlines being output to the printer. UNIT is not coded when a DD statement is coded with SYSOUT = A or another SYSOUT output class. For print data sets being output to the print spool via SYSOUT the system automatically uses the designated spooling disk. A job step has no control over the device used for the spool.[2]

WHEN UNIT MUST BE SPECIFIED

If the data set being referenced is written in this job step—it does not yet exist and has never been allocated even as an empty data set—then UNIT must be specified.

If the data set already exists and is being read or written to but is not cataloged, then UNIT must be specified because the system has no way of ascertaining the appropriate unit type needed by the data set.[3]

If a data set is cataloged and UNIT is coded in the JCL anyway, then the coded JCL must be consistent with the information recorded in the system catalog. If the JCL UNIT specifies something not consistent with the catalog, the job will fail and an error message will state that an "incorrect device type" has been specified. The catalog is always right; JCL may not be and the JCL overrides the catalog. If UNIT is omitted but is needed, the same error message results.

It is common to see UNIT coded in JCL for DD statements even when it is technically redundant. This results from force of habit and from the fact that for tapes being read the UNIT's "DEFER" subparameter is usually coded for efficiency.

UNIT CODING—SHORT FORM AND LONG FORM

UNIT can be coded in a DD statement as simply as this

```
// UNIT=xxx,
```

and in some cases this is done. The "xxx" can take the form of a hexadecimal hardware address, a device type identifier, or a symbolic device name. The UNIT parameter in its long coding form takes the appearance:

```
// UNIT=( device, device-count, DEFER ),
```

An actual example of this coding is

```
// UNIT=(TAPE,4,DEFER),
```

and is sometimes but not often seen in practice.

Device Coding by Hardware Address

Every I/O device attached to the computer carries a unique hardware address, expressed as a three-position hexadecimal value. In its most elementary form it is possible to specify the required I/O device on a DD statement by its hardware address. Thus, if the system is configured with a given disk device at address A49, it is possible to code the UNIT parameter as

```
// UNIT=A49,
```

to access this device. This coding, however, is almost never done by applications programming personnel.

MVS is smarter than we are when it comes to being informed of device status. It should be; that is one major job it was designed to handle. If device allocation is coded using a hardware address, MVS must withhold processing of the job step until the specific device indicated is available. The device may be busy on behalf of another job or jobs running concurrently, or it may be offline and not currently accessible by any job, but a similar device or devices may be free for use. Unless there is some definite reason that one specific disk, tape drive, or printer must be used, it is not reasonable to code a UNIT specification using hardware address. Hardware address coding is, however, sometimes employed by an operating system support group because certain MVS data sets must be housed at specific device addresses.

Device Coding by Device Type

It is possible to code the UNIT parameter by indicating a device type or, in other words, its IBM-assigned common name or model number. Because a mainframe installation usually has a quantity of similar disk and tape drives, this is a more general way to specify a needed device. This type of specification can take the form

```
// UNIT=3380,
```

to request use of any available 3380 disk unit. When specified in this manner, MVS will check its current information about disk unit usage and will automatically allocate an available 3380 to the data set being written. As we have already discussed, coding UNIT for an existing cataloged data set is superfluous but will not fail if the coded UNIT is an accurate reflection of the actual unit on which the data set resides.

Coding a device by device type allows MVS to satisfy a unit need even when some devices of the type are out of service or busy. The device assigned to the request is indicated in the messages output by MVS; that is why these messages are called allocation and deallocation reports.[4]

The mechanism that allows UNIT to be specified as a device type relies on a list of the hardware addresses of devices. The device type, such as the characters "3380" is really a reference to a list of hardware addresses at which 3380 devices are attached. This list is maintained by MVS and is supported as a convenience in designating device requirements. An installation also has the ability to prepare and maintain a list of device addresses grouped under a purely symbolic name, which is the third way in which a UNIT parameter can be coded.

Device Coding by Symbolic Device Group Name

It is possible for an installation to build lists of addresses of devices, grouping devices together for purposes of access. A given device address may appear in any number of lists; therefore the lists may overlap. Each list is given a symbolic name. Three of the most common lists and names are provided by IBM: SYSALLDA, SYSDA, and SYSSEQ. SYSALLDA and SYSDA are lists of addresses of devices that can support direct access operations and SYSSEQ is a list of addresses of devices that can support sequential data set operations. SYSDA is the most commonly seen symbolic device name. If UNIT is specified as SYSDA, any available disk device can be allocated by MVS to a data set.[5] Even if an installation has not established any of its own symbolic device group address lists, SYSDA can be coded since MVS is provided with it.

An installation will typically create device address lists under at least two other symbolic names: DISK and TAPE. Under the symbolic name DISK the installation will list the addresses of all its production-preferred disk devices—most likely it newest, highest capacity, and fastest access disk drives. JCL written for production purposes in such an installation specifying UNIT = DISK for disk files will access these drives. *UNIT = DISK and UNIT = TAPE will not be recognized as legitimate if an installation is running with plain vanilla, IBM-supplied device lists and has not explicitly created DISK and TAPE as local symbolic device group lists.*

Under the symbolic name TAPE an installation will usually list the addresses of its production-preferred tape drives. In the contemporary environment these will most likely be the addresses of 3420s or 3480s but not a combination of the two. Why not a combination? Because 3420 and 3480 drives are not compatible; a tape reel written on a 3420 cannot be read on a cartridge-loading 3480. If these different devices were put into the same symbolic device list, tape reels would soon be directed to mount on 3480s and 3480 tape cartridges would be directed to reel-to-reel drives. When phasing in 3480s an installation may code JCL for the new drives by their device type, as UNIT = 3480, or create a symbolic device list of 3480 addresses using a name like TAPE3480 or TAPEHI.

An installation may also create other symbolic device names, perhaps many of them. A name TEST may be used to identify a list of addresses at which are located disk drives devoted to test data sets only. Personnel testing new job streams are directed to code UNIT = TEST in JCL to confine test files to these units. The list "behind" the symbolic device name TEST may include only a few addresses.

Symbolic group name device coding is the most prevalent form of UNIT parameter specification. Installations strongly prefer it because this makes it easier to cope with the ever-changing progression of peripheral equipment attached to the mainframe. As older disk devices are replaced by newer ones, an installation can attach new devices to the system, add their addresses to the lists named DISK and TAPE and "migrate"—gradually move—production data sets to the new devices. JCL does not have to be changed at all. If JCL had been coded for device types such as UNIT = 3350, the JCL would have to be extracted from production libraries, modified and replaced as the equipment complement changed.

An installation may change the hardware addresses associated with various devices. When symbolic name device grouping is used, this requires only a matching change in the device group list. The task is much more difficult, however, if hardware addresses have been coded directly in the thousands or hundreds of thousands of lines of JCL in the installation.

SPECIAL FEATURES

Device Count

```
// UNIT=(TAPE,4,DEFER),
```

The device specification in the UNIT parameter is actually one of three subparameters that can be indicated. All of the parameters for UNIT are positional; they are recognized by MVS based on their position following the word UNIT. When only device type is specified on the UNIT parameter, the two remaining subparameters are omitted; hence the short form of coding for UNIT.

The second of the subparameters allows specification of the count of devices required for the data set. It can be a number from 1 to 60, and if omitted it defaults to 1. It is rarely used and has no meaning when a data set resides on only one unit of media, such as one tape reel or one disk volume.

Device count may be used when a data set spans more than one storage volume *and* all volumes must be mounted at the same time, "in parallel." For very large indexed file disk data sets on demountable media it has some relevance. It should be noted, however, that the newer disk drives like the 3350 and 3380 are fixed-media units; the disk packs mounted on their spindles cannot be removed. Therefore the issue of explicitly requesting parallel mounting has fallen by the wayside, even for large VSAM disk data sets.

For tape data sets, which can be read only serially anyway, parallel mounting has almost no relevance at all. When device count is not coded for a multiple volume tape data set, MVS automatically notifies the operator to demount a tape reel that has been completely read or written and mount the next volume. Thus a multiple volume data set is read one volume at a time using only one drive. This is the customary processing method for large sequential data sets on tape.

Instead of indicating the number of devices needed to achieve parallel mounting it is possible to accomplish it by coding P in this subparameter if the associated VOL parameter identifies all of the volumes or if the data set is cataloged. In these cases MVS can determine for itself how many devices are needed to achieve parallel mounting because it knows how many volumes the data set spans:

```
//    UNIT=(TAPE,P,DEFER),
```

The "P" stands for "parallel." When it or a number of units is coded, MVS executes the job step by seeking the number of devices necessary to mount all volumes of the data set concurrently; it issues messages to the computer console to give the operator the volume serial number of each disk or tape and the drive on which to mount each.

Parallel mounting of the several tape reels that store large data sets may appear appealing because the job doesn't wait for an operator to demount one tape and mount another. But an effect just the opposite of parallel mounting is nearly always desirable: the minimization of the number of tape drives used by any given job step. The fewer significant resources, such as tape drives, that a job uses, the more able MVS is to find and supply the resources the job needs. Jobs that require more than a few tape drives will receive less scheduling priority, often via a distinct low priority job class processed in nonpeak usage hours. The UNIT device count, the VOLume parameter volume count, and the "AFF" specification all affect device and volume allocation and the serial/parallel mounting of media. AFF is described at the end of this chapter.

In certain rare instances it is necessary to expedite the creation of tape data sets to the maximum extent, even at the expense of devices. See the discussion under *VOL and UNIT Parameter Interplay* in Chapter 9 which concerns a parallel mounting for this purpose.

Deferred Mounting of Tape or Disk

```
// UNIT=(TAPE,4,DEFER),
```

The third subparameter of UNIT, DEFER, is provided in keeping with the desire to minimize unnecessary media mounting and mounting bottlenecks. If not present, MVS sends a message to the computer console to request the mounting of the media *when the job step starts.* If DEFER is coded, the transmission of this media mount message is deferred until the program being executed in the step *opens* the data set.

The advantage of coding DEFER, especially for tape data sets, is that if a given job step never opens a data set, MVS never requests the mounting of media for it. This is significant for job steps such as executions of IEFBR14 being used to allocate, scratch, or find a data set because this null program never opens any data sets.[6] Failing to code DEFER on the DD statements for such a job step causes media to be mounted for no purpose. DEFER has no effect on device *allocation*, the assignment of resources to a job. For an IEFBR14 that deletes a tape data set a tape drive is still allocated to the step; the DEFER only blocks the mounting of media. The AFF specification *does* offer the capability to affect device allocation, as discussed below.

DEFER has relevance for programs other than IEFBR14; many programs do not open all data sets at beginning of job, but only as needed. Deferred tape mounting may allow a job to start running faster because manual intervention to mount tapes for data sets not yet opened will be put off.

DEFER has no meaning for new disk data sets because space for these is allocated by MVS before the step starts; for the space allocation to occur the media must be accessible to MVS. Because 3350 and 3380 disk units do not have demountable media, the issue of mounting disk volumes in connection contemporary disk devices is moot.

When the device count or "P" is not specified but the third positional parameter is coded, the empty positional parameter slot is indicated by coding the comma that normally follows it:

```
// UNIT=(TAPE,,DEFER),
```

It is possible to omit both the unit type and device count subparameters to totally generalize a UNIT specification for an existing data set while still specifying deferral of mounting:

```
//  UNIT=(,,DEFER),
```

This makes it possible to avoid changes in JCL as it moves from a testing environment with disk test files to a production environment in which tapes are used.

Unit "Affinity" Specification AFF

UNIT can be specified to be the same as for a preceding DD statement in the step by using the AFF specification

```
//SORTIN      DD  DSN=AK00.C99.TRANSIN,
//  DISP=(OLD,KEEP)
//SORTOUT     DD  DSN=AK00.C99.TRANSORT,
//  UNIT=AFF=SORTIN,
//  DISP=(NEW,CATLG,DELETE),
//  DCB=(RECFM=FB,LRECL=71,BLKSIZE=6177),
//  LABEL=RETPD=180
```

even if the specific device is to be assigned by MVS. This allows the number of devices needed by the step to be minimized. This is advantageous for tape drives when a program like the sort utility completely finishes using the device for one data set—as in reading the SORTIN data set and copying it to sort work space—before directing any use to the other DD statement, such as the sort's SORTOUT. The AFF specification also allows the minimization of device allocation to IEFBR14 housekeeping steps by arranging for the second and subsequent tape data sets to be assigned to the same tape drive as the first data set.

An important but often overlooked application of the AFF specification lies in the area of concatenated tape inputs at a DD statement. As illustrated in Chapter 17 item 12, more than one data set can be input at a DDname and MVS will automatically arrange to demount a finished volume and begin accessing the next. However, a separate unit will be allocated to each data set named in the concatenation unless UNIT = AFF = DDname is coded at the second and subsequent data set names. In this case DDname is the *same* DDname:

```
//SYSUT1      DD  DSN=AK00.C99.TESTTRAN,
//  UNIT=(TAPE,,DEFER),
//  DISP=(OLD,KEEP)
//          DD  DSN=AK00.C99.MORETRAN,
//  UNIT=AFF=SYSUT1,
```

```
//    DISP=(OLD,KEEP)
//            DD   DSN=AK00.C99.HISTTRAN,
//    UNIT=AFF=SYSUT1,
//    DISP=(OLD,KEEP)
```

For data sets on permanently mounted disk media the AFF specification is not applicable but for tape data sets being concatenated the use of AFF will considerably reduce the device requirements of the job step.

An opposite-sounding SEP parameter for "channel separation" formerly existed within the syntax of the UNIT parameter. SEP is not supported under MVS and is ignored if coded.

REVIEW QUESTIONS AND (*)EXERCISES

1. Cite the three methods of specifying a device on a DD statement for a data set to be created and the limitations or advantages of each.

2. Name three instances when UNIT can be omitted from a DD statement.

3. Identify three instances when coding of UNIT is mandatory on a DD statement.

4. Explain what type of device will be used to house a data set when UNIT=SYSDA is coded at the DD statement creating it.

5. A programmer new to an installation coded the DD statement at which a new data set was to be created as UNIT=DISK and experienced a job failure, with MVS indicating that an incorrect device type had been specified. Explain the likely reason for this failure.

6. Why wouldn't an installation group a combination of its 3420 reel-to-reel tape drives and its 3480 cartridge tape drives under the same symbolic device group list?

7. Cite the purpose served by the UNIT device count parameter and describe its level of usage in the contemporary environment.

8. Explain what the DEFER subparameter of UNIT accomplishes in regard to device allocation as well as handling of storage media.

9. Describe the circumstances under which the UNIT AFF affinity feature is relevant to use of the IEFBR14 utility.

*10. Code the JCL to perform a sort of tape-stored data using the IBM sort utility and only one tape drive in the step.

NOTES

1. Due to the way that VSAM files are defined, MVS consistently knows so much about every VSAM file that DD statements for them are nearly always composed of only the data set name, or DSN, and the short form disposition parameter, either DISP = SHR or DISP = OLD.

2. UNIT can be coded for printlines being sent directly to a printer outside of the SYSOUT mechanism by coding a UNIT parameter and hardware address or model number for the printer. Such an action is usually not permitted and will occur rarely in a production environment; "direct allocation" of a printer is extremely inefficient and limits job processing speed to the speed of the printer.

3. The device type is not recorded in the data set label. Even if the data set carries a standard label, as tapes can and all disk data sets do, UNIT must be given to MVS either via the catalog or JCL. Anything else would be a paradox. If the device type were carried in the data set label, how could the system know on what type of device to mount the data set in order to read the label to determine the device type?

4. For UNIT requests by device type and symbolic device group the job log will show in printed form the messages issued to the console operator as MVS attempts to find devices suitable for the job. If devices needed for the job, such as tape or disk drives, are configured in the system but are in a nonaccessible condition, having been taken offline with the operator-issued "VARY" command, informational message will remind the operator of this condition.

    The job log and allocation/deallocation report indicate the volume serial numbers of media associated with the job. These reports provide a programmer with the means of learning the identity of the media to which data sets created in a run were written. For data sets not being cataloged this is vital information. For cataloged data sets the serial numbers of the media to which data sets were consigned by MVS are of much less interest.

5. If a given DD statement uses a symbolic device name and more than one unit is assigned for the data set, as with parallel mounting of volumes, all units assigned by MVS are of the same type, even if the symbolic device group list contains a mixture of device types.

6. Learning what is contained in IEFBR14 is a rite of passage in the IBM environment, as was finding the left-handed monkey wrench in the steam locomotive roundhouse or locating the can of grid leak bias in the 1930s radio repair shop. The newcomer is usually made to feel foolish by the fact that the answer is in the name. The program contains only the assembler instruction BR 14, "branch to the address pointed to by register 14." This register contains the address to which control must return when the program completes execution; BR14 equates to the FORTRAN "STOP" or COBOL "STOP RUN" statement. As discussed in Chapter 6 in connection with the DISP parameter and cataloging, IEFBR14 exists simply to provide a convenient excuse for interaction with MVS. It contains no logic to open data sets or, for that matter, to do anything at all.

6

DISP: Data Set Disposition

The DISP parameter provides the means of indicating whether a data set is supposed to exist when a job step begins, whether it can be shared with other jobs during the step, what is to be done with it after the job step concludes, and what is to be done with it if the job step fails. *DISP is always required on a DD statement unless a data set is created and deleted in the same step.*

DISP GENERAL FORMAT

The general form and possible values of the DISP parameter are shown here and although some combinations of the three subparameters are not permitted or would make no sense, most combinations are reasonable

```
DISP=( start-status , end-status-normal , end-of-status-abend )
         NEW                DELETE                 DELETE
         OLD                PASS                   KEEP
         SHR                KEEP                   CATLG
         MOD                CATLG                  UNCATLG
                            UNCATLG
```

and allowed. "Start" means the start of a *job step*, not the start of the job itself. The coding for a typical DISP parameter appears as

```
DISP=(OLD,KEEP,KEEP)
```

when all three subparameters are coded. It is possible to omit coding of the last two subparameters and to code only the first one without parentheses as in:

```
DISP=OLD
```

In such a case the second and third subparameters default to the preservation of the data set status as it existed before the job step started. The two statements illustrated above are equivalent. If the start-status is omitted and the DISP is coded as

```
DISP=(,DELETE)
```

it is implied that the start-status is NEW. *If the DISP parameter is not coded, the start-status defaults to NEW and the end-status defaults to DELETE to preserve the condition of the data set—nonexistent—prior to the step.* It defaults in this case to an explicit coding of the form:

```
DISP=(NEW,DELETE,DELETE)
```

This is the reason that DISP is usually omitted on DD statements for work files like those used by the compiler and the sort utility. Although this default condition of DISP is handy, it can be dangerous. If DISP is inadverdently omitted on a new data set that should be retained and will be accessed in later jobs, *no error will result in the job that creates the data set by the omission of DISP.* A job subsequently seeking the data set will experience a "data set not found" problem or will read an older generation of the data set.

START-STATUS VALUES

```
DISP=( start-status , end-status-normal , end-status-abend )
```

Start-status in some ways mixes apples and oranges: it indicates the status of the data set at the start of the job step, and also the *manner of access* desired for an existing data set.

NEW means that the data set does not presently exist and will be created during this step. It implies that the program or JCL will supply data set characteristics that are needed by the system to create the data set.

OLD indicates that the data set exists, and it must exist or an error will result. OLD also specifies exclusive use of the data set; OLD does not permit the sharing of data sets between jobs running concurrently. A job that carries a DISP of OLD for a data set will await execution until the end of all other jobs already using the data set. For VSAM data sets only OLD or SHR are appropriate.[1]

SHR, or in its long form SHARE, specifies that the data set must exist but indicates that it can be accessed by other programs executing at the same time. By the same token, a job step with a DD statement carrying a disposition of SHR will not be forced to wait for disk data set access if other jobs are already accessing the data set with SHR. SHR is the start-status disposition normally coded to read a disk data set. (SHR,DELETE) is contradictory and is treated as (OLD,DELETE) by MVS.

MOD means that the data set can be a new one or can already exist; MOD is the "permissive" start-status disposition. Like OLD, it dictates exclusive use of a data set. If the data set does not already exist, MOD causes it to be created *if these conditions are met:*

- no specific VOL parameter is coded, and
- the data set characteristics are supplied by the program or the DCB parameter of JCL, and
- the appropriate UNIT parameter is provided in JCL, and
- for disk data sets, the SPACE parameter is coded.

MOD also allows extension of an existing data set as discussed at the end of this chapter.

END-STATUS-NORMAL VALUES

```
DISP=( start-status , end-status-normal , end-status-abend )
```

The end-status-normal specification for the DISP parameter tells MVS what is to be done with the data set when the job step ends, assuming that the step ends without a problem.

DELETE indicates that the data set is to be deleted when the step ends. When DISP is omitted entirely, end-status defaults to the status that preserves the pre-job step status quo. A NEW data set did not exist before the step; therefore, lacking an end-status specification, this case defaults the end-status to DELETE. An OLD data set did exist before the step and lacking end-status in that case defaults the end-status to KEEP. It is not necessary for the program executing in the job step to open and close the data set in order for MVS to process the end-status of DELETE. A member of a partitioned data set cannot be deleted with an end-status of DELETE. *If (OLD,DELETE) is coded when a member of a partitioned data set is being processed, the entire PDS is deleted.* DELETE does not work when a data set carries an expiration date that has not yet been reached.

PASS tells MVS to place information about the data set into a "pass list." A step that follows can access the data set and need not include UNIT or VOLUME parameters on the DD statement for it. *A passed data set is retained in a mounted condition, speeding repeated access to it.* A permanent or temporary data set can be passed, and passing a cataloged data set is possible. Temporary data sets, named with simple names prefaced with two ampersands, are always created to be PASSed and their use can in some ways approximate the "piping" capability of UNIX and MS-DOS. PASS is not used for VSAM data sets. The internal operation of PASS is discussed in depth at the end of this chapter.

KEEP is coded as the end-status when the data set is to be retained but not cataloged. Most new data sets are created by using CATLG instead of KEEP, because of the advantage of having information about the data set recorded in the system catalog. An end-status of KEEP or CATLG is inconsistent with a temporary data set.

CATLG indicates the same retention action as KEEP but also tells MVS to record the data set name, volume identifier of the media, unit type, relative generation number for generation data group data sets, and tape data set relative file number in the system catalog. Cataloged data sets can be accessed simply by data set name. Duplicate names cannot be cataloged, but cause only an inconspicuous "NOT CATLG 2" warning message on the allocation/deallocation report for the job and *not* a job failure. It is possible to catalog an uncataloged data set by using the CATLG specification with a start-status of OLD or SHR.

UNCATLG is coded to ask that MVS remove the catalog entry for a data set but retain the data set itself. Subsequent reference to the data set will have to specify the volume on which it resides and the unit or device type, or within the same job stream a VOL referback can be employed as discussed in Chapter 9 and illustrated in Appendix B.

END-STATUS-ABEND VALUES

```
DISP=( start-status , end-status-normal , end-status-abend )
```

The third DISP subparameter is optional and if coded indicates the desired disposition of the data set if the *job step* abends. This specification is also known as the "conditional disposition." If it is not coded, it defaults to the same value as end-status-normal. If neither end-status-normal or end-status-abend is coded, both default to DELETE for NEW or PASSed data sets and KEEP for all others.

End-status-abend is deceptive in that it might be assumed to provide a way to clean up unwanted data sets in case a job stream fails, so that a rerun of it is possible. However, end-status-abend comes into play only if the step in which it is coded is the step that fails and causes the abend. If this step concludes successfully but a later one fails and terminates the job the data set is not affected by this specification. That is why it is necessary to take special precautions to use condition code testing and explicit data set deletion actions to clean up after a failed run, as discussed in Chapter 14.[2]

Once the values permitted for end-status-normal are understood, the values for end-status-abend will also be understood. All of the values for the former are permitted for the latter, except PASS. PASS is not legitimate as an end-status-abend because PASSed data sets are automatically eliminated by MVS at job end.

There is no simple convention for the coding of the end-status-abend value. The value required for a given step depends entirely on how job recovery has been planned, in other words, how the run will be redone or restarted if it fails at some point. If a data set normally deleted at a step must be retained so that the job can be restarted there in case of failure, DISP might be coded:

```
DISP=(OLD,DELETE,CATLG)
```

or

```
DISP=(OLD,DELETE,KEEP)
```

In this case the data set would still be available after an abend at this step. In other cases it is desirable to eliminate a data set being created in a step that fails, so that it need not be manually deleted to do a complete rerun. If this is applicable, then this coding

```
DISP=(NEW,CATLG,DELETE)
```

may apply. But *this only eliminates the data set if this particular step fails.* A failure later in the job that will be cured by rerunning the entire job still requires extra action to eliminate this data set before doing the rerun.

THE SYSTEM CATALOG

Functions of the Catalog

It is accurate to picture the catalog as a system-wide clearinghouse of data set information. The catalog automates the handling of technical information MVS needs to access data sets. Entries for data sets are placed in the system catalog by using the DISP parameter.

Several data sets with the same name may exist on the computer system, each on a different disk or tape volume. Only one occurrence, however, of a given data set name can exist in the catalog and only one occurrence of a given name can exist on any single disk volume. If more than one data set of a given name exists and the name is coded on a DD statement without the VOL and UNIT parameters, the data set that is cataloged is accessed. *Not specifying VOL and UNIT for an existing data set implies that it is cataloged.* A DD statement at which an existing cataloged data set is read, containing only the DSN and DISP parameters, is the minimal DD statement possible and is an example of implied catalog access. Such a DD statement is applicable to cataloged disk and tape data sets.

If a data set name is indicated on a DD statement and the VOL and UNIT parameters are provided, *MVS will not look in the catalog,* a fact that can cause trouble when a data set spans multiple disk or tape volumes and only one or some of the volume serial numbers are coded in the JCL. This is how noncataloged data sets with a name that duplicates a cataloged data set name are referenced. Overspecifying information in a DD statement for a cataloged data set is dangerous—all you can do is duplicate what the catalog knows, but if you encode the volume serial number or numbers incorrectly or do not code all relevant volume serial numbers the job will fail, access only part of the data set, or access a same-name data set that you do not want to access.

Tape reels can contain more than one data set, one after another. Each data set can be cataloged and the catalog retains the volume id of the media—the tape volume serial number—and the relative "data set number" of the data set on the tape. Thus a tape is not cataloged but rather the individual data sets; a given tape volume serial number may appear in the system catalog many times, just as may a disk volume serial number.

Partitioned Data Sets, DISP, and the Catalog

For partitioned data sets the data set itself, not the members, is cataloged. The members of a data set cannot be accessed without stating the data set name; it is the directory within the PDS that locates the member, not the catalog entry for the PDS.

When a new member is written to an existing partitioned data set, it is essential to remember that DISP refers to the data set as a whole and not to the member. Therefore in this case—as it exists when a new load module is added to a load module PDS at a linkage edit step—DISP is specified as DISP = SHR or DISP = OLD and not as NEW or MOD. Coding DISP = (NEW,CATLG,DELETE) when attempting to add a member to an existing PDS will result in a JCL error.

The DDname //STEPLIB serves a special purpose at any job step by indicating the partitioned data set at which the program named in the EXEC statement PGM= is to be found. The name following PGM is the member name of the program load module in the PDS pointed to by //STEPLIB. In other regards, however, //STEPLIB is a normal DD statement and the DISP coded at it will be processed by MVS as usual. It is therefore possible to delete an entire load module library by specifying DISP = (OLD,DELETE) at //STEPLIB. This could cause terrible inconvenience to many programmers and installations normally do not allow widespread delete access to shared program load module libraries; an installation without access security software is vulnerable to this problem. Individual programmers executing programs out of their own load module libraries are more prone to experience the problem, especially when first gaining experience with MVS JCL.

UPGRADING THE SEQUENTIAL UPDATE JOB STREAM

In the initial sort, update, and report job stream of Figure 3.4, the master file to be updated is presumed to be a cataloged data set named AK00.C99.TELMAST. You can now understand how the reference to it in //STEPB at DDname //BT3708E2 carries simply the data set name and the DISP; the system catalog supplies the volume id and the unit information necessary to access the data set. The new master file output by the test update job at //BT3708U2 is called AK00.C99.TELMAST.UPDATED; it is created as a cataloged data set.

At least one of the reasons that this is a test job stream should be apparent at this time: the job is good for one run, period. Once it has run, the JCL would have to be modified if a second update run were needed. Aside from the fact that the same transaction file is drawn in, the old master file drawn into the update is always AK00.C99.TELMAST.

We do not "cure" the problem of one run's updated master file automatically becoming the old master file for the next run until Chapter 13, when we discuss generation data groups. But in this chapter, we will address another problem in our initial JCL that limits its utility even for testing purposes. As it stands in Figure 3.4, not only does the job always bring in the same old master file but the JCL itself can be run only once! If we run it, successfully creating a new master file at //BT3708U2, and then attempt to run it again, the second run will fail with an error that indicates the existence of a duplicate data set name or will complete but result in duplicate ".UPDATED" data sets on different disk volumes. Only the first created such data set will be cataloged.

The source of the error in a repeat run of the job stream is that our first run creates an entry for AK00.C99.TELMAST.UPDATED in the system catalog, as our disposition coding of DISP = (NEW,CATLG,DELETE) at DDname //BT3708U2 has requested. When we again run the job, the system attempts to create a catalog entry for another data set of this same name, finds that it cannot, and gives us the NOT CATLG 2 warning message. If we want to run the job a second time, we must somehow uncatalog or delete the .UPDATED data set created in an earlier run.

It is possible to use TSO to delete a data set with the 3.2 function. A programmer who was testing a program and ran into the problem just described would be tempted to do so. But we are seeking a data set housekeeping solution that does not require human intervention; after all, when a need arises for a production job to run something on a cyclical basis it is impractical for programmers to intervene and clean data sets off the system. How do we make JCL take care of the deletion of the data set before we create another data set by the same name?

DATA SET HOUSEKEEPING WITH IEFBR14 AND DISP

Deleting Data Sets to Be Recreated

Data set housekeeping is interesting because it involves the use of a program that is supplied free with MVS, IEFBR14. The only instruction in this program is the assembler instruction, BR 14, which is the equivalent of the FORTRAN "STOP" or the COBOL "STOP RUN" statement. IEFBR14 is called the "null" program because it does nothing; it is simply an excuse for a job step to interact with MVS, much as the coquette's dropped handkerchief is a pretext to interact with a party of interest. IEFBR14 exists to provide a place to code DISP statements and have MVS act on them.

The resolution of the data set housekeeping problem is interesting in a second way because we must face the fact that the data set we wish to eliminate may not always be present for deletion. Our goal is to create JCL that will always run. This means that the same JCL should work the very first time we run the update test and every time thereafter. The first time we run it no new, updated master file named AK00.C99.TELMAST.UPDATED will exist. Subsequent runs will probably encounter a new master file but may not. Therefore, on an initial deletion step in the job stream we cannot simply code DISP = (OLD,DELETE) because OLD as a start-status disposition means that the data set to be referenced *must* exist. If it does not exist and OLD is coded, an error results and the job is terminated.

The revised JCL for the test sequential update run shown in Figure 6.1 contains an initial deletion step named //DELSTEP. The step name can be any eight-character value composed of letters and numbers, starting with a letter. If we were starting the development of the JCL and realized that we needed such a step, we might have named it //STEPA.

The //DELSTEP executes the null program IEFBR14. The program contains no SELECT/ASSIGN or OPEN statement carrying the DDname DEL1 because it contains no logic at all. How did we determine that //DEL1 was a legitimate DDname for IEFBR14? The issue is not at all as Humpty Dumpty thought it to be:

"My *name* is Alice, but—"

"It's a stupid name enough!" Humpty Dumpty interrupted impatiently. "What does it mean?"

"*Must* a name mean something?" Alice asked doubtfully.

"Of course it must," Humpty Dumpty said with a short laugh: "*my* name means the shape I am—and a good handsome shape it is, too. With a name like yours, you might be any shape, almost."[3]

DDnames can be any shape, almost. The DDname //DEL1 means nothing; MVS really doesn't care what DDnames are coded in JCL in association with a program. It is perfectly acceptable to MVS to see extra DDnames associated with a step, the "extra" meaning "more than the program requires." MVS always processes all the DD statements, acting on the DISP parameters, if the step is executed at all, even if a program doesn't do anything with a given DD statement.[4]

In DD statement //DEL1 we see this coding for the updated data set name:

```
//DELSTEP   EXEC   PGM=IEFBR14
//DEL1         DD   DSN=AK00.C99.TELMAST.UPDATED,
//   UNIT=SYSDA,
//   DISP=(MOD,DELETE),
//   SPACE=(TRK,0)
```

```
//FSBT686A  JOB AK00TEST,'DP2-JANOSSY',CLASS=E,MSGCLASS=X,
//   MSGLEVEL=(1,1),NOTIFY=BT05686
//*
//*     TEST RUN OF SEQUENTIAL UPDATE FSBT3708 -- VER 2
//*     THIS JCL = BT05686.SOURCE.CNTL(BT3708V2)
//*
//*************************************************************
//*                                                          *
//*     DELETE EXISTING UPDATED DATA SET              DEL    *
//*                                                          *
//*************************************************************
//DELSTEP   EXEC  PGM=IEFBR14
//DEL1      DD    DSN=AK00.C99.TELMAST.UPDATED,
//   UNIT=SYSDA,
//   DISP=(MOD,DELETE),
//   SPACE=(TRK,0)
//*
//*************************************************************
//*                                                          *
//*     SORT TRANS FILE                               A      *
//*                                                          *
//*************************************************************
//STEPA     EXEC  PGM=SORT
//SORTLIB   DD    DSN=SYS1.SORTLIB,
//   DISP=SHR
//SORTIN    DD    DSN=AK00.C99.TRANSIN,
//   DISP=SHR
//SORTOUT   DD    DSN=&&TRANSORT,
//   UNIT=SYSDA,
//   DISP=(NEW,PASS,DELETE),
//   DCB=(RECFM=FB,LRECL=71,BLKSIZE=6177),
//   SPACE=(6177,(32,7),RLSE)                    '2800 TRANS
//SYSOUT    DD    SYSOUT=*
//SYSUDUMP  DD    SYSOUT=*
//SORTWK01  DD    UNIT=SYSDA,SPACE=(CYL,2,,CONTIG)
//SORTWK02  DD    UNIT=SYSDA,SPACE=(CYL,2,,CONTIG)
//SYSIN     DD    *
    SORT FIELDS=(1,4,CH,A,9,2,CH,A,5,4,CH,A,14,1,CH,D)
/*
//*
//*************************************************************
//*                                                          *
//*     UPDATE MASTER FILE                            B      *
//*                                                          *
//*************************************************************
//STEPB     EXEC  PGM=FSBT3708
//STEPLIB   DD    DSN=BT05686.TEST.LOADMODS,
//   DISP=SHR
//BT3708E1  DD    DSN=&&TRANSORT,
//   DISP=(OLD,DELETE)
//BT3708E2  DD    DSN=AK00.C99.TELMAST,
//   DISP=(OLD,KEEP)
//BT3708E3  DD    DSN=AK00.C99.AREAREF,
//   DISP=SHR
//BT3708U1  DD    SYSOUT=*
//BT3708U2  DD    DSN=AK00.C99.TELMAST.UPDATED,
//   UNIT=SYSDA,
//   DISP=(NEW,CATLG,DELETE),
//   DCB=(RECFM=FB,LRECL=314,BLKSIZE=5966),
//   SPACE=(5966,(4210,850),RLSE)                '80000 RECS
//BT3708U3  DD    DSN=&&TRANSFIN,
//   UNIT=SYSDA,
//   DISP=(NEW,PASS,DELETE),
//   DCB=(RECFM=FB,LRECL=102,BLKSIZE=6222),   '2800 TRANS
//   SPACE=(6222,(46,9),RLSE)
//SYSOUT    DD    SYSOUT=*
//SYSUDUMP  DD    SYSOUT=*
```

```
//*************************************************************
//*                                                         *
//*      PRODUCE TRAN REPORT (INTERNAL SORT)          C     *
//*                                                         *
//*************************************************************
//STEPC     EXEC  PGM=FSBT3719
//STEPLIB    DD   DSN=BT05686.TEST.LOADMODS,
//  DISP=SHR
//SORTLIB    DD   DSN=SYS1.SORTLIB,
//  DISP=SHR
//BT3719E1   DD   DSN=&&TRANSFIN,
//  DISP=(OLD,DELETE)
//BT3719U1   DD   SYSOUT=*
//BT3719U2   DD   SYSOUT=*
//SORTWK01   DD   UNIT=SYSDA,SPACE=(CYL,2,,CONTIG)
//SORTWK02   DD   UNIT=SYSDA,SPACE=(CYL,2,,CONTIG)
//BT3719SM   DD   SYSOUT=*
//SYSOUT     DD   SYSOUT=*
//SYSUDUMP   DD   SYSOUT=*
//
```

FIGURE 6.1. Test sequential update job stream upgraded to perform new data set "housekeeping"

Because this data set, if it does exist from a prior run, is cataloged, why do we specify the UNIT and SPACE parameters as if we were creating it? And why is this combination of parameters present when the end-status-normal disposition is DELETE?

The answer to these questions lies in the operation of the MOD start-status disposition value. MOD is usually defined as the start-status option that permits extension of an existing data set; that definition is correct but it obscures MOD's greater utility as the start-status that is *permissive of finding or not finding a given data set.* MOD operates in this manner: if the named data set is on the system, it can be extended; if the named data set is not on the system, MOD creates it and then allows extension of it. In this DD statement we have coded UNIT and SPACE to make sure that they will be present if MOD needs them. This is what happens when MVS processes this DD statement:

- MVS looks in the catalog for a reference to the data set because no VOL parameter is coded for AK00.C99.TELMAST.UPDATED.

- If MVS finds the data set name in the catalog, that data set is made available to IEFBR14, which does absolutely nothing with it. When IEFBR14 finishes execution, MVS processes the DELETE end-status disposition. Because the data set was cataloged, processing the DELETE involves uncataloging the data set and then deleting it, actions reported by two IEF285I messages in the system deallocation report.

- If MVS does not find the data set name in the catalog, MOD creates it using the UNIT and SPACE specifications indicated. UNIT = SYSDA specifies that any available disk volume on the system can be used

to house the data set, and the SPACE specification provides the minimal amount of space imaginable: none. After creating the data set,
control is given to IEFBR14, the program being executed. When
IEFBR14 completes execution, MVS processes the DELETE end-status
disposition. Since the data set was not cataloged, processing the
DELETE involves simply deleting it. The actions are documented with
IEF285I messages in the system deallocation report.

One housekeeping step such as //DELSTEP is sufficient at the start of
a job stream to delete any data sets that must be eliminated to allow
the job stream to run. If there were more data sets like
AK00.C99.TELMAST.UPDATED in the job stream, all could be listed
in //DELSTEP, one DD statement after another. The DD statements would
usually carry different names—perhaps //DEL1, //DEL2, and so forth—
and each would be processed as indicated here. Some data sets could
exist and be deleted; others might not be present, but no error message
would be received in connection with their absence. The //DELSTEP is
typical of a general purpose data set housekeeping job step.
    The data set given the housekeeping treatment here is a disk data set.
If it were a tape data set, the DD statement would be coded slightly
differently, as

```
//DELSTEP  EXEC  PGM=IEFBR14
//DEL1        DD  DSN=AK00.C99.TELMAST.UPDATED,
//   UNIT=(TAPE,,DEFER),
//   DISP=(MOD,DELETE)
```

and no SPACE parameter is used because the SPACE parameter is associated only with disk data sets. The DEFER in the UNIT parameter is
particularly important in this case because it tells MVS that the mounting
of the tape can be deferred until the program opens the data set. Since
IEFBR14 never opens any data set, the DEFER means that an operator
will not be asked to mount a tape. If DEFER is omitted and only
UNIT=TAPE is coded, a tape that will not be used will have to be
mounted. Because this is a manual action, omitting DEFER will waste
time and slow the job considerably and will justifiably irritate operations
personnel.
    In both cases only one data set is indicated for deletion in the IEFBR14
step. If more than one tape data set were to be handled, using a DD
statement for each, it would be highly desirable to minimize the number
of devices assigned to the step by using the affinity specification, AFF,
on the second and subsequent tape data sets, pointing to the first tape
DDname. The DEFER subparameter of UNIT delays mounting the media
until actually needed, but there is no way to escape the assignment of
a device to a step and a tape drive will be assigned to the above step

when it executes. If we were deleting more than one tape data set we would use the AFF feature of UNIT to avoid the need for MVS to assign several tape drives:

```
//DELSTEP   EXEC  PGM=IEFBR14
//DEL1         DD   DSN=FS62.A31.ACCTSLOG,
//   UNIT=(TAPE,,DEFER),
//   DISP=(MOD,DELETE)
//*
//DEL2         DD   DSN=FS62.A31.JOURNLOG,
//   UNIT=AFF=DEL1,
//   DISP=(MOD,DELETE)
//*
//DEL3         DD   DSN=FS62.A31.VOUCHLOG,
//   UNIT=AFF=DEL1,
//   DISP=(MOD,DELETE)
```

Data Set "Finder" Step

The null program has many uses related to the DISP parameter. Under MVS it is truly amazing what can be accomplished by a program that has nothing in it.

In some job streams it is important to find out early if a certain data set is present and accessible. It is possible to do so in the first step of the job stream, even if the data set will not actually be used until later, by coding a first step that invokes IEFBR14 and carries a disposition that does not alter the current status of the data set:

```
//STEPA     EXEC  PGM=IEFBR14
//DD1          DD   DSN=FS62.A31.PAYMASTER,
//   DISP=(OLD,KEEP)
```

If this step does not find the data set or cannot obtain access to it, the step will fail and the job will terminate.

Target for VOL Referback

For some jobs a "finder" role is played by an initial IEFBR14 step. In //STEPA of the partitioned data set reorganization job stream of Appendix B we see a reference to the partitioned data set that will ultimately be copied to another PDS and deleted. The information will then be copied back to a newly allocated PDS of the original name. The IEFBR14 step here insures that the data set exists and is accessible, but it also makes MVS identify the volume on which the PDS now resides. The VOL referback lets JCL specifications take on a value from an earlier step. *It is possible in a step to refer back to a former step and pick up information that MVS acquired for us.* In the case here this information is the identity of the disk volume on which the PDS resides, and //STEPA is where MVS obtains it.

In the PDS reorganization the steps that actually copy the PDS to be processed from one place to another use the IEBCOPY utility, and the DD statements for it must specify the disk volume serial number on which the new PDS copy will reside. It is desirable to have the data set remain on the same disk volume on which it is presently located. It is also desirable not to have to know and enter this volume id manually when running the reorganization. By using the IEFBR14 finder step, coded with a disposition that does not alter the data set status, MVS is forced to look in the system catalog to determine the location of the data set. In a later step, when we need to specify the volume serial number of the disk on which to place the new copy of the data set, we refer back to //STEPA and use the volume serial number associated with the original data set without ever having to know it ourselves. The reorganization JCL is generalized in this manner.

Cataloging and Uncataloging Data Sets

IEFBR14 can be used to catalog an existing data set that is not currently cataloged. To do this the UNIT and VOL parameters must be specified to tell the system how to find the data set and obtain its other characteristics from its data set label:

```
//STEPX     EXEC  PGM=IEFBR14
//CAT1       DD   DSN=AK00.C99.TELMAST,
//   UNIT=SYSDA,
//   DISP=(OLD,CATLG),
//   VOL=SER=FSDC03
```

The DDname is arbitrarily chosen but the data set must actually exist. If the data set is already cataloged, this step causes the catalog entry to be updated. If a data set of the same name exists on a different disk or tape and is already cataloged, a "NOT CATLG 2" warning error is received and the catalog is not changed. In the majority of cases data sets are cataloged at the time of their creation. Although manual cataloging of a data set is possible, its utility is usually limited to actions taken to "patch up" an application system after a job failure, to restore such a system to operation. Data sets may be uncataloged with (OLD,UNCATLG) or uncataloged and deleted in one action with a disposition of (OLD,DELETE).

DISP TRIVIA

Writing Data Sets with OLD or MOD

Most commonly, when OLD is specified for start-status, the data set in question is being opened by the program for INPUT; that is, reading. An existing data set, however, can be accessed by coding OLD and opening it for OUTPUT; in other words, for writing. When this is done, the former contents of the data set are completely obliterated by the open action. Any data written out to that data set overlays the data formerly in the data set. The open for output action and subsequent data set closure writes an end-of-file marker in the data set; once this has occurred the former contents of the data set are no longer accessible even if no data writing actions were initiated by the program. For COBOL, coding OLD in the JCL and opening the data set for EXTEND produces the same result as coding MOD; COBOL's EXTEND overrides the JCL's OLD.

MOD dictates exclusive control of a data set as does OLD, but it allows the extension of an existing data set, something that no other start-status allows. It is in this latter capacity that its primary purpose was originally thought to lie; hence the name MOD, a shortening of "modify." A disk data set can, for example, be allocated using IEFBR14 so that space for it is assigned and reserved; the data set will have no contents. A subsequent job step, or a different job running later, can access the data set by using the MOD start-status disposition and place information in the data set. In fact, several jobs can run, one at a time, each adding data to the data set. Each access places more data at the end of the data set, moving the end-of-file marker in the data set farther back in the allocated disk area. Opening a data set for OUTPUT in a program and coding MOD in the JCL accomplishes the extension process.

MOD is a lesser used start-status disposition because it is preferable to know the actual status of a data set to be updated—existing or not existing—when a job starts. In addition, its use is made less appealing by the fact that attempting to extend a data set carries some risk of its corruption if a job step is interrupted or abends. If a job step MODding onto a data set abends, the data set is usually left in an unusable condition.

How PASS Works

When a data set is passed, information about it such as the unit and volume on which it resides is placed by MVS into a pass list. This list is a creation of MVS and is used in a behind-the-scenes "first in, first out" or "FIFO" manner. If data sets are created under the same name by successive steps in the same job—*as will happen with multiple executions of the same cataloged procedure in a job*—each will generate an entry on the pass list because the pass list mechanism makes an entry every time PASS is coded.

When a job step accesses the pass list with a disposition such as (OLD,PASS), the OLD removes the oldest entry of the given data set name on the pass list. The PASS end-status-normal disposition causes another entry for the name to be placed at the bottom of the list. When (OLD,DELETE) or (OLD,KEEP) is coded for a data set passed from a prior step, no new entry to the pass list is made for the name.

A given step that receives a passed data set, in a job stream in which many passed data sets have been created under the same name, is not necessarily going to get the physical data set one might assume. It will get the data set referenced by the then-oldest entry in the pass list for that data set name. The actual data set pointed to by this entry will depend on prior accesses by other job steps. This can cause a problem if the same &&name has inadvertently been used for different temporary data sets or if a given instream or cataloged procedure is being invoked repeatedly in the same job stream. The elimination of potential problems with PASS lies in the application of two simple rules:

- Within a job stream or JCL two different steps should not create temporary data sets using the same name.
- Every instream or cataloged procedure should cause any named temporary data set to be deleted explicitly in the last step to receive it by using a disposition of (OLD,DELETE) at that point.

Abiding by the first of these rules prevents potential problems in the job stream by eliminating the ambiguous nature of the reference to passed data sets. Application of the second of these rules results in the creation of procs that clean up after themselves by their own end points, deleting explicitly all passed temporary data sets and not relying on MVS to delete them at the end of the job. When a job invokes more than one instream or cataloged procedure, or the same procedure more than once, "end of job" is not synonymous with "end of procedure."[2]

REVIEW QUESTIONS AND (*)EXERCISES

1. What is the default for DISP if it is not explicitly coded in a DD statement?

2. What is the effect of coding OLD as opposed to SHR in terms of other jobs that attempt to use a data set and in terms of the initiation of processing for a given job?

3. If DISP = (NEW,CATLG) is coded on a DD statement at a job step that fails in execution, what is the status of the data set named on this DD statement?

4. DISP = (,KEEP) is coded on a DD statement. Explain what this means and how a data set created at this DD statement must be accessed afterwards.

5. What types of data sets can be PASSed, when is PASSing appropriate, and what are some of its advantages?

6. What are the two significant aspects of the start-status of MOD and which of them is more commonly employed in the contemporary environment?

7. Assume that in //STEPC of Figure 6.1 the DISP for &&TRANSFIN at DD statement //BT3719E1 is coded as DISP = (OLD,PASS) instead of DISP = (OLD,DELETE). What happens to the report produced by program FSBT3719 if two copies of the JCL are placed end-to-end and executed as one job?

*8. Create a data set by using JCL as illustrated in *Creating a PDS and Adding or Deleting Members* in Chapter 2. Specify that the data set is to be allocated zero tracks of disk space as illustrated in the //DELSTEP of Figure 6.1 and cataloged. Develop and run another one-step job stream using IEFBR14 to uncatalog the data set. Finally, develop a one-step job stream to catalog the data set; remember also to include the VOL parameter for this operation. Compare the MVS allocation/deallocation messages for each run. Using an IEFBR14 step, delete the data set you created.

*9. Create a data set by using JCL as illustrated in *Creating a PDS and Adding or Deleting Members* in Chapter 2. Specify that the data set is to be allocated zero tracks of disk space as illustrated in the //DELSTEP of Figure 6.1 and cataloged. Include a VOL specification for a disk volume accessible to you in your installation, the identity of which can be found in allocation/deallocation listings from jobs you have already run. After running the creation job once, run it a second time and note the type of error message received. Using an IEFBR14 step, delete the data set you created unless you are also doing exercise 10.

*10. After performing exercise 9, modify the VOL identification on your data set creation JCL to specify a disk volume different from that on which you have already created a data set. Run this job and note how the data set is created on the second disk volume; identify the NOT CATLG 2 warning message issued by MVS which indicates that while the data set was created it could not be cataloged. Using an IEFBR14 step, delete the data sets you created and note that to delete the second one you will need to specify the volume on which it resides; use the VOL parameter.

NOTES

1. VSAM provides it own safeguards against concurrent access, beyond the DISP parameter. VSAM manages the sharing of data sets via a SHAREOPTIONS attribute established at the time that the data set is defined using the IDCAMS utility. VSAM SHAREOPTIONS and OLD can both prevent data set access.

2. For passed data sets MVS will act on the end-status-abend value even after the step in which the data set was created. It is possible to create a new, permanent data set in a step and to use a disposition such as (NEW,PASS,CATLG). Subsequent steps can receive this passed data set and pass it on with a disposition such as (OLD,PASS,CATLG). A final step receiving it can specify (OLD,CATLG,CATLG) to retain and catalog it. The purpose of the end-status-abend or "conditional" disposition of CATLG on the creating and receiving accesses is to cause the data set to be cataloged if a job step abends after the point of data set creation. This coding presumes that the retention of the data set is desired.

   A disposition such as (OLD,PASS) is sometimes said to have no end-status-abend or conditional disposition. In fact, it has one because the end-status-normal disposition of PASS is taken as the end-status-abend by default. PASS is not regarded as a legitimate end-status-abend, however, because a passed data set cannot "live" beyond the end of a job. End of job is not necessarily the same as end of instream or cataloged procedure, as discussed in this chapter at *How PASS Works* and in Chapter 16.

3. *The Annotated Alice—Alice's Adventures in Wonderland & Through the Looking Glass*, by Lewis Caroll, illustrated by John Tenniel; introduction and notes by Martin Gardner. Bramhall House Publishers, 1960.

4. What actually does the DD statement DISP processing? It is an "initiator," one of the MVS "nanny" programs that pick up an application program from the input queue, usher it along, and finally free its resources at job step end. The only time DD statements are not processed is when a step is not executed because of condition code testing and the MVS skipping of the step, or when the name for a data set is coded as NULLFILE or DUMMY on a DD statement. Including a DDname for an unneeded data set that carries a disposition of OLD excludes any other program from using the data set, even though the program executed at this step does not use it.

7

DCB: Data Set Control Block

The DCB parameter of the DD statement has more subparameters associated with it than do other parameters. The need for the DCB itself may be somewhat difficult to comprehend, especially when one has had experience with other types of computers and operating systems. The DCB is, however, easily mastered once some background is understood. Further easing of the situation results from the fact that only a relatively small number of DCB subparameters are actually used in contemporary work because the majority deal with the requirements of obsolete or little used I/O devices and access methods.

THE MVS DATA CONTROL BLOCK

When a callable routine is developed in an applications programming environment, one of the first items determined is what the interface between such a module and its "caller" will be. MVS makes heavy use of callable modules. Literally thousands of specialized routines exist within MVS to perform tasks associated with memory management, job initiation and monitoring, communication between subsystems, data set opening and closing, and so forth. These programs are written in assembler language. The linkage area for these programs consists not of precoded copybook or "copylib" record definitions but of documented "control blocks" of memory. Fields within such an interface memory area are located by a positive or negative displacement relative to a memory address.

When one MVS routine calls another for service, it first locates a portion of memory to which it has access and control, and establishes it as a place for the necessary linkage area. The calling routine fills the fields in the linkage area with the values or parameters required for the routine being invoked. The calling logic then gives control to the called routine and passes the starting address of the linkage area to it in a specified register. The called routine accepts the address from the register, retrieves the parameters it requires from the fields in the linkage area, and does its work.

Linkage areas shared by MVS routines are called "control blocks." Scores of different control blocks exist; some are better known than others. Different types of control blocks are different—they have different numbers of fields, different lengths, and are used by different service routines and modules. Control block fields and formats are documented in *System/360 Control Blocks*, GC28-6628. Included in this publication are the formats for volume table of contents or "VTOC" data set control block or "DSCB" records and even the VOL1, HDR1 and HDR2 80-byte records that constitute tape labels. *OS Data Management Macro Instructions* GC26-3794, provides information to the assembler language programmer concerning the macros that IBM provides for dealing directly with I/O control blocks. Neither of the publications cited is commonly useful to a contemporary COBOL, PL/I, FORTRAN or fourth generation language programmer.

THE "DCB MERGE"

The data control block—not the DCB parameter of JCL but the actual area of memory that serves as the control linkage to MVS I/O routines—is one of the many MVS control blocks. It is formed in memory by MVS from a variety of sources before the invocation of I/O services on behalf of a program. Three sources can contribute to the formation of the data control block by MVS:

• The program being executed, via file description statements and/or language compiler defaults

- The DCB parameter of JCL
- The label of the data set being accessed

MVS extracts information from these three sources in the hierarchy shown. If an item of data control block information is obtained from the program, it is not sought from the DCB parameter of JCL or from the data set's label. If the item is coded in JCL, it is not sought from the data set label. Thus the program overrides both the JCL and data set label, and JCL overrides just the data set label. The process of building the actual data control block for the I/O routines from these three sources is called the "dcb merge." JCL errors can seem strange, arbitrary, and frustrating if this background on the JCL DCB and the "real" data control block is not understood.

Data set blocking, specified as block size by the BLKSIZE subparameter, is commonly specified via the DCB. Although many minicomputer operating systems and IBM's DOS mainframe operating system require record blocking to be specified in programs themselves, MVS allows a program to pass up its opportunity to specify this. To do so, one codes "BLOCK CONTAINS 0 RECORDS" in the file description in a COBOL program. In response to this, the COBOL compiler does not supply a block size to MVS, and MVS uses the block size stated in the JCL DCB for data control block formation.[1] For an assembler program to pass up the opportunity to specify a block size and allow it to be done in JCL, BLKSIZE can be omitted in the DCB instruction in the program. In PL/I, BLKSIZE is omitted from the ENVIRONMENT option to allow blocking to be specified in JCL.

THE JCL DCB FOR NEW DATA SETS: WHEN NOT NEEDED

Sometimes new data sets, or work data sets, are output by a program and no DCB parameter appears in the DD statements in JCL. This is possible when the program itself has access to all aspects of the actual data control block needed by the I/O routine, and the program itself supplies all the information to complete the data control block. Assembler language is more commonly associated with this capability. When a program itself provides the information to complete the data control block, the DD statement for the data set may need to contribute only the data set name, which is optional, and provide the physical disk or tape resources needed by the data set.[2] Only the DD statement can supply the disk or tape storage resources; in this instance only a UNIT and, for disk, a SPACE parameter, are found on the DD statement.[3]

Examining the DD statements for the //SYSUT1 through //SYSUT4 work data sets required by the COBOL compiler, in Figure 1.2, we see such DD statements. Here the compiler program, written in assembler, has coded within it the data set characteristics necessary to fill the MVS data control block; the //SYSUT1 through //SYSUT4 DD statements specify only the physical disk resources needed. The //SORTWKnn data sets of the sort utility are similar. The DD statements for the COBOL compiler's work data sets, and for the work data sets of the sort utility, carry no DISP parameter; omitting DISP results in the implication of a disposition coded as // DISP = (NEW,DELETE). These DD statements do not carry a data set name; we can be lazy and allow MVS to generate its own unique identifier to name for them because the data sets will not be referenced in subsequent steps.

Let's look now at the DD statement appearing in JCL for a new data set being output by a typical COBOL application program. FSBT3708 is such a program and the JCL executing it appears in //STEPB of Figures 3.4 and 6.1. Here we see, in addition to the DSN, UNIT, DISP and SPACE parameters, a DCB parameter:

```
//BT3708U2   DD   DSN=AK00.C99.TELMAST.UPDATED,
//   UNIT=SYSDA,
//   DISP=(NEW,CATLG,DELETE),
//   DCB=(RECFM=FB,LRECL=314,BLKSIZE=5966),
//   SPACE=(5966,(4210,850),RLSE)
```

This DCB is present for a very good reason. The program being executed is either unable to supply the necessary data set characteristics information needed by MVS to form the data control block for this data set or it has been judged better to supply this information via JCL, external to the program. Coding the characteristics in the JCL DCB parameter will allow the block size to be changed without modifying and recompiling the program.

The DCB parameter in the //BT3708U2 DD statement explicitly conveys three items of information: record format, record length, and block size. This is more than is needed. The program itself indicates the record length in its file description and also specifies the recording mode. Coding the DCB parameter with these three items of information is customary, however, because it allows visual validation, using JCL alone, of the block size as a multiple of record length. For blocked, fixed length records the block size must be a multiple of the record length, because blocks are assembled by MVS I/O routines by combining integral numbers of records into packages written or read as a whole.

DCB SHORT FORM CODING WITH A SINGLE "KEYWORD"

All DCB subparameters are "keywords" and the order of specifying them makes no difference. When only one keyword subparameter is specified, the DCB can be coded as

```
//   DCB=keyword=xxxx
```

with parentheses omitted. This short form coding applies in only a few
instances, but it is used consistently in connection with DUMMY data
sets. It is possible to "shut off" an output from a program in JCL by
consigning the output emerging from a DD statement to a "bit bucket"
or "sink." For example, if we coded the //BT3708U2 DD statement in
Figure 3.4 or 6.1 in this way

```
//BT3708U2    DD   DUMMY,
//   DCB=BLKSIZE=314
```

or more compactly

```
//BT3708U2    DD   DUMMY,DCB=BLKSIZE=314
```

we would be disposing of the output. Note, however, that even in this
case the information needed by MVS to complete the data control block
must be supplied. Although the program supplied the record format and
record length in its FD, it did not give the block size. For output emerging
from application programs and from utility programs we must have at
least the minimal DCB shown here when output is consigned to DUMMY
status.
    A block size is needed by MVS I/O routines to allocate the memory
buffer to which output is directed from the program. This buffer is needed even if that output will not be conveyed subsequently to an external
storage device. DUMMY causes MVS to omit the last stage of output
handling, never transferring the output to an actual I/O device, but it
cannot cut off the outputting actions of the program that places the data
into a buffer. *The size of the buffer required by the DUMMY statement
can be as small as one record length; it need not be the same size as
the actual block length if the record had been output and written to
disk or tape.*

DCB I/O SUBPARAMETERS

The actual data control blocks used by different I/O routines differ in
content but many contain dozens of fields. Because JCL can be used to
supply these items of information, it is reasonable to conclude that several DCB subparameters besides RECFM, LRECL, and BLKSIZE could
exist and they do. In fact, 37 DCB subparameters are recognized by MVS,
of which RECFM, LRECL, and BLKSIZE are three. When multiple DCB
subparameters are coded, the format of the DCB specification is as illustrated in Figures 3.4 and 6.1. DCB coding can span more than one
line if the line is broken at a comma between subparameters.

Not all DCB subparameters are relevant to any one data set organization and some apply only to highly specialized I/O tasks that deal with communication lines, optical readers, and device controllers. The following summary presents DCB subparameters applicable to the types of I/O encountered in contemporary COBOL, PL/I, FORTRAN and assembler applications programming. It includes, for background purposes, coverage of certain obsolete items related to direct and ISAM data sets that may still be seen in "ancient" pre-VSAM JCL.

BLKSIZE=nnnnn   ***Block size in bytes***   **Usage: common**

BLKSIZE specifies the maximum length of the block, which can range between 18 and 32,760. The lower limit is imposed by circuitry that cannot distinguish between noise on the storage media and a real data block shorter than 18 bytes. The upper limit is imposed by the manner in which block size is handled by MVS, stored as a 16-bit, half-word binary item, less seven bytes. For data sets coded in ASCII, not EBCDIC, on magnetic tape that carries ASCII standard labels, the upper limit is only 2,048 bytes per block. See the discussion under LRECL concerning block size and record length coding for variable length records.

BUFL=nnnn   ***Size of buffers in bytes***   **Usage: rare**

The length of each data buffer defaults to the size of the block. BUFL can be specified as a value as low as the block size and as high as 32,760. An example of the syntax is BUFL = 13000. For disk data sets it is possible to gain efficiency by having the buffer size larger than the default and allowing more blocks from the same track or cylinder to be brought into program-accessible memory with a given revolution of the media. *But BUFL is not relevant to VSAM data sets, where the AMP subparameter BUFSP serves an analogous purpose, as discussed in Chapter 11.*

BUFNO=nnn   ***Number of buffers for I/O***   **Usage: slight**

This value can range from 1 to 255; each buffer is one block length of memory or the size set by the BUFL subparameter. The default is two buffers so that physical I/O occurs in parallel with the processing of data. The default is usually sufficient but may be made larger to speed processing of large sequential data sets at the expense of memory. An example of the syntax is BUFNO = 6. BUFNO and BUFL can be specified together to control the size and number of data buffers used by the MVS "IOCS" or input/output control system. *BUFNO is not applicable to VSAM data sets, for which the AMP subparameters BUFND and BUFNI govern the number of buffers for data and index components, as discussed in Chapter 11.*

DEN=x   ***Tape recording density***   **Usage: slight**

Values from 0 to 4 are valid and signify the recording density in bits per inch:

0	200 bpi
1	556 bpi
2	800 bpi
3	1,600 bpi
4	6,250 bpi

The default for DEN is defined by the installation and is dictated by the specific tape equipment in local use. In a contemporary mainframe installation densities under 1,600 bpi are obsolete. Recording densities of 200 and 556 bpi are associated only with seven-track tape drives, which were rendered obsolete in the 1960s by the introduction of the eight-bits-per-byte architecture of the System/360. An installation may now have one or more 800-bpi drives only to be able to read low density nine-track tapes created by a key-to-disk data entry operation. IBM's newest tape drive, the 18-track, cartridge loading 3480, records only at a density of 38,800 bpi and does not respond to the DEN subparameter.

DSORG=xx   ***Data set organization***   **Usage: slight**

DSORG specifies the basic nature of a data set. Four real DSORG codes exist and three additional codes appear for descriptive purposes:

  PS   Physical sequential (default)
  PO   Partitioned organization; partitioned data set
  IS   Indexed-Sequential Access Method (ISAM)
  DA   Basic Direct Access Method (BDAM)
 *CX   Basic Telecommunications Access Method (BTAM) line
      group
 *GS   Graphic Access Method (GAM) control block
 *VS   Virtual Storage Access Method

The DSORG codes marked with an asterisk are not commonly seen in application program JCL. In fact, "VS" is not specifiable as a DSORG at all because VSAM data sets are not created using this form of JCL but by the access method utility program IDCAMS. "VS" is, however, shown on TSO screens as the DSORG for VSAM data sets when displaying a volume table of contents (VTOC).

A "U" may be appended to PS, PO, IS, and DA codes to denote that a data set is unmovable, which means that the data set contains device dependent information such as relative track addresses. Unmovable data sets are rarely used because they impose limitations on disk space management.

EROPT=xxx,   ***Error option***   Usage: slight

EROPT can take one of three values and interacts with the error detection provisions of the program being executed:

ABE (Abend).   MVS is to initiate an abend with a system completion code and a memory dump if an I/O error occurs. This is the default and ordinarily the most appropriate treatment.

SKP (Skip).   MVS is to skip over a bad block or blocks if an I/O error occurs. Most often this action is not acceptable because it can result in the loss of an unpredictable amount of data. At times, however, it is useful as a means of salvaging data from a flawed tape when it cannot be recreated.

ACC (Accept).   MVS is to accept the block or blocks on which an I/O error occurred. This is not often satisfactory because the data accepted may be garbled and of unknown integrity. If an assembler program is to deal with low-level I/O errors, EROPT = ACC should be coded to prevent MVS from abending at the error and pass the occurrence on to the program. It is unusual for an application program to perform low-level I/O error recovery; the normal course of action is to allow an abend for true I/O errors. Declaratives, file status, and "invalid key" tests are used only to deal with record "found/not found" read, write, rewrite, browse, and delete actions and EROPT is *not* coded in the DCB, allowing the default ABE to prevail.

KEYLEN=nnn,   ***Key length***   Usage: obsolete

Key length is specified only with Basic Direct Access Method (BDAM) or Indexed Sequential Access Method (ISAM) data sets. Ranging in value from 0 to 255, this indicates the length of the access method primary key. It is not used with unkeyed files such as sequential data sets or partitioned data sets, and *it is not used with VSAM.*

LIMCT=nn   ***Limit count***   Usage: obsolete

Used only with "direct" files, this specifies how many additional blocks or tracks are to be searched seeking a record if the intended block or track to house the record is already filled. Obtaining the effect of LIMCT also requires coding the OPTCD = E subparameter, where the "E" has meaning only for this type of data set organization. *LIMCT is not used with VSAM.*

LRECL=nnn   ***Maximum record length***   **Usage: common**

LRECL is expressed in bytes. This is the actual record length for fixed length records and the size of the largest record for variable length records. This value can range from 1 to a high of 32,760; it can be even higher for specialized record formats and can exceed block size when the record format is "variable spanned." For common fixed (F), fixed-blocked (FB), variable (V), and variable-blocked (VB) record formats these values typically range from less than 100 bytes to several thousand bytes.

Unblocked and blocked fixed length records are also known as COBOL "F" mode records. The most common types of data sets are those that contain fixed length records grouped into blocks that provide efficient I/O and media usage. In such cases block size must be specified as a multiple of record length and no larger than 32,760 bytes.

For *variable length unblocked* records LRECL is specified as four bytes more than the longest length record in the data set to allow for MVS-generated "record length written" information, called the "record descriptor word," to be appended to the front of each record. BLKSIZE is specified as a value four bytes more than LRECL even though the variable length records are not blocked. Unblocked variable length records are handled as a subset of blocked variable length records, and MVS automatically appends "block length written" information to the front of each. Such "block length written" information is called the "block descriptor word." Variable length *unblocked* record usage is rare.

For *variable length blocked* records LRECL is specified as four bytes more than the longest record in the data set and BLKSIZE is specified as a quantity at least four bytes greater than LRECL, but usually much greater, as great as is prudent given the storage media used. MVS automatically places information at the front of each block to indicate the actual size of the block written. With variable length blocked records there is no way to predict how many records will fit in a block or how long any specific block will actually be. Block size is usually coded as track size in order to maximize variable length blocked record storage on disk.

Both variable length unblocked and variable length blocked records are known as COBOL "V" mode records. The handling of variable length unblocked and blocked records limits their block size to no more than 32,752 bytes because of the record and block length written information applied by MVS and the normal I/O limit of 32,760 bytes per data access or EXCP.

LRECL for "undefined" format records, which are known as COBOL "U" mode records, is specified as zero and BLKSIZE is indicated as the maximum record length or greater. RECFM = U essentially tells MVS to omit any record deblocking actions on each burst of information between inter-record gaps oon the storage media. The primary use for format U data sets is to house program load modules, which are continuous streams of program storage areas and machine language instructions. For these, block size is most efficiently coded as the maximum usable track size of the disk that contains the data set: 23,476 bytes on 3380 disks, or the 3330/3350/3380 compromise value of 6,233 bytes.

OPTCD=xxxx   ***Optional services code***   **Usage: slight**

A total of 35 optional input/output services may be specified, with code values of one letter each. Some letter codes have a different meaning for different data set organizations and not all optional services are relevant for each of them. Some letter codes can be specified in combination, for example:

```
DCB=(RECFM=FB,LRECL=64,BLKSIZE=1280,OPTCD=QB),
```

The most common of the still-relevant optional services codes are these:

B The logic routine that handles end-of-volume tasks ordinarily regards the end-of-file (EOF) trailer label on a data set as the basis to end reading the data set. Sometimes, however, it is useful to treat an end of file indication as if it were simply the end of one volume or reel of a multivolume data set that spreads across several reels of tape. Coding OPTCD = B allows this to happen. The end-of-volume routine encounters the EOF trailer labels but regards them as if they were end-of-volume (EOV) labels. EOV labels are not a signal for the end of the data set; their presence is an indication to mount the next specified volume in the volume serial number list— VOL = SER = (aaaaaa,bbbbbb,cccccc)—and so forth. This allows multivolume data sets to be read in a specified volume sequence instead of actual sequence, but more importantly it allows several tapes with the same data set name to be cited in a VOL = SER specification and be read as one multireel data set. This is useful when data from several sources or covering several data entry cycles is conveyed on tapes to a mainframe application.

J Applicable only to data sets to be printed on the IBM 3800 printing subsystem laser printer, this indicates that each line begins with a print control character and a second print control character, known as the table reference character or "TRC."

Q Requests that the data from a tape being read be converted from ASCII to EBCDIC as it is input. For a tape being output this requests that the EBCDIC encoding of the IBM system be converted to ASCII as the data is written. This code applies only to tape and cannot be used for disk data sets.

RECFM=xx   ***Record format***   **Usage: common**

RECFM is a basic specification that describes the nature of the records stored in a data set. Four types exist:

F   fixed length records   "RECORD MODE IS F"
V   variable length records   "RECORD MODE IS V"
U   undefined length records   "RECORD MODE IS U"
D   variable length ANSI records   Not supported by COBOL

Each of these format codes can be modified by the association of other codes with them; for example, F, V, and D record formats can be blocked:

FB   fixed length blocked records
VB   variable length blocked records
DB   variable length ANSI records, blocked

Figures 7.1 to 7.5 are graphic illustrations of each of the record formats and how they appear on storage media.

Additional codes can be appended to specify variations in record content, format, and in some cases, treatment:

A Record contains device control characters in an ANSI standard format; mutually exclusive to M. Additional information on these values is found in Chapter 12 which deals with printed output.

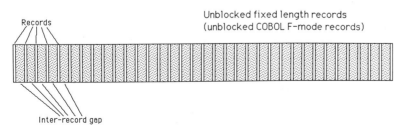

FIGURE 7.1. Organization of unblocked fixed length records (COBOL F-MODE records)

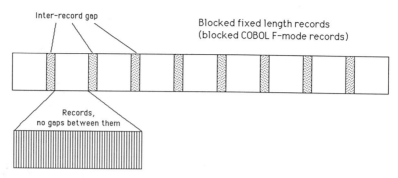

FIGURE 7.2. Organization of blocked fixed length records (COBOL F-MODE records)

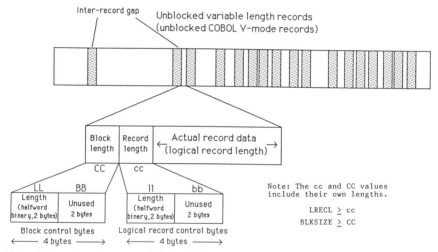

FIGURE 7.3. Organization of unblocked variable length records (COBOL V-MODE records)

M Record contains device control characters in a machine-specific format; mutually exclusive to A.

S Record is not to be written with truncated blocks (fixed length files) or records span blocks (logical record exceeds block size, variable length record).

T Records can exceed or overflow track size on disk.

The valid combinations of these format specifications are:

```
FB       FBA       FBM
FS       FSA       FSM
FT       FTA       FTM
FBS      FBSA      FBSM
FBT      FBTA      FBTM
FBST     FBSTA     FBSTM
```

VB	VBA	VBM
VS	VSA	VSM
VT	VTA	VTM
VBS	VBSA	VBSM
VBT	VBTA	VBTM
VBST	VBSTA	VBSTM

For undefined format records, which are data written or read without MVS blocking/deblocking services, the following code combinations are valid:

| U | UA | UM |
| UT | UTA | UTM |

Undefined format data cannot be blocked because, by definition, MVS does not know how to interpret its content. For writing this format the LRECL is specified as zero and BLKSIZE is coded to be large enough to accommodate the largest record. The block size can be anything up to 32,760; specifying blocks the same size as disk track size is preferred for efficiency. Blocks actually written need not all be the same length. A program reading undefined format data has to code a file description entry defining a record size as large as the largest record and the program has to know, for itself, how to interpret the data. Such programs are rare. They are not in the mainstream of general applications work; when encountered, they are usually involved with reading and translating data

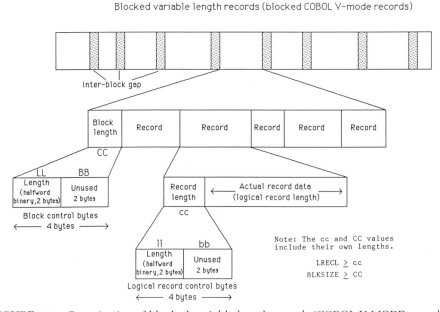

Blocked variable length records (blocked COBOL V-mode records)

FIGURE 7.4.   Organization of blocked variable length records (COBOL V-MODE records)

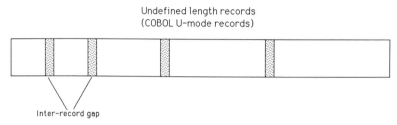

FIGURE 7.5. Organization of undefined format records (COBOL U-MODE records)

from minicomputer, microcomputer, or cassette tape data entry sources to MVS formats. Load modules are written as undefined format data sets but are not normally "read" by applications programs; they are the programs.

In practice, the most commonly used and encountered record formats are FB and VB. Source code and JCL card images are stored as fixed length, blocked 80-byte records. TSO command lists, or CLISTs, are normally stored as variable length, blocked records, with a maximum record length of 255 and a block size chosen as a value efficient for storage on the type of disk housing the data set. Chapter 17, item 6, illustrates the JCL to explore different MVS data formats firsthand. IDCAMS can be used to dump FB and VB data sets normally and, using RECFM = U, to see the content of MVS-applied control bytes in variable length records and blocks.

RKP = n   ***Relative key position***   **Usage: obsolete**

The starting position of the record key relative to the first byte of the record. The value indicated for RKP is a displacement from the first byte; therefore RKP = 0, which is the default, means the first byte. You will encounter this DCB if you work with ISAM data sets, which are now obsolete. *RKP is not applicable to VSAM.*

REVIEW QUESTIONS AND (*)EXERCISES

1. What purpose do control blocks serve within the framework of MVS?

2. Three sources of information contribute to the formation of the MVS data control block. What are these sources, what is the hierarchy of their contribution, and what is the process of data control block formation named?

3. When is a JCL DCB parameter not needed for a new data set?

4. Why is DCB not coded in a DD statement when an existing labeled data set is being read?

5. When BLKSIZE is coded in a DCB for a data set being written, why are RECFM and LRECL usually coded, even if a program specifies recording mode and record size?

6. How small might a record be, in bytes, on an MVS system, how small can a block be, and how large can a block be?

7. Why must BLKSIZE be specified when the output emerging at a DD statement is to be discarded by using the DUMMY feature?

*8. A mainframe application receives transaction input from a data entry unit that keys data on a minicomputer. The data are conveyed via a data set on tape each day. Because of a delay in delivery, three input tapes arrive on the same day and all must be input in the same job and processed together. Code a DCB parameter that handles this situation when the record length is 92 bytes, the block size is 1,840 bytes, and the data are conveyed in ASCII rather than EBCDIC encoding.

*9. Compile a COBOL program to read a blocked data set and intentionally omit the BLOCK CONTAINS 0 RECORDS phrase in its file definition. Execute the program and observe the system completion code returned by MVS. Interpret and explain why this situation results.

*10. Create a blocked, variable length record PDS by using the JCL shown in *Creating a PDS and Adding or Deleting Members* in Chapter 2, and coding

```
DCB=(RECFM=VB,LRECL=255,BLKSIZE=6233)
```

instead of the DCB illustrated. Use TSO to create a member within this data set. Use the JCL illustrated in Chapter 17, item 6, to dump this PDS member in "normal" form, and with RECFM=U. Highlight the "block descriptor word" and "record descriptor word" generated by MVS in the RECFM=U version of the dump; interpret them by using Figure 7.4 and the hexadecimal-to-decimal reference table in Appendix C.

NOTES

1. Omitting the BLOCK CONTAINS 0 RECORDS phrase does not accomplish the same purpose as coding the phrase. Omitting the phrase causes the COBOL compiler to default to a blocking factor of one record; that is, a block size the same as the record

size. If the program in question is reading a data set that already exists, which was created with records blocked in some way, an inconsistency then results in the data control block, and an abend occurs. You can see immediately why the abend, associated with a system completion code of 001-4, is encountered; even if the correct block size is stated in the JCL DCB, COBOL's default blocking factor of 1 has been used by MVS to form the actual data control block.

Sooner or later everyone inadvertently forgets to include BLOCK CONTAINS 0 RECORDS in a program and experiences a job abend with system completion code 001-4. The hidden COBOL compiler default and the dcb merge strike again.

2. The data set name or DSN subparameter of the DD statement can be omitted and MVS will assign a unique name of its own making. The name is formed from the Julian date, job name, time, and certain literal characters, as shown in the IEF285I messages associated with the sort work data sets of //STEPA in Figures 3.4 and 6.1. When a temporary data set name prefaced by two ampersands is used to name a data set, a similar system-generated name format is used, with the exception that the &&name is used as the last part of the name. The IEF285I message for the output data set from //STEPA in Figure 3.6, named &&TRANSORT, is an illustration.

It is actually possible to reference a data set not assigned a name in JCL, by using the DSN referback feature. Doing so, however, is on par with the use of the most esoteric and arcane features of a programming language for their own sake; it represents the height of willful obfuscation.

3. The DCB can also be omitted in certain cases when the custom model data set label technique is being used for generation data group data set creation. See Chapter 13 for a discussion related to that obsolescent technique.

=== 8 ===

SPACE: Disk Data Set Space Allocation

The SPACE parameter exists for one reason alone: it is the means by which a quantity of physical direct access storage device resources, or "DASD," is specified for use by a data set. SPACE is coded on the DD statement for a disk data set only when it is being created and it tells MVS and MVS/XA how much disk resources the data set will be allocated. Unlike minicomputer or microcomputer operating systems that assign disk space on an "open ended" basis as needed for files, MVS requires disk space usage to be planned and calculated in advance. SPACE, if coded for a tape data set, is ignored.

DISK STORAGE BACKGROUND

The space used by a data set on a disk device is identified in entries in the disk volume table of contents, or VTOC, which corresponds to the disk directory on minicomputer and microcomputer disk storage devices. The SPACE parameter interacts with the entries in the VTOC at the time a data set is created because it is the VTOC that carries the information indicating how much space on the disk media is currently free. Understanding the makeup of the VTOC is not terribly important to a programmer. However, knowing the role of the VTOC is valuable background because many JCL error messages associated with data set allocation mention it as if the nature of its "DSCB" or data set control block records—the records in the VTOC were common knowledge.[1]

Physical Organization of Mainframe Disks

The most commonly used direct access storage device in the contemporary mainframe world is the movable head hard disk. Hard disks employ a magnetic recording technique similar to that used by the floppy disk, audio and video cassette, and computer tape. Information is stored by placing the bits of each byte of information onto the media as tiny magnetized spots, in a pattern in which magnetization mirrors the on/off pattern of bits. Each spot is created by passing an electrical current through the coils or traces of the read/write head as media passes under it. When reading takes place, each spot becomes a "generator" of a minute electrical current in the disk read/write head as it passes under it.

Hard disks are different from other magnetic media in that the read/write head *does not* contact the media surface. The media, a group of platters joined at a central hub, rotates at a rate of 60 revolutions per second, dragging a film of air along its surface. The read/write heads are positioned over the disk surfaces on arms that can move the heads across a concentric portion of the surface as illustrated in Figure 8.1. Each disk arm is shaped like an aircraft wing. Each head "flies" a few millionths of an inch above a disk surface in the air being dragged by the rotating media because this air passes the head at a speed of about 170 miles per hour. A head cannot fly when the disk and air film stop rotating; stopping a hard disk suddenly allows the read/write heads to descend and damage the magnetic surfaces. Normal shutdown of a hard disk lets the heads retract to a position away from the data recording area of the surface before the media can slow and stop.

The disk surfaces in the data recording area present distinct tracks of recording space. Each incremental position of the head assembly between the outer circumference of the disk recording area and its inner edge constitute a track. The IBM 3350 provides 555 tracks per disk surface, the IBM 3380 provides 885 or 1,770 tracks, and the older IBM 3330 Model 11 disk provides 808 tracks.[2]

The IBM 3350 disk media, a nonremovable disk pack sealed within the unit, contains 15 disk platters joined at the hub. The 3380 provides sealed, nonremovable disk media that places 15 recording surfaces under

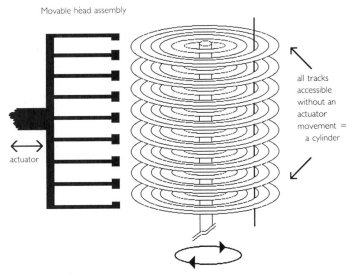

FIGURE 8.1. Terminology associated with mainframe direct access storage devices (DASD)

read/write heads at each track location with the spindle mounted horizontally, not vertically. The older IBM 3330 disk media, a demountable disk pack, contains 10 individual disks joined at a central hub. In all cases each of the recording surfaces has its own read/write head. The disk arms, each carrying a read/write head, are rigidly joined to a mechanism that moves all of them laterally at once. The net effect is that all tracks at a given distance from the hub are accessible at the same time. Such a group of tracks is called a cylinder because the tracks define this geometric shape. At an elementary level disk space can be specified in terms of specific tracks or cylinders. Application programmers have no need to be concerned with any particular tracks or cylinders; all tracks and cylinders on a given disk are alike for applications data storage.

Data Storage Architecture and "Extents"

Disk devices in the MVS and MVS/XA environment employ a storage architecture that is known as "count, key, data" or "CKD." This is different from the sectored organization of minis and micros in which tracks are premarked into same-length units, such as 512-byte sectors. Under CKD architecture the formatting of a disk establishes the concentric tracks on the media and flags bad spots on the surfaces, but does not "carve up" the tracks into sectors.[3] There is no inherently efficient record size related to a sector size and the smallest unit of allocatable space is quite large: the entire track. This is the reason that partitioned data sets were invented; PDSs allow storing more than one item—each as a member—on each track. The IBM 3350 provides 19,069 bytes per track, and the IBM 3380 provides 47,476 bytes per track. The older IBM 3330 provides 13,030 bytes per track.

Track capacity has a significant bearing on the choice of physical data block size, as discussed later in this chapter. *The single most burdensome thing connected with disk space is the development of an appropriate block size for records.* The calculation of the amount of space needed is based on the block size and the anticipated number of records in a data set.

Space is specified at the time a data set is created and a figure for the *primary* allocation and an optional *secondary* allocation figure can be stated. Each "piece" of the data set is called an "extent" and, although this may seem to be a shortening of the word "extension," it is not. Even the primary allocation of space counts as one of the extents of the data set.

A data set can have 16 extents on a given unit of disk media. Some types of data set, such as sequential and VSAM, can span more than one unit of disk media but a partitioned data set cannot. The extent limitation of 16 applies only within each unit of disk media and is imposed by the way that the VTOC functions.[4] If more than one volume is specified for a sequential data set, it can spread to 16 secondary allocations on each additional volume. Extreme data set fragmentation carries serious performance penalties and is therefore seldom permitted. Chapter 9, however, illustrates how this is specified in the discussion *VOL and UNIT parameter interplay.*

The ability to receive secondary allocations and the size of secondary extents is a characteristic of the data set; this information is retained in the format 1 DSCB record in the VTOC of the disk on which the data set starts. Even though the SPACE parameter that specified the secondary allocation criteria is coded for the data set only when it is created, a data set allowed secondary allocations will receive them if it is later updated and it expands. A TSO PDS allowed secondary extents will receive them as necessary as new members are added to it and/or old members are changed and saved.

OVERVIEW OF SPACE PARAMETER SYNTAX

The general format of the SPACE parameter is as follows. All the SPACE subparameters are positional; if any are omitted, the commas that delimit their positions are required to identify the appropriate "slots" in the parameter. The entire "(primary,secondary,dir-blocks)" is one positional parameter and both "secondary" and "dir-blocks" are optional within it.

```
SPACE=( units, primary,secondary,dir-blocks), RLSE, force, ROUND )
       nnn  --------- quantity  ---------  RLSE  CONTIG ROUND
       TRK                                       MXIG
       CYL    aaa      bbb         ccc           ALX
```

where: nnn is a number representing block size
       TRK and CYL are literals
       quantity is one positional subparameter
       aaa is the number of units for the primary allocation
       bbb is the number of units for each secondary allocation
       ccc is the number of directory blocks for a PDS
       RLSE, CONTIG, MXIG, ALX, and ROUND are literals

The shortened form of the parameter omits all but the units and primary specification and results in coding that eliminates the internal parentheses of the second subparameter:

```
//   SPACE=(CYL,15)
```

When secondary space allocations are provided, the internal parentheses are required:

```
//   SPACE=(CYL,(15,5))
```

If the data set being created is a partitioned data set, the third element of the second parameter tells how many directory blocks are to be created at the start of the primary allocation:

```
//   SPACE=(CYL,(15,5,20))
```

If the data set being created is a PDS, but no secondary allocation is desired, the missing middle element of the second subparameter is still delimited by the comma that follows it:

```
//   SPACE=(CYL,,(15,20))
```

Finally, if the data set being created is not intended to contain more space than presently needed and no secondary allocation is desired, the RLSE subparameter can be coded to release unused tracks when the data set is closed by the program writing it:

```
//   SPACE=(CYL,(15,,20),RLSE)     for a PDS
```

or

```
//   SPACE=(CYL,15,RLSE)                  for a sequential data set
```

SPACE Short Form Coding

The SPACE parameter contains five positional subparameters, but it is easier to consider the simpler, more common forms first. This SPACE parameter specifies that 15 tracks of space are to be allocated

```
//   SPACE=(TRK,15)
```

and this coding specifies that 22 cylinders are to be allocated:

```
//   SPACE=(CYL,22)
```

In both cases the space allocation is for the primary allocation only, no secondary allocation is coded. In both cases the allocation is crude and the amount of space acquired is dependent on the type of disk device that is used.

The first allocation acquires 15 tracks that contain 195,450 bytes on an IBM 3330, 15 tracks that contain 286,035 bytes on an IBM 3350, or 15 tracks that contain 712,140 bytes on an IBM 3380, based on the device characteristics summarized in Appendix G. Because an installation may have several different types of disk configured with the system at any time, all accessible with the UNIT=SYSDA designation or another locally created symbolic device group identifier, the use of TRK or CYL space allocation is a "meat axe" approach. It is akin to telling the butcher "give me a side of animal" without specifying whether part of a pheasant, turkey, lamb, calf, or cow is desired.

A third method of assigning the amount of disk space is by data block. To illustrate this we must also describe the DCB parameter of a DD statement for a new data set. Suppose we are creating a data set that contains fixed length records of 100 bytes each. Via the DCB we might tell MVS to write these in 62-record groupings in blocks or "physical records" of 6,200 bytes each. "Physical record" is a synonym for block, and when this term is used, the actual record, such as the 100-byte record here, is called a "logical record." This DCB parameter and SPACE parameter work in conjunction with one another

```
//   DCB=(RECFM=FB,LRECL=100,BLKSIZE=6200),
//   SPACE=(6200,300)
```

to request that space for 300 blocks of 6,200 characters each be allocated. When this is specified, MVS computes the number of tracks needed to provide sufficient space, after it has chosen the disk device that will receive the data set.

A prevalent practice in the contemporary environment is to specify space for sequential and partitioned data sets in terms of data blocks

whenever possible. This reduces the development of SPACE requirements to estimating the number of records involved, calculating the
number of blocks required at the block size chosen, and coding the DCB
and SPACE parameters to match in this way.

There are times when the block size of a data set to be written to disk
is not known, as in the case of sort work data sets. Here the program
itself, not a DCB parameter, supplies the record length to MVS. It is in
such a case expedient to provide disk resources by using TRK or CYL.
Specifying space by track or cylinder has no effect on the record format
or length; those characteristics are set by the program or DCB parameter.[5]

Secondary Space Allocation

SPACE coding of the form

```
//    DCB=(RECFM=FB,LRECL=100,BLKSIZE=6200),
//    SPACE=(6200,300)
```

is adequate but it provides no secondary allocation, meaning that when
the data set is created and we keep on writing records to it in excess of
the estimated 300 blocks, the job will fail. We can provide as many as
15 secondary allocations on the disk volume by coding

```
//    DCB=(RECFM=FB,LRECL=100,BLKSIZE=6200),
//    SPACE=(6200,(300,60))
```

and in this case have specified that each secondary allocation will house
60 more blocks of data. In the coding shown the data set would have a
maximum of about 300 + 15 times 60 or 1,200 blocks of space. The
"about" applies because the real amount of space available to the data
set is the integral number of tracks necessary to house the specified
number of blocks.

The second positional parameter of the SPACE has three parts: primary
quantity, secondary quantity, and a third optional part that applies only
to partitioned data sets or the now obsolete ISAM data sets. Comparing
the coding for the same primary allocation, with and without secondary
allocations, you will note that an extra set of parentheses exists when
the secondary is requested. *This is because the "300,60" is really the
second subparameter, not the second and third subparameters.*

There is nothing to guarantee that any given disk to which the data
set is assigned will actually have a contiguous amount of space for the
full primary allocation, or full secondary allocations. If the space available on a given disk is fragmented in such a way that the primary allocation cannot be fulfilled in one extent, it is allocated the largest
amount of space that can be found within the requested amount, and

up to four additional, noncontiguous extents may be allocated to complete the primary request. Thus is it possible, on a very crowded disk pack, to use TSO function 3.7, the VTOC listing, and see multiple extents for a data set even when secondary allocation was not requested for it. If secondary allocations are specified but the primary goes into multiple extents to be fulfilled, the number of possible extents on the disk still remains at 16. The overall amount of space that the data set can acquire is then more limited than it would otherwise have been.

Although secondary allocations are handy as a means of preventing job stream abends when the volume of records being processed exceeds an estimate, they are somewhat inefficient. The system must refer to the VTOC every time it accesses another extent of a data set. For two secondaries the effect is not usually significant, but it would be unwise to have a data set normally extend to four or more extents because access time to it degrades. This can cause other jobs using data sets on the same disk to suffer delays because their access also relies on the use of the VTOC. This degradation becomes more serious with disk drives of large capacities. The original VTOC mechanism was created more than 20 years ago when disks were small. A modern IBM 3380 disk that supports many TSO users may have a VTOC that spans 15 cylinders and take several seconds to search when data set access is required.[6]

Space Coding with Release (RLSE)

Requesting primary and secondary space allocations for a sequential data set is usually sufficient in SPACE parameter coding. An additional subparameter, however, is often coded on the SPACE parameter to perform a housekeeping task—the relinquishing of space requested but not used. Suppose we had asked for enough space to house 300 blocks of 6,200 bytes each:

```
//    DCB=(RECFM=FB,LRECL=100,BLKSIZE=6200),
//    SPACE=(6200,300)
```

When this is executed, space for 300 blocks of this size will be allocated. If we wrote only a few records to the data set, the remaining space would still be allocated to it and would not be usable by any other data set. We could cause the unused tracks that result in such a situation to be returned to a free status by coding the RLSE or "release" subparameter:

```
//    DCB=(RECFM=FB,LRECL=100,BLKSIZE=6200),
//    SPACE=(6200,300,RLSE)
```

If we had coded secondary allocations, we would code:

```
//   DCB=(RECFM=FB,LRECL=100,BLKSIZE=6200),
//   SPACE=(6200,(300,60),RLSE)
```

When RLSE is coded, it is the third positional subparameter and follows the second—the (300,60)—after a comma. When a data set "goes into secondaries" and RLSE has been coded, it releases unused tracks in the last active secondary. Because tracks cannot be split between data sets, the release here, as in a partly used primary space allocation, really means "release any unused tracks." Unused space on the last track written on cannot be released. If a single 80-byte card image is written to a sequential data set, specifying

```
//   DCB=(RECFM=F,LRECL=80,BLKSIZE=80),
//   SPACE=(80,1,RLSE)
```

nothing is released.

RLSE works only when a data set is accessed by a DD statement that carries the RLSE on a SPACE parameter and the data set is closed normally. If a data set is allocated by using IEFBR14, which does not open or close any data sets, RLSE is meaningless and does nothing. RLSE does not work when another job is sharing the data set or another job task—such as another DD statement in the same step, which is unusual but possible—is opening, closing, or using the data set. RLSE does not work if the step abends and the data set for which RLSE has been coded on the SPACE parameter is not closed by the program being executed.

RLSE is not a retained characteristic of the data set. If the data set is permitted secondary allocations and is later opened with a disposition of MOD and extended or OLD and rewritten completely, no space release action occurs. RLSE is just a one-time communication to MVS that may alter the last stages of its initial space allocation actions.

SPACE CODING FOR PARTITIONED DATA SETS

Directory Block Specification

Although PDSs are most commonly used to house TSO-created and maintained source code and JCL statements, they also house program load modules and all the other MVS libraries. There is no inherent connection between PDSs and 80-character records. The partitioned data set is a creature of BPAM, the MVS Basic Partitioned Access Method, and BPAM handles records of lengths appropriate to most record formats.

A PDS is established just as any other data set: it is allocated by a DD statement that names it and carries a disposition, such as DISP = (NEW,CATLG,DELETE) and other parameters, and a SPACE allocation. *The only thing that distinguishes the creation of the data set as a PDS, and not a simple sequential data set, is an indication in the second SPACE subparameter that tells how many PDS directory blocks are to be carved out at the start of the primary space allocation.*[7] A new sequential or partitioned data set can also be allocated using the allocate option of TSO's 3.2 function, and that is the way a programmer would normally create a new PDS library. When this is done, space can be specified in blocks, tracks, or cylinders, as dictated by local conventions.

If we wished to create a partitioned data set without provision for secondary allocations, the coding could take the form

```
//    SPACE=(6200,(300,,10))
```

or

```
//    SPACE=(TRK,(44,,10))
```

where the internal positional parameter in nested parentheses is omitted but its location is still delimited by the comma that follows it. The specific values shown here are roughly equivalent for an IBM 3380 disk. The value 10 is no magic number in regard to the quantity of directory blocks; it has been used in these examples solely for consistency.

PDS Directory Block Calculation

Calculation of the number of directory blocks needed for a PDS depends on two factors: the number of members that the PDS is intended to house and the amount of "user statistics" that will be recorded in each member entry in the PDS directory. The directory itself is composed of unblocked, 256-byte records, each of which is prefaced by an inaccessible eight-byte key.

Each directory block can house information for as many as 18 members if no user information about the member is retained there. The minimum directory block room needed for a given member entry is 12 bytes. These consist of eight bytes of member name, and four bytes containing binary stored values, manipulated by the Basic Partitioned Access Method. These four bytes, called the "TTRC," indicate the relative track and data block within the track in which the member starts, and how many half-words of user data follow this information in the directory entry. BPAM allows a given PDS application to house user data in the directory entries for each member via assembler macros provided with MVS and MVS/

XA. When use is made of this capability, for example, by TSO/ISPF, the directory entries for a member are larger than the minimum 12 bytes. TSO/ISPF/PDF makes use of 42-byte directory member entries, because it is here that all statistics, viewable whenever a PDS member list is displayed, are stored. This use of the directory means that a directory block of a PDS maintained by TSO as a library will house only six member entries.[8]

The space for a PDS directory is established at the time that the data set is allocated and is located at the start of the primary space allocation. The directory never extends into secondary allocations even though the PDS data area might. A PDS may have more member storage space available but no ability to house more members because the directory is filled. In such a case, TSO function 3.5 can be used to delete user statistics from the PDS, allowing the directory to house additional member entries. A better solution is to delete members no longer needed and/or reorganize the PDS using the JCL found in Appendix B, using the symbolic parameters provided to increase the number of directory blocks in the new version of the PDS.

SPACE LONG FORM CODING

The fourth and fifth SPACE positional subparameters are less commonly used than the first three, representing one-time communication to MVS concerning allocation options available at the time a data set is created.

SPACE "FORCE" Subparameter

The fourth subparameter of SPACE, if specified, can take on one of three values, all of which force MVS to accord special attention to the way that space is grouped in the primary allocation. The "force" subparameter represents one-time communication to MVS to alter its method of establishing the primary allocation for the data set.

CONTIG forces the primary allocation to be contiguous in one extent only. This means that all tracks in the allocation are in the same or adjacent cylinders; no cylinder allocated completely to other data sets intervenes. Normally the primary allocation is rendered in this condition. But if available space on a disk is fragmented into parts that are all smaller than that requested for the primary allocation, MVS will normally make the primary allocation using as many as five noncontiguous disk extents: the primary as large as possible and up to four secondary allocations. If CONTIG is specified, MVS is precluded from taking that expedient.

With CONTIG, if enough contiguous space to satisfy the primary allocation is not available, the job will fail. CONTIG is useful only if there is some real performance necessity to have the primary allocation in one chunk—so great a necessity that the job should be prevented from running if the condition cannot be met. Work files for large amounts of data being sorted usually fall into this category. CONTIG is a benign specification that if misused adversely affects a job but not a disk volume.

MXIG is a dangerous specification. MXIG is an abbreviation for "maximum extent contiguous." It tells MVS "I'll settle for my requested primary allocation as a minimum, but if you have more in a contiguous chunk I'll take the biggest piece." In other words, it sends MVS on a fishing expedition for the largest available contiguous space on the disk.

Use of MXIG can result in obtaining as much space as requested or, conceivably, the entire disk. The extra space obtained will be released if RLSE is coded, but RLSE works only if the data set that is allocated the space is opened for writing and is closed normally. Using IEFBR14 to allocate a data set and MXIG with any stated amount of space will tie up much of the disk because IEFBR14 does not open and close data sets; therefore RLSE is not effective with it. *Do not use MXIG unless you have explicit authorization.*

ALX is MXIG five times over. It stands for "all largest extents," and asks that MVS inventory the available contiguous space on the disk and identify the five largest pieces of space. Then any of these five that are as large or larger than the amount of space requested for the primary allocation are to be allocated to the data set. If specified, ALX can tie up most or all of a disk. ALX is useful only when a very large data set is being allocated and must reserve space immediately to insure that subsequent access to it will be as efficient as present disk conditions allow. *Do not use ALX unless you have explicit authorization.*

ROUND Subparameter

ROUND, the fifth SPACE positional subparameter, is useful when space is requested by data blocks, not tracks or cylinders, but for performance reasons it is desirable to allocate complete cylinders of disk. It asks MVS to calculate the number of tracks needed to house the specified blocks, round up to the next integral number of cylinders needed to provide that many tracks, and then allocate the number of complete cylinders. By concentrating the allocation in complete cylinders access time is reduced because no disk arm movement is needed to reach groups of tracks. An example of this coding is:

```
//   SPACE=(6200,22000,,,ROUND)
```

Use of ROUND requires that commas be coded to delineate the fifth subparameter slot. If RLSE and the force subparameters are not coded, their positions must still be delimited by the commas that follow them.

ROUND by itself can allocate noncontiguous cylinders for the primary allocation. CONTIG can also be specified if the primary allocation must consist of complete cylinders adjacent to one another. Because access efficiency is the basis for the use of ROUND, concurrent use of CONTIG is customary:

```
//   SPACE=(6200,22000,,CONTIG,ROUND)
```

It is of course possible that the number of blocks of space requested far exceeds the number of blocks of data actually written. RLSE can be coded to cause the release of unused space when the data set is closed. When this is done with ROUND, any unused *cylinders* are released; unused tracks on the last cylinder written on are not released:

```
//   SPACE=(6200,22000,RLSE,CONTIG,ROUND)
```

Secondary space allocation is not precluded when ROUND is used; it can also be specified. Secondary allocations, however, are not accorded the same "round up to the cylinder" calculation treatment if they are allocated in subsequent updating actions as the data set grows. Similarly, CONTIG applies only to the primary space allocation; there is no guarantee, and the overwhelming potential is against it, that the additional extents for the secondary allocation will be contiguous with the primary allocation's extent.

BLOCK SIZE AND ITS IMPORTANCE

Block Size Efficiency

Although it is natural to focus on the syntax of the SPACE parameter and its subparameters in considering JCL, the syntax is not the real meat of the issue. When it comes to disk space, the item of overwhelming importance is the use of an efficient block size for data sets. The true importance of this aspect of disk use may be masked in a learning environment when only small amounts of data are involved. In a production environment, with real data sets of hundreds of thousands or millions of records, efficient disk space utilization is critical.

The records—logical records—in data sets are grouped into blocks—physical records—to minimize the number of "execute channel program" or EXCP requests required to process a data set. Each EXCP brings into memory or writes one block of data at a cost of approximately 5,000 machine language instruction executions and significant time for physical device actions. Both disk and tape data sets also require relatively large nondata gaps, written automatically by MVS, between data blocks to separate them. Blocking records so that a minimum number of blocks are needed to store a given number of records economizes the use of media, since the number of inter-block gaps is minimized. In exchange for the execution and media use economies a tradeoff is made: larger memory buffers are needed to store the larger blocks handled, to permit MVS to block or "deblock" the logical records for the program.

The virtues of blocking having been recited, why is the issue of disk block size potentially troublesome? Because certain factors are peculiar to disks:

- Track capacity dictates the maximum efficient block size; writing a block larger than track capacity by using the DCB record format code T to allow track overflow is inefficient.

- Track capacity varies from one model of disk to another, and an installation will typically have a mixture of disk models configured in a system at any one time.

- Because of disk overhead, track utilization efficiency versus block size does not vary in a strictly linear manner. An efficient block size on one model of disk is not necessarily efficient on another; in fact, it might be quite inefficient.

- The needs of teleprocessing systems that access disk data sets make it desirable to minimize block size to avoid response time degradation, whereas batch usage of the same data sets improves with larger block sizes.

- Each member of a partitioned data set, such as a member of a TSO library, starts in a new block; small members in large blocks waste space but small blocks are less efficient for disk utilization.

These factors combine to create a complex situation. Figure 8.2 illustrates track utilization efficiency on a vertical scale of 0 to 100% versus block size on the horizontal scale for the IBM 3380 disk unit. It becomes apparent that storage efficiency can vary dramatically—from about 98% down to 65% or less—simply by making a block one byte too large. For example, three blocks of 15,476 bytes can be housed on a 3380 track. Because of disk overhead, once a block is any larger than this, no more than two blocks can be housed on a track. Using a block size of 15,477 on a 3380 makes it possible for the track to accommodate only two blocks. Above a block size of 23,476 bytes only one block will be accommodated on a 3380 track. Performance characteristics of the IBM 3330 and 3350 disk units, when graphed, produce charts similar to Figure 8.2, except that the sawtooth is compressed to the left due to lesser track capacities.

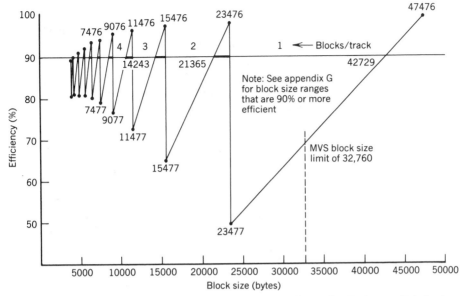

FIGURE 8.2.   Disk track utilization efficiency versus block size for IBM 3380 disk devices

The areas above the horizontal line on the utilization graph represent those in which 90% or better disk utilization is experienced. Appendix G summarizes the block size ranges that provide 90% or better track utilization for the 3330, 3350, and 3380 disks.[9]

Compromise Block Size for 3330s, 3350s, and 3380s

Each of the three types of disk commonly found in IBM mainframe installations have different characteristics concerning block size efficiency. One block size, 6,233, is adequately efficient on all three devices. If an installation has a mixture of these devices under one symbolic device group name, it is desirable to shoot for 6,233 as a good compromise figure on which to base block size determinations.

To use 6,233 as the target block size first divide it by the record size to be housed in the data set. For a record size of 133, the length of an ordinary printline, this division yields a value of 46.865. Drop the fractional part to get an integer value, the number of whole records that will fit in 6,233: in this case it is 46. Multiply the record size by this integer value to find the block size nearest to but not exceeding the target value of 6,233. Here, 133 × 46 = 6,118. For printline records a block size of 6,118 will provide adequate efficiency on all three disk devices: 93.9% efficiency on an IBM 3330, 96.25% efficiency on an IBM 3350, and 90.2% efficiency on an IBM 3380.[10]

Use of the compromise figure of 6,233 as a starting point for block size determination is generally adequate but on occasion it may be desirable to tailor a block size to a specific device. Perhaps it is known that an IBM 3350 or 3380 will always house the data set; perhaps the installation has only 3380s in its complement of disk devices used for production purposes. Performing the block size computation in such a case is identical to that already described except that the starting point is chosen as the track capacity of 19,069 on the IBM 3350 or as 23,476 or 15,476 on the IBM 3380.

Track capacity on the IBM 3380 is 47,476 bytes, which exceeds the block size that can be handled by the MVS and MVS/XA access methods. This limitation is 32,760 bytes; to write a record longer than this it is necessary to perform I/O directly, outside of MVS I/O support. This is something that is not feasible in the normal applications environment. Therefore in using the IBM 3380 we assume for block size determination purposes that 23,476 is the track capacity and get two blocks of the size developed on the track; alternatively, we use 15,476 as the track capacity and get three blocks on the track. Whether you start with 23,476 or 15,476 as the largest block size for a 3380 disk depends on whether you consider the lower buffer size requirements of the smaller block size or the greater disk storage efficiency of the greater block size more important.

Repeating the 133-byte printline record computations for 3350s and 3380s, we obtain these block sizes and efficiencies:

Device	Record Size	Block Size	Efficiency
3350	133	19,019	99.7%
3380	133	15,428	97.5%
3380	133	23,408	98.6%

An old "rule of thumb" for blocking says "multiply the record length by 10" to get the block size. Let's do it for the IBM 3350 and 3380 and throw in a blocking factor of 100 as well:

Device	Record Size	Block Size	Efficiency
3350	133	1,330	83.7%
3350	133	13,300	69.7%
3380	133	1,330	72.8%
3380	133	13,300	84.0%

The old rule of thumb serves us poorly in connection with contemporary disk storage; to make effective use of disk you must do the arithmetic indicated or use one of the computational CLISTs discussed in the following sections.

Automating the Block Size Calculations

Although the tables of Appendix G can be used to formulate an efficient block size for a sequential file or PDS based on the length of record to be housed, it is more expeditious to automate the logic to perform this chore. A natural way to do this is to use a TSO CLIST or a microcomputer. We'll discuss CLISTs here; both the CLISTs and microcomputer routines are available to you on diskette; see Appendix D.

The CLISTs of Appendix D entitled DISKINFO and DISKJCL generate DCB and SPACE parameters. These CLISTs merely ask you to indicate the type of disk on which you wish to base your block size: for the IBM 3330, 3350, or 3380 or the compromise block size target figure of 6,233. They ask for the record size and compute and tell you the most suitable block size. They then ask for the number of records you will house in the data set; from this they compute the number of blocks you need, assuming a secondary allocation level of 20% of the primary allocation, and they compose workable DCB and SPACE parameters which are displayed on the screen. Then, just for the fun of it, DISKINFO computes the efficiency of storage for the block size developed on the device indicated. If you specify that the compromise maximum block size of 6,233 is to be used in developing the block size, DISKINFO will give you the efficiency of the computed block size for all three devices: the 3330, 3350, and 3380.

You will find the CLISTs of Appendix D helpful in your work with fixed record length disk data sets. If you have not worked with CLISTs, you may also find the code for them interesting and potentially useful as a pattern for other computational CLISTs. You can enter these CLISTs into a library allocated as described in Appendix D. They are also available on diskette as described in Appendix D, for upload to a mainframe via a suitably equipped PC. These CLISTs, similar IBM PC and compatible ready-to-run utilities and other major items from this book have been placed on several microcomputer-based bulletin boards in the United States and Europe under the generic name PRACJCL for convenient downloading. These are original to this book.

Block Sizes for TSO Libraries

TSO libraries are partitioned data sets. They are no different than other types of data sets in disk space allocation and storage; PDSs predate TSO in origin and TSO made use of this already-present data set organization. When TSO library data sets are allocated or fully reorganized, the block size specified should be carefully considered. An appropriate block size for a PDS is not only dependent on the nature of the disk housing it but also on the nature of the members to be stored in it.

A partitioned data set is arranged in such a way that its members are located by relative track and block number within that track. Every member of the PDS starts in a new block. Extra space in the last block holding a member is unusable. If a PDS carries a large block size but houses small members, much space can be wasted in each block. On the other hand, using an especially small block size for source code PDSs is wasteful because it suffers from the penalty of disk overhead associated with housing many small blocks on each track.

For several years a TSO library PDS blocksize of 3,120 has been common for both source code and JCL data sets. This figure produced a high track utilization efficiency of 95.8% for fixed length 80-byte records on the IBM 3330 disk, much used in the 1970s when TSO was released. It was also appropriate for teleprocessing access because it was not overly large. As time moved on so did disk technology and the IBM 3350 replaced the 3330. On the IBM 3350 a block size of 3,120 for 80-byte records produces only 81.8% efficiency; a better choice of block size is 3,600, which provides track utilization of 94.4% and is still within the size typical of good teleprocessing system practice.

For the contemporary environment in which IBM 3380s predominate the optimal TSO block size changes once again:

Device	Record Size	Block Size	Efficiency
3380	80	3,120	85.4%
3380	80	3,440	86.9%
3380	80	3,520	81.6%
3380	80	3,600	83.4%
3380	**80**	**3,840**	**89.0%**
3380	80	4,000	86.3%
3380	80	4,240	89.3%
3380	80	4,560	86.4%
3380	80	4,800	91.0%
3380	80	5,440	91.7%
3380	80	6,000	90.6%
3380	80	6,160	90.8%
3380	80	6,320	93.2%
3380	80	7,440	94.0%
3380	80	9,040	95.2%
3380	80	9,440	79.5%

Specifying a block size of 3,840 for TSO data sets on the IBM 3380 gains an advantage while not inclining too much toward overly large blocks for online access.

Block Sizes for Non-TSO Libraries

Some PDSs by their nature hold only small, one or two line members. A PDS that exists in an installation to hold the sort control cards for all production jobs, which cannot be carried as DD * in-stream data in cataloged procedures, is of this nature. Let's say this data set held 1,600 sort control statement members, not really a huge number for a mainframe installation that has been in operation for many years. Because each PDS member starts in a new block, 1,600 blocks will be needed for the data set. Blocking this on an IBM 3380 at a block size normally suitable for TSO use, such as 3,840 bytes, will result in much unused space in each block, because each block holds 48 card image records but each member has only one or a few records. At this block size only 11 blocks fit onto a 3380 track; the data set will require 1,600/11 tracks; 146 tracks.

Blocks of 240 bytes hold only three card image records. Blocking a sort control card partitioned data set at 240 bytes per block, which is normally inefficient, means that 1600 of the smaller blocks will be required. The small block size won't hurt access to this data set; nearly all of its members are smaller than three records. As Appendix G indicates, 65 blocks of 240 bytes fit onto a 3380 track. The data set will now require 1,600/65 tracks or only about 28 tracks. Saving 118 tracks is certainly not an earthshaking accomplishment, but why waste them if you can help it by suiting the block size to the purpose? Depending on how your installation buys or leases disk resources, this amounts to $500 to $1,000 in 3380 disk space.

We need not meditate and weigh assumptions concerning an optimum block size applicable to PDSs; it is possible to pinpoint an optimal value empirically. Take a copy of a PDS like a sort control card library and run on it the batch reorganization JCL illustrated in Appendix B; specify a block size that seems appropriate by using its QBLK symbolic parameter. Once the job finishes look at the data set information presented by TSO function 3.2, see the amount of space that the data set consumes, and compare it with the space requirement at the data set's current block size. Repeat the process a few times with different QBLK values and a suitable block size will become evident. Then run the batch PDS reorganization on the actual PDS using the block size value found to be the most efficient.

REVIEW QUESTIONS AND (*)EXERCISES

1. Explain the similarities and significant differences between floppy and mainframe hard disks.

2. What is a disk track and what is a disk cylinder?

3. Explain what an "extent" is in terms of the disk storage architecture employed by MVS and some limitations that exist in connection with it.

4. Can the primary and secondary space allocations for a data set be the same value?

5. In what types of disk space allocation is the use of the CONTIG subparameter beneficial?

6. A data set was created at a DD statement in which the SPACE parameter did not specify secondary allocation. After the successful creation of the data set, examination of the data set information provided by TSO screen 3.2 indicates that a primary allocation and three secondary allocations exist for it and that it spreads to four extents. Has there been a malfunction of MVS or is this an acceptable condition? Explain the basis for your conclusion.

7. Your installation just replaced its 3350 disk units with 3380s and has requested all programmers to modify the block size of their TSO libraries to a value efficient on the new units. Your data sets have been blocked at 3,120 bytes per block. What has been your disk utilization efficiency on the 3350s, what value are you going to use now on the 3380s, and why? (Note that you can easily accomplish this task once you make your decision by using the PDS reorganization JCL of Appendix B.)

*8. A data set to be written will contain 15,000 fixed length records each of 92 byte length. Using Appendix G, *compute an efficient block size* for this data to be housed on an IBM 3380 disk unit and *code the SPACE parameter* for it, allowing secondary allocations 20% the size of the primary allocation. Assume that the installation standard is to make disk storage usage as efficient as possible.

*9. *Code a one-step IEFBR14 job* to allocate a new cataloged partitioned data set named BT80000.DEVCOPY.COBOL to house an estimated 600 blocks of data in which the block length is 3,840 bytes. Anticipated growth suggests that a secondary allocation equal to 25% of the primary is suitable. The PDS will serve as a shared developmental copy library used by several programmers and will house about 300 members edited by TSO/ISPF. The installation provides 3350 and 3380 disks for programmer use mixed under the symbolic device group list TEST.

*10.   The //SYSPRINT printline image output from a series of large
compiles, stored in one data set on tape, is to be written to disk.
A total of 110,000 lines of print image exists. The installation has
a mixture of 3330, 3350, and 3380 disk devices under locally created symbolic device group name PRDISK to be used to house
this kind of information. Compose suitable DCB and SPACE parameters to load this sequential data set; allow no secondary allocation and release any unused space. Compiler //SYSPRINT
records are 121 bytes in length.

NOTES

1.   MVS and MVS/XA error message manuals cite disk error conditions in low level
terms; error messages refer to the various formats of DSCB records contained in
the disk volume table of contents or VTOC. The VTOC itself is allocated as a disk
data set by an installation when new disk media is initialized. The amount of space
the VTOC consumes is up to the installation and is established at initialization;
even the location of the VTOC on the media is under local control. The VTOC is
a keyed, unblocked data set that contains records with a separate key 44 bytes long
and a data portion of 96 bytes. The VTOC contains "data set control block" or
DSCB records that exist in seven different formats. Although they have a special
significance to the disk, they are really just records like any others.

   Format 0 DSCB records are place holders created when the VTOC is established
as a disk is initialized; they contain binary zeros, in other words, "low-values."
To create a new data set on the disk MVS looks for format 0 DSCB records in the
VTOC and overwrites them with format 1, 2, 3, and 6 DSCB records as appropriate.
The different formats of DSCB records used for a data set may not be sequential
or even close to one another in the VTOC; they are tied together by internal pointers.
The formats of DSCB records carry varied information:

Format 0.   An unused DSCB record suitable for overwriting by MVS.

Format 1.   A data set identifier, one for each data set on the disk; can contain
information for as many as three of the 16 separate extents that the data set can
be allocated on the disk.

Format 2.   Index information used only by ISAM data sets, now obsolete.

Format 3.   Extension information, describes up to 13 data set extents in excess of
the three identified in the format 1 DSCB. The three extents described in the format
1 DSCB plus the 13 described here form the basis of the limit of 16 extents for a
data set on a given volume.

Format 4.   VTOC DSCB, contains information about the VTOC itself, not other
data sets. This is always the first record in the VTOC and provides some of the
disk volume information that appears at the top of the TSO function 3.7 screen.

Format 5.   Free space DSCB, these are housekeeping records each of which describes up to 26 extents free for use by new data sets or for secondary allocation
to existing data sets that are permitted to receive secondaries. As data sets are
allocated and later deleted the format 5 DSCBs in the VTOC are updated by MVS.
Additional format 5 DSCBs are created as needed by overwriting format 0 records,

to document fragments of space that become free for allocation. These format 5 records are chained to one another by pointers; the format 4 DSCB points to the first format 5 DSCB and each format 5 then points to another if another exists.

Format 6. Shared cylinder allocation information, contains data on cylinders that are split between two or more data sets. The format 4 DSCB points to the first format 6 DSCB and from there on each format 6 DSCB points to the next format 6 record.

For disks that are large and heavily loaded with hundreds or thousands of frequently accessed data sets such as TSO libraries the VTOC can become a bottleneck. It must be accessed every time a data set is created, deleted, opened, or updated, and chains such as those for the format 5 DSCB traversed. The VTOC must be large enough to house DSCB records for each data set on the disk, and on IBM 3380s it may be as large as 10 to 20 cylinders in size. The unblocked nature and sequential searching of the VTOC presents an impediment to efficient disk utilization. An IBM enhancement, DF/DS, provides an option to use the VTOC in an indexed manner to increase efficiency. The IBM IEHLIST utility can produce detailed listings of VTOC contents; the JCL that executes IEHLIST is somewhat unusual and is illustrated in item 20 of Chapter 17.

2. The early IBM 3380 disks, the IBM 3380 single density models AA4 and BA4, provided 885 tracks per surface, or 885 cylinders when considering the disk pack as a whole. This provided 630 megabytes of storage per disk arm assembly. The double density 3380 models AE4 and BE4 squeeze twice the number of data tracks on the surface, thus allowing each disk arm to access 1,260 megabytes of storage. Because four disk arms are housed in a 3380 device, each accessing its own area on one of two spindles, the capacity of the device is 5,400,000,000 bytes, or 5.4 gigabytes.

3. DOS/VSE and the VM operating system make use of 3340, 3370, and 9370-series disk devices on which track space is divided into 512-byte sectors. This form of disk storage architecture is called "fixed block architecture," or "FBA," not to be confused with the JCL record format code FBA often used with stored printline images that contain a carriage control byte.

4. The limitation of 16 extents per data set on a given unit of disk media no longer applies to VSAM data sets when the Integrated Catalog Facility, or ICF, is used. ICF has a newer type of system catalog and small ancillary portions of housekeeping information called the "VVDS" for "VSAM volume data set" stored on each disk itself. With this means of keeping track of data set extents VSAM data sets can grow to 123 extents. Performance considerations dictate, however, that such extreme fragmentation of data sets be avoided by appropriately large specification of the VSAM primary allocation.

5. The block length figure in the first positional subparameter of a SPACE parameter is actually the *average* block length; for fixed length records this is the same as each record length. For variable length records the fact that this figure is the average block length underscores its purpose not as establishing the characteristics of the records but as the basis for MVS to compute the number of disk tracks needed. There is no internal relationship between a numeric value coded in the SPACE parameter instead of TRK or CYL and the actual block length. The number that represents block size in the SPACE parameter can be erroneously specified as a value inconsistent with the block size, resulting in the allocation of too few or too many tracks for the data set.

6. The author wishes to thank William Fairchild, Vice President, Research and Development, Software Corporation of America (now a division of UCCEL Corpo-

ration), for many insights on internal disk operation, presented in a paper entitled "DASD Management and Measurement in the TSO Environment."

7. Some IBM JCL manuals contain the emphasized note: "When you specify TRK or CYL for a partitioned data set, the space for the directory is specified twice: once as a part of the primary quantity and a second time separately as the directory quantity." What the statement means is that when space is specified in tracks or cylinders the specification includes *all* the space the data set will obtain. When SPACE is specified by data block for a PDS, the space for the number of directory blocks requested is added by MVS to the number of tracks computed for the data blocks. The number of directory blocks desired is really *coded* only once in the SPACE parameter, regardless of whether space is requested for the PDS in units of cylinders, tracks, or blocks.

8. TSO/ISPF function 3.5 allows the resetting or elimination of statistics on a PDS. If statistics are eliminated the PDS directory blocks of a TSO library can accommodate more than six members and the directory is automatically reorganized. TSO statistics are handy to have and it is not a good tradeoff to eliminate them to economize on TSO library PDS directory block space.

9. The disk track utilization plot shown in Figure 8.2 deals with data sets in which the records have no separate physical key. Keyed files have a greater overhead and different block size efficiency characteristics. In the contemporary environment applications programmers will have little or no contact with physically keyed data sets. IBM's ISAM, Indexed Sequential Access Method, made use of physically keyed data sets, but ISAM was replaced in the 1970s by VSAM, an indexed data set access method that resolves many of the inefficiencies of ISAM and conforms more fully to ANSI standards for indexed file support.

   VSAM handles record keys, indexing, and record access in a manner unto itself, without regard to physical disk keys. The DCB and SPACE parameters are not used in connection with VSAM; instead, IDCAMS, the Access Method Services utility, provides a completely separate language to define, establish, and manipulate VSAM files. Disk space efficiency for VSAM is related to the nonkeyed graph and tables illustrated. VSAM imposes rigid requirements for 512, 1,024, 2,048, 4,096, 8,192, and increments of 8,192 byte "control interval" sizes, roughly analogous to traditional blocks as far as disk storage is concerned. See *Practical VSAM For Today's Programmers* by James Janossy and Richard Guzik, Wiley, 1987, for information on the selection of VSAM control interval size.

10. It is not necessary for any JCL purpose to calculate disk storage efficiency. If you wish to derive it, you need to determine first how many blocks of the size you have developed will fit on a track on the device or devices in question. Obtain this figure by looking at a standard chart for the disk unit that shows block size ranges and the number of records within each range that fit on a track. Then multiply the block size by this figure to get the number of bytes you will actually store on a track. Divide the number of bytes you will store on the track by the track capacity and the efficiency percentage will result. *Note that you can't simply divide the track capacity by the block size and hope to find out how many blocks will fit on the track.*

   The DISKINFO computational CLIST shown in Appendix D automatically computes the most efficient block size for you when told the length of record you wish to store. It also computes and indicates the disk storage efficiency of this block size.

9

VOL: Disk and Tape Volume Specification

In the mainframe environment every storage volume—unit of storage media—carries a unique identifier. The only exception to this requirement lies with "unlabeled" tapes, which lack the small internal data set that prefaces the actual application data and carries the identifier.[1]

The identifier for all forms of storage media is called the volume serial number. "Number" is a misnomer; the six-byte identifier can be and often is alphanumeric in nature. Thus 012587 is a volume serial number; E03762, PUBL93, STOR19, ACSCAC, VSLIB1, and FSDC03 are other legitimate identifiers. Sometimes with tapes the volume serial number is indicated sloppily as a number shorter than six positions; for example, 12587 instead of 012587. This is poor form but the identifier is still six positions. The identifiers used by an installation for its volume serial numbers typically follow some locally adopted naming convention. They are applied to media using the IEHINITT, IEHDASDI, or IEHDASDR utilities by the installation itself. This is a one-time task for each unit of media, performed by operations personnel, not applications programmers. Once assigned the volume serial number on a given item of media does not change, regardless of the data sets written to the tape or disk.

VOL PARAMETER PURPOSE

The VOL parameter in the DD statement exists primarily to provide the means of specifying the volume serial number of the media on which a given data set is to be written or on which it now resides. The extent to which it is necessary to code the VOL parameter in DD statements varies considerably, depending on the extent to which an installation supports disk and tape media allocated to specific users and the extent to which the system catalog facility is used.

When a data set is written to disk in a contemporary MVS installation, the volume serial number is usually specified only if there is a real need to house the data on a specific disk volume. For many data sets there is no requirement to do so and VOL is therefore not coded. When the volume serial number is not specified, the request for storage space is called, quite plainly, "nonspecific." In this case MVS itself determines and uses an accessible disk volume with sufficient space for the initial space allocation. Such a data set would commonly be cataloged with specification of the DISP parameter as (NEW,CATLG,DELETE). The identity of the disk on which the data set was placed would be of little or no concern.

When a data set is written to tape, VOL can be specified to use a specific tape volume. It is also uncommon in this case, however, to specify the volume serial number. If VOL is omitted, MVS will find an available "scratch" tape already on a tape drive or tell the console operator to mount a scratch tape. When the operator mounts a tape in response to a scratch tape mounting request, MVS reads the data set label on the tape to determine whether the expiration date carried in the first data set label has been reached. If the date has not been reached, the operator is informed that the media carries unexpired data. Only if the operator indicates that MVS should overwrite the data will an unexpired tape data set be overwritten. In most cases this is not desirable and instead the operator removes the tape, which was not a scratch tape after all, and mounts another scratch tape candidate. Scratch tapes are usually stockpiled near the tape drives ready for reuse.[2]

VOL PARAMETER SHORT FORM AND LONG FORM CODING

VOL must be coded on a DD statement to identify the media housing an existing data set to be accessed if it has not been cataloged. The most common coding of the VOL parameter to meet this requirement is the short form VOL parameter. It is coded

```
//   VOL=SER=xxxxxx,
```

where xxxxxx is the volume serial number. If the data set spans more than one volume, it can be specified as

```
//   VOL=SER=(xxxxxx,yyyyyy,zzzzzz)
```

and up to 255 volumes can be cited. When a data set is cataloged, all volume serial numbers of media that contain it are recorded by the system; therefore a VOL specification like this is rarely needed. Four lesser used positional subparameters of the VOL parameter also exist. If they are used in connection with VOL, these positional subparameters must be listed before SER. The general format of the VOL parameter is

```
VOL=( private, retain, vol-seq-no, scratch-vols, SER=xxxxxx )
```

and a specific, full length example is

```
VOL=(PRIVATE,RETAIN,2,4,SER=(038272,013267,020133))
```

This example, however, is for syntax illustration purposes rather than real life because the circumstances for using some of the subparameters are mutually exclusive. When a given subparameter is not coded, its empty "slot" is still delimited by the comma that follows it:

```
VOL=(PRIVATE,RETAIN,2,,SER=(038272,013267,020133))
```

The short form for this coding shortcuts the specification of the positional subparameters:

```
VOL=SER=(038272,013267,020133)
```

The four positional subparameters provide the ability to:

- Preclude use of a storage volume by other data sets during mounted condition, making a volume "private,"

- Retain the media in a mounted condition after the job step,
- Begin access to a multivolume data set at a volume other than the first,
- Specify how many scratch media volumes an output data set requires.

Private Volumes

```
VOL=( private, retain, vol-seq-no, scratch-vols, SER=xxxxxx )
//  VOL=(PRIVATE,RETAIN,2,4,SER=(038272,013267,020133)),
```

Tapes, by their nature, cannot be accessed by more than one job at a time for either reading or writing. Tapes are therefore always regarded as private volumes even without the coding of PRIVATE. No nonspecific request for media arising from some other job being executed concurrently can possibly be satisfied by MVS selecting the tape to receive data. This is what "private" means to MVS; access to media that is private is limited to the job that caused it to be mounted.

Disk volumes can and typically are used to store many different data sets, and many data sets may be open concurrently on a given disk for different jobs and programs. PRIVATE can be coded for a disk volume and the nonspecific requests for disk space made by other jobs will not be directed to it. Permanently mounted disk packs, either physically unremovable or designated as "always mounted" by an installation, cannot be treated as private media. If PRIVATE is coded in JCL for these volumes, it is ignored.

If PRIVATE is not coded but the subsequent subparameters are, the comma normally coded after it is still used to delimit the empty subparameter slot.

Keeping Media Mounted with RETAIN

```
VOL=( private, retain, vol-seq-no, scratch-vols, SER=xxxxxx )
//  VOL=(PRIVATE,RETAIN,2,4,SER=(038272,013267,020133)),
```

In many job streams a tape created by one step is read by a following step and then kept for a period of time. But at the end of a job step MVS normally rewinds a tape and issues a message for the operator to remove it from the tape drive. RETAIN provides the means of overriding this inclination of MVS and of leaving a tape, or demountable disk treated as PRIVATE, in a mounted condition.

RETAIN can be coded as a second positional parameter on the VOL parameter. Although it is redundant to code PRIVATE in the case of tape data sets, it is often coded when RETAIN is specified simply as a matter of form:

```
//UNIT=(TAPE,,DEFER),
//VOL=(PRIVATE,RETAIN)
```

Coded on the DD statement for a tape being read or written, the tape will not be rewound and ordered to be demounted from the tape drive; MVS will rewind it and position it to its "load point," meaning that it is ready for access by another job. The same effect is obtained when a data set on tape is PASSed to subsequent steps.

A retained tape may still be dismounted if during an intervening step the tape drive is not allocated to the same job stream. Be that as it may, RETAIN allows production JCL to conserve operator actions and to expedite the processing of jobs. RETAIN is effective even when steps access different data sets on the same tape volume. For a data set spanning multiple volumes, RETAIN retains in a mounted condition only the last volume processed; RETAIN does not avoid the operator intervention that is needed to remount the first tape reel in a subsequent step reading a multivolume data set.

Volume Sequence Number

```
VOL=( private, retain, vol-seq-no, scratch-vols, SER=xxxxxx )
//  VOL=(PRIVATE,RETAIN,2,4,SER=(038272,013267,020133)),
```

The third positional parameter is not often useful. This number can legitimately be 1 to the number of volumes occupied by the data set, a maximum of 255. If coded, it denotes the volume of an existing multivolume data set with which we wish to begin processing. For example, if a data set were named AK00.C99.PAYMAST, cataloged, occupied five tape volumes, and we knew that for the read access we were going to conduct in a program data from only the fourth and fifth reels would be needed, we could code the DD statement

```
//BT9947E1    DD   DSN=AK00.C99.PAYMAST,
//  DISP=(OLD,KEEP),                        clear form
//  UNIT=(TAPE,,DEFER),
//  VOL=(PRIVATE,,4)
```

Much less plainly, taking the default to PRIVATE that always prevails for a tape data set and coincidentally foregoing the deferral of tape mounting until the data set is opened, we could code:

```
//BT9947E1    DD   DSN=AK00.C99.PAYMAST,
//  DISP=(OLD,KEEP),                        harder to read
//  VOL=(,,4)
```

This circumstance isn't likely to occur often. The main reason it is necessary to know that this subparameter exists is that when the next subparameter is coded, which occurs at least slightly more frequently, the omission of coding the volume sequence number must be indicated by coding the comma that normally follows it.

Using the DISP = (MOD,CATLG) disposition for a data set being extended, the volume sequence number *overrides* MOD. MOD normally dictates that processing will begin at the end of the data set on the last volume. If the volume sequence number is coded, processing begins with the volume indicated by the volume sequence number. There is little reason to code a volume sequence number if MOD is being used to extend a data set. Extension of tape data sets is not in itself a common practice because it forces operator approval to perform write operations on an unexpired data set. This requires operator confirmation to an MVS-generated computer console prompt, which indicates that the unexpired tape should be "used"—the operator must reply "U." Operators are usually trained to respond negatively to this prompt because it almost always stems from an erroneous attempt to use as scratch a tape containing live data.

Scratch Volume Count

```
VOL=( private, retain, vol-seq-no, scratch-vols, SER=xxxxxx )
 //   VOL=(PRIVATE,RETAIN,2,4,SER=(038272,013267,020133)),
```

The fourth positional subparameter of the VOL parameter specifies the number of scratch volumes that may be required to house an output data set. It is relevant only for data sets being created or extended. If this value is not coded, it will, on a plain vanilla system supplied by IBM, default to a maximum of five volumes. It is possible for an installation to modify this default.

For large data sets written to tape it is impossible to predict exactly how many volumes the data set will require. Although new reel tapes on 10½-inch reels are 2400 feet long, they often "become" shorter in use. Many data sets are small enough to be contained in the first few feet of a tape and some installations recycle tapes when they wear by removing a hundred feet or more from a reel, applying a new adhesive reflective marker, and reinitializing the tape with the same or a new volume serial number.

Because the actual number of reels needed to house a large tape data set may vary, the scratch volume count is treated by MVS as an estimate and is handled in steps:

• If the volume count is omitted or coded as a value of 1 to 5, the system provides up to five volumes,

- If the volume count is coded as a value of 6 to 20, the system provides up to 20 volumes,
- If the volume count is coded as a value greater than 20, the system provides a multiple of 15 volumes plus 5, up to a maximum of 255 volumes; for example, if the volume count is coded as 24, the system allows a maximum of $2 \times 15 + 5 = 35$ volumes.

Personnel often first encounter the volume count parameter when they are assigned to handle a large backup or historical archival job. The system default allowance of five scratch volumes is quite generous and is rarely exceeded except by such runs.

VOL and UNIT Parameter Interplay

If the number of scratch volumes is indicated for a data set to be housed on disk, the VOL parameter does not specify PRIVATE, and no specific volume serial numbers are coded, MVS ignores the volume count. Instead, it allocates the number of volumes in the device count subparameter of UNIT. To have a new sequential data set extend to more than one disk volume, code UNIT=(SYSDA,n) for it, where "n" is the number of disk volumes over which the data set can extend. Up to 16 separate "extents" can exist for the data set on each volume as additional secondary allocations but access to them can be inefficient. Partitioned data sets cannot extend to more than one volume. Although TSO can access sequential disk data sets, it cannot access a sequential data set that extends to more than one volume.

The VOL parameter in combination with the UNIT parameter can be used to govern serial mounting of multiple media volumes on the same drive, or parallel mounting of all volumes on several drives at the same time. For example, if we coded

```
//   UNIT=(TAPE,,DEFER),
//   VOL=SER=(038272,013267,020133),
```

one tape drive would be allocated for the data set. The three volumes of the data set would be mounted one after another on this single drive as the data set spanning them was read. The same holds true if the data set were cataloged; the VOL parameter is not needed and is not coded. This is by far the most desirable situation because tapes can be processed only sequentially. If we did code this, however:

```
//   UNIT=(TAPE,3),
//   VOL=SER=(038272,013267,020133),
```

MVS would attempt to allocate three separate tape drives to the job and would issue messages to the operator to mount all three volumes at once, in parallel. This is somewhat inconsistent with the DEFER subparameter because the explicit intention of coding for parallel mounting is to have the stated number of volumes mounted and awaiting job use. For tapes, this would be an extreme luxury and nearly always unnecessary; it would also tend to impede the initiation of the job because finding several tape drives free at the same time would usually be difficult.

If we desired parallel mounting of all the volumes in the example above for access after data set creation, and the data set was cataloged, we would not have to concern ourselves with specifying their volume serial numbers or a precise unit count. The system catalog records the volume serial numbers of all volumes used to store a data set, and their sequence. We could achieve parallel mounting by omitting the VOL parameter and coding

```
//    UNIT=(TAPE,P),
```

or

```
//    UNIT=(,P),
```

The latter example would eliminate the TAPE symbolic device device group name because the catalog retains the device type. But once again, parallel mounting of existing multivolume tape data sets is not normally done.

For a data set being written the combination of P in the unit count subparameter of the UNIT specification and a number in the volume count subparameter of the VOL specification, such as

```
//    UNIT=(TAPE,P),
//    VOL=(,,,2),
```

causes multiple devices to be assigned to the step. The number of devices is the higher of the volume count or the number of volume serial numbers coded in the VOL parameter, if any. If an installation has a particularly large volume of online VSAM data set backups to perform in a limited off-hours "window," the process can be somewhat accelerated, at the expense of other batch jobs, by having tape drives tied up in this manner. A much better approach is to increase the number of buffers allocated to the backup steps, at the expense of memory, by using the appropriate AMP subparameters BUFND and BUFNI as illustrated in item 9 of Chapter 17.[3]

VOL = SER and Catalog Interplay

Specification of the VOL SER subparameter when it is not necessary can produce undesirable results as existing data sets are accessed. The problem results from the simple fact that *when volume serial number and unit are specified MVS does not refer to the catalog*. Its philosophy is that because the JCL has taken it upon itself to specify the volume serial number, the JCL has become entirely responsible for specifying any volumes of the data set that exist or are to be accessed. This has two major impacts:

- Access to one or a few volumes of an existing cataloged multivolume data set is possible by specifying only the volume serial numbers of the volumes desired for access. Specification of VOL = SER, however, means that MVS will not "know" from the catalog about any other volumes that house parts of the data set. You can be surprised if you think you are jumping into the middle of a large cataloged data set by specifying a particular volume in the middle of it, because that is the only volume that will be accessed; volumes following it will not be accessed unless you code their volume serial numbers also, even though the entire data set is cataloged.

- Specification of VOL = SER for a VSAM data set, sometimes done in a DD statement to which IDCAMS control cards refer, prevents MVS from "knowing" that the data set is of VSAM organization. Because that information is stored in the system catalog and the presence of VOL in the DD statement causes MVS to omit reference to the catalog, it is necessary to tell MVS explicitly that the data set is VSAM. This is done by coding the AMP parameter in the form

```
//   AMP='AMORG',
```

on the DD statement. As discussed in Chapter 11, "AMORG" stands for "Access Method ORGanization."

An additional admonition is warranted concerning the extension of a data set to additional volumes using the disposition of MOD. If a data set has already been created and is subsequently being extended, the disposition of (MOD,CATLG) should be specified whether or not specific volume serial numbers of media to receive the additional data are coded. In this case CATLG causes the system catalog to be updated with volume serial numbers of the additional volumes. If (MOD,KEEP) is coded in such a case, the catalog will not be updated and it will know only about the volumes on which the data set originally existed.

Multiline VOL Parameter Coding

There is usually little need for multiline coding for any JCL parameter, but in the case of an uncataloged multivolume data set it may occur. If a large number of volumes is involved, it is possible for the list of volumes to span more than one line. This coding

```
//   VOL=(PRIVATE,,5,,SER=(038272,013267,020133,015364,
//   001845,013444,032883,012713)),
```

or

```
//   VOL=SER=(038272,013267,020133,015364,001845,
//   013444,032883,012713),
```

is an example for syntax illustration. Data sets are nearly always cataloged and the catalog will retain the list of volumes on which a multivolume data set resides. The first example, in which the volume sequence number of 5 is stated to start processing in the fifth volume of the data set, would be coded

```
//   VOL=(PRIVATE,,5)
```

or

```
//   VOL=(,,5),
```

for a cataloged data set.

VOL REFERBACKS

It is possible to code the keyword "REF" instead of "SER" on the VOL parameter when the actual serial number of media is not known but has been established in an earlier DD statement within the step or job stream. This provides the means of accessing an uncataloged data set created earlier in the job, a feature used more in earlier days prior to widescale adoption of the convention to catalog all data sets. VOL referbacks are more commonly used now when the same scratch tape is to house several data sets, as in a backup operation. The PDS reorganization JCL in Appendix B uses volume referback for a different purpose. There an IEFBR14 "finder" step locates the volume on which a data set is housed so that we can specify it to house another data set without actually knowing its precise identity beforehand.

Example: Many Backup Data Sets onto the Same Scratch Tape

Let's say that an online system is supported by several VSAM data sets, all of which are to be copied to tape in a backup job. If the data sets are small enough to all fit on one or two tape volumes, it is advantageous to "stack" them onto tape, one after another. This conserves media and helps to secure synchronization of data set backups.

The first step in this job stream carries no VOL parameter, meaning that its request for a tape to carry the first data set is nonspecific. MVS will issue a message to the operator to mount a scratch tape on a drive to receive this data set. The next step of the job stream has to specify that the same volume mounted in the first step be used to receive the second data set, to be written as the second file on the tape. But how do we know what volume serial number was actually used in the earlier step? We do not know and actually do not need to know. It is enough to specify that it be the *same*, without knowing the precise serial number. Suppose the first step were called //STEPA and the second was //STEPB, and that the first step's output was written at DDname //OUTMASP with customary DCB and LABEL parameters:

```
//STEPA     EXEC  PGM=IDCAMS
//OUTMASP      DD  DSN=AK00.C27.ARCVMASP,
//  UNIT=(TAPE,,DEFER),
//  DISP=(NEW,CATLG,DELETE),
//  VOL=(PRIVATE,RETAIN),
//  DCB=(RECFM=FB,LRECL=212,BLKSIZE=32648),
//  LABEL=RETPD=180
```
   (additional DD and IDCAMS statements follow as in item 9 of
   Chapter 17)

For the second step to place the next backup on the same tape volume, making it the second file sequence number, the "REF" volume referback is used in conjunction with the data set sequence number on the LABEL parameter coded as 2:

```
//STEPB     EXEC  PGM=IDCAMS
//OUTINV9      DD  DSN=AK00.C27.ARCVINV9,
//  UNIT=TAPE,
//  DISP=(NEW,CATLG,DELETE),
//  DCB=(RECFM=FB,LRECL=628,BLKSIZE=32656),
//  VOL=(PRIVATE,RETAIN,REF=*.STEPA.OUTMASP),
//  LABEL=(2,SL,RETPD=180)
```
   (additional DD and IDCAMS statements follow)...

For this purpose all data sets on the same tape should have the same retention period and each is cataloged separately because it is the data set, not the tape, that is cataloged. In the first step the DEFER specification on UNIT may be useful, but it is not meaningful in subsequent steps where the same tape will be used because the tape is already mounted. The RETAIN specification in the first step is used to prevent the tape from being dismounted at the end of the step. It will remain on the drive for use by the second step to avoid unnecessary operator actions. The second step here is presumably not the last one because it, too, uses the RETAIN specification to keep the tape mounted for use by the steps that follow. The VOL and LABEL parameters of the third and last step to write a data set to the same tape could be coded

```
//    VOL=REF=*.STEPA.OUTMASP,
//    LABEL=(3,SL,RETPD=180)
```

completely omitting the first four VOL subparameters, which are positional. These steps contain more than one DD statement each; this partial example is focused only on the DD statement for the output data set.

Syntax Variations

The volume referback can be coded to refer back to another data set by name within the same step, to another DDname within the same step, or to a DDname in an earlier step:

```
REF=data-set-name           referback to data set in same step
REF=*.DDname                 referback to DDname in same step
REF=*.stepname.DDname        referback to DDname in prior step
```

The third format was used in the preceding example. It is also possible to refer back to a DDname in a cataloged procedure invoked by an earlier step in the job stream. For example, a job stream may, in one or more of its steps, invoke a cataloged procedure, which itself contains steps. A subsequent step may execute a program rather than a proc. This is somewhat unusual and is not in the mainstream of production JCL because it makes the "run deck" a mixture of procedure invocations and raw JCL rather that purely a set of procedure invocations. If this is done, however, the referback takes the form of

```
REF=*.stepname.procstepname.DDname
```

where "stepname" is the name of the step in *this* JCL that invoked the cataloged procedure, "procstepname" is the name of the step *within the cataloged procedure* in which the DDname occurs, and "DDname" is the DDname at which the backward referenced data set and volume are stated. The net effect of this coding is to make a DD statement coded in the JCL refer back to a DD statement contained within a proc invoked in an earlier step.

One final form of volume referback exists but is subject to special confusion. It is possible to refer back to a DDname that occurs at a step within a cataloged procedure invoked from the *current* step in JCL; the current step is invoking a proc and some step within that proc contains a DDname that is to be referenced

```
REF=*.procstepname.DDname
```

where "procstepname" is the name of the step within the cataloged procedure at which the DDname occurs and "DDname" is the DDname at which the referenced data set and volume are stated. The only purpose of this type of volume referback is to allow specification of the same volume for an override of another DD statement within the proc, or for a DD statement not contained within the proc but supplied by the execution JCL. This has some relevance to one-shot overrides of production cataloged procedures but it is not a common or often used capability, and has no relevance for the coding of cataloged procedures themselves.

REVIEW QUESTIONS AND (*)EXERCISES

1. What is the nature of the unique identifier assigned to every item of storage media under MVS?

2. How is a "non-specific" volume request coded on a DD statement?

3. What is the effect of coding the PRIVATE subparameter of VOL for a tape data set?

4. A large, cataloged, sequential data set spans five reels of tape. How many volume serial numbers are recorded for the data set in the system catalog?

5. What is the impact of achieving parallel mounting of a three-volume tape data set?

6. Cite two instances in which a volume referback may be useful.

7. Discuss alternative ways of enhancing the speed of backing up a large VSAM data set to tape.

*8. Give an example of efficient VOL parameter coding for a DD statement at which a tape data set will be read, where the tape will also be read by a step following.

*9.   A large accumulation of historical data from a major application system is to be purged from disk to tape. Calculations indicate that 10 to 12 3840 tape cartridges may be required to contain the data, recorded at 38.8K bpi. Code a VOL parameter for the DD statement at which the data will emerge, taking note of the data set size.

*10. An uncataloged data set named FS62.A35.CASHHIST exists on tape volumes 001637, 018443, 008720, 010573, 012002, and 000892. We wish to access records in this data set onward from a record that we know is contained on tape 008720. Code an appropriate VOL parameter for the DD statement at which this data set will be input.

NOTES

1. The internal label of a tape is nothing more than an 80-byte record at the immediate start of the tape after its reflective spot load point. Chapter 10 discusses tape labels in detail. Disk data sets also have labels. The analog to the tape's VOL1 label is contained in the disk's VTOC, its volume table of contents, and exists as different formats of DSCB or "data set control block" records, as discussed in note 1 of Chapter 8.

2. A third-party software adjunct to the MVS system catalog called a "tape management system" is often present in installations to serve as a storehouse of information about data sets. UCCEL-1, distributed by UCCEL Corporation, is a prominent product of this kind. This system intercepts MVS actions that deal with the creation of new data sets and captures the data set name, expiration date, and the volume serial number on which new data sets reside. The information is stored in a data set open to online inquiry from which reports are produced.

    Because a tape management system captures the expiration date of tape data sets, just as does the data set label, it can report the identity of scratch tapes. The catalog does not record data set expiration date. Although MVS will not wantonly allow overwriting an unexpired data set, it is unproductive for machine operators to have to mount a tape to determine whether it carries unexpired data. A tape management system makes this unnecessary and allows scratch tapes to be identified readily from a listing. Scratch tapes are commonly stockpiled near the tape drives of a mainframe according to tape management system reports.

    A tape management system has no inherent connection with the system catalog. Although it stores some of the same information, its entries are not governed by the disposition parameter's CATLG subparameter. The information "picked off" from MVS by such a product is always picked off. A tape management system readily provides management of the media housing uncataloged as well as cataloged data sets, including unlabeled tapes.

3. The number and length of data buffers for non-VSAM data sets is governed by the BUFNO and BUFL subparameters of the DCB parameter, as discussed in Chapter 7. The default without coding BUFNO is two, to achieve "double buffering," in which I/O can occur to one buffer while processing proceeds on the other, in alternation.

A larger value can be coded to increase the number of buffers at the expense of memory. For VSAM data sets the JCL AMP parameter must be used to increase the size or number of buffers. See Chapter 11, which deals with the AMP parameter, and *Practical VSAM For Today's Programmers*, James G. Janossy and Richard E. Guzik, John Wiley and Sons, Inc., 1987.

═══ 10 ═══

LABEL: Data Set Labels and Tape Data Sets

The LABEL parameter is almost totally irrelevant to disk data sets; it exists primarily for use with tape data sets. In this chapter we consider several aspects of tape background, the LABEL parameter and tape usage. We again enhance the sequential update job stream, presented initially in Figure 3.4 and upgraded in Figure 6.1, by adapting it to the use of tape for transaction input and sequential master file storage.

TAPE BACKGROUND

Reel-to-Reel Tapes

Tape is a familiar medium in most households in the form of cassette recording tape. Tape media used in the mainframe environment are similar but wider than audio tape, resembling the media found in video cassettes; this tape is 1/2 inch wide.

Until 1985 the most common packaging for computer tape was 10½ inch plastic reels; these open reels and smaller diameter reels are still widely used. The standard 10½-inch reel holds 2,400 feet of tape and is stored with a protective edge-locking band when not mounted on a tape drive. About 2,370 feet at most is usable; the leading 10 to 15 feet and a like amount at the trailing end do not carry information because that amount is needed for threading.

The IBM 3420 and compatible tape drives have been the staple of mainframe tape equipment since the early 1970s. These are large, heavy devices that resemble a household refrigerator in size and shape. Regardless of how JCL specifies the unit or device to be used for a tape data set, MVS ultimately issues console messages to the person who will do the mounting by designating what tape—what volume serial number—to mount on what drive. A drive at hardware address 54C, for example, is named by MVS and MVS/XA messages as 54C. A small sign that carries the device hardware address is normally placed on each tape drive.

Tape drives are manually loaded devices. The person who handles the tapes and mounts them on the drive is an operator, not a programmer; programmers do not handle tapes or disks or operate printers in a mainframe environment. When instructed to mount a tape on a drive, an operator must first locate the tape and place it physically on the assigned drive. Mounting a tape takes effort and time. As discussed in connection with the UNIT and VOL parameter, it is possible and desirable to minimize operator intervention by the use of the DEFER and RETAIN subparameters.

Tape Recording Density and Capacity

Reel-to-reel tapes are recorded with nine longitudinal tracks. All nine tracks, or on 3480 cartridge tape, all 18 tracks, are recorded in the forward direction; there is no "other side" on a computer tape as there is on audio cassette or eight-track auto stereo tapes. Eight of these tracks carry one bit of a byte each. The ninth track carries a parity bit that is identical in operation to the parity bit in the memory of the IBM-PC: it allows the detection of a recording or read back error. Error detection and correction capabilities exist in the drive itself and are out of sight of the programmer.

In the distant past "density" and "tape recording technique" were significant issues in JCL composition because several different parity schemes and tape hardware capabilities existed. *Tape recording tech-*

nique and tape density issues are now irrelevant; nine-track tape has a standard parity and standard recording densities and so does 3480 cartridge tape. Tape recording density is measured in "bpi" which has the distinction of being an abbreviation with two legitimate meanings. It can be taken as "bits per inch" when considering one of the nine recording tracks on tape. When referring to all nine tracks in cross section, bpi means "bytes per inch." Since tracks exist in parallel and are not separable from one another, the two values are the same for tape.

Various models of the IBM 3420 tape drive can read and write at 800 and 1,600 bpi or 1,600 and 6,250 bpi. Unlike the case with video cassette tape, there is no fidelity advantage to the lower densities, and sheer media consumption disadvantages. Installations typically use the 3420 models 4, 6, or 8, which can read and write at 1,600 and 6,250 bpi, leaving one or two model 1, 2, 3, 5, or 7 units, if any, to read 800 or 1,600 bpi tapes produced on older key to disk equipment or minicomputers. The tape drives on many minis can create only 1,600 bpi tapes and in some cases only 800 bpi. The recording density DCB subparameter, in which DEN = 2 indicates 800 bpi, DEN = 3 indicates 1,600 bpi, and DEN = 4 indicates 6,250 bpi, deals with reel type tapes only; it does not apply to the 3480 cartridge drives, which do not read or write at such low densities.

Some simple calculations based on the standard 2,400 foot tape length—approximately 2,370 usable feet—at a recording density of 6,250 bpi and a maximum blocksize of 32,760 bytes will quickly confirm that this maximum size block requires 5.24 inches of media for storage. Blocks are read one at a time, and the drive must be able to stop the tape physically after each block and accelerate it again for another read. This requires a small 0.3-inch gap between blocks, called the "inter-block gap."[1] Therefore our example 32,760-byte block requires a total of 5.54 inches of tape, including the inter-block gap; about 5,130 blocks will fit on the 28,440 inches of usable tape on a full 10½-inch reel. Thus the theoretical storage capacity of this reel is 32,760 × 5,130 or about 168 megabytes. The actual capacity declines from this value the smaller the block size used, because smaller blocks require more inter-block gaps.

When tape storage was introduced in the early 1960s it was often compared to punched cards in terms of storage density. The comparison was interesting even then, when technology limited recording density to 200 or 556 bpi. To continue the comparison is also informative, although it is more meaningful to include microcomputer diskette capacity comparisons as well as cards. A 10½-inch reel of tape recorded at 6,250 bpi can store the equivalent of 2.1 million punched cards, 466 IBM PC 360K double-sided diskettes, 233 3½-inch micro diskettes, 140 PC-AT 1.2 megabyte floppies, or 1,175 Apple-II 143K single-sided diskettes.

The 3480 Tape Cartridge Drive

The IBM 3480 tape cartridge and drive are replacing reel tapes and 3420/3422 drives. Both media and drive occupy less space than their older counterparts—60% less space—yet offer higher information storage capacity, greater read/write speed, and an increase in reliability estimated to be 5 to 20 times that of the older reel-to-reel drives in spite of a much higher recording density.

The 3480 cartridge is physically smaller than a 10½-inch reel; its 4 × 5 inch casing houses 505 feet of special 1/2-inch wide chromium dioxide tape. The cartridge stores 200 megabytes of information and the IBM 3480 drive transfers data at a rate of three megabytes per second. The 3480 drive records data in 18 longitudinal tracks with a format of information coding that differs from earlier technology. Although it packs much more information into a unit of tape—38,800 bpi—its error detection and correction capabilities actually make it more reliable than older reel-to-reel magnetic tape. The device uses semiconductor "thin film" heads similar to those of the IBM 3380 disk drive, not wire-wound metallic spools as on earlier tape drives, and the heads do not actually contact the tape surface. The drive contains its own large data storage area to buffer data between the computer's channel and the read/write mechanism and allows the drive to keep the media in more constant motion.

Because advancing technology is delivering increases in disk storage recording density more rapidly than tape storage density, it still requires six of the 3480 cartridges to store the data from one 1.2 gigabyte IBM 3380 disk unit. An installation that uses 3480 cartridge drives does not typically reduce its complement of drives from the level that applied for reel-to-reel units.[2]

TAPE LABELING

Media Labeling: The Volume Label

Every unit of storage media is assigned a unique identifier, its "volume serial number," often coded in JCL as VOL = SER. The volume serial number of the media is recorded on it; with tape the volume serial number is recorded immediately after a physical "reflective spot" that denotes the end of the leader threading. This position is called the "load point."

The volume label is a single 80-byte card image that contains the literals VOL1 in positions 1 through 4 and the tape volume serial number in positions 5 through 10. Figure 10.1 illustrates this record. When a tape is mounted for any purpose, MVS directs the tape drive to position

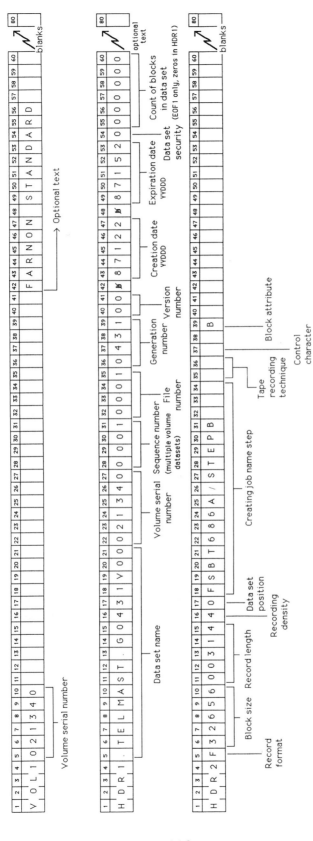

FIGURE 10.1. Tape volume, HDR1 and HDR2 label formats

169

itself at the load point, reads the VOL1 tape volume label, and thereby identifies the tape.

When new tapes are acquired by an installation, they must be initialized before use with the IEHINITT utility. This is a process performed by an operations group in an installation; it is not done by programmers. Although initialization may at first glance seem to be analogous to the formatting that is necessary before microcomputer diskettes are used, this is not a good comparison because diskette initialization does much more than tape initialization. The only thing that happens when a tape is initialized is that the VOL1 record is applied to it carrying a volume serial number that must not duplicate an existing tape or disk volume serial number. An operator will also attach a gummed label with the assigned volume serial number to the side of the tape reel or cartridge. This makes it possible to locate the tape among the thousands of others that may exist in the installation. The outside label, often called the "external label," is *not* what is indicated when a tape is said to be labeled. "Labeled" refers to the presence of the VOL1 and data set HDR1/HDR2 internal labels recorded on the tape.

The end of recorded information on the tape is denoted by two "tape marks." A tape mark is a long series of unique signals that can be detected by MVS. One tape mark separates different data sets on tape and two tape marks denote the end of recorded data on the tape. For a tape just initialized two tape marks follow the VOL1 label immediately.[3]

Data Set Labeling: HDR1 and HDR2

Data sets written to tape are by default individually labeled when they are created. The labels are known as "IBM standard labels" and consist of two 80-byte card image records that carry "HDR1" and "HDR2" in their respective first four bytes, as illustrated in Figure 10.1. Positions 5 through 80 of these label records contain various fields used by MVS to store information about the data set itself, such as its name, record length, and block size. The HDR1 and HDR2 records are commonly referred to as "header" labels, hence the HDR designation.

The end of a data set on tape is denoted by one tape mark, followed by copies of the HDR1 and HDR2 records with the front literals now changed to EOF1 and EOF2. The EOF label records are identical in composition to the HDR records except that the field within the EOF1 record that carries the number of blocks in the data set now contains a count. The EOF labels are commonly known as "trailer" labels.

Most often only one data set is recorded on a given tape. Figure 10.2 illustrates the VOL1 and HDR records and the data set and EOF records. For this one standard labeled data set three distinct pieces of recorded information exist on the tape, separated from one another by tape marks:

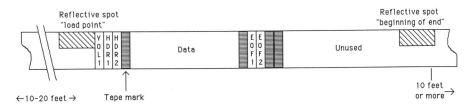

FIGURE 10.2. Volume and header labels, data set, and trailer labels for a single data set on one tape

the VOL1/HDR1/HDR2 labels, the data set, and the EOF1/EOF2 trailer labels.

Multiple Reel Data Sets

Figure 10.3 illustrates the arrangement of data set labels when a large data set spans more than one tape volume. The data set is prefaced by the VOL1, HDR1, and HDR2 labels and is followed by a tape mark. The approaching end of the tape is denoted by a reflective marker similar to that at the load point. This marker does not signal the actual end of the recordable area; just its approach. The last part of the last data block written *follows* the trailing reflective spot and is followed in turn by a tape mark and a copy of the HDR1 and HDR2 labels, with the first four characters changed to EOV1 and EOV2, then two tape marks. "EOV" signifies "end of volume." The second reel of the data set begins as usual with VOL1, HDR1, and HDR2 labels, followed by a tape mark. The end of the data set on the last volume is denoted by the customary tape mark and EOF labels, then two tape marks.

It is possible to use the volume-sequence-number of the VOL param-

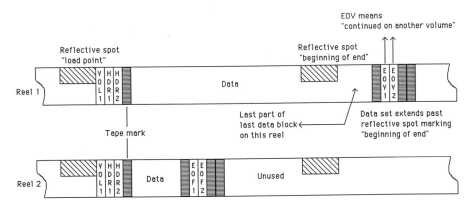

FIGURE 10.3. Volume and header labels, data set, and trailer labels for a single data set spanning more than one tape

eter to "jump into the middle" of a multivolume data set and begin reading it at that point. There is no backward pointer on the second and subsequent reels of a multivolume data set to indicate that other volumes exist carrying preceding portions of the data set. In addition, although the EOV labels denote that one or more volumes will follow, they do not reveal the identity of those volumes.

Multiple Data Sets on One Tape

It is possible to record more than one data set on the same tape. These data sets are separated from one another by a single tape mark. As illustrated in Figure 10.4, the sequence of information on the tape begins with the VOL1 record and is followed immediately by the HDR1 and HDR2 label records of the first data set. There is then a tape mark, the first data set, another tape mark, and the EOF1 and EOF2 records for the first data set's trailer labels. Then comes another tape mark, the HDR1 and HDR2 label records for the second data set, a tape mark, the second data set, a tape mark, and the EOF1 and EOF2 records for the second data set. If the second data set is the last one on the tape, its EOF records are followed by two tape marks. If more data sets exist, the pattern repeats, and finally ends in two tape marks.

When more than one data set exists on a tape reel, the need for the first positional subparameter of the DD statement LABEL parameter becomes apparent. Accessing any but the first data set requires that MVS know its relative data set number or "file sequence number"; the LABEL

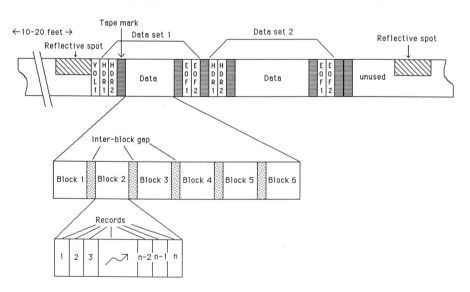

FIGURE 10.4. Volume and header labels, data set, and trailer labels for a multidata set tape

parameter provides the means of making this specification if the data set is not cataloged. For example, to read an uncataloged fifth data set on a tape that carries volume serial number 023472 the following DD statement could be used

```
//BT3712E1    DD   DSN=AK00.C18.HISTDATA,
//   UNIT=(TAPE,,DEFER),
//   DISP=(OLD,KEEP),
//   VOL=SER=023472,
//   LABEL=5
```

but the need for this coding would be rare. In the contemporary environment it is customary to catalog data sets at the time of their creation. When a data set is cataloged, *everything* necessary to access it is recorded by MVS in the catalog. The data set and not the media is cataloged; therefore when a tape data set is cataloged, its relative data set number on the tape is stored in the catalog. Every one of many data sets on a tape can be cataloged and each receives its own catalog entry. Each such catalog entry identifies the same tape volume serial number but a different relative data set number.

This example deals with *accessing* an existing data set on a multiple data set tape. In *creating* this data set, there is no escaping the need to specify the relative data set number because there is no default in MVS that allows it to determine the next available relative data set number on a given tape. The mechanism for multiple data set storage on tape is simple; there is no single repository of information about tape contents as exists for disk in its volume table of contents. For example, to output a new data set as the seventh one on standard labeled tape 034112 the following would be coded:

```
//BT3722U1    DD   DSN=AK00.C27.ARCVMASP,
//   UNIT=(TAPE,,DEFER),
//   DISP=(NEW,CATLG,DELETE),
//   DCB=(RECFM=FB,LRECL=173,BLKSIZE=32697),
//   VOL=SER=034112,
//   LABEL=(7,RETPD=180)
```

This would write a new data set as the seventh on tape 034112, overwriting whatever existed as the seventh data set on this tape *if its expiration date had been reached*. The expiration date of a data set is contained in its HDR1 and EOF1 data set labels. If there were not already six data sets on the tape, this coding would cause a job failure. If there were an existing seventh data set and its label did not carry an expiration date that been reached, MVS would prompt the console operator for permission to overwrite this unexpired data set. Most likely an operator would not allow it because operators do not usually regard such an attempt as legitimate. The job would then fail.

In this example the second positional subparameter of the LABEL specification is omitted, defaulting to "SL" for IBM standard label. The third entry is the keyword parameter for retention period, and we have specified that the data set label for this new data set should carry an expiration date 180 days later than the current date.

In all, there are five subparameters for LABEL, the first four of which are positional and the fifth, RETPD/EXPDT, which is a keyword parameter. In actual practice coding that involves the first positional subparameter data-set-sequence-number and the RETPD keyword is entirely sufficient. The middle subparameters are useful only for work with tapes "foreign" to an installation and are of little contemporary relevance.

Data Set Sequence Number

The complete form of the LABEL parameter is

```
LABEL=(data-set-seq-no,label-type,PASSWORD,in-out,RETPD/EXPDT=)
```

where all but the last subparameter are positional. Defaults are in effect for all parameters so that it is possible to create a data set on tape without the use of the LABEL parameter at all. Use of at least the final specification, however, to indicate a retention period or expiration date is customary so that MVS does not immediately regard the tape as expired and a candidate for use by another output.[4]

The data set sequence number defaults to a value of 1 if not coded; in the majority of cases only one data set is written to a tape and the default applies. This subparameter and the three that follow are positional. If data set sequence number is not specified but label-type, PASSWORD, or in-out are to be coded, the empty positional slots for the unspecified items must be indicated by the comma that normally follows them:

```
//  LABEL=(,SL)
```

This, for example, shows that the first data set on a standard labeled tape is involved. SL happens also to be the default for standard label, which we discuss next, and the foregoing coding is normally not necessary. It is identical in meaning to the omission of the LABEL parameter altogether or to:

```
//  LABEL=(1,SL)
```

LABEL "TYPE" CODING

```
LABEL=( data-set-seq-no, label-type, PASSWORD, in-out, RETPD/EXPDT )
```

A fascination for the different types of label possible on a tape data set is a carryover from the wild and woolly days of the 1960s. In the period immediately following the introduction of the System/360 in 1964 many installations faced the task of reading data from other systems, forcing recognition of the then current variations in tape labeling between different lines of equipment. Beyond the variations some installations felt that their circumstances were so unusual that it was necessary to develop their own special formats of data set labels to supplant or add to IBM's standard data set labeling format.

Tape data set labels are almost trivial in their purpose, composition, and functioning; in the contemporary environment programmers will not typically encounter any but IBM standard labels. These are written and read by MVS by default and handle tape data set identification tasks automatically. It's not that there is a choice in the matter; most installations have a rigid policy of standard labeling. But a total of eight codings is possible in the second positional specification. In the overwhelming majority of instances this value will be left to the default, SL.

IBM Standard Labels

HDR1 and HDR2 and the corresponding end of data set EOF1 and EOF2 labels are the IBM standard labels denoted by SL in the label-type subparameter. At times SL may be coded in the second position even though it is redundant to the default when another following parameter such as RETPD is coded:

```
//    LABEL=(2,SL,RETPD=180)
```

However, this is simply due to force of habit. This coding is identical in effect to

```
//    LABEL=(2,RETPD=180)
```

because the final keyword subparameter is discernible by the JCL parsing software without regard for intervening positional parameters. When the default value of 1 for data set sequence number and the default of standard labels are to apply, the statement is sometimes written

```
//    LABEL=(1,SL,RETPD=180)
```

but it could just as well be expressed as:

```
//    LABEL=RETPD=180
```

NL Specification for Nonlabeled Tapes

Nonlabeled tapes are written by MVS when NL is coded in the label-type field for an output data set. When this is done, the existing VOL1 volume label of the tape is obliterated and no HDR1 and HDR2 data set labels are written. The tape is created with the data set immediately following the reflective spot load point—no leading tape mark—and the data set is followed immediately by two tape marks. MVS refers to the tape in the job log by a system-concocted volume serial number consisting of an "L" and five digits.

Writing nonlabeled tapes on a mainframe serves no purpose; because MVS does not record an expiration date for the data set, the tape becomes available immediately for use as a scratch tape by other jobs running concurrently.[5] Attempting to write tapes in this manner is more or less like an aircraft pilot choosing, just for fun, to take off with one of three engines out, low fuel, and no radio. It can be done but it is foolish. It also requires operator involvement for reinitialization if this tape is to be used again as a standard labeled tape.

Reading nonlabeled tapes on a mainframe is fairly commonly done, given the variety of key-to-disk equipment in existence. Much of this equipment employs minicomputer operating systems of varying degrees of sophistication. Some of this equipment is programmed to generate IBM standard labels but much of it requires data entry personnel to compose and output explicitly the fields of the VOL1, HDR1, and HDR2 records and the requisite tape marks. This often leads to trouble when an installation requires that data entry tapes be standard labeled because it is easy in such cases for an inconsistency to develop between the volume serial number on the external gummed label of a reel and the volume serial number written into the VOL1 label by the data entry operator.[6]

Data entry tapes are typically created without labels, meaning without the VOL1 label or data set labels. NL can be specified for label-type in the JCL reading and copying these tapes to mainframe data sets. When this is done, it is necessary to code VOL = SER on the DD statement and customary to code DSN even though the tape has no HDR1 and HDR2 labels that carry the data set name. This following coding could be used when the IEBGENER utility is employed to copy the data set to disk or tape:

```
//*****************************************************
//*     COPY NL TRANS DATA TO DISK                    *
//*****************************************************
//STEPA      EXEC  PGM=IEBGENER
//*
//SYSUT1     DD   DSN=AK00.C99.KEYTRANS,
//   UNIT=(TAPE,,DEFER),
//   DISP=(OLD,KEEP),
//   DCB=(RECFM=FB,LRECL=122,BLKSIZE=1220),
//   VOL=SER=LB0809,
//   LABEL=(1,NL)
//*
//SYSUT2     DD   DSN=AK00.C99.KTRNDISK,
//   UNIT=SYSDA,
//   DISP=(NEW,CATLG,DELETE),
//   DCB=(RECFM=FB,LRECL=122,BLKSIZE=6222),
//   SPACE=(6222,(100,20),RLSE)
//*
//SYSPRINT   DD   SYSOUT=A
//SYSIN      DD   DUMMY
```

//SYSIN is dummied out and the records are copied to the output data set in the same format as input to IEBGENER. //SYSUT1 is IEBGENER's input data set; //SYSUT2 is its output data set. Because the tape being read carries no label to convey the characteristics of the data set, we need to code the complete DCB for it. If the tape were keyed in the ASCII character set, we would also need to include the OPTCD = Q DCB subparameter to invoke the optional service of ASCII to EBCDIC code translation at //SYSUT1:

```
//   DCB=(RECFM=FB,LRECL=122,BLKSIZE=1220,OPTCD=Q),
```

If the installation in which this job is being run also used a tape management system such as UCC-1 from UCCEL Corporation, one additional item might have to be coded in the LABEL parameter. This item has no relationship to JCL but rather to the tape management system data set maintained by such independent housekeeping software. The LABEL parameter would be coded with the EXPDT specification:

```
//SYSUT1     DD   DSN=AK00.C99.KEYTRANS,
//   UNIT=(TAPE,,DEFER),
//   DISP=(OLD,KEEP),
//   DCB=(RECFM=FB,LRECL=122,BLKSIZE=1220),
//   VOL=SER=LB0809,
//   LABEL=(1,NL,EXPDT=98000)
```

This has no effect on the tape itself but is simply the means of telling the tape management system not to search its own housekeeping data set in an attempt to find a reference to the data set and tape—in this case data set AK00.C99.KEYTRANS on tape LB0809. UCC-1 is a widely used product that intercepts all system data set creation tasks and makes entries into its housekeeping data set, whether or not a data set is cataloged. When data sets are accessed, UCC-1 attempts to find the data set in its housekeeping records. If the installation uses UCC-1 and EXPDT = 98000 is not coded for reference to a "foreign" tape data set, an error will result.[7]

In a case as above, the VOL = SER and the DSN are coded for practical reasons. The VOL = SER carries the identification written on the external gummed label on the tape and MVS uses it to formulate the tape mount message it issues to the operator when this job is run. The person who conveys the tape to the mainframe isn't the one who runs the job; the operator running the job must be able to find this tape among the hundreds or thousands present near the tape drives. Even though there is no internal label on the tape that the system can compare with this JCL specification—as there would be with standard labels to make sure that the correct tape had been mounted—the VOL = SER is needed in the JCL to allow a useful mount message to be generated. The DSN is specified only to aid in the formulation of the message to the operator. In this case it can be anything at all within the permitted scope of the installation's naming conventions and security arrangements.

If NL is specified as the label-type, the data set *must not* have a VOL1 label as the first record. MVS searches for this record and regards it, if found, as a label record; its presence is taken as inconsistent with the NL indication. If this contradiction is apparent, the job will fail.

Although it is possible to place more than one data set on an tape on an unlabeled basis, it becomes potentially confusing for the person reading the tape to interpret what is being conveyed. Reading such a tape can be especially troublesome because the DCB for each of the separate data sets can be different and must be coded.

BLP to Bypass Label Processing

Sometimes confused with NL as a means of reading an unlabeled or foreign tape, "BLP" really isn't a label format at all. It tells MVS to omit invoking the routines it normally uses to check for the presence of VOL1 and HDR1/HDR2 labels when processing a tape. If BLP is coded as the second positional subparameter of LABEL, then everything on the tape is regarded as data: the initial VOL1 and HDR1/HDR2 labels, if present, the first data set, its EOF1/EOF2 labels, the HDR1/HDR2 data set labels of the next data set, and so forth. Each of these items becomes accessible by using the data set sequence number, but in this case the data set sequence number counts each item between tape marks as a data set:

	BLP Data Set Sequence Number
VOL1/HDR1/HDR2 labels	1
-------------------------------------	----------------------------
First data set	2
First data set EOF1/EOF2 labels	3
-------------------------------------	----------------------------
Second data set HDR1/HDR2/ labels	4
Second data set	5
Second data set EOF1/EOF2 labels	6
-------------------------------------	----------------------------
Third data set HDR1/HDR2 labels	7
Third data set	8
Third data set EOF1/EOF2 labels	9

(and so forth)

BLP is not a production method to read data sets but a tool for use when some conveyance of data or program source code originating outside the installation is made via tape. In such a case BLP allows dumping any item on the tape for examination. In many installations BLP is rendered inaccessible because it allows tape data set security based on data set name to be circumvented. If BLP is not active in MVS it is treated as NL if coded; if a tape carrying a label is coded to be read under these conditions, the job fails because *NL will not process a standard labeled tape.*

Miscellaneous Label Types and ASCII Labels

Five other label-type designations exist, none of which find much use in the majority of mainframe installations:

"AL" means ANSI standard labels, in a form defined by the ANSI Version 1 or Version 3 standard, documented in *American National Standard Magnetic Tape Labels for Information Interchange, ANS X3.27-1969.* AL and AUL automatically trigger ASCII-to-EBCDIC conversion, identical to that achieved by coding OPTCD=Q in the DCB parameter. The first-time conveyance of data from a mini to the mainframe often requires more than simply creating the data set on the mini and reading it with AL on the mainframe. The actual format of records created by the non-IBM system may be far different from formats normally used on the IBM system and tapes from such sources often require the dumping and analysis of the ASCII tape to see what is actually being conveyed. Unlike IBM standard labels, AL labels carry not only HDR1 and HDR2 records, but also a third label record HDR3.

"AUL" indicates that the tape carries AL labels and in addition that data set header records beyond HDR1, HDR2, and HDR3 are also present. User labels are extra labeling records that a given installation might cause to be written by locally developed operating system enhancements.

"NSL" indicates that a tape and its data sets carry nonstandard labels. This means that no MVS standard label processing is to be done and that control for label processing is to be handed over to custom-written, locally maintained routines. The installation has decided to "roll its own" data set labeling software, something that few installations now do.

"LTM" stands for "leading tape mark," a characteristic of the way that the IBM *mainframe* DOS operating system writes tapes. LTM indicates that a tape mark is to be found immediately after the reflective spot load point on the tape and that this tape mark is to be ignored. In other regards it functions the same as BLP.

"SUL" means "standard user labels" and is the same as SL for standard labels except that additional custom user labels may follow the HDR1/HDR2 label records. User labels are extra labeling records a given installation might cause to be written by locally developed software that intercepts data set creation actions. User labels are a carryover from earlier days. It would now be rare for an installation to develop and employ user labels and assume the responsibility to maintain this nonstandard adjunct to MVS.[8]

LITTLE-USED LABEL SPECIFICATIONS

PASSWORD

```
LABEL=(data-set-seq-no,label-type,PASSWORD,in-out,RETPD/EXPDT)
```

The password LABEL subparameter is the means by which the OS password indicator in a tape data set label is set to one of the two levels of security available in the limited OS password access security arrangement. This subparameter can take the form of the literal PASSWORD or the literal NOPWREAD. The subparameter can affect only the contents of the security indicator in the tape label and the actual password is not assigned by this parameter or specified within it. Instead, the password must be placed in the system password data set and associated with the data set name in advance by using the IEHPROGM utility as illustrated in item 21 of Chapter 17.

If PASSWORD is indicated in this subparameter for a tape data set when it is created, subsequent access to the data set will cause MVS to issue a prompt to the computer console operator to enter the password. If NOPWREAD is coded at tape data set creation, subsequent jobs will be able to read the data set without operator intervention, but the operator will be prompted to supply the password when a job tries to write to the data set by MODding onto it or tries to delete it.

The level of security provided by OS passwords is minimal because for a batch job many machine operators will have to be aware of the password. Mechanisms far more sophisticated than OS passwords have been developed and marketed by IBM and by third party vendors. IBM's product is called RACF, for Resource Acquisition Control Facility. Other products, such as ACF2 by SKK Inc. and Top Secret marketed by Computer Associates also enjoy a following. Some of these systems and others such as Guardian and Omniguard by Online Software International address the needs of the online environment.

IN-OUT

```
LABEL=(data-set-seq-no,label-type,PASSWORD,in-out,RETPD/EXPDT)
```

The fourth positional subparameter of LABEL is rarely used. It has the effect of overriding the options of a program's OPEN statement. IN-OUT is a carryover from early FORTRAN programming and was provided to overcome that language's manner of opening data sets for both reading and writing in all cases. That manner of operation complicated the reading and writing of files and forced operator involvement and special actions. This subparameter can be coded as the literal IN or the literal OUT to match actual data set usage in the program being executed. This subparameter plays no part in JCL for COBOL, PL/I, or utility program execution.

EXPDT AND RETPD: DATA SET EXPIRATION DATE

```
LABEL=(data-set-seq-no,label-type,PASSWORD,in-out,RETPD/EXPDT)
```

Data sets can be made to carry an expiration date that is placed into the data set label. MVS will prevent the data set from being deleted or modified until this date has "expired." *Expiration occurs on the date coded with EXPDT or computed by the system as a result of indicating RETPD.* When the current date and the expiration date are *equal*, the data set has expired and can be overwritten. Only the date is carried, not a time of day.

If RETPD is used to specify the retention period, it is specified in terms of a number of days, ranging from 1 to 9999. MVS uses this number and the current date to compute a date in the future, which is stored as the expiration date. The computation is a simple one that ignores leap years and assumes 365 days for every year. There is an overall limit on retention periods that IBM is expected to remedy before the end of the century. OS was originally developed in 1964 when the end of the century was far distant. At this point the year 2000 looms much nearer but retention is limited to January 1, 2000. By the mid-1990s IBM or a creative third party will have no doubt produced a software patch to remove this limitation.

EXPDT, if used to establish an expiration date, must be coded as a Julian date in the form YYDDD. Julian dates express the date as a two-digit year, followed by a number 1 to 365, the days of the year numbered ordinally without regard to month. The use of EXPDT for expiration date is not desirable because it requires that the JCL be changed continually to create and retain new data sets for consistent periods. RETPD is coded with a period in days and lets MVS compute the expiration date that reflects the desired time span.

The specification of a retention period or expiration date is optional; if omitted, retention defaults to zero days—the current date—or to another installation-defined value. If no other LABEL parameter is coded, only RETPD or EXPDT needs to be coded, without the commas usually present indicating the omitted positional parameters:

```
//   LABEL=RETPD=180
```

If only some of the first four positional parameters are coded, the empty positional slots for the last missing ones do not need to be coded:

```
//   LABEL=(,SL,RETPD=180)
```

THE SEQUENTIAL UPDATE JOB STREAM USING TAPE

Let's take a look at the test sequential update job stream that we first used in Chapter 3 and revised in Chapter 6. We'll now modify it again, changing the master file to a tape-stored data set, making the new master file a tape-stored data set, and reading the update transactions from a data entry tape.

The changes reflected in the job stream, listed in Figure 10.5, lie in //DELSTEP, //STEPA and //STEPB. In all of these cases we are now interested in specifying TAPE instead of SYSDA for the UNIT parameter of certain DD statements. SYSDA is a symbolic device group name or "esoteric" name that identifies a list of hardware addresses for all the disk devices in an installation; some installations may have established other device group names, perhaps calling one of them DISK. The TAPE specified in the UNIT parameters of this job stream is an installation-created symbolic device group list; TAPE is not a default device group name supplied by IBM. IBM supplies no symbolic device group list for the tape devices analogous to SYSDA.

In //DELSTEP we have added the UNIT parameter carrying the DEFER option. The disposition parameter will uncatalog and delete the data set if it exists or create a dummy data set and delete it if it does not. A tape-stored data set is not overwritten or deleted; only the uncataloging occurs. DEFER will defer mounting of the tape until it is opened. *IEFBR14 never opens or closes any data sets; therefore DEFER here saves unnecessary mounting and dismounting of tapes.* A tape device is allocated for this step, but not used.

In //STEPA, which executes the sort utility, we now find that the DDname //SORTIN deals with a tape rather than a disk test data set. This particular data set is created by a data entry operation using key-to-disk equipment within the installation, by a service bureau, or perhaps by a "lockbox" operation of a bank. It is conveyed on a nonlabeled tape that lacks VOL1, HDR1, and HDR2 labels; we must code the DCB parameter on the //SORTIN DD statement. Data entry key-to-disk systems typically have a much lower block size limit than the mainframe, and in this case a figure under 2,048 bytes has been used to create the tape. In addition, the recording density is specified as DEN=3, which denotes that the tape is recorded at 1,600 bpi, and OPTCD=Q is coded because the tape carries data encoded in ASCII rather than the mainframe's EBCDIC.[9]

We still code the DSN with a legitimate data set name for the nonlabeled tape and we code the VOL parameter specifying the volume serial number as the unique number on the external gummed label on the reel. The VOL=SER is how MVS tells the computer operator what tape to mount when the job runs.

The LABEL parameter is coded for the //SORTIN DDname because MVS must be told that the tape is not labeled; otherwise, it will assume that it carries standard SL labels. Because there is only one data set on the tape, the "1" in

```
//   LABEL=(1,NL,EXPDT=98000)
```

is really superfluous. Here is a case in which coding consumes little effort and adds much to the clarity. It could have been coded as

```
//   LABEL=(,NL,EXPDT=98000)
```

```
//FSBT686A  JOB AK00TEST,'DP2-JANOSSY',CLASS=T,MSGCLASS=X,
//  MSGLEVEL=(1,1),NOTIFY=BT05686
//*
//*     TEST RUN OF SEQUENTIAL UPDATE FSBT3708 -- VER 3B
//*     STILL FOR TESTING, OLD MF IS ALWAYS ".TELMAST"
//*     BUT OLD AND NEW MASTER FILES ARE NOW TAPE, AND
//*     INPUT IS ON A 1600 BPI NON-LABELED TAPE KEYED ON
//*     AN ASCII-BASED DATA ENTRY SYSTEM OR MINI.
//*
//*     THIS JCL = BT05686.SOURCE.CNTL(BT3708V3)
//*
//************************************************************
//*                                                          *
//*     DELETE EXISTING UPDATED DATA SET          DEL  *
//*                                                          *
//************************************************************
//DELSTEP  EXEC  PGM=IEFBR14
//DEL1        DD  DSN=AK00.C99.TELMAST.UPDATED,
//  UNIT=(TAPE,,DEFER),
//  DISP=(MOD,DELETE)
//*
//************************************************************
//*                                                          *
//*     SORT TRANS FILE                           A   *
//*                                                          *
//************************************************************
//STEPA    EXEC  PGM=SORT
//SORTLIB     DD  DSN=SYS1.SORTLIB,
//  DISP=SHR
//*
//SORTIN      DD  DSN=AK00.C99.TRANSIN,
//  ·UNIT=(TAPE,,DEFER),
//  DISP=(OLD,KEEP),
//  DCB=(RECFM=FB,LRECL=71,BLKSIZE=1420,DEN=3,OPTCD=Q),
//  VOL=SER=HXR452,
//  LABEL=(1,NL,EXPDT=98000)                'EXPDT ONLY FOR UCC-1 TMS
//*
//SORTOUT     DD  DSN=&&TRANSORT,
//  UNIT=SYSDA,
//  DISP=(NEW,PASS,DELETE),
//  DCB=(RECFM=FB,LRECL=71,BLKSIZE=6177),
//  SPACE=(6177,(32,7),RLSE)                '2800 TRANS
//SYSOUT      DD  SYSOUT=*
//SYSUDUMP    DD  SYSOUT=*
//SORTWK01    DD  UNIT=SYSDA,SPACE=(CYL,2,,CONTIG)
//SORTWK02    DD  UNIT=SYSDA,SPACE=(CYL,2,,CONTIG)
//SYSIN       DD  *
    SORT FIELDS=(1,4,CH,A,9,2,CH,A,5,4,CH,A,14,1,CH,D)
/*
//*
//************************************************************
//*                                                          *
//*     UPDATE MASTER FILE                        B   *
//*                                                          *
//************************************************************
//STEPB    EXEC  PGM=FSBT3708,REGION=2048K
//STEPLIB     DD  DSN=BT05686.TEST.LOADMODS,
//  DISP=SHR
//BT3708E1    DD  DSN=&&TRANSORT,
//  DISP=(OLD,DELETE)
//BT3708E2    DD  DSN=AK00.C99.TELMAST,
//  UNIT=(TAPE,,DEFER),
//  DISP=(OLD,KEEP)
//BT3708E3    DD  DSN=AK00.C99.AREAREF,
//  DISP=SHR
//BT3708U1    DD  SYSOUT=*
//*
//BT3708U2    DD  DSN=AK00.C99.TELMAST.UPDATED,
//  UNIT=(TAPE,,DEFER),
//  DISP=(NEW,CATLG,DELETE),
//  DCB=(RECFM=FB,LRECL=314,BLKSIZE=32656),
//  LABEL=RETPD=30
//*
```

184

```
//BT3708U3    DD   DSN=&&TRANSFIN,
//   UNIT=SYSDA,
//   DISP=(NEW,PASS,DELETE),
//   DCB=(RECFM=FB,LRECL=102,BLKSIZE=6222),   '2800 TRANS
//   SPACE=(6222,(46,9),RLSE)
//SYSOUT      DD   SYSOUT=*
//SYSUDUMP    DD   SYSOUT=*
//*********************************************************
//*                                                       *
//*      PRODUCE TRAN REPORT (INTERNAL SORT)         C    *
//*                                                       *
//*********************************************************
//STEPC     EXEC  PGM=FSBT3719,REGION=2048K
//STEPLIB     DD   DSN=BT05686.TEST.LOADMODS,
//   DISP=SHR
//SORTLIB     DD   DSN=SYS1.SORTLIB,
//   DISP=SHR
//BT3719E1    DD   DSN=&&TRANSFIN,
//   DISP=(OLD,DELETE)
//BT3719U1    DD   SYSOUT=*
//BT3719U2    DD   SYSOUT=*
//SORTWK01    DD   UNIT=SYSDA,SPACE=(CYL,2,,CONTIG)
//SORTWK02    DD   UNIT=SYSDA,SPACE=(CYL,2,,CONTIG)
//BT3719SM    DD   SYSOUT=*
//SYSOUT      DD   SYSOUT=*
//SYSUDUMP    DD   SYSOUT=*
//
```

FIGURE 10.5. Revised sequential update job stream using tape-stored master files and transaction files

but that requires someone who does not carry all the JCL defaults around in his or her head to confirm the data set sequence number default. It is better to be explicit here in JCL; it costs nothing to do so.

The EXPDT = 98000 is coded because the installation that uses this JCL has in place a tape management system. This specification informs the tape management system that the data set is a foreign one and that it should not attempt to locate it in its housekeeping information concerning data sets.

The //SORTOUT DD statement of //STEPA does not change from the earlier job stream. The sort will read data from tape but write it out to disk. The sort does not care what media conveys the input or what media carries the output. It's the purpose of JCL to handle this interface to free individual programs from having to know the nature of the storage media used.

//STEPB executes program FSBT3708, a sequential update routine. At DDname //BT3708E2 the old master file is input on tape. The UNIT parameter is coded here, simply to carry the DEFER specification. Because the data set is cataloged, there would be no need for the UNIT parameter if it were not for our desire to code DEFER. The system catalog stores information on the type of unit on which a data set resides and it is not necessary to specify the unit in JCL for a cataloged data set.

At //BT3708U2 the new master file emerges on tape. We specify that it is to be cataloged and MVS records its name, characteristics, and the volume serial number on which it is placed. The characteristics of the new data set not specified by the program must be conveyed on a DCB parameter, establishing most importantly the block size. For tapes we use the largest possible block size within the 32,760 byte limit to speed read/write operations and conserve media. We did not use the density subparameter DEN; instead we allowed density to default to whatever the installation has established as its default. In this case allowing the default to take effect serves a definite purpose: the installation can upgrade its equipment to higher density tape drives and JCL will not have to be changed to take advantage of it.

Not specifying the VOL parameter indicates a *nonspecific* volume request; MVS will direct that a suitable scratch volume that matches the UNIT type be mounted. We specify the LABEL parameter, coding only the retention period, from which MVS will compute an expiration date. By not specifying the relative data set number or label-type they default to 1 and SL. *The expiration date is recorded in the data set label but not in the system catalog.* This is the single most significant reason that a tape management system became a desirable product for mainframe installations in the 1960s. Without such support software, locating scratch tapes relies on a purely manual tape inventory and quite a bit of mounting of tapes to let MVS see if the tape is a scratch tape by reading the expiration date of the first data set on it.

//STEPC of the original job stream is not affected by the modification from disk to tape storage because it does not deal with the transaction input or the master file itself.

DISK DATA SETS AND THE LABEL PARAMETER

Under normal circumstances the LABEL parameter is not coded when disk data sets are created; the result is standard SL labeling by default. Disk data sets must always be created standard label SL or standard and user labels, SUL. For disk data sets the label exists as part of the disk volume table of contents, or VTOC, which serves as the directory on each unit of disk media; the disk data set label is the VTOC's format 1 data set control block or "DSCB" record. In practice, few installations add locally written user label processing routines to enhance the information already retained in standard disk data set labels. In addition to the burden inherent in providing the logic to handle extra user labels, there is a significant performance penalty as well: user labels on disk data sets, if employed, require an additional full track to be allocated to the data set. The default SL standard label processing, obtained when the LABEL parameter is omitted, is consistently appropriate for disk data sets.

Data set sequence number is irrelevant for disk because a disk and the VTOC are designed to deal with multiple data sets on the media in a much more sophisticated way than by sequence number. The IN-OUT and PASSWORD subparameters have as little utility in connection with contemporary disk data set usage as they have with tape data sets. Therefore the only subparameter of LABEL that has any real relevance to disk is RETPD/EXPDT, but it has more of a negative relevance than a positive one because expiration date is most often not used with disk data sets.

Expiration dates on a disk data set are undesirable because unlike tape data sets, disk data sets must be able to be moved, copied, deleted, and reorganized in the normal course of operation. If expiration dates were coded for them, the ability to take these housekeeping actions would be severely constrained.[10]

REVIEW QUESTIONS AND (*)EXERCISES

1. When MVS calls for a tape to be mounted by a computer operator as a result of JCL non-specifically for a tape volume, how is the drive on which to mount the tape specified to the operator in the system message?

2. Why does reel-to-reel tape use nine longitudinal recording tracks instead of eight, even though bytes are expressed with eight bits?

3. What are the two highest recording densities used with open reel tapes, and how are they explicitly coded using the DCB DEN parameter?

4. In what ways does the 3480 tape cartridge differ from the open reel tapes of the 3420 equipment series?

5. What would happen if an installation created a symbolic device group list that included the addresses of 3420 open reel devices and 3480 tape cartridge drives?

6. A tape carries a single data set with an expiration date of 93365. What is the earliest Gregorian (MMDDYY) date that this tape, if mounted as a scratch tape to receive a new data set, will be written upon by MVS without question?

*7. A new data set that contains normal printline images is to be written to reel-to-reel tape at default density instead of directed to SYSOUT. The data set is to be named FS62.A31.HREP23PR and emerges at DDname //BT3731E4. Code the complete DD statement to meet this requirement, blocking the data set as efficiently as possible and writing the data set as the third on standard labeled tape volume 011483. The installation uses a symbolic device group name of REELTAPE for its open-reel tape drives.

*8. An existing cataloged data set written at 1,600 bpi resides as the fifth one on standard label tape 038872. This data set is named FS62.A37.CURRTRAN and is to be read at DDname //BT3757U1. Code the necessary DD statement.

*9. A large data set is written to standard labeled tape and spans three volumes. Draw a simple diagram of each tape as a horizontal rectangle and illustrate the arrangement of volume and data set labels and tape marks.

*10. A large data set that contains fixed blocked records each 2,802 bytes in length is to be written to open-reel tape at 6,250 bpi. Compute the most efficient block size for the data set and determine how many 10½-inch tape volumes will be required to house 450,000 records, taking into account the 0.3 inch inter-block gaps between data blocks.

NOTES

1. The terminology associated with the inter-block gap is sometimes confusing. A block of data that contains many logical records is sometimes called a "physical record" in the technical literature and the gap then referred to as an "inter-record gap." There are no physical gaps between records in a block; this is why it is desirable to block records in the first place. The size of the gap was 0.6 inches with tape recording densities less than 6,250 bpi.

2. As an illustration, when Phillips Petroleum Corporation, a major IBM mainframe user with several contemporary mainframes, converted 70,000 active tapes from its 120,000-reel tape library from open reels to 3480 cartridges in 1985, it replaced its complement of 57 IBM 3420 drives with 58 IBM 3480 drives. Of the original 3420 drives 15 were retained to access less active tape reels not immediately converted.

3. Because the drive detects the end of recorded data when it encounters two tape marks, it is possible to run to end of reel and cause an abend if a tape without two tape marks is mounted and read. This occurs occasionally when a tape produced by a key-to-disk data entry operation that employs a minicomputer is processed. Minicomputer operating systems usually provide no automatic IBM labeling or tape mark generating facility, requiring the operator who sets up a keying job to issue explicit commands to write the two tape marks that denote the end of recorded data. It is possible on such systems to inadvertently omit the final tape marks.

4. The MVS and MVS/XA default for a data set expiration date is the current date; in other words, a retention period of zero. Some installations modify this for tape data sets and cause a default such as seven days to apply. Programmers are then told *not* to code a retention period or expiration date on test tapes. This is done to avoid the accumulation of unexpired test tapes that are forgotten and left to rot ignominiously in an installation's tape library.

5. The immediate reuse of the newly created, nonlabeled tape can be prevented by

causing the dismounting of the tape, using a disposition of DISP = (NEW,DELETE). The DELETE does not cause actual deletion of the data set even though the system allocation/deallocation report IEF285I message will so indicate.

6. MVS doesn't create problems of inconsistent external and internal labels because it doesn't change the content of the VOL1 label even when a tape on a multidensity IBM 3420 tape drive recorded at one density is made to carry a new data set of another density. On the other hand, the VOL1 label, which carries the volume serial number, does not enjoy this sacrosanct treatment on many data entry key-to-disk systems. When a labeled tape is created on such equipment the VOL1 label present on the tape, if one exists, is overwritten with whatever the data entry operator or program supplies as the label records. This amounts to reinitializing the tape each time such a system writes on it. Because of this fact, *a significant potential for external label/internal label inconsistency exists in the creation of labeled tapes by many types of data entry or minicomputer equipment.* As a practical matter these inconsistencies cause failed runs on the mainframe and can impede the operation of a production application system.

7. UCC-1 is representative of tape management system software. UCC-1 is a trademark of UCCEL Corporation, formerly University Computing Company, UCCEL Tower, Exchange Park, Dallas, Texas 75235. An installation licenses UCC-1 separately from MVS. Systems programmers at a computer site handle the installation of third party software such as UCC-1.

8. The terminology associated with tape labels is sometimes confusing when any but default standard labels are involved. SUL means that IBM's standard labeling is being used but that additional user-generated and processed labels also follow the data set's HDR1 and HDR2 labels. Up to eight user 80-byte labels can be carried, starting with UHLn or UTLn in the first four bytes, where "n" is a number, 1 to 8.

   AUL presents nearly the same situation as SUL except that ASCII coded data and standards are followed for the VOL1, HDR1, HDR2, and an additional HDR3 label. The label records must be 80 bytes in length, but there is no limit to the number of additional user labels that can exist on the tape. Neither AL or AUL can exist on mainframe disk; all data sets written to disk must be EBCDIC encoded and labeled SL or SUL. The OPTCD = Q optional services code is part of MVS tape processing routines and is not accessible in connection with disk data sets.

   NSL means that labels exist but that the customization in labeling is not a supplement to IBM's default labels; it completely replaces IBM labeling. If this gross customization is used, the installation has assumed complete responsibility for tape labeling routines and MVS will seek user-supplied label processing routines instead of any of its own. For NSL labeled tapes the first four bytes of the VOL record *cannot* be VOL1 because this is associated with SL or SUL labeling. The format and content of NSL labels is not otherwise constrained by MVS. The labels do not need to be 80 bytes in length but can be any length up to 4,096 bytes, and any number of them can exist. NSL can be used with tape data sets only.

9. See Appendix C for information on how the ASCII encoding scheme differs from that of EBCDIC, IBM's Extended Binary Coded Decimal Interchange Code.

10. A programmer testing production programs that have been modified sometimes copies production JCL that executes the programs to his or her own library and modifies it for test runs. If the production JCL specifies tapes but the programmer overlooks dropping the LABEL parameter when changing data set UNITs to disk, disk data sets that carry expiration dates can be created unintentionally. A disk data set with an expiration date can be deleted in advance of that date by using the IDCAMS utility, as illustrated in item 7 of Chapter 17.

11

AMP: Access Method (VSAM)
Parameter

AMP is a parameter that was added to MVS job control language in the early 1970s when the Virtual Storage Access Method, VSAM, was introduced. AMP, an acronym for "access method parameter," provides the means of feeding parameters to the subsystem software that manages VSAM data sets.

Before the introduction of VSAM IBM took the approach of supporting diverse and separate mechanisms, such as Basic Sequential Access Method (BSAM), Basic Direct Access Method (BDAM), and Indexed Sequential Access Method (ISAM), with "normal" JCL parameters and optional services codes, OPTCDs. Data sets for each of the earlier access methods were created and manipulated solely with JCL. VSAM, a more complex data storage mechanism, requires the services of the separate major Access Method Services utility program, IDCAMS, for data set definition and manipulation. The then existing facilities of JCL were inadequate to provide communication to Access Method Services support software and AMP was "tacked on" to the syntax of JCL.

PURPOSE OF AMP ON THE DD STATEMENT

The AMP parameter is actually a means of supplying information to the ACB, or "access method control block." One of the newer MVS subsystem control blocks, ACB serves the same access method intercommunication purpose for VSAM data sets that the data control block does for non-VSAM data sets. In fact, two of the lesser used AMP subparameters, OPTCD and RECFM, are identical in syntax to those of the DCB parameter. ACB *cannot* be coded in JCL to provide a source of information to the access method control block as the DCB does to the data control block; AMP serves that purpose.

AMP provides 10 keyword subparameters. Of these, four are more commonly used than the others: AMORG, BUFSP, BUFND, and BUFNI. AMORG identifies the data set as having VSAM organization, and the three BUF. . specifications deal with input-output buffer space, as the DCB BUFL and BUFNO subparameters do for non-VSAM data sets. The remaining AMP subparameters are highly specialized.

AMP SYNTAX

Because of its nature as an "added on" parameter of JCL, the syntax of AMP is unlike that of other JCL parameters and similar to that of the EXEC statement PARM, discussed in Chapter 15. AMP subparameters are all keywords of five characters. Most contain an imbedded equal sign:

```
//   AMP=('AMORG,BUFSP=13000,BUFND=12,BUFNI=5')
```

When split between JCL lines, it is even more apparent that the same apostrophe framing conventions that apply to PARM also apply to AMP:

```
//   AMP=('AMORG,BUFSP=13000,BUFND=12',
//      'BUFNI=5')
```

The coding supplied at the AMP parameter framed by apostrophes is handed over by MVS to VSAM support software as a whole for interpretation instead of being parsed and interpreted by MVS itself. This is identical to the way in which compiler parameter options are handed over to a language compiler and the reason that AMP syntax resembles that of a PARM string.

COMMONLY USED AMP SUBPARAMETERS

AMORG

AMP = 'AMORG' must be coded when a VSAM data set is cited on a DD statement with VOL and UNIT parameters. This communicates to appropriate support software that the data set is of "Access Method ORGanization." The data set organization is carried in the system catalog but the presence of explicit VOL and UNIT parameters on a DD statement causes MVS to omit access to the catalog. AMORG must also be coded if the DD statement for the VSAM data set is to carry DUMMY.

BUFSP = nnnn

BUFSP allows specification of the I/O buffer size for the data set. If the value coded is greater than the buffer space defined for the VSAM data set in the catalog, this value will override the catalog value. At the time a VSAM data set is created the BUFFERSPACE parameter of the IDCAMS DEFINE command can specify a value for this attribute. If not specified, a default large enough to accommodate two data control intervals and one index control interval will apply. Although this subparameter may be used to provide greater buffer resources to speed sequential access to a data set, it is customary to use the BUFND and BUFNI subparameters for this purpose.

If BUFSP is set too low to accommodate the default or number of buffers specified in the BUFND and BUFNI subparameters, the number of buffers will be reduced to fit the BUFSP buffer space. If BUFSP is coded larger than needed to accommodate the number of buffers, the number of buffers will be increased by VSAM to use the space. There is no need to specify BUFSP because VSAM will compute the value of BUFSP needed to accommodate the buffers specified by explicit or default BUFND and BUFNI values.

BUFND = nn

BUFND specifies the number of data component I/O buffers that will be used to access the VSAM data set. This value defaults to two. The default is adequate for random access to the data set by teleprocessing or batch programs.

For purely sequential or start/browse sequential access a greater number of data buffers can lessen processing time significantly. The specific number of data buffers that will optimize sequential I/O processing depends on the number of control intervals contained on a given track. A common starting point to search for an efficient BUFND value for sequential processing, including REPRO backups, assumes 10 control intervals of 4,096 bytes per track on a 3380 disk device, and suggests coding BUFND=12. The BUFND value can be increased to 24, 36, and even higher values until enhanced processing speed is no longer achieved or the virtual memory requirement for buffers becomes unsupportable. Use of up to 255 buffers is possible.[1]

BUFNI = nn

Analogous to BUFND, BUFNI deals with the number of I/O buffers allocated to index control intervals. The default is one, which is sufficient for sequential processing of a data set, including REPRO backup. For random or start/browse access by a batch program a larger value is desirable to allow the highest levels of the data set index component to be held in memory. This avoids repetitive disk I/O into these levels of the index for each access. For this processing BUFNI=5 is often adequate. Index control interval size is normally smaller than data control interval size and this imposes minimal additional memory requirements on the job.

LESS COMMONLY USED AMP PARAMETERS

CROPS

An unusual acronym, CROPS stands for Checkpoint/Restart Options. Four such options are available:

RCK. The default, this causes tests on the data set to be applied when restarting at a checkpoint: the "data-erase" test and the "post-checkpoint modification" test. The data-erase test is valid only for data sets being written.

NCK. The data-erase test is performed when a checkpoint restart is made but no post-checkpoint modification test is performed.

NRE. The post-checkpoint modification is performed when a checkpoint restart is made but no data-erase test is performed.

NRC. Neither the data-erase or the post-checkpoint modification test is made when a checkpoint restart is performed.

The default is commonly suitable but moot unless the checkpoint restart facility is used. Checkpoint restart requires coordinated arrangements for job recovery and is not usually employed. CROPS is not normally coded. See *OS/VS2 MVS Checkpoint/Restart*, GC26-3877 for detailed information on the job restart options of MVS.

OPTCD = IL

OPTCD is a subparameter of AMP solely for the purpose of carrying codes I, L, or IL to the ISAM interface program, a bridge between IDCAMS and the now obsolete ISAM data set organization.

The ISAM interface program allowed programs originally written to access ISAM data sets to access key sequenced VSAM data sets instead, as a conversion aid. Data sets were first converted from ISAM to VSAM in a definition and load process. Older programs could then be operated by revised job streams in which the lengthy DD statement coding for ISAM data sets was replaced by the simpler JCL needed for VSAM access. The interface program intercepted attempts by the unmodified program to use ISAM-specific verbs and made the necessary translation to VSAM actions on behalf of the program until it could be changed to use VSAM-specific verbs like DELETE.

The only function of the AMP OPTCD subparameter lies in the area of records to be deleted. ISAM did not provide a DELETE verb. Records to be regarded as deleted were marked with high-values (hexadecimal FF) in the first byte. If OPTCD = IL is coded in the AMP parameter, it tells the ISAM interface program that if the program being executed reads a record from the data set and is now rewriting it with high-values in the first byte, to delete the record from the VSAM data set.

RECFM

RECFM conveys the format of the records being processed to the ISAM interface program. It should be coded when the VSAM interface is used to allow a program coded for ISAM to access a VSAM data set. The same meanings for F, FB, V, and VB apply here as for the DCB RECFM subparameter. The default is V.

STRNO = n

STRNO specifies the number of request parameter lists or concurrent processes that may access a VSAM data set. The number coded indicates the number of requests that require concurrent data set positioning as with the START verb.

SYNAD = modulename

"Modulename" is the up to eight-character name of an error routine that is to be loaded by the ISAM interface program if a physical or logical error is encountered when the program being executed is accessing a data set. This is relevant only when the ISAM interface program is used.

TRACE

The Generalized Trace Facility, "GTF," can be made to run concurrently with the program being executed by specification of this subparameter. GTF logs information about data set access and provides a program to list the accumulated information, as documented in *OS/VS2 MVS System Programming Library: Service Aids*, IBM publication GC28-0674.

REVIEW QUESTIONS AND (*)EXERCISES

1. What specialized purpose is served by the AMP parameter of the DD statement?

2. Why does the syntax of the AMP parameter resemble that of the EXEC statement PARM, often used to pass a parameter string to a language compiler?

3. In what instance is it necessary to code AMP = 'AMORG' on a DD statement?

4. What corresponds to the MVS data control block in connection with VSAM data sets?

5. The input-output buffer size for non-VSAM data sets can be altered by the DCB BUFL subparameter. What provides the analogous capability for VSAM data set I/O?

6. The number of input-output buffers for non-VSAM data sets can be specified with the DCB BUFNO subparameter. What provides the analogous capability when dealing with VSAM data sets and why is this more complex than with non-VSAM data sets?

7. If the ISAM interface program is being used, how can it be instructed to delete any records that an ISAM-coded program is marking with high-values in the first byte?

*8. A VSAM data set accessed online during business hours is to be backed up to tape using the REPRO command of the IDCAMS utility. Code a representative AMP parameter for the DD statement at which the VSAM data set will be specified, to enhance the processing rate of the job.

*9.   Use the JCL and IDCAMS coding of item 8 in Chapter 17 as a pattern, omitting statements that deal with alternate indexes, to define and load a VSAM data set with only a primary key. Use test data convenient for your purposes and run the job, loading at least 100 records to the VSAM data set. Examine the summary information produced by the LISTCAT command at the bottom of the example IDCAMS control statements and identify the item that describes the buffer space default for access to the data set.

*10. After performing exercise 8 use the JCL of item 9 in Chapter 17 as a pattern to create an IDCAMS REPRO step to copy the VSAM data set to a sequential disk data set. Run the job with and without an AMP parameter that enhances sequential processing speed and note any differences between these in the MVS system allocation/ deallocation reports in terms of memory requirements. (Unless several thousand records are used to load the VSAM data set, processing speed enhancement will most likely not be detectable.)

NOTE

1.   For specific formulas to determine the optimal number of data and index buffers, see *Practical VSAM for Todays Programmers*, James G. Janossy and Richard E. Guzik, John Wiley and Sons, Inc., 1987.

=== 12 ===

SYSOUT: Printed Output

SYSOUT is the generalized print handling mechanism of MVS. SYSOUT is a parameter of the DD statement, as are DSN, UNIT, DISP, DCB, and others. But SYSOUT is relevant only to print and its use is mutually exclusive to many other DD statement parameters. More DD statement parameters that deal with print include BURST, CHARS, COPIES, DEST, FCB, FLASH, OUTLIM, OUTPUT, and UCS and can be present only when SYSOUT is coded; they modify the way print is handled. In a parody of Orwell's *Animal Farm*, "all DD parameters are created equal, but some are more equal than others."

SYSOUT buffers print output between a job and the printer. Material destined to be printed is "handed over" to SYSOUT, one printline at a time. SYSOUT stores the lines and arranges to funnel them through to the one or more print output devices attached to the computer. SYSOUT

exists to allow several jobs to output printlines at the same time without
having each job attached to a separate printer. In order to function
SYSOUT requires disk storage space for its own use. This space is referred to as the "system spool" and printlines residing in it awaiting
print are said to be "queued for print." You might think of SYSOUT in
the same light as a software or hardware print buffer on a microcomputer
but it is orders of magnitude more capable and competent than such a
device.

MAINFRAME PRINT VERSUS ASCII PRINT

A significant difference between the IBM mainframe environment and
the ASCII minicomputer and microcomputer world lies in the nature
of print image data—printlines. In the ASCII world a line of data to be
printed is stored in text file format, where the line contains only the
characters to be printed, including control characters such as horizontal
tabs. A carriage return and line feed are found after the last printable
character in each line. These line-delimiting control characters direct
the printer to move to the left margin of the paper and the printer to
advance the paper after a line has been printed. Text file lines or "stream
file" data can be displayed on a screen as well as printed because the
carriage-control characters are handled in the same manner on both types
of output device and produce the same text formatting effects.

IBM mainframe print output is not in text file format. It is analogous
to punched cards, except that printlines may carry 132 or more bytes
of data, not just 80. Like the punched card, blanks are present for each
unprinted position; there is no such thing as a horizontal tab character.
The entire printline is transmitted to the printer, character for character.
A "vertical tab" is present in the IBM mainframe printing arrangement.
This role is performed by the carriage control byte, which is the first
byte in any line of print. Printlines are different from data records because of the carriage control byte; this byte *does not* produce the appropriate vertical tabbing on mainframe video terminals, which simply
display it.

THE MVS PRINT SPOOL

The spool is a large community buffering device that resides between
programs of all types and the printers configured with the system. Pic-
tured as simply as possible, it is a heap of printline images in which
each printline is identified by nonprinting prefacing information attached to it to allow the images to be assembled into the intended print
order by job and DDname. Although this description may seem chaotic,

the spool is really very orderly; it functions superbly to allow myriad outputs to be directed to far fewer printing devices.

The spool is housed as a disk data set and is typically allocated an entire disk pack. As various jobs executing on the system direct output to SYSOUT, SYSOUT appends identifying information to the lines of the print image. Output is identified not only by the job, step, and DDname that produced it but also by a *print class*. Print class has nothing to do with *job class*, a parameter of the job card discussed in Appendix A. The print class is, in effect, a subdivision of the print spool. By having print segregated into classes it is possible to treat the types of print differently and to withhold printing some items from the spool until it is desirable to print them.[1]

The "A" in the typical SYSOUT = A specification means "place this print output into the spool in print class A." The A in the job card parameter MSGCLASS = A is also stating that certain print is to go into print class A; in this case it is the job log for the run and the allocation/ deallocation reports. By tradition, print class A represents ordinary "no special treatment required" paper print. Print class B is the established output class for punched output. If a job is outputting information with record lengths up to 80 bytes and you want to have MVS punch it out on cards, the output can be sent to SYSOUT = B.

A third print class ordinarily covered by convention is "X." This class is called the "hold queue" and output directed to it is called "held output;" it is not printed automatically. Held output assumed a significance when TSO became available as a programming tool in the 1970s because it is possible to use TSO's 3.8 function or the Spool Display and Search Facility, or "SDSF," to view spool contents.[2] By directing the output of a compile or program to SYSOUT = X the output remains on the spool and can be viewed.

Print Class: How Output Leaves the Spool

Printline image output remains on the spool until picked off and directed to a printer. The software that picks material from the spool and prints it is called an "output writer." Several output writers may be running at once. These tasks run at the direction of the computer operator and are not visible to applications programming personnel or end users.

An output writer is directed by the console operator to pick certain print classes off the spool and print them. It is possible that at a given time no output writer will be picking off and printing some print classes. If a mistake is made in coding the SYSOUT parameter, and a little-used or nonexistent print class is specified, the output may sit on the spool indefinitely. It can, however, be requeued by the console operator to another print class.

In addition to A, B, and X other print classes may be employed by installations that use laser printers like the IBM 3800 printing subsystem or the Xerox 9700 family. Some of this equipment can produce two-sided printing automatically. The default printing mode may be set by the installation as two-sided to take advantage of this economy for most print. One-sided print is then assigned a special print class such as "S" which gives an appropriately tailored output writer the means of handling the bulk of print images in a two-sided manner while allowing outputs that must remain one-side printed to be handled by an output writer tailored for that type of print.

Print class is a single position code and can be any letter or number. Installations may decide on other print class identifiers than A, B, and X and arrange for output writers to handle them in different ways. A firm or school with several programmer groups or computer labs at a number of geographical locations can establish a print class for each location. People submitting jobs can then indicate, via the print class, the location at which the print is to appear. The output writers assigned to handle each print class are tailored to direct print to the communication line for the location associated with the print class.

Multiple Simultaneous Print Outputs

Personnel who have worked with microcomputers or with low-horse-power minis envision programs that will generate one printed output at a time. With the foregoing information about MVS output spool operation it should be clear that *there is no artificial limit, within practicality, to the number of print outputs that a given program can generate.*

Whether a program generates one print output or a dozen, each is handled in the same way. In a COBOL program that writes many print outputs each output is accorded its own SELECT/ASSIGN statement and its own file description. In a FORTRAN program each print output is assigned to a different unit number and emerges from the program at a different DDname in JCL. Each DDname print output is turned over to the SYSOUT printing mechanism, usually, but not necessarily, to the same print class. For example, if a COBOL program outputs two user reports and a status report, its SELECT/ASSIGN statements might appear as:

```
SELECT REPORT1-FILE    ASSIGN TO UT-S-P165REP1.
SELECT REPORT2-FILE    ASSIGN TO UT-S-P165REP2.
SELECT STATREPT-FILE   ASSIGN TO UT-S-P165STAT.
```

The relevant portion of the JCL executing the program might appear as

```
//P165REP1   DD SYSOUT=A
//P165REP2   DD SYSOUT=A
//P165STAT   DD SYSOUT=A
```

and each report would simply be assigned to SYSOUT. If SYSOUT is coded as SYSOUT = *, the print class is taken from the MSGCLASS parameter of the JOB statement, which makes it easier to change the print classes of all outputs with one action. This feature is most often used by programmers testing new job streams.

SYSOUT does a good job of managing print output, so good that the other way of handling print—sending printline records directly to a printer by coding its hardware address or model number with the UNIT parameter—is rarely permitted. Here are some salient facts about SYSOUT and mainframe print:

- SYSOUT can accept lines longer than a printer can handle. Excess length lines on the spool can be viewed by the TSO 3.8 outlist function or SDSF. TSO 3.8 wraps around at the 134th print position, whereas SDSF does not. The length of line actually printed is limited by the printing device.

- Impact printers are generally limited to 132 printable positions, whereas laser printers have an upper limit as high as 200 or more printable positions per line. Mainframe printers generally drop the excess positions of printlines sent to them and, unlike microcomputer printers, do not wrap around an excessively long printline.

- If a given job step produces more than one print output, the order in which the reports are printed is *the order in which the DD statements for the job step appear in JCL.* You can choose whatever print output you wish to appear first in a stack of reports just by arranging the DD statements for the outputs in that order in the JCL, regardless of the sequence in which the program writes the reports.

- Several parameters can follow SYSOUT on the DD statement to indicate that the printlines being output have carriage control information in the first byte, that a specific character set or print chain is to be used for the output, to produce multiple copies of the output, to route print to a remote printer, to limit the number of lines of print output allowed, and to issue special print formats to IBM compatible printers.

SYSOUT PARAMETER LONG FORM

The common SYSOUT = A or SYSOUT = * coding of the SYSOUT parameter is actually the short form of the parameter. Its long form conveys the fact that it really has three positional subparameters:

```
SYSOUT = ( print-class, writer-name, form-id/code-id )
```

Print-class identifies the figurative category or subunit of the spool into which the print image output will be directed. It has a bearing on when, how, and where the print will be reduced to paper by the action of an output writer routine.

```
SYSOUT = ( print-class, writer-name, form-id/code-id )
```

If an output writer picking a given print class is not operative, nothing in that print class will print. By definition, no output writer is normally set to pick material from the held output print class X.

Print-class is a one-position code that customarily follows the pattern that A denotes "no special requirement" printing on an installation-standard plain paper. Print class B by tradition is associated with punched card output. Print class X is the customary held class that remains on the spool for viewing via TSO's 3.8 and SDSF functions. A given installation may establish other print classes according to local requirements.

Writer-name Subparameter

```
SYSOUT = ( print-class, writer-name, form-id/code-id )
```

Writer-name identifies a program similar to an output writer but one that is external to the SYSOUT mechanism. When a writer-name is specified, the name must represent a member within SYS1.LINKLIB or another default load module library on the system. When this SYSOUT specification is executed, the named program is loaded by MVS and used to process the output rather than one of the customary output writers.

One special output writer provided by MVS and MVS/XA is called INTRDR, or "internal reader." When output is directed in this manner

```
SYSOUT=(A,INTRDR)
```

the program INTRDR is given control to remove the material from the spool and process it. To what does INTRDR feed the material? To the input queue, another part of the system spooling mechanism, also known as the "card hopper." INTRDR allows a program to form or copy JCL statements, complete with a job card, and to submit them for execution as if the material were being read in via the system input hopper on punched cards or via the TSO SUBMIT command. This is useful in the production environment when it is necessary to provide the means of initiating a job, yet security requirements dictate that it is not desirable to provide access to the complete JCL for the run. The user is provided with and submits only the small amount of JCL needed to invoke a job that executes a utility like IEBGENER to copy the execution JCL from a data set into the internal reader.

There is little need in the majority of cases for customized output writers and, aside from the occasional use of INTRDR, you will probably not see a writer-name coded in SYSOUT. When writer-name is not coded but the third subparameter is, the comma that follows writer-name is coded.

Form-id/code-id Subparameter

```
SYSOUT = ( print-class, writer-name, form-id/code id )
```

Form-id may be specified in the third positional subparameter slot. It is a name that may be one to four characters long. The value placed here is provided to the computer console operator in what is commonly called the "print zone" near the impact printer when the output is about to be printed, so that the necessary custom form may be mounted on the printer. For certain laser printers that store forms images electronically and print them at the same time program-supplied form print occurs the printer responds automatically to the form-id.

Code-id is a value similar to form-id. However, it represents a code name for an /*OUTPUT statement that must be included in the JCL immediately after the job card. /*OUTPUT is an "appendage" statement that was created for JCL when it became apparent that supplying parameters to the 3800 printing subsystem laser printer required more coding than could conveniently be tacked on to every DD statement carrying a SYSOUT parameter. If a SYSOUT is coded in the form

```
DD  SYSOUT=(A,,T890)
```

the JCL has to contain a statement similar to the following immediately after the job card

```
/*OUTPUT T890 . . . . .
```

or T890 will be regarded as a form-id. If an /*OUTPUT statement is coded, it potentially carries many items of print specification for various printing devices. The name following /*OUTPUT can be any four characters or numbers, starting with a letter; T890 is an arbitrary example here. /*OUTPUT provides several DD statements that carry the SYSOUT parameter with the ability to refer to one perhaps complicated definition of a printing requirement. /*OUTPUT has been superseded by an even more powerful capability called "OUTPUT JCL" that allows processing of portions of print to different printers in different formats. Both /*OUTPUT and OUTPUT JCL are beyond the scope of work most programmers encounter. Installations that make use of these facilities provide documentation on local standards.

REMOTE JOB ENTRY STATION PRINT

Print output may be routed to different destinations. Every printer station configured with a mainframe has a unique identifier assigned to it that can be specified with the DEST parameter or the /*ROUTE job parameter statement. Mainframe systems, themselves, can be tied together into a network, in which case each remote device is associated with a node name as well as its unique identifier.

Printer work stations are usually "remote job entry" stations or RJEs. They are known as "3780" units because this is the most recent IBM model of a device that functions as an RJE; the 3780 superseded the 2780 in the 1970s. RJEs are typically large devices that combine a card reader with a high-speed line printer. The communication protocol that RJEs use is one of the two standard communication arrangements offered by the mainframe, the other being "3270" interactive communication. The 3270 protocol is used by terminal devices that communicate with TSO or a teleprocessing monitor such as CICS.

The RJE station identifier is a number from 1 to 1000; the entry and print station local to the computer itself is remote 0, synonymous with the identifier "LOCAL." The designation for stations can take any of the following forms:

```
REMOTEnn
RMTnn
Rnn
```

Therefore an RJE identified as number 17 can be indicated as REMOTE17, RMT17, or simply R17; REMOTE0, RMT0, R0, or LOCAL refer to the printer local to the computer itself. The word "local" can be confusing because what is local in the colloquial sense to an RJE user is not local to the mainframe. The mainframe understands and abides by itself alone as the center of the universe and "locality." Once assigned, remote printer identifiers are not usually changed. Unless otherwise specified in an installation, SYSOUT = A will default to printing items local to the mainframe.

DEST: Selective Routing

It is possible to use the RJE remote number designator in two ways to tailor the destination of print: with a scalpel and with an axe. The scalpel allows routing of individual print outputs to different stations with DEST coded on individual SYSOUT DD statements. The axe uses one statement, /*ROUTE, at the top of the job to send all outputs not otherwise indicated for routing to a given destination. The two facilities can be used together.

Suppose three reports are emerging at a job step. One is to print local to the computer. The second is to print at a remote job entry point located some distance away, identified as remote 5. The third is to print at a microcomputer that emulates an RJE, identified as remote 14 located hundred of miles distant.[3] The JCL for the job step can be coded as:

```
//BT3766U1   DD   SYSOUT=A,DEST=LOCAL
//BT3766U2   DD   SYSOUT=A,DEST=R5
//BT3766U3   DD   SYSOUT=A,DEST=R14
```

In this case print class A is specified because among all print classes it is the most likely to have an active output writer. In response to the coding shown MVS takes the printlines as they are output to it by an output writer and directs each of them to the appropriate communication path.

/*ROUTE: Overall Output Routing

The axe or bulk approach to routing output affects all print outputs of a job *that lack explicit DEST parameters*; if any DEST parameters are specified they are handled as the individual DEST directs. This method of overall print output routing uses a statement of the form

```
/*ROUTE PRINT R15
```

and it follows the JOB statement immediately. It is somewhat unusual, beginning with a slash and an asterisk rather than two slashes; it is technically not a JCL statement but one of several job entry subsystem control statements.[4] The R15 in this example can be any legitimate RJE station identifier. Punched output can also be routed in this manner by using the word PUNCH instead of PRINT but it is very nearly an extinct specification. Output routed with /*ROUTE but placed in the print class X hold queue can be viewed by the TSO 3.8 outlist function as usual; the routing applies when and if the output is requeued to a print class that prints using the TSO 3.8 screen or SDSF.

/*JOBPARM for Multiple Copies

/*JOBPARM COPIES = nnn can be used to produce nnn copies of all print items from the job, including the system allocation/deallocation reports. The nnn can be a number from 1 to 255. When used after a top-of-job /*ROUTE PRINT statement, it causes nnn copies of all job print outputs to be directed to the specified remote printer. If directed to the held printout class, SYSOUT = X, and the MSGCLASS parameter of the JOB statement is also the held class, /*JOBPARM is ignored and only one copy is ultimately printed if the print is requeued. The COPIES parameter, discussed below, does not suffer from this limitation.

SPECIAL DD PARAMETERS USED WITH SYSOUT

BURST: Burst Output into Separate Sheets

BURST is a one-position specification that can take on the value of Y or N; N is the default. It is valid only for the IBM 3800 printing subsystem, a large laser printer. Continuous form paper is burst into separate sheets in the subsystem if BURST = Y is coded; if BURST = N is coded or BURST is omitted, continuous form paper is not separated. An example is

```
//BT3768U1    DD   SYSOUT=A,BURST=Y
```

CHARS: Character Set

The IBM 3800 printing subsystem accepts the CHARS parameter to specify one to four table names, indicating character sets to be used for printing. The name of a given character table can be one to four alphanumeric or national symbols. If one character set is coded, the syntax is:

```
//BT3768U2    DD   SYSOUT=A,CHARS=HV12
```

If several character table names are coded, the syntax is

```
//BT3768U2    DD   SYSOUT=A,CHARS=(HV12,PP10,LG10,OCRB)
```

and the optional services specification OPTCD=J is coded on the DCB parameter; if more than one character table name is coded, printline records must have two prefacing bytes of carriage control. The first is the standard carriage control byte that dictates the degree of vertical tabbing to be accorded before printing the line. The second byte must carry the number 0, 1, 2, or 3 to indicate the entry in the CHARS parameter coding that represents the character set table to be used in printing the line. The first entry in the larger example, HV12, corresponds to a second control byte value of 0. CHARS=DUMP can be coded on //SYSUDUMP and //SYSABEND DD statements to request a special IBM 3800 printing subsystem 204 character per line format suitable for memory dumps, under JES3 only.

Character tables are stored as members in a partitioned data set named SYS1.IMAGELIB. All character table names start with "XTB1" and the one to four character name by which they are referenced in a CHARS specification is really the last four positions of the full member name.

COPIES: Multiple Copies of Print

The default mode of operation for the SYSOUT print mechanism is to print one copy of a given print output from the spool and then delete the item from the spool. Using the COPIES parameter, it is possible to have SYSOUT print 1 to 255 copies of the printlines for an item from the spool before deleting them. COPIES can be coded with or without other parameters:

```
//BT3766U1    DD    SYSOUT=A,COPIES=3
//BT3766U2    DD    SYSOUT=A,DEST=R5,COPIES=6
```

Each copy of the output receives its own MVS-generated job separator pages. If the output is small—a page or two—COPIES will often generate more separator pages than actual desired output.

The COPIES parameter can be coded in a more complex manner in a form such as

```
//BT3766U4    DD    SYSOUT=A,COPIES=(7,(2,5,4))
```

but this is relevant only to an installation that uses as one of its printing devices the IBM 3800 printing subsystem. When the device to which this output is written is not the IBM 3800, the "7" in the foregoing specification acts like the 7 in a COPIES=7 and the remaining coding is ignored. When the output device is an IBM 3800, the first specification is ignored and the second part of the COPIES coding comes into play. In this case three groups of output will be printed, represented by the numbers coded in the nested parenthesis. The sum of the number values—2,5,4 or 11, in this case—indicates how many copies of each page will be printed in each "output group." Up to eight output groups can be coded on this statement. The example has three output groups; three separate piles of paper output are involved. The first of the three groups will have two copies of each page printed, the second will have five copies of each page printed, and the last will have four copies of each page printed. Use of the COPIES output group specification is not common.

FCB: Forms Control Buffer

```
FCB= ( fcb-name, operator-action )
```

On some printers physical carriage-control tapes have been replaced by an electronic "forms control buffer." The image of a carriage control tape, stored as a member in a partitioned data set called SYS1.IMAGELIB, is fed into this buffer automatically at print time to govern certain print characteristics. Names of FCB members in SYS1.IMAGELIB may all start with "FCB2" or "FCB3" and the fcb-name coded in JCL consists of only the last four characters, such as "F12A." When this feature is available in an installation, the appropriate electronic carriage-control tape can be sent to the printer via coding such as

```
//BT3722U2  DD  SYSOUT=A,FCB=F12A
```

using the FCB parameter. IBM supplies three standard FCB images: STD1 that defines six lines per inch printing for paper 8½ inch high, STD2 for six lines per inch printing for paper 11 inch high—standard computer paper—and STD3 for eight lines per inch compact dump printing.

If the printer is equipped to handle an FCB, but FCB is not coded, MVS loads the printer with whatever FCB image has been defined by the installation as a default. If FCB is coded but the printer is not capable of handling it, MVS provides a message to the operator to ask that a carriage-control tape of the fcb-name name be mounted.

Operator-action is an optional specification. ALIGN specified here produces a prompt to the operator which asks that form alignment be checked before printing. VERIFY specified here causes MVS to send the operator a message to check the printer's chain or train printing elements to confirm that the appropriate font is in place.

The FCB parameter is closely associated with the IBM 3800, a large high-speed laser printing device, and IBM's newer post-1403 impact printers. Additional information on specialized device-specific printer parameters can be found in the *IBM 3800 Printing Subsystem Programmer's Guide*, GC26-3846, and in an installation's locally developed documentation.

FLASH: Forms Overlay

```
FLASH=( overlay-name, count )
```

Applicable only to the IBM 3800 printing subsystem, FLASH causes a message to be sent to the operator to insert a photographic forms overlay frame in the printer. The 3800 can flash or expose the laser printer drum with this output image to place the image and the print itself on the paper at the same time. MVS, however, cannot insure that the operator mounted the form overlay image requested and it is possible for an incorrect image to be used. Photographic forms images have been superseded by electronically defined and stored form images.

"Overlay-name" is a four-character identifier. Each overlay image carries a unique identifier, such as "R407" or "AK62." The optional "count" subparameter makes it is possible to produce multiple copies of output but to apply the overlay image only to some of the copies. If the COPIES parameter is specified as a value larger than the FLASH count subparameter, only the "count" number of copies will be produced with the overlay; it will not be applied to the remainder. Typical syntax for the FLASH parameter is:

```
//BT3754U2   DD  SYSOUT=A,
//  COPIES=4,
//  FLASH=(R407,3)
```

A simpler example is:

```
//BT3717U1  DD  SYSOUT=A,FLASH=AK62
```

The count specification can be 0 to 255. If not coded, it defaults to 255 and the form overlay is applied to all copies. Selective flashing and non-flashing of certain copies does not require operator intervention, but it is a little used capability.

OUTLIM: Limiting the Quantity of Print

It is desirable for many types of jobs to place a ceiling on the amount of print that the job or a given DD statement can produce, as a safety measure. Test jobs that execute programs newly developed or modified are the best examples. A small error that causes a loop involving a WRITE statement can quickly generate enormous amounts of print output. The danger in this occurrence is more than just the potential waste of paper. It is possible for a job run wild to generate enough printline output to degrade spool operation seriously or to fill the spool data set completely.

If the spool fills up, the entire computer system must be stopped to resolve the situation.

The OUTLIM parameter takes the form OUTLIM = n and an example is

```
//BT3766U1   DD   SYSOUT=A,COPIES=3,OUTLIM=1000
```

where the OUTLIM value can range from 1 to 16,777,215 coded without commas. If the output limit is reached, the job is terminated with a brief message; the lines already output to the spool remain there and are printed.

OUTLIM is a limit of records written to the spool, not of lines taken from the spool and printed. If COPIES is coded for a job that ends prematurely because it has reached an OUTLIM limit, multiple copies of the partial output are generated. OUTLIM is a limit of logical records written to the spool and each printline is treated as a record. Thus it is still possible to consume large quantities of paper even with a relatively low OUTLIM limit if many of the lines being output have a page eject carriage control character of "1" in the first byte. Student or programmer routines that inadvertently involve page heading generation logic within a loop can create large quantities of output even if the OUTLIM for a report has been set to a value of only a few thousand lines.

Potential problems with the quantity of print output from programs caused by coding errors is one reason that installations often establish rigid guidelines for the logic in programs that write output and trigger page ejects. These mundane aspects of program coding are no place to reinvent the wheel; once an installation has well functioning standard logic modules in place for output writing their use is enforced.[5]

UCS: Character Set Specification

```
UCS=( character-set, FOLD, VERIFY )
```

Certain IBM printers and some made by third parties can automatically respond to a JCL-coded specification to use a certain character set for a print job. Other printer models cannot automatically make use of a specially indicated character set but can at least check to see what character print train is mounted and ask the operator to mount the one wanted if it is not on the printer. The IBM 3800 printing subsystem is of the first variety; it can obtain the image of the character set desired from SYS1.IMAGELIB. On the other hand, the 3211 impact printer requires operator intervention to mount a print chain if it is different from that already in place.

The specification for the print character set is the UCS parameter, for "universal character set:"

```
DD   SYSOUT=A,UCS=SN
```

Depending on the printer and local presence of one print chain font or another, as many as 12 character sets may be available as options, each recognizable by a one to four position identifier. The CHARS parameter also affects the character set used by the IBM 3800 laser printer and overrides the UCS parameter if it also is coded. Additional information on these device-specific parameters is found in the *IBM 3800 Printing Subsystem Programmer's Guide*, GC26-3846.

Common IBM print chain identifiers are:

```
1403   3211
  AN    A11    EBCDIC (48 character set)
  HN    H11    EBCDIC (full character set)
  --    G11    ASCII
  PN    P11    Alphanumeric (PL/I)
  TN    T11    Text printing
  SN    --     Text printing
```

UCS can be coded with FCB if it is necessary to specify a character set and also to load the printer with an electronically stored carriage control tape image. UCS is used sparingly with impact printers because of the delays introduced by changing the printing element. If at all possible, application design is generally biased against reliance on special print chains.

The optional FOLD subparameter does not deal with paper processing as it may appear; instead it causes printers that can respond to it to print lower case letters in upper case. The optional VERIFY subparameter requires the operator to confirm that the correct print chain or train is in use.

SEQUENTIAL UPDATE JOB STREAM WITH REPORT REPRINT

Reprint Capability for Production Job Streams

There is no reason that the printline records output by a program need to be handed over to SYSOUT immediately on generation. This is a convenience and has been employed up to this point in the test sequential update job stream to minimize complexity. The printlines generated by a program like FSBT3708 at DDname //BT3708U1 are shown in Figures 3.4, 6.1 and 10.5 output as

```
//BT3708U1   DD   SYSOUT=*
```

or

```
//BT3708U1   DD   SYSOUT=A
```

but they can instead be output and stored on disk as shown in Figure 12.1. This is a revision of our example sequential update job stream. We again upgrade it by modifying the job stream to store its end-user print outputs in printline form to allow reports to be reprinted if necessary.

In //STEPB of the revised job stream we see the update report emerging at //BT3708U1 and being placed into a disk data set. The convention shown here for the name of the printline data set is a common one. The higher level qualifiers of this name follow the installation convention of identifying the major system and application with which the data set is associated. The last part of the printline data set is the same as the DDname. For a report output stored on disk or tape this is often the handiest way to identify the contents of the data set meaningfully if the DDname itself is unique. The data set name, however, could be anything acceptable to MVS and local conventions.

The revised method for handling the output of printlines results in their being written out to disk as cataloged data sets. The record format indicates that the records have a fixed length and that the first byte contains carriage control information. The 133-byte printlines are blocked with 9,044 characters per block, a blocking factor of 68.[6] The SPACE requested here for the printline data set allows 45 blocks of data to be stored, or just over 3,000 records, in a primary space allocation. If necessary, as many as 15 secondary allocations of 20 blocks each are also requested. The space figures are an estimate. It will take just under one block to store the 60 or so lines of a typical report page, and for this run it is estimated that a 50-page report is typical. RLSE will release unused disk space when the job step concludes.

The print step in Figure 12.1 uses IEBGENER to print report printlines from the three major reporting points in the job stream. IEBGENER is a vintage utility that is part of MVS. IEBGENER, or "GENER" for short, can accept control card input at the DDname //SYSIN to tell it to reformat fields within records, to fill fields with specified literal characters, or to change the representation of fields from zoned decimal (PIC 9) to packed decimal (PIC 9 COMP-3) and vice versa, as illustrated in item 13 in Chapter 17. But GENER can also be executed without supplying control cards at //SYSIN, in which case //SYSIN is coded as DD DUMMY and the utility simply copies the input file from //SYSUT1 to //SYSUT2.

At //SYSUT1 in the IEBGENER step we concatenate the printline data sets for the three reports into the copy process. MVS will automatically read one concatenated data set after another in sequence and make it appear to the program being executed that the input is all coming from

```
//FSBT686A  JOB AK00TEST,'DP2-JANOSSY',CLASS=T,MSGCLASS=X,
//  MSGLEVEL=(1,1),NOTIFY=BT05686
//*
//*     TEST RUN OF SEQUENTIAL UPDATE FSBT3708 -- VER 4B
//*     STILL FOR TESTING, OLD MF IS ALWAYS ".TELMAST"
//*     BUT OLD AND NEW MASTER FILES ARE NOW TAPE, AND
//*     INPUT IS ON A 1600 BPI NON-LABELED TAPE KEYED ON
//*     AN ASCII-BASED DATA ENTRY SYSTEM OR MINI.
//*
//*     PRINT OUTPUT IS NOW DIRECTED TO DATA SETS TO MAKE
//*     REPRINT POSSIBLE, AND IS PRINTED AT END OF JOB
//*
//*     THIS JCL = BT05686.SOURCE.CNTL(BT3708V4)
//*
//************************************************************
//*                                                          *
//*     DELETE EXISTING UPDATED DATA SET          DEL        *
//*                                                          *
//************************************************************
//DELSTEP  EXEC  PGM=IEFBR14
//DEL1       DD  DSN=AK00.C99.TELMAST.UPDATED,
//  UNIT=(TAPE,,DEFER),
//  DISP=(MOD,DELETE)
//DEL2       DD  DSN=AK00.C99.BT3708U1,
//  UNIT=SYSDA,
//  DISP=(MOD,DELETE),
//  SPACE=(TRK,0)
//DEL3       DD  DSN=AK00.C99.BT3719U1,
//  UNIT=SYSDA,
//  DISP=(MOD,DELETE),
//  SPACE=(TRK,0)
//DEL4       DD  DSN=AK00.C99.BT3719U2,
//  UNIT=SYSDA,
//  DISP=(MOD,DELETE),
//  SPACE=(TRK,0)
//*
//************************************************************
//*                                                          *
//*     SORT TRANS FILE                           A          *
//*                                                          *
//************************************************************
//STEPA    EXEC  PGM=SORT
//SORTLIB    DD  DSN=SYS1.SORTLIB,
//  DISP=SHR
//*
//SORTIN     DD  DSN=AK00.C99.TRANSIN,
//  UNIT=(TAPE,,DEFER),
//  DISP=(OLD,KEEP),
//  DCB=(RECFM=FB,LRECL=71,BLKSIZE=1420,DEN=3,OPTCD=Q),
//  VOL=SER=HXR452,
//  LABEL=(1,NL,EXPDT=98000)                  'EXPDT ONLY FOR
//*                                           'UCC-1 TMS
//SORTOUT    DD  DSN=&&TRANSORT,
//  UNIT=SYSDA,
//  DISP=(NEW,PASS,DELETE),
//  DCB=(RECFM=FB,LRECL=71,BLKSIZE=6177),
//  SPACE=(6177,(32,7),RLSE)                  '2800 TRANS
//SYSOUT     DD  SYSOUT=*
//SYSUDUMP   DD  SYSOUT=*
//SORTWK01   DD  UNIT=SYSDA,SPACE=(CYL,2,,CONTIG)
//SORTWK02   DD  UNIT=SYSDA,SPACE=(CYL,2,,CONTIG)
//SYSIN      DD  *
   SORT FIELDS=(1,4,CH,A,9,2,CH,A,5,4,CH,A,14,1,CH,D)
/*
//*
//************************************************************
//*                                                          *
//*     UPDATE MASTER FILE                         B         *
//*                                                          *
//************************************************************
//STEPB    EXEC  PGM=FSBT3708,REGION=2048K
//STEPLIB    DD  DSN=BT05686.TEST.LOADMODS,
//  DISP=SHR
```

FIGURE 12.1. Revised sequential update job stream using stored printlines and IEBGENER print step

215

```
//BT3708E1    DD   DSN=&&TRANSORT,
//   DISP=(OLD,DELETE)
//BT3708E2    DD   DSN=AK00.C99.TELMAST,
//   UNIT=(TAPE,,DEFER),
//   DISP=(OLD,KEEP)
//BT3708E3    DD   DSN=AK00.C99.AREAREF,
//   DISP=SHR
//BT3708U1    DD   DSN=AK00.C99.BT3708U1,
//   UNIT=SYSDA,
//   DISP=(NEW,CATLG,DELETE),
//   DCB=(RECFM=FBA,LRECL=133,BLKSIZE=9044),
//   SPACE=(9044,(45,20),RLSE)
//*
//BT3708U2    DD   DSN=AK00.C99.TELMAST.UPDATED,
//   UNIT=(TAPE,,DEFER),
//   DISP=(NEW,CATLG,DELETE),
//   DCB=(RECFM=FB,LRECL=314,BLKSIZE=32656),
//   LABEL=RETPD=90
//*
//BT3708U3    DD   DSN=&&TRANSFIN,
//   UNIT=SYSDA,
//   DISP=(NEW,PASS,DELETE),
//   DCB=(RECFM=FB,LRECL=102,BLKSIZE=6222),    '2800 TRANS
//   SPACE=(6222,(46,9),RLSE)
//SYSOUT      DD   SYSOUT=*
//SYSUDUMP    DD   SYSOUT=*
//***********************************************************
//*                                                         *
//*       PRODUCE TRAN REPORT (INTERNAL SORT)           C   *
//*                                                         *
//***********************************************************
//STEPC     EXEC  PGM=FSBT3719,REGION=2048K
//STEPLIB     DD   DSN=BT05686.TEST.LOADMODS,
//   DISP=SHR
//SORTLIB     DD   DSN=SYS1.SORTLIB,
//   DISP=SHR
//BT3719E1    DD   DSN=&&TRANSFIN,
//   DISP=(OLD,DELETE)
//BT3719U1    DD   DSN=AK00.C99.BT3719U1,
//   UNIT=SYSDA,
//   DISP=(NEW,CATLG,DELETE),
//   DCB=(RECFM=FBA,LRECL=133,BLKSIZE=9044),
//   SPACE=(9044,(45,20),RLSE)
//BT3719U2    DD   DSN=AK00.C99.BT3719U2,
//   UNIT=SYSDA,
//   DISP=(NEW,CATLG,DELETE),
//   DCB=(RECFM=FBA,LRECL=133,BLKSIZE=9044),
//   SPACE=(9044,(45,20),RLSE)
//SORTWK01    DD   UNIT=SYSDA,SPACE=(CYL,2,,CONTIG)
//SORTWK02    DD   UNIT=SYSDA,SPACE=(CYL,2,,CONTIG)
//BT3719SM    DD   SYSOUT=*
//SYSOUT      DD   SYSOUT=*
//SYSUDUMP    DD   SYSOUT=*
//*
//***********************************************************
//*                                                         *
//*     PRINT THE REPORT OUTPUTS                        D   *
//*                                                         *
//***********************************************************
//STEPD     EXEC  PGM=IEBGENER
//SYSUT1      DD   DSN=AK00.C99.BT3708U1,DISP=SHR
//            DD   DSN=AK00.C99.BT3719U1,DISP=SHR
//            DD   DSN=AK00.C99.BT3719U2,DISP=SHR
//SYSUT2      DD   SYSOUT=A,
//   DCB=(RECFM=FBA,LRECL=133,BLKSIZE=9044)
//SYSIN       DD   DUMMY
//SYSPRINT    DD   SYSOUT=*
//SYSUDUMP    DD   SYSOUT=*
//
```

FIGURE 12.1. (con't.)

one file. //SYSUT2 is IEBGENER's output spigot. Here we see the now-familiar SYSOUT = A, followed by DCB coding to tell the printing device that each record being supplied to it via the spool contains carriage control information in the first byte.[7]

The ability of a report reprint mechanism is limited in coverage to the number of cycles of print images retained. As we explore in Chapter 13, generation data groups or GDGs provide the capability to store successive generations of data sets named in the same way and are a natural support mechanism for print image data sets. A production MVS job stream most often employs GDG storage for printline data sets as well as for master files and other data sets created on a cyclical basis.

When RECFM = FBA Is Needed

When a program outputs information to a DDname and it is fed to SYSOUT, how does SYSOUT know that the first byte of each record contains carriage control information? *Unless the printing device is aware of this fact, it defaults to printing each line on the next available line, single spaced.*

COBOL programs that write printlines can make use of the WRITE verb with the ADVANCING option. ADVANCING exists in COBOL only to be used with printline output. When it is used—and almost all print output does so—COBOL marks the record format of the output with the RECFM adjective of "A" as in "FBA." This conveys to the printing device that ANSI standard carriage control information is carried in the first byte of each record.

It is possible for a COBOL program to output printlines to a DDname without ever having used the AFTER ADVANCING option. It is also possible for printlines stored on disk or tape to be copied to SYSOUT by a utility like IEBGENER. In such cases the printing device will assume its default mode of operation and advance a single space before printing each record. Unless the printing device is informed that the records it is being given carry carriage control information in the first byte that byte will not be used to control vertical tabbing, it will be printed. To overcome this problem we need to supply the DCB parameter, at least in its short form, with the RECFM subparameter coded. The format of the SYSOUT statement with this specification is

```
//BT3752U1    DD   SYSOUT=A,
// DCB=RECFM=FBA
```

without parentheses unless, in addition to RECFM, other subparameters are coded.

The "F" in the "FBA" indicates that the records emerging from the DDname are fixed length. The "B" indicates that the records are blocked.

Because this DCB is not for the spool, but for the ultimate printing device, it has no effect on the way that the spool stores the records given to it. The "A" in the "FBA" is the important item in this specification; it means that the first byte of each record contains carriage control information and it tells the printing device, via SYSOUT as the messenger, to use this byte to print the line. When it is necessary to specify UCS, FCB, DEST, and perhaps COPIES, all of it can be done in combination:

```
//BT3752U1    DD   SYSOUT=A,
//   COPIES=6,
//   DEST=R5,
//   FCB=(F12A,,VERIFY),
//   UCS=(SN,,VERIFY),
//   DCB=RECFM=FBA
```

Selective Reprint

On occasion it is necessary not only to provide the ability to store print-line images for later reduction to paper but also to allow an end user to reprint selectively from this repository of stored printlines. This may occur when the print output from a large application system conversion run is so massive that trying to run it out to the system spool all at once would overload the spool. It may also be that only parts of the print output from a large conversion run are needed on paper at any point or that selective retrieval from a historical archive is required.

The technique of storing the printline images is similar to that discussed for normal production print output, but tape is used rather than disk to house the printlines. The JCL to output the printlines may then take the form:

```
//BT3708U1    DD   DSN=AK00.C99.BT3708U1,
//   UNIT=(TAPE,,DEFER),
//   DISP=(NEW,CATLG,DELETE),
//   DCB=(RECFM=FBA,LRECL=133,BLKSIZE=32718),
//   LABEL=EXPDT=93365
```

With tape we have the latitude on mainframes of specifying a much larger block size than with disk and we do so to increase the speed and efficiency of I/O. Tape block sizes are limited only by the MVS overall block size limit of 32,760 bytes. A blocking factor of 246 for 133 byte printline records produces a block size of 32,718 bytes, the maximum that can be specified. When a block size that large is used, the default memory allocation for the step may be insufficient to provide for the I/O buffers required. As discussed in Appendix A, it may be necessary to specify a larger region size by using the REGION parameter on the EXEC statement of the step.

In the DD statement illustrated for tape output printlines we see no

SPACE parameter because SPACE specification is relevant only to disk storage. We use the RETPD or EXPDT subparameter of the LABEL parameter to provide a future expiration date for the data set to prevent it from expiring prematurely. We do not specify the volume serial number of the tape because we really do not care what particular scratch volume or volumes are selected to house the data set. The volume serial numbers of the tapes used will be recorded for us in the system catalog by the second positional subparameter of the DISP specification, CATLG.

To output selectively from this store of print images something more capable than IEBGENER is required. Ideally, the routine should be able to accept controlling information such as starting page number and quantity of pages to print from that point onward. The handiest way to arrange for the control information to enter a program is via a PARM coded on the EXEC statement in the step executing the program. A program to accomplish this tests the carriage control byte in each printline record and identifies the start of each new page of printlines by the "1" carriage control code that indicates a page eject.[8] The program would never use AFTER ADVANCING in copying the selected printlines to output; therefore RECFM=FBA would be coded on its output DD statement.

REVIEW QUESTIONS AND (*)EXERCISES

1. Nine of the more than 30 DD statement parameters can be coded only in conjunction with SYSOUT. Cite at least six and explain briefly what each does.

2. Describe how printlines output by a mainframe under MVS are intrinsically different than those output by a typical mini- or microcomputer.

3. What is the MVS print spool and what function does it perform?

4. A certain installation still maintains a card punch to create small card decks for customers desiring this service. Code the output DD statement for a program that will convey 80 character records to the punch.

5. Explain why SYSOUT=X is called the held print class.

6. A student erroneously coded SYSOUT=E on the DD statement at which a program's print output emerged. The run gave no indication of error but the output never materialized. Indicate why this happened and what could be done to provide the output.

7. What happens to a job and its output if a program being executed erroneously outputs a printline that exceeds the impact printer limit of 132 printable positions?

*8.   A program outputs four reports:

        `//BT4315U1`   list of all inventory items
        `//BT4315U2`   list of items with activity in last 30 days
        `//BT4315U3`   list of items with no activity for 365 days
        `//BT4315U4`   list of items with inventory level less than
                          reorder point

Code the appropriate DD statements to place the list of all inventory items onto tape with a block size no greater than 8,000 bytes for conveyance to a microfiche vendor, to send two copies of the list of items with activity in the last 30 days to the RJE printer known as remote 32, to discard the list of items with no activity for 365 days, and to route the list of items with an inventory level less than the reorder point to the local printer using the electronic form image stored under FCB3FL55 in SYS1.IMAGELIB.

*9.   A program outputs a summary report at DDname //BT3725U1, a list of master file records updated at //BT3725U2, and a transaction disposition listing at //BT3725U3. All are to be directed to print class A. Code appropriate DD statements to accomplish this, arranging for the transaction listing to come first in the print outputs, then the list of master file records updated, and at the bottom of the outputs, the summary report.

*10.   Printline images have been stored in a disk data set named FS41.A01.FS4146U3 and must now be made to appear on paper. Code a one-step job stream that executes IEBGENER to do this, routing all print in duplicate, including MVS allocation/deallocation reports, to remote printer 20.

NOTES

1.   There is a similarity between print class as a factor that distinguishes between print queues and job class as a factor that distinguishes between job queues. The print arrangement of the spool—the output queue—and a similar spool arrangement for the job entry subsystem—the input queue—are both handled in the same manner by the Job Entry Subsystem, JES2 or JES3. This portion of MVS has the duties of handling the JCL submitted and awaiting execution as well as print spooling.

    If your installation uses job classes to distinguish between jobs that require various resource levels you will see two class indicators on the job card: CLASS= that specifies job class and MSGCLASS= that specifies the output print class of the system job log and allocation/deallocation reports. CLASS has nothing to do with print; it would be clearer if this parameter of the job card was "JOBCLASS" instead of just CLASS.

2.   The JES2 or JES3 spooling function also performs services for the input queue. Using the Spool Display and Search Facility SDSF, the input queues to the system can be viewed by selecting the "I" function. This is directly analogous to the "O" or output

spool display function and can be limited to display by job class, just as the "O" function can be limited to display by print class.

3. An installation might use ASCII printers as remote printing devices and drive them with a protocol converter attached to a computer channel; real RJEs attach to the 3725 communication controller. When a protocol converter is used, the computer may not be aware of all of the printers because the converter appears as one device. In such a case, each remote printer may not have its own remote identifier and the technique for routing print is limited to SYSOUT print class.

4. Job entry subsystem control statements—not JCL statements, but those like /*ROUTE and /*JOBPARM that can follow a job statement—are formatted differently for JES2 and JES3. With JES2 they begin with /* whereas under JES3 they begin with //*.

5. A fundamental tenet of software engineering is that generalized basic structures exist that can be proved logically and applied to practical situations with certainty of the result. This is identical to the process by which the engineering of new buildings and other tangible creations proceeds. However, for the first several years in which "structured programming" was discussed in business data processing a major gap existed between theory on the one hand and mundane syntax debate on the other. If you would like to see the bridging of that gap with detail-complete generic models for business data processing, you may enjoy *Commercial Software Engineering*, ISBN 0-471-81576-4, published by John Wiley and Sons in 1985. It was developed specifically for day-in, day-out COBOL programming and illustrates in detail the engineered source code for standard printing, control break, internal sorting, tables, sequential update and VSAM random access handling.

6. A blocking factor of 68 for 133-byte printline records stored on disk produces a block size of 9,044 bytes. This is fairly efficient for 3350 and 3380 disk units. See Chapter 8 for a comprehensive discussion of block size and data storage efficiency. *See also Chapter 1, note 3, for information on the VSCOBOL ADV/NOADV PARM option, which affects FD coding for printlines.*

7. The DCB carrying RECFM=FBA on the //SYSUT2 for a GENER step that copies printlines out to SYSOUT is needed only if the printlines were originally stored using RECFM=FB instead of FBA. It is customary, however, to code RECFM=FBA here for safety because not all personnel always remember to code printlines with FBA when they are written to disk or tape. When specified in JCL, the DCB characteristics override those in the data set label.

   One might reasonably ask why there is an LRECL and BLKSIZE following the RECFM=FBA on the //SYSUT2 output in this JCL because these are carried in the data set label and neither SYSOUT or the printer respond to the BLKSIZE subparameter of the DCB. The reason is that IEBGENER, one of the oldest utilities in the OS stable, demands LRECL and BLKSIZE on the //SYSUT2 output statement for its own purposes. IEBGENER contains logic to specify record length and block size of the output data set for itself if none is specified in JCL for the //SYSUT2 output. If none is explicitly specified, GENER copies these characteristics from the DCB of the input data set, //SYSUT1. When it does this, it issues a warning message in its //SYSPRINT housekeeping output:

```
DATA SET UTILITY- GENERATE
IEB352I WARNING : OUTPUT RECFM/LRECL/BLKSIZE COPIED FROM INPUT
PROCESSING ENDED AT EOD
```

This message means nothing, however. It merely indicates that GENER has made the output data set assume the same characteristics as the input data set. In the old days, GENER was commonly used to copy and "reblock" data sets; for example, to copy a card deck to tape. The warning message meant something in those ancient times, for if blocking had not been specified in the //SYSUT2 output DD statement a card deck could have been placed on tape in a very inefficient one card per block format.

When we wish to use IEBGENER to copy stored printlines to SYSOUT and the lines already have carriage control in the first byte but were written to tape or disk with FB and not FBA, it is necessary to specify one subparameter of the DCB: the RECFM = FBA. But GENER cannot cope with this partial DCB specification. If we try to do this:

```
//SYSUT2   DD SYSOUT=A,DCB=RECFM=FBA
```

IEBGENER will complain that LRECL AND BLKSIZE were not specified and fail. GENER demands that if you spell out one feature of the DCB on the //SYSUT2 output, you must also spell out the LRECL and BLKSIZE. Going further, GENER demands that at least the LRECL must match the LRECL of the input. GENER does not care about the BLKSIZE being an even multiple of the LRECL, but it is customary to code BLKSIZE as a reasonable figure when LRECL is coded.

The old OS utilities like IEBGENER do much more of their own I/O handling than do applications programs or more modern software. Many of the utility I/O actions and error messages overlap areas now regarded as the purview of MVS. Certain I/O errors that would cause an abend if encountered during execution of a COBOL program will cause only a nonzero return code to be posted if encountered when a utility is being executed, as illustrated in Appendix E. This makes it essential in production job streams to anticipate carefully the consequences of nonzero return codes to continued job stream processing and recovery, as discussed in Chapter 14.

8. It is not necessary to know the actual values used in the carriage control byte to cause the limited range of vertical tabbing possible. When printlines are examined using the TSO/ISPF outlist function 3.8 or SDSF, they will be visible. The values are:

+	no advance; overstrike last line printed
space	advance one line; single space
0	advance two lines; double space
–	advance three lines; triple space
1	advance to top of page; page eject
2 through 9	advance to channels 2 through 9
A	advance to channel 10
B	advance to channel 11
C	advance to channel 12

The COBOL "AFTER POSITIONING" option requires insertion of these literal values in the carriage control byte. The "AFTER ADVANCING" option is more powerful and equates a specification coded as a quantity of lines to an appropriate combination of triple-and single-spaced blanks lines and the print line, to accomplish the intended action. PL/I provides similar page control facilities. In FORTRAN we must produce printlines that carry the appropriate carriage control character by moving the appropriate values explicitly to the first position of the printline. One could mimic this same practice in COBOL programs, avoiding the AFTER ADVANCING or AFTER POSITIONING options entirely and coding RECFM = FBA on the DD statement with SYSOUT, but there is no reason to do so.

PART 3

THE PRODUCTION MVS AND MVS/XA ENVIRONMENTS

Haru no umi,
   Hinemosu notari,
      Notari kana.

Taniguchi Buson
(1716–1783)

(The sea at springtime,
   All day it rises and falls,
      Yes, rises and falls.)

Making job streams capable of being run repeatedly by personnel other than programmers is different from simply putting JCL together and running it. In this section we cover four advanced areas of MVS JCL: generation data groups or "GDGs," the COND parameter for return code testing and job stream failure recovery, PARM or "parameter" passing to programs via JCL, and how "procs" or cataloged procedures are composed, built, tested, and employed.

Taniguchi Buson, a Japanese painter and poet of the eighteenth century, captured the relentless motion of the sea in an onomatopoetic haiku. Like the sea, a mainframe is a surging leviathan. Its potential is harnessed by MVS. It is the subjects of this part that allow individual units of business data processing automata to interact concurrently on a reliable production basis with MVS.

═══ 13 ═══

GDG: Generation Data Groups

Unlike research or analytical programming in which programs are written and run by their authors and then perhaps not run for a long time or ever again, programs and systems developed under MVS usually form a regular part of an organization's everyday operation. A file maintenance routine such as FSBT3708, a sequential update program that has figured in several earlier examples, is executed on a regular schedule by personnel other than the author. Each time it is run it draws in newly prepared transactions and updates what was the preceding run's new master file. MVS provides the generation data group or "GDG" feature to support this cyclical processing.

SEQUENTIAL UPDATE JOB STREAM WITH GDG MASTER AND PRINT FILES

Figure 13.1 is similar to Figure 3.1, the original diagram used to describe the sequential update job stream. As a diagram more typical of a production sequential file maintenance routine, it has been modified to indicate the cyclical nature of the master file update by showing how one run's new master file becomes the next run's old master file.

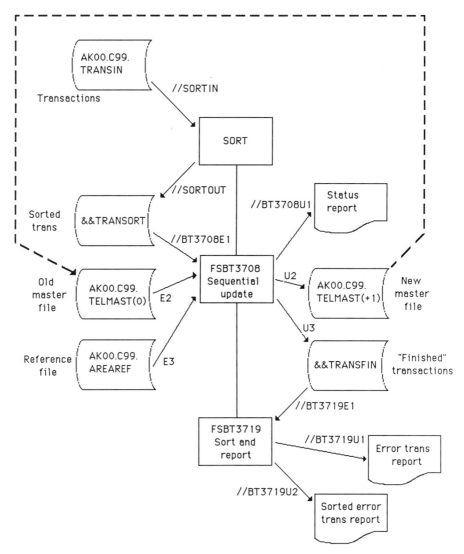

FIGURE 13.1. Upgraded sequential update job stream diagram illustrating use of generation data group master file

Generation data groups are conceptually much like human generations, except that a programmer or systems analyst specifies when new
generations are "born" and when—how far "back"—an old generation
will exist before it "dies." Figure 13.2 presents the sequential update
job stream modified to use GDGs for the AK00.C99.TELMAST master
file and reporting printline data sets; //DELSTEP is no longer present.
That housekeeping step, introduced in Chapter 6, was necessary because
the run created a new copy of AK00.C99.TELMAST.UPDATED and the
reporting printline data sets each time it was run. Now, with GDGs, each
run will create the next generation of these data sets. The next generations will be cataloged and will have different names, although *the
names we see in the JCL will appear to be identical.* MVS itself will
manage the trailing portion of the GDG names and allow us to refer to
the data sets by unchanging names and a "relative generation number."

"Sliding forward" of Relative Generation Number

In //STEPB of the revised job stream we see that the old master file enter
the update program at DDname //BT3708E2:

```
//BT3708E2   DD  DSN=AK00.C99.TELMAST(0),
//   UNIT=(TAPE,,DEFER),
//   DISP=(OLD,KEEP)
```

The trailing parentheses on the data set name are reminiscent of the
syntax associated with partitioned data sets, but they have nothing to
do with a PDS. The number at the trailing end of the name identifies
which of the generations of AK00.C99.TELMAST we wish to access.
These generation numbers always exist in the following relationships
at the start of a job:

Grandparent	(-2)
Parent	(-1)
Current generation	(-0) or $(+0)$ or just (0)
Children	$(+1)$
Grand children	$(+2)$

"At the start of the job" is emphasized. If "offspring" generations are
created during a job, the highest generation number of the offspring becomes the current generation *when the run concludes.* This is an important point because it affects the way that newly created GDG data
sets are referenced during a given job and how they are referenced differently in jobs afterward. It is this "sliding" of the generational reference
that delivers the automatic cycling capability GDGs provide.[1] Genera-

```
//FSBT686A  JOB AK00TEST,'DP2-JANOSSY',CLASS=T,MSGCLASS=X,
//    MSGLEVEL=(1,1),NOTIFY=BT05686
//*
//*     TEST RUN OF SEQUENTIAL UPDATE FSBT3708 -- VER 5B
//*     STILL FOR TESTING, OLD MF IS ALWAYS ".TELMAST"
//*
//*     OLD AND NEW MASTER FILES ARE NOW TAPE GDG DATA SETS
//*     INPUT IS ON A 1600 BPI NON-LABELED TAPE KEYED ON
//*     AN ASCII-BASED DATA ENTRY SYSTEM OR MINI.
//*
//*     PRINT OUTPUT IS NOW DIRECTED TO DISK GDG DATA SETS
//*     THAT ARE PRINTED AT END OF JOB
//*
//*     THIS JCL = BT05686.SOURCE.CNTL(BT3708V5)
//*
//*************************************************************
//*                                                          *
//*     SORT TRANS FILE                              A   *
//*                                                          *
//*************************************************************
//STEPA    EXEC  PGM=SORT
//SORTLIB   DD  DSN=SYS1.SORTLIB,
//  DISP=SHR
//*
//SORTIN    DD  DSN=AK00.C99.TRANSIN,
//  UNIT=(TAPE,,DEFER),
//  DISP=(OLD,KEEP),
//  DCB=(RECFM=FB,LRECL=71,BLKSIZE=1420,DEN=3,OPTCD=Q),
//  VOL=SER=HXR452,
//  LABEL=(1,NL,EXPDT=98000)                   'EXPDT ONLY FOR
//*                                            'UCC-1 TMS
//SORTOUT   DD  DSN=&&TRANSORT,
//  UNIT=SYSDA,
//  DISP=(NEW,PASS,DELETE),
//  DCB=(RECFM=FB,LRECL=71,BLKSIZE=6177),
//  SPACE=(6177,(32,7),RLSE)                   '2800 TRANS
//SYSOUT    DD  SYSOUT=*
//SYSUDUMP  DD  SYSOUT=*
//SORTWK01  DD  UNIT=SYSDA,SPACE=(CYL,2,,CONTIG)
//SORTWK02  DD  UNIT=SYSDA,SPACE=(CYL,2,,CONTIG)
//SYSIN     DD  *
    SORT FIELDS=(1,4,CH,A,9,2,CH,A,5,4,CH,A,14,1,CH,D)
/*
//*
//*************************************************************
//*                                                          *
//*     UPDATE MASTER FILE                           B   *
//*                                                          *
//*************************************************************
//STEPB    EXEC  PGM=FSBT3708,REGION=2048K
//STEPLIB   DD  DSN=BT05686.TEST.LOADMODS,
//  DISP=SHR
//BT3708E1  DD  DSN=&&TRANSORT,
//  DISP=(OLD,DELETE)
//*
//BT3708E2  DD  DSN=AK00.C99.TELMAST(0),
//  UNIT=(TAPE,,DEFER),
//  DISP=(OLD,KEEP)
//*
//BT3708E3  DD  DSN=AK00.C99.AREAREF,
//  DISP=SHR
//*
//BT3708U1  DD  DSN=AK00.C99.BT3708U1(+1),
//  UNIT=SYSDA,
//  DISP=(NEW,CATLG,DELETE),
//  DCB=(XX90.A00.DUMMYLBL,RECFM=FBA,LRECL=133,BLKSIZE=9044),
//  SPACE=(9044,(45,20),RLSE)
//*
//BT3708U2  DD  DSN=AK00.C99.TELMAST(+1),
//  UNIT=(TAPE,,DEFER),
//  DISP=(NEW,CATLG,DELETE),
//  DCB=(XX90.A00.DUMMYLBL,RECFM=FB,LRECL=314,BLKSIZE=32656),
//  LABEL=RETPD=30
//*
```

228

```
//BT3708U3    DD   DSN=&&TRANSFIN,
//  UNIT=SYSDA,
//  DISP=(NEW,PASS,DELETE),
//  DCB=(RECFM=FB,LRECL=102,BLKSIZE=6222),   '2800 TRANS
//  SPACE=(6222,(46,9),RLSE)
//*
//SYSOUT      DD   SYSOUT=*
//SYSUDUMP    DD   SYSOUT=*
//**********************************************************
//*                                                        *
//*      PRODUCE TRAN REPORT (INTERNAL SORT)         C    *
//*                                                        *
//**********************************************************
//STEPC    EXEC   PGM=FSBT3719,REGION=2048K
//STEPLIB     DD   DSN=BT05686.TEST.LOADMODS,
//  DISP=SHR
//SORTLIB     DD   DSN=SYS1.SORTLIB,
//  DISP=SHR
//BT3719E1    DD   DSN=&&TRANSFIN,
//  DISP=(OLD,DELETE)
//*
//BT3719U1    DD   DSN=AK00.C99.BT3719U1(+1),
//  UNIT=SYSDA,
//  DISP=(NEW,CATLG,DELETE),
//  DCB=(XX90.A00.DUMMYLBL,RECFM=FBA,LRECL=133,BLKSIZE=9044),
//  SPACE=(9044,(45,20),RLSE)
//*
//BT3719U2    DD   DSN=AK00.C99.BT3719U2(+1),
//  UNIT=SYSDA,
//  DISP=(NEW,CATLG,DELETE),
//  DCB=(XX90.A00.DUMMYLBL,RECFM=FBA,LRECL=133,BLKSIZE=9044),
//  SPACE=(9044,(45,20),RLSE)
//*
//SORTWK01    DD   UNIT=SYSDA,SPACE=(CYL,2,,CONTIG)
//SORTWK02    DD   UNIT=SYSDA,SPACE=(CYL,2,,CONTIG)
//BT3719SM    DD   SYSOUT=*
//SYSOUT      DD   SYSOUT=*
//SYSUDUMP    DD   SYSOUT=*
//*
//**********************************************************
//*                                                        *
//*      PRINT THE REPORT OUTPUTS                    D    *
//*                                                        *
//**********************************************************
//STEPD    EXEC   PGM=IEBGENER
//*
//SYSUT1      DD   DSN=AK00.C99.BT3708U1(+1),DISP=SHR
//           DD   DSN=AK00.C99.BT3719U1(+1),DISP=SHR
//           DD   DSN=AK00.C99.BT3719U2(+1),DISP=SHR
//*
//SYSUT2      DD   SYSOUT=A,
//  DCB=(RECFM=FBA,LRECL=133,BLKSIZE=9044)
//SYSIN       DD   DUMMY
//SYSPRINT    DD   SYSOUT=*
//SYSUDUMP    DD   SYSOUT=*
//
```

FIGURE 13.2. Revised sequential update job stream using generation data group (GDG) master and print data sets

tions earlier than (-2) and later than $(+2)$ are possible; the foregoing list is a subset for discussion purposes only.

At DDname //BT3708U2 in //STEPB the next generation of the master file emerges. It is assigned to a data set by the name

```
//BT3708U2   DD   DSN=AK00.C99.TELMAST(+1),
```

and if referenced further in the job must be referenced as the (+1) generation. In this particular job stream, however, the new master file is not referenced further. We see something different in the DCB parameter of //STEPB: the presence of what appears to be a data set name ahead of the actual DCB subparameters. We discuss that difference later in this chapter.

In //STEPB we create the (+1) generation of another data set as well. At DDname //BT3708U1 we see emerge the printlines for an update report produced by FSBT3708. These are assigned to a data set as follows

```
//BT3708U1   DD   DSN=AK00.C99.BT3708U1(+1),
```

even though we have not referenced the current (0) generation of this data set in the job stream. *There is no requirement within a job stream for the current generation of a data set to be referenced in order to create the next generation; the next generation of a data set need not be the progeny of the current generation.* In this regard our comparison of human generations to MVS and MVS/XA data set generations becomes less directly analogous. In this DD statement we are more or less "putting the next volume of the same name on the shelf," much like one might place the newly received issue of a magazine on a shelf by pushing all the older issues a bit to the left to make room.

In //STEPC of this job stream we are reading a temporary data set that carries "finished" transactions from the update routine and are using these records to produce two additional reports. Each of these reports emerges at its own DDname and creates the (+1) generation of a uniquely named data set. The generations of these report printline data sets and those of the report produced in //STEPB will be "synchronized" in that the (+1) generations—later the (0) generations—will be related. All will represent print outputs from this invocation of the job stream. This synchronization is not a facet of GDGs; it could be upset by some other job that independently creates a (+1) or greater generation of only one or some of these data sets.

The final step in the revised sequential update job stream is //STEPD; it was added in Chapter 12. This step exists to reduce the stored printlines of the three reports to paper—one produced by FSBT3708 and two by FSBT3719. This step invokes the IBM utility program IEBGENER to copy the printlines to SYSOUT. We now see that the inputs to IEBGENER here, under the DDname //SYSUT1, are the three (+1) generation data sets created before, concatenated as were the earlier simple data sets. The fact that we reference a data set by relative generation number has no effect on its ability to be concatenated with other GDG or non-GDG data sets.

In //STEPD we refer to the three report printline data sets created in the run with the (+1) relative generation number. These data sets will carry this number until the job ends. Up until this time you have seen only one set of JCL, or job stream, making up a job. In Chapter 16, which deals with cataloged procedures, we examine how one or more sets of JCL may be invoked under one job card, making everything invoked one job, and the effect this has on relative generation numbers coded in JCL. For now it is important to remember that once the job represented by the JCL in Figure 13.2 ends execution, the sliding forward of generation references occurs.

Reprinting GDG-Stored Printlines

We may wish to reprint the reports carried in the three stored printline data sets of this job, using another, separate invocation of IEBGENER later. If that is done, that subsequent run must reference the data sets as the current (0) generation

```
//FSBT686A  JOB AK00TEST,'DP2-JANOSSY',CLASS=E,MSGCLASS=X,
//  MSGLEVEL=(1,1),NOTIFY=BT05686
//*THIS BT05686.SOURCE.CNTL(REPRINT)
//****************************************************
//*     REPRINT THE REPORT OUTPUTS                   *
//****************************************************
//REPR1      EXEC  PGM=IEBGENER
//*
//SYSUT1     DD    DSN=AK00.C99.BT3708U1(0),DISP=SHR
//          DD    DSN=AK00.C99.BT3719U1(0),DISP=SHR
//          DD    DSN=AK00.C99.BT3719U2(0),DISP=SHR
//*
//SYSUT2     DD    SYSOUT=A,
//  DCB=(RECFM=FBA,LRECL=133,BLKSIZE=6118)
//*
//SYSIN      DD    DUMMY
//SYSPRINT   DD    SYSOUT=*
//SYSUDUMP   DD    SYSOUT=A
//
```

because of the sliding forward of the generation reference that occurred at the end of the update job. The current generation here could have been coded as (−0) instead of (0). This may be desirable for coding consistency when the generation is specified as a symbolic parameter to a cataloged procedure. In the discussion of cataloged procedures in Chapter 16 we show how the use of a symbolic parameter at the relative generation number allows the same procedure to handle normal print as well as reprint runs.

MECHANISM BEHIND GENERATION DATA GROUPS

The GDG Base

The mechanism by which MVS supports GDGs relies on two components, established by utility program executions. One of these is a "generation data group index" unique to a given GDG. It is established in the system catalog and keeps track of the generation numbers used for data sets in the group. Under the obsolete System/360 catalog structure, which employs OS "CVOLs" or "control volumes," the IEHPROGM utility was used to create the GDG index. Under the contemporary VSAM and ICF catalog structures the IDCAMS general purpose utility is now used for this purpose and the GDG-defining entity is called a "base" rather than an index.

The Model Data Set Label

A second component necessary for GDG use is a "model data set label," sometimes referred to as a "model DSCB." This is a pattern for the data set label created for any data set named as part of the GDG group. "Model DSCB" is somewhat confusing because DSCB stands for "data set control block," a part of a disk volume table of contents, and several different record types exist in the VTOC for a disk volume. The VTOC's format 1 DSCB record houses the disk data set label; every disk data set has its own format 1 DSCB, as discussed in note 1 of Chapter 8. Generation data sets need not be housed on disk and the association between a DSCB record and a tape GDG may appear strange. It is the use of a model of a data set label on which the GDG mechanism rests, not the "magic" of the DSCB as a record format in a disk VTOC. Model DSCB really does mean, in plain language, model data set label.

Absolute Data Set Name

Every data set handled by MVS must carry a data set name, whether specified in JCL or left to formation by MVS. The data sets making up a generation data set group are no exception to this requirement. In every respect they are normal data sets; the GDG mechanism just provides a uniquely convenient way to access them. All GDG data sets must be cataloged; there is no choice in this matter. Users of MVS see GDGs as something special because of a layer of software that works with the GDG index or base, stored in the system catalog.

The real name of a data set in a generation data group consists of the name as we know it and a final name portion made up of "GxxxxVyy" where "xxxx" is the generation number and yy is the version number.

MVS always creates the final name portion incrementing the Gxxxx number and making the Vyy a V followed by zeros. It is possible to manually create a "replacement" for a given generation by creating a cataloged data set with the same absolute name and "Gxxxx" number, with the Vyy incremented upward by one, such as V01. This is not a very commonly performed action. An overall data set name can be up to 44 characters in length, and the presence of the final "GxxxxVyy" portion of a name on GDG data sets, preceded by a period, means that the portion of the name over which we have control is limited to 44 minus 9 or 35 characters. For example, the absolute name of the master file related to the JCL of Figure 13.2 at one point in time could be:

```
AK00.C99.TELMAST.G0278V00
```

Using LISTCAT to See GDG Base Contents

If you want to see what data sets are part of a generation data group at any given time, technically called entries in the GDG base, you can run a job

```
//FSBT686A   JOB AK00TEST,'DP2-JANOSSY',CLASS=E,MSGCLASS=X,
//   MSGLEVEL=(1,1),NOTIFY=BT05686
//*   THIS JCL = BT05686.SOURCE.CNTL(LISTCAT)
//STEPA      EXEC   PGM=IDCAMS
//SYSPRINT   DD    SYSOUT=*
//SYSUDUMP   DD    SYSOUT=A
//SYSIN      DD    *
    LISTCAT GDG ENTRIES('AK00.C99.TELMAST') ALL
/*
//
```

that uses the LISTCAT or "list catalog" function of the IDCAMS utility. This provides the output shown in Figure 13.3.

```
GDG BASE ------ AK00.C99.TELMAST
     IN-CAT --- SYS6.PRODCAT.FSDC01
     HISTORY
         OWNER-IDENT-------(NULL)       CREATION----------87.139
         RELEASE---------------2        EXPIRATION--------00.000
     ATTRIBUTES
         LIMIT-----------------6        SCRATCH         NOEMPTY
     ASSOCIATIONS
       NONVSAM--AK00.C99.TELMAST.G0273V00
       NONVSAM--AK00.C99.TELMAST.G0274V00
       NONVSAM--AK00.C99.TELMAST.G0275V00
       NONVSAM--AK00.C99.TELMAST.G0276V00
       NONVSAM--AK00.C99.TELMAST.G0277V00
       NONVSAM--AK00.C99.TELMAST.G0278V00
```

FIGURE 13.3. Typical IDCAMS "LISTCAT GDG" report

CREATING GENERATION DATA GROUPS

Creating the GDG Base

The GDG base is created by a batch run of the IDCAMS utility[2]:

```
//FSBT686A  JOB AK00TEST,'DP-JANOSSY',CLASS=E,MSGCLASS=X,
//  MSGLEVEL=(1,1),NOTIFY=BT05686
//*   THIS JCL = BT05686.SOURCE.CNTL(DEF1GDG)
//ONEGDG    EXEC  PGM=IDCAMS
//SYSPRINT   DD   SYSOUT=*
//SYSUDUMP   DD   SYSOUT=A
//SYSIN      DD   *
     DEFINE -
       GDG     (    NAME(AK00.C99.TELMAST) -
                    OWNER(FSBT0003) -
                    FOR(9999) -
                    LIMIT(6) -
                    NOEMPTY -
                    SCRATCH                    )
  /*
  //
```

More than one GDG base can be established in one run by repeating the GDG specification and appropriate items:

```
//FSBT686A  JOB AK00TEST,'DP2-JANOSSY',CLASS=E,MSGCLASS=X,
//  MSGLEVEL=(1,1),NOTIFY=BT05686
//*   THIS JCL = BT05686.SOURCE.CNTL(DEF2GDG)
//MANYGDG   EXEC  PGM=IDCAMS
//SYSPRINT   DD   SYSOUT=*
//SYSUDUMP   DD   SYSOUT=A
//SYSIN      DD   *
     DEFINE -
       GDG     (    NAME(CC19.F72.PAYMAST) -
                    OWNER(FSBT0162) -
                    FOR(9999) -
                    LIMIT(5) -
                    NOEMPTY -
                    SCRATCH                    ) -

       GDG     (    NAME(CC19.F72.PARTSTOC) -
                    OWNER(FSBT0162) -
                    LIMIT(7) -
                    EMPTY                      )
  /*
  //
```

NAME is the base name of the generation data set and can contain up to 35 characters. This is the name that precedes the relative generation number when relative generation access is used.

OWNER is optional descriptive information. It may be up to eight bytes in length and serves as a comment. It is often omitted but is shown here to illustrate syntax. It is carried in the catalog entry that establishes the GDG base but it serves no purpose for data set access.

FOR is the number of days for which the GDG base itself is to exist, *not* the retention period for individual generations of data sets. FOR can be a number from 0000 to 9999, but if it is more than the value 1831 the specific value does not matter; it is interpreted as retention to the year 1999. The retention can be specified as a date by using TO instead of FOR and coding the date in Julian form as YYDDD. Neither FOR or TO is necessary; when used, they act as does the data set expiration date for a disk data set. That is, this retention period does not imply automatic deletion of the GDG base after a period of time, it only makes it possible to do a deletion after a period of time. Even without a retention date IDCAMS will not readily allow deletion of a GDG base as long as it has any generations associated with it.

LIMIT is the number of generations that the GDG will contain. This value can be as little as 1 or as high as 255. Note, however, that unlike some of the other specifications for the GDG that can be changed afterward by using the IDCAMS ALTER command, LIMIT cannot be changed once the GDG is established; it must be chosen appropriately in the first place.

NOEMPTY and **EMPTY** are two mutually exclusive specifications that establish what data sets in the GDG are affected when the LIMIT is reached. NOEMPTY means that when the generation LIMIT of the base has been reached and another generation is to be created the *oldest* existing generation is to be affected according to the SCRATCH specification. EMPTY indicates that when the generation LIMIT of the base has been reached and another generation is to be created *all* existing generations are to be affected as specified by the SCRATCH specification. NOEMPTY is the default but is coded here for example purposes. In the vast majority of cases NOEMPTY is the desired specification. "Affected" always includes removal from the GDG base and uncataloging, but the SCRATCH and NOSCRATCH options specify possible additional treatment of the affected data sets.

SCRATCH and **NOSCRATCH** are two mutually exclusive specifications. SCRATCH indicates that affected data sets are to be uncataloged and deleted. NOSCRATCH indicates that affected data sets are simply to be uncataloged. In both cases the affected data sets are removed from membership in the generation data set group and are no longer accessible by relative generation number. Data sets uncataloged and removed from the GDG can be referenced by absolute name. NOSCRATCH is the default, but this is usually not desired and SCRATCH is explicity coded. SCRATCH can delete disk data sets only, not tape-stored data sets. The retention of a tape data set is governed by its expiration date, as discussed later in this chapter under *Interplay Between GDG SCRATCH and Data Set Expiration Date*.

The GDG base must be established before any generations of the data set can be written. Once it is established and the first generation written, the presence of that generation can be seen by using the JCL described earlier to perform a LISTCAT with IDCAMS. The first generation will appear carrying its absolute name, which will end with G0001V00.

In some installations control is exercised over the creation of GDG bases by stipulating that only a technical support group is allowed to create them. In such cases it is usually necessary to file a simple form with the installation librarian or other designated party, stating the information for the IDCAMS control statements. The actual base creation run takes only a fraction of a second.

Creating the Model Data Set Label

The issue of the model data set label for a generation data group stretches all the way back to the earliest days of System/360 OS. It was originally thought that a separate model data set label would be created for each generation data group and that the data set attributes resulting from the DCB statement that established the label would apply to all data sets in the group. If this were the case, then it would be unnecessary to code the DCB parameter in the DD statement at which a new data set generation emerges.

The use of the model data set label actually did not work out as expected; in fact, none of the information in the model data set label usually applies to the specifics of a given new GDG data set. The reason is that it became burdensome to create a separate model data set label for every generation data group and unwieldy to have to modify the DCB characteristics of that model label when things occurred that made it necessary to change the characteristics of data sets in the GDG. *There is no requirement that all members of a GDG have the same DCB characteristics or even that they reside on the same type of media.* The requirement for a model data set label, however, remains in connection with GDGs.

A disk data set label is contained in a record known as the format 1 data set control block in a disk volume table of contents or VTOC. Several formats of VTOC records exist; each is a 144-byte record as described in note 1 of Chapter 8. The format 1 DSCB record carries the data set name, DCB characteristics, and housekeeping data about the first of three disk data set extents. Just because it can carry information about three disk extents does not mean it must actually point to any disk space at all.

A data set label on disk can be created by invoking any program, including IEFBR14, with a DD statement for the data set that carries appropriate disposition and other parameters. The typical JCL which follows would cause a data set label—a format 1 DSCB record—for data set CC19.F72.PAYMAST to be created in the volume table of contents for disk volume FSDC01. It could serve as the model for a generation data group in which data sets carried this name. For this to work FSDC01 would have to be the same disk volume on which the system catalog resided. In addition, this model data set label could *not* be cataloged; that's the reason for placing it on the same disk volume as the catalog. It could not be cataloged because its name, CC19.F72.PAYMAST, is the same as that of the GDG base for the data set.

Using the Model Data Set Label

If the model data set label were established with JCL such as this

```
//FSBT686A   JOB AK00TEST,'DP2-JANOSSY',CLASS=E,MSGCLASS=X,
//   MSGLEVEL=(1,1),NOTIFY=BT05686
//*   THIS JCL = BT05686.SOURCE.CNTL(MODLDSCB)
//MAKEMOD   EXEC   PGM=IEFBR14
//MAKE1      DD   DSN=CC19.F72.PAYMAST,
//   UNIT=SYSDA,
//   DISP=(NEW,KEEP,DELETE),
//   DCB=(RECFM=FB,LRECL=200,BLKSIZE=6200),
//   SPACE=(TRK,0),
//   VOL=SER=FSDC01
//
```

and the characteristics of the data sets really were as defined in the foregoing DCB, a generation could be written in a step coded as:

```
//CC6723U1   DD   DSN=CC19.F72.PAYMAST(+1),
//   UNIT=SYSDA,
//   DISP=(NEW,CATLG,DELETE),
//   SPACE=(6200,(3000,300),RLSE),
//   VOL=SER=FSDC25
```

The data set is cataloged. This DD statement contains no DCB parameter and it is not necessary for the data set to reside on the same volume as the model data set label, or even on disk. If the VOL parameter were omitted completely, thus implying a nonspecific volume request, MVS would as usual pick out a suitable disk volume for the data set. The

DCB is not needed because MVS will find and use the model data set label of the same name on the disk volume that contains the catalog.

Let's see why it is not necessary to bother with a unique, uncataloged model data set label for every different generation data group. Under a rather arcane capability of JCL it is possible to code a DCB parameter in a "piggyback" fashion to specify an existing data set label as a "starter" for a new one. This is done by first coding the data set name defined by that existing data set label in the DCB parameter and then following with any DCB subparameters that are to vary from it. Suppose we needed to write a new data set named CC19.F72.SELCDATA and it was to contain fixed length records of 110 bytes in blocks of 6,160 bytes. If we knew that another cataloged data set called FS67.A13.TRANREC3 already existed with these characteristics, we could code the DD statement at which the new data set would be written as:

```
//STEPG     DD  DSN=CC19.F72.SELCDATA,
//    UNIT=SYSDA,
//    DISP=(NEW,CATLG,DELETE),
//    DCB=(FS67.A13.TRANREC3),
//    SPACE=(6160,(90,30),RLSE)
```

By placing the existing data set name first in the DCB parameter MVS will act like a word processor and will "drag in" the data set label of that data set to use its characteristics to build the data control block for the new data set.

We may want to make use of an existing data set label in this way but wish to change one or more data set characteristics. We could do so by coding the DCB subparameters we want to be different after the existing data set name:

```
//STEPG     DD  DSN=CC19.F72.SELCDATA,
//    UNIT=SYSDA,
//    DISP=(NEW,CATLG,DELETE),
//    DCB=(FS67.A13.TRANREC3,BLKSIZE=15400),
//    SPACE=(15400,(36,12),RLSE)
```

We have used the existing data set label as a pattern to create a new data set but have replaced the block size with a value more efficient for 110-byte records on an IBM 3380 disk.

It is this particular feature of JCL that allows us to dispense with the burden of creating a unique, uncataloged model data set label for every generation data group. It is possible to meet the model data set label requirement for *all* generation data groups by creating a standard model label that actually pertains to *none* of them. Then every DD statement that relates to a new generation of a GDG to be written simply carries a

DCB parameter, naming the model, and follows this with the DCB sub-parameters that would usually be coded. In effect, we use the model data set label not for its intended purpose but simply to meet the requirement of GDGs that we have a model. Because with the DCB sub-parameter coding we replace every relevant DCB characteristic in each case, the model really provides no characteristics of use whatsoever, and it doesn't matter what is coded in the DCB that establishes it. The model data set label has become much like the human appendix: everybody has one but the need for it has disappeared.

This JCL creates a general model data set label named in a manner that makes apparent the contemporary function of the model:

```
//FSBT686A   JOB AK00TEST,'DP2-JANOSSY',CLASS=E,MSGCLASS=X,
//   MSGLEVEL=(1,1),NOTIFY=BT05686
//*  THIS JCL = BT05686.SOURCE.CNTL(MODELXX)
//STEPA    EXEC  PGM=IEFBR14
//MAKEMODL  DD  DSN=XX90.A00.DUMMYLBL,
//   UNIT=SYSDA,
//   DISP=(NEW,CATLG,DELETE),
//   DCB=(RECFM=FB,LRECL=80,BLKSIZE=3840),
//   SPACE=(TRK,0),
//   VOL=SER=FSDC01
//
```

This model can be cataloged because no GDG base will ever be established for this name. The model must still be on the same volume as the system catalog in which the GDG bases are stored. If we now wished to create the next generation of CC19.F72.PAYMAST, we would do it in this manner:

```
//CC6723U1   DD  DSN=CC19.F72.PAYMAST(+1),
//   UNIT=SYSDA,
//   DISP=(NEW,CATLG,DELETE),
//   DCB=(XX90.A00.DUMMYLBL,RECFM=FB,LRECL=200,BLKSIZE=6200),
//   SPACE=(6200,(3000,300),RLSE),
//   VOL=SER=FSDC25
```

We could have dropped the VOL parameter if we did not want to force placement of the data set on a specific disk volume such as FSDC25; this nonspecific volume request would be customary. The generation data set could, of course, be directed to tape instead of disk

```
//CC6723U1   DD  DSN=CC19.F72.PAYMAST(+1),
//   UNIT=(TAPE,,DEFER),
//   DISP=(NEW,CATLG,DELETE),
//   DCB=(XX90.A00.DUMMYLBL,RECFM=FB,LRECL=200,BLKSIZE=32600),
//   LABEL=RETPD=30
```

because *there is no requirement that all members of a generation data group be on the same type of media or even that they have the same record length or block size.*

In going to tape, the block size has been increased to the maximum possible to gain I/O efficiency and the SPACE and VOL parameters have been dropped; the LABEL parameter, however, has been added. If the installation is using a tape management system, the label parameter may have been coded in an unusual way, such as LABEL = EXPDT = 99000, to gain the benefit of tape retention until the tape is uncataloged by the GDG mechanism. Here, without the use of a tape management system, we specify a retention period during which the job will be run enough times to exceed the generation LIMIT. If we did not code the LABEL parameter with a retention period of sufficient length, the tape could "dry up" on us while the data set is still carried in the GDG base as a generation. *Simply being a member of a generation data group does not ensure tape data set retention.*

When a general dummy model data set label is used, there is no requirement ever to create a model data set label in addition to the dummy. A model data set label like XX90.A00.DUMMYLBL could be referenced by all DD statements at which new generations of GDG data sets are written, a practice followed in many installations.

GDG TRIVIA

Interplay Between GDG SCRATCH and Data Set Expiration Date

It is important to keep in mind that the GDG mechanism deals with three distinct aspects of data sets: access to them via a relative generation number, their continued cataloged nature, and their existence. The aspects are separate but often joined in the case of disk data sets. GDGs, however, are also used for tape data sets, and it is possible for some generations of a GDG to be on disk and some on tape.

The "limit" of the GDG index or base establishes how many generations will be given support for relative generation number access. With most GDGs, when this limit is reached, it is desirable to have the oldest existing generation drop off the GDG and become inaccessible by relative generation number. At this point it is possible to have the GDG mechanism itself uncatalog and delete the data set *if* the data set is housed on disk and *if* it carries no expiration date or an expired date. Because tape data sets are not always present in a mounted condition and the expiration date is contained in the data set label on the tape itself, the GDG mechanism can uncatalog a tape data set but cannot actually scratch it.

It is customary not to code expiration dates for disk data sets. For these, the GDG mechanism can readily handle the removal of the oldest generation from the GDG and uncatalog and delete it. Deletion is accomplished by the GDG mechanism initiating the overwriting, with binary zeros, of the format 1 DSCB for the data set in the volume table of contents, or VTOC, of the disk on which the data set resides. This is an unnecessarily technical explanation of the action; it is sufficient to simply say that the data set is deleted. The full explanation is given here only because many technical manuals express disk data set deletion in arcane terms of VTOC DSCB manipulations and it is essential to dispel the confusion that sometimes results.

Tape data sets *are* usually given expiration dates by using the LABEL subparameter RETPD or EXPDT. *The retention of tape data sets is wholly dependent on their expiration dates.* Simply because a tape data set is carried in a GDG as one of the generations does not mean that it will continue to exist if its expiration date is reached. Unlike disk data sets, an installation will handle its identification of scratch tapes in a manner that singles out the tapes carrying data sets that have reached their expiration dates. This does not necessarily involve any checking to determine whether the tape data set is carried as a generation in a GDG base.

For tape-stored GDG data sets the LABEL subparameter of the DCB must be used to insure continued access to the data. The value specified for the retention period must be great enough to keep the data set alive until it drops off the GDG because of the cyclical operation of the application in which it is created. The determination of a retention period, even for a system run regularly, is not possible with extreme precision. Therefore the retention period for tape GDGs is usually specified conservatively long, or a tape management system is employed to automate the process of managing scratch tapes.

TSO Access to a GDG

A generation data group data set can be accessed by TSO/ISPF by specifying either the data set name and relative generation number, or the absolute data set name, at the "OTHER" data set name at the bottom of the screen. When this access is made, the *absolute* data set name is shown by TSO/ISPF at the top of the screen.

Because the TSO 1 "browse" function has more liberal line length display capabilities than the TSO 2 edit function, browse is more appropriate when attempting to see the contents of a GDG data set with a record length greater than 80. A given installation may, however, have in place a security system that prevents programmers from having TSO access to production data sets.

Retrieval or Deletion of Generations en masse

It is possible to access easily all the existing generations of a data set. When a GDG is accessed with a DSN parameter omitting the relative generation number, the access takes this form:

- All generations are accessed.
- The generations are accessed in reverse order of creation; the most current or (0) generation, then the next most current or (-1) generation, then the (-2) generation, and so forth.
- The generations are received by the program reading them as if they were continuous; in other words, they are concatenated in the foregoing sequence.

One common use of this capability involves a GDG to house data sets transmitted over a remote job entry line, or RJE, to "pool" data on the mainframe. A data entry unit or an end-user may transmit data in batches in this manner and the job receiving the data on the mainframe may park it in the next generation of a data set, perhaps named AK22.T95.TRANDATA($+1$).[3] After many transmissions several generations of the data set will exist. Then an update run may be initiated, reading all the transaction input generations en masse into a sort step with a DD statement such as:

```
//SORTIN      DD  AK22.T95.TRANDATA,
//  DISP=OLD
```

A final action of this job would be to uncatalog and delete all generations of the GDG to clear the decks for subsequent transmissions of additional data batches. This is readily accomplished by executing a delete step of IEFBR14 without a specific generation number:

```
//ENDDEL     EXEC  PGM=IEFB14
//DEL1            DD  DSN=AK22.T95.TRANDATA,
//  DISP=(OLD,DELETE)
```

This uncataloging and deletion takes place in reverse order of the creation of the data sets just as en masse access to GDG data sets for retrieval occurs. When this is done, the GDG base remains but contains no data set references. When the next generation of the data set is created as the ($+1$) generation, its absolute name will end with G0001V00.

Deletion of GDG Base

IDCAMS is used to delete a generation data group base:

```
//FSBT686A   JOB AK00TEST,'DP2-JANOSSY',CLASS=E,MSGCLASS=X,
//  MSGLEVEL=(1,1),NOTIFY=BT05686
//*   THIS JCL = BT05686.SOURCE.CNTL(DELGDGA)
//DELGDG    EXEC  PGM=IDCAMS
//SYSPRINT   DD   SYSOUT=*
//SYSUDUMP   DD   SYSOUT=A
//SYSIN      DD   *
    DELETE -
            AK00.C99.TELMAST -
            GDG
/*
//
```

This will delete the GDG base *if* it had no expiration date or the GDG
base expiration date has been reached or passed, and *if* there are no
generations of the data set at the time the step executes. When either of
these conditions is not met, the DELETE will fail. It is possible to allow
IDCAMS to delete a GDG base even if it has an expiration date that has
not been reached; the PURGE specification does this. It is also possible
to delete a GDG base even when there are data set generations still associated with it; the FORCE specification does this. The "no holds
barred" DELETE step would appear as:

```
//FSBT686A   JOB AK00TEST,'DP2-JANOSSY',CLASS=E,MSGCLASS=X,
//  MSGLEVEL=(1,1),NOTIFY=BT05686
//*   THIS JCL = BT05686.SOURCE.CNTL(DELGDGB)
//DELGDG    EXEC  PGM=IDCAMS
//SYSPRINT   DD   SYSOUT=*
//SYSUDUMP   DD   SYSOUT=A
//SYSIN      DD   *
    DELETE -
            AK00.C99.TELMAST -
            GDG -
            PURGE -
            FORCE
/*
//
```

The removal of incorrectly created GDG bases, the elimination of test
data sets and materials, and the abandonment of older systems are the
three instances in which GDG base removal may occur. If the GDG base
is deleted by force and data sets still exist under the generation data

group data set name, they will no longer be accessible by relative generation number but must be accessed by their absolute names. DELETE with FORCE does not delete the data sets themselves, it deletes only their entries in the GDG base and the base itself.

Resetting the Absolute Generation Number

The Gnnnn number for generations in a GDG increases by the amount specified in the "(+n)" each time a data set is created named with the GDG base and a positive relative generation number. Creating the (+1) generation causes the next highest Gnnnn number to be generated; more generally stated, using (+n) produces a Gnnnn equal to the current generation number plus the (+n) number. It is possible to skip absolute generation numbers, accidentally or intentionally, by creating a (+2) generation and no (+1). This generates no error at creation or later but it does leave a "hole" in the absolute data set names. This hole will not affect any reference to the data set by the relative generation number of a *subsequent* job.

If all generations currently in a GDG index or base are deleted, the Gnnnn numbering will be extinguished and the next generation created will carry the generation number G0001. Deletion en masse can be made with an IEFBR14 step that carries the GDG base, but no generation number.

For GDGs approaching the maximum Gnnnn number of G9999 it is possible to reset the absolute generation number. The latest generation of the GDG can be copied by relative generation number (0) access to a simple data set of some other name; all generations can then be deleted en masse and the latest data copied back to the (+1) generation of the GDG. The result will be the latest generation of the data set carrying an absolute generation number of G0001. If it is necessary to preserve all current generations of the data set, each can be copied to other data sets, the original generations deleted en masse, and the data sets copied back in generation order. This will result in the oldest generation carrying absolute generation number G0001 and more recent generations with successively higher numbers.

REVIEW QUESTIONS AND (*)EXERCISES

1. Explain what a relative generation number is in terms of access to generation data group data sets.

2. The next generation of a data set is created within a certain job stream. Another job executing after this one will need to read the

then-current generation. How would the relative generation number be coded in that subsequent job and why?

3. How is the GDG base created?

4. What is a "model DSCB" and why is its name sometimes confusing in relation to tape-stored GDG data sets?

5. AK00.C99.TRANHIST(0) is the name of a generation data group data set. Give an example of what its absolute name might be and explain what the portions of the absolute name are.

6. Explain the interaction between the GDG attributes LIMIT, EMPTY/NOEMPTY, and SCRATCH/NOSCRATCH. Indicate also any defaults that may apply to any of these attributes.

*7. Create a model DSCB for your own use by placing it on the same disk volume on which your default system catalog resides. You can find the identity of this volume by examining the MVS allocation/deallocation report for any job accessing a cataloged data set. Use the IEHLIST JCL illustrated in item 20 of Chapter 17 to produce a formatted disk volume table of contents of the catalog disk volume. Because this can result in voluminous print, use TSO/ISPF 3.8 or SDSF to view it and avoid actually printing it. Find the model DSCB you created in this listing and identify the quantity of disk space assigned to it.

*8. Create a GDG base for a data set that will contain five generations by using your installation's standard model DSCB or the model DSCB you created in exercise 7. Then copy three members of your CNTL library to this GDG by using three job executions and coding the appropriate DCB parameter in the DD statement at which output to the GDG emerges. Perform an IDCAMS LISTCAT with the appropriate control statements to see the contents of the GDG base after the copy process.

*9. Copy a fourth item into the GDG you created in exercise 8 but specify it to be the (+2) generation of the GDG instead of the (+1), as customary. Then run an IDCAMS LISTCAT to see the contents of the GDG base. Explain why the relative generation numbers are as you find them. Use TSO to view the (0) generation and the (−1) generation and match them to the LISTCAT based on your knowledge of the content you stored in each GDG generation.

*10. Delete all generations of the GDG you used for exercises 7, 8, and/ or 9 by accessing them en masse. Then use IDCAMS to delete the GDG base.

NOTES

1. The sliding reference to the current generation is also typical of common language usage. For example, adults of today are regarded as the current generation; children are the next or (+1) generation. In the year 2010, when the children of the current generation are themselves adults, reference to them as members of the then current (0) generation would be appropriate. Today's adults would at that point be of the old generation, the (−1) generation. Humans slide into the next generation simply as a function of time, whether or not they themselves are parties to begetting the next generation. MVS generation data group data sets slide into the geriatric ward of automata only as new generations are "born."

2. IDCAMS is a multipurpose utility that deals with far more than VSAM data sets. In older days, under the now obsolete System/360 OS "CVOL" control volume catalog structure, the IEHPROGM utility was employed to create the GDG index instead of IDCAMS:

```
//GDGB4      EXEC  PGM=IEHPROGM
//SYSPRINT   DD   SYSOUT=A
//SYSIN      DD   *
     BLDG      INDEX=AK00.C99.TELMAST,ENTRIES=6,DELETE
/*
//*
```

Except for DELETE, the meaning of the fields on the control statement is obvious. In addition, one possible entry on the control statement is not shown—the word EMPTY.

EMPTY, if coded in the statement, stipulates that when the number of generations created exceeds the ENTRIES limit all existing data sets in the group are to be removed from the index. If EMPTY is not coded, then only the oldest data set generation is removed. The corresponding IDCAMS specification is EMPTY/NOEMPTY.

DELETE, when coded, specifies that any disk data set removed from the index is to be uncataloged and deleted. If DELETE is omitted, any disk data set that is removed from the index simply loses membership in the generation data group and is uncataloged but it remains on the system. Tape data sets are affected by DELETE only to the extent that they are uncataloged; they are not deleted. The corresponding IDCAMS specification is SCRATCH/NOSCRATCH.

The control statements for the creation of a GDG base under VSAM/ICF catalog structures with the IDCAMS utility are similar in function but differ in syntax. The VSAM/ICF catalog structures provide additional features not available in the old CVOL catalog and *IEHPROGM does not work with the newer catalog structures.* Like IEHLIST, which performed catalog display tasks in older times, IEHPROGM has had its wings clipped by progress.

3. RJE transmission of keyed data, as opposed to conveyance via magnetic tape, has been featured since the 1970s. However, it carries limitations inherent in the 3780 communication protocol. This protocol specifies that the record size is fixed at 80 bytes for sending to the mainframe and a maximum of 133 bytes in length for transmission from the mainframe to a remote job entry station. Records longer than 80 bytes must be broken into 80-byte portions, transmitted, and then reassembled by a program that picks up the data from a disk data set to which it has been sent.

The transmission of card image data is often addressed by the invocation of the IEBGENER utility, feeding in the 80-byte records to be transmitted as SYSIN DD * instream card image data. The destination of the data is usually specified as a generation data set, so that the data resulting from several transmissions can be pooled and processed at one time.

14

COND: Job Stream Control and Recovery

Every step in a job stream begins with an EXECute statement. Although coding of the EXEC statement can be as simple as

```
//STEPD   EXEC   PGM=FSBT3708
```

it is possible for other parameters to be placed after the program or procedure name. COND is one such parameter and PARM, discussed in Chapter 15, is another. The COND specification allows testing of the *user return code* set by preceding job steps. Coded with COND, the foregoing EXEC statement could be:

```
//STEPD   EXEC   PGM=FSBT3708,COND=(0,LT)
```

COND is fairly simple, but its documentation has suffered through the years from overly complex examples that describe intricate, atypical usage. We concentrate here on the applications of COND prevalent in business data processing work: controlling job steps for "recoverability," or the ability to resubmit a job that has been interrupted at some point, and communication between one job step and another. This statement expresses the general mandate of the COND parameter:

> *COND allows the indication of one or more conditions which, if satisfied, allow a step coded with it to be skipped.*

The syntax of COND does *not* provide the means of indicating directly any condition under which a step *should* be executed, but that can also be arranged.

SYSTEM COMPLETION CODES AND RETURN CODES

One of two different codes may be posted by a job step. "Posted" means left as a residual with MVS after step execution. To use COND successfully it is essential to understand that COND deals differently with each code. The *system completion code* is a three-position identifier controlled by MVS; programs have no access to it. If a job step executes successfully, its system completion code is 000. The code is printed in hexadecimal on the job log and in the allocation/deallocation report for a step that failed, prefaced under MVS with a literal "S" in the form "S001." *The system completion code is not the same as the user return code.*

A program that fails in execution is said to have suffered an "unresolvable program interruption." This interruption occurs when a program attempts something that cannot be accomplished, such as arithmetic on a nonnumeric quantity or reading a data set with an incorrect record size. For such conditions MVS constructs a nonzero system completion code. It could theoretically express any one of 4,095 different nonzero values between hexadecimal 001 and FFF. Despite its capacity, however, only about 480 distinct system completion code values, many of which are listed in Appendix F, are used by MVS to indicate the general nature of a problem.

Some system completion codes are well known: those beginning with the characters "0C" are associated with program logic-induced failures. One of these, an 0C7 or, as printed by MVS, S0C7, is the most common, representing an attempt to do arithmetic manipulations on nonnumeric data. When received, the system completion code is printed in the MVS job log and system report, as illustrated in Chapter 3, Figures 3.9 and

3.10. The analysis of the system completion code on a failed job is the starting point for problem resolution.

When we talk about one step of a job receiving communication from a preceding one, the discussion is *not* concerned with the system completion code. The system completion code is communication to the installation, not communication to subsequent steps. When a nonzero system completion code is posted by MVS at a step, the steps that follow are skipped unless special provisions are made.

USER RETURN CODE: THE "CONDITION" CODE

The program executed at each step posts it own code, called the user return code. This code, like the system completion code, can range from zero through 4,095. This code, however, is not printed by MVS in hexadecimal but in decimal as a four-position value. A step that completes successfully and does not take explicit action to place a value in the user return code by default returns a value of 0000. This value is labeled the COND or "condition" code by MVS and appears in the allocation/ deallocation listing for the job as:

```
IEF142I FSBT686A STEPG - STEP WAS EXECUTED - COND CODE 0016
```

A step that is never executed does not post a user return code. The MVS allocation/deallocation report carries a default literal of 0000 in such cases and implies that a code of zero is posted when a step is skipped but in fact, no such action occurs. The 0000 printed is a misleading default of the routines that reduce MVS generated information to printed form.

A program can place a value in the return code register by using the syntax of its language. In COBOL the statement is simple:

```
MOVE 0058 TO RETURN-CODE.
```

RETURN-CODE is not defined in working storage, it is provided without explicit definition. The MOVE could be coded as 58 or +58 instead of 0058, but it will print as 0058 regardless of the format. In PL/I the return code is set by coding

```
CALL IHESARC(58);
```

or

```
CALL PLIRETC(RCODE)
```

where RCODE is a variable into which the desired return code value has been placed. In FORTRAN it is set by issuing STOP with the value following:

```
STOP 58
```

In assembler whatever value is in register 15 at the immediate end of program execution is posted as the return code. The move of a value to the return code must be the last action the program takes before ending execution or the value in register 15 may be overlaid.

It is the convention of IBM software such as the compilers and utilities, which are merely programs to MVS, to use return code values of 0004, 0008, 0012, 0016, and 0020 as indications of increasingly serious errors. These values represent only conventions, but they are easily recognized and are documented in Appendix E.

Why do we care about having a program post a user return code? If a program executes but no action is taken to set such a code, it defaults to zero. Certain IBM programs such as the compiler, linkage editor, sort, and utilities, post a number of codes as noted above; the COBOL compiler unconditionally inserts logic into compiled programs to post unusual values like 0187, 0203, 0295, 0303, 0304, 0519, 1301, 3361, 3440, and 3505 in various error situations.[1] We care about the facility to post a user return code for two reasons:

- In combination with the COND parameter it allows a program of our own making to have control over the execution of programs that follow within a job stream.
- It allows a program to tell, in a crude way, why it stopped prematurely; in other words, what situation was detected that the program was designed to recognize as unresolvable.

The compiler tells subsequent steps, such as the linkage editor, not to execute if serious source code errors that would prevent a successful compile are encountered. Various IBM utilities tell other steps that follow not to execute if some type of control statement or I/O error is detected that would make probable the production of incorrect or incomplete output. An application program can tell a subsequent step not to run because no output to be processed by that step has been produced. A program that failed to run properly can tell special cleanup steps, that normally do not execute, to execute and delete the data sets created before the step that failed. This allows a complete rerun of the job stream, often the most reliable way to handle an I/O abend when all but huge data sets are involved.

A considerable amount of imprecision has crept into the technical vernacular in the more than two decades since OS was invented. In

connection with system completion and user return codes this imprecision is made apparent by the fact that texts and even IBM manuals
tend to lump both into the same pot. In common expression system
completion code, user return code, completion code, return code, and
condition code may at times refer confusingly to one or the other of
these two codes.[2]

COND PARAMETER OF THE EXEC STATEMENT

Simple COND Tests

Let's take a common example that uses COND, one with which you are
already familiar. Figure 1.2 presented the JCL for the usual IBM compile,
linkage edit, and go, or run, of a program. Reproduced here are the EXEC
statements for these three steps:

```
//COB     EXEC PGM=IKFCBL00,PARM=('SXR,DMA,CLI,APOST',
//  'NOSEQ,NOADV,LIB,DYN')
  -
  -
//LKED    EXEC PGM=IEWL,PARM='LIST,XREF,LET',COND=(5,LT)
  -
  -
//GO      EXEC PGM=GO,COND=(5,LT)
```

We note that at the end of the EXEC statement for the second and third
steps the COND parameter is coded.

COND has three subparameters: COND = (value, operator, stepname)

The "value" portion of the COND parameter must be a literal value,
such as the 5 in the above example. The "operator" can be one of six
different indications: EQ, NE, LT, LE, GT, GE. These well chosen ac-
ronyms have fairly obvious meanings:

EQ	equal
NE	not equal
LT	less than
LE	less than or equal
GT	greater than
GE	greater than or equal

"Stepname" is an optional indication that can tie the test to a specific
step that preceded the one on which the COND is coded. For example,

//COB is the stepname of the first step illustrated above. At the //LKED step COND could have been coded as COND=(5,LT,COB). If stepname is coded, it limits the test to the return code of a specific prior step. If stepname is omitted, it means that the COND test is made on the user return codes of all prior steps that executed; *any one such return code fulfilling the COND test is sufficient to cause the step carrying the COND to be skipped.* All return codes from every step that executed successfully are retained during the run by MVS and are accessible for COND tests.

"NERTS" as a Mnemonic Device

A corny but effective way to remember how COND works is embodied in the mnemonic device "NERTS" which can be pronounced as a silly word—its silliness is what helps remember it. The first three letters stand for whole words as phonetic sounds; "N-E" when spoken as letters form the word "any" and "R" is "are." The mnemonic means:

```
  N-E   R     T     S
 "any are true, skip"
```

The COND parameter of (5,LT) at //LKED means: "if 5 is less than the return code of any prior step, skip this step." The condition—5 being less than any prior step's return code—will be true if the return code from //COB, the only prior step here, is 6 or more. The compiler sets a return code of 0000 when no source code errors are detected; it sets a return code of 0004 for trivial warning errors and a return code of 0008 or greater for serious source code errors. Therefore the COND test will be false for trivial errors and true for serious errors. The //LKED step will execute when the COND test is false—trivial errors or no errors—and will be skipped when the COND test is true—serious errors.

The identical COND parameter is coded at the //GO step because we do not want to execute it when the compile was unsuccessful or when the compile was successful and the linkage edit was not. NERTS: any are true, skip. If *any* prior step satisfies a condition coded for a COND, the present step is skipped. Synonymous terminology has it that the step is "bypassed."

Compound COND Tests

In our compile JCL example we could have coded stepnames in the COND parameter tests at //LKED and //GO; it was not necessary, but we'll do it here to illustrate some additional aspects of COND. This is equivalent in operation to the foregoing example:

```
//COB     EXEC PGM=IKFCBL00,PARM=('SXR,DMA,CLI,APOST',
//        'NOSEQ,NOADV,LIB,DYN')
   -
   -
   -
//LKED    EXEC PGM=IEWL,PARM='LIST,XREF,LET',COND=(5,LT,COB)
   -
   -
   -
//GO      EXEC PGM=GO,COND=((5,LT,COB),(5,LT,LKED))
```

We now see a compound test at the //GO step. Two tests, one tied to the //COB step and the other to the //LKED step, are cited. It is possible to code up to eight such tests in a single COND. Although this may be appealing initially, the occasions on which it is useful are few. When a multiple test is coded, it is essential to keep in mind what it really means:

> The COND mechanism *always* operates to try to skip a step. It will skip a step if any of eight tests coded for a COND are true.

Once again the mnemonic NERTS can be recalled. With no step coded on a given COND test the return code from any prior step can potentially satisfy it. With steps coded on the test just those steps can potentially satisfy it. Yet any one or more coded tests being satisfied causes the step to be skipped. There is no way to make COND treat individually coded tests on a COND, as at the //GO step above, as if there were an "and" between them. COND is like the cowboy O. D. Cleaver's well seasoned whiskey jug: each one of the up to eight tests in a compound COND is like one of eight patched up holes in the jug. We can't tell the contents of the vessel to leak out "just when all the holes are open." Each hole has its own capability to drain the jug completely.

Coding one stepname on a COND test limits the COND to that particular step's return code. Multiple COND tests on a step broaden the basis for skipping a step but do so on a particular, step by step basis. Coding COND=(value,operator) omitting a stepname is tantamount to coding an individual test for each prior step. If this were really done, there would be an implied *or* between each test, not an *and*. There is no way of making a test like COND=(5,LT) be true just when *all* prior steps meet the condition; if *any one* of the prior steps satisfies the condition, the COND is satisfied and step skipping occurs. It is quite easy to overlook this fact, with very frustrating results.

COND has major applicability in the area of job stream recovery after an abend. It is more common to want the COND test broadened to the maximum amount, which is exactly what is conveyed when no stepname is coded. When no stepname is coded, only one test is needed after the COND to detect any previously posted "problem" user return code.

COND CODING FOR JOB FAILURE RECOVERY

Making a Cleanup Step Execute only Under Error Conditions

In the example of the compile, linkage edit, and run JCL we accomplished *positive* control over steps in a job stream: we allowed a final step, the //GO step, to execute when both prior steps executed successfully. The normal mode in the compile, linkage edit, and go job stream is for all steps to execute; that is, barring source code errors caught by the compiler, we expect and want all three steps to be executed.

We now turn our attention to a different situation, one more typical of a production job stream. Suppose we have the shortest possible job stream—one step—to sort a data set into sequence for an update. We want this job to produce a sorted output. We could picture the JCL in this form:

```
//FSBT686A  JOB AK00TEST,'DP2-JANOSSY',CLASS=E,MSGCLASS=X,
//  MSGLEVEL=(1,1),NOTIFY=BT05686
//*   THIS JCL = BT05686.SOURCE.CNTL(TESTSORT)
//STEPA    EXEC  PGM=SORT
//SORTLIB    DD  DSN=SYS1.SORTLIB,
//  DISP=SHR
//SORTIN     DD  DSN=FS12.C05.RAWDATA,
//  DISP=(OLD,KEEP)
//SORTOUT    DD  DSN=FS12.C05.SORTDATA,
//  UNIT=SYSDA,
//  DISP=(NEW,CATLG,DELETE),
//  DCB=(RECFM=FB,LRECL=50,BLKSIZE=6200),
//  SPACE=(6200,(40,5),RLSE)
//SYSOUT     DD  SYSOUT=*
//SYSUDUMP   DD  SYSOUT=A
//SORTWK01   DD  UNIT=SYSDA,SPACE=(CYL,5,,CONTIG)
//SORTWK02   DD  UNIT=SYSDA,SPACE=(CYL,5,,CONTIG)
//SYSIN      DD  *
     SORT FIELDS=(15,6,CH,A)
/*
//
```

When we run this one-step job, we execute the IBM sort utility. We read data from an existing data set named FS12.C05.RAWDATA and output the sorted data to FS12.C05.SORTDATA.

The sort will usually run successfully. It is possible, however, that it will encounter a problem resulting from an I/O error within the data set it is reading or an incorrect control statement. Some types of error will cause the sort or other IBM utility programs to abend, post a system completion code, and allow the end-status-abend of the DISP parameter on the output file to take effect. The output data set, which might have been partially created, will then be deleted, because we have specified DELETE for the disposition end-status-abend.

Certain levels of error may occur but will not cause the sort to abend; instead it will post a user return code of 0016 or 0020 and conclude without an abend.[3] When this happens, it occurs with the philosophy of *caveat emptor*; let the buyer, or user of the sorted data, beware. The data may or may not be usable for a given purpose. Ordinarily it is not productive to try to analyze the sorted output in such a case; it is more expeditious to delete the data set that contains the questionable sort output and run the sort again. It would be convenient if we could add some steps to our simple sort job to take care of necessary housekeeping for us. We can put an IEFBR14 ahead of the sort to delete any copy of the sort output that may exist from a prior run and eliminate the chance of rerun failure due to attempted creation of a duplicate data set name. Can we put a step following the sort that will delete the sort output and make that last step execute only if the sort *does not* run successfully?

What is desired is the reverse of our arrangement for the compile, linkage edit, and go job stream: it is *negative* job-stream control. Here we are interested in a normal sequence of executions that involves the first steps running—the IEFBR14 and the sort—and the third step *not executing unless there is a problem*. If the sort posts a nonzero return code, let's have the last step execute and delete the sort output for us, to prevent any job we run subsequently from trying to run with a flawed sorted data set. Better for the next job to find no sorted data set and fail outright than to find a flawed data set and use it to produce incorrect or incomplete output. Figure 14.1 illustrates the revised JCL, which now includes //DELSTEP and a final //CLEANUP step. The step names in this example are merely descriptive; in a production job stream the step names would follow an installation naming convention.

The //DELSTEP is an invocation of IEFBR14, the null program, which serves as an excuse for MVS to interact with our DD statement. At this point FS12.C05.SORTDATA, if it exists, is uncataloged and deleted. If it does not exist, the disposition of MOD causes a dummy data set by this name to be created and then deleted. This is the basis for the presence of the UNIT and SPACE parameters; they are used only in the latter case.

The //CLEANUP step carries a condition code of COND=(0,EQ,STEPA). This means "skip this step if zero is equal to the user return code of //STEPA." It will cause the following action:

- In the normal case, when the sort executes successfully, it will post a return code of zero. For this case the COND test will be true: 0 will

```
//FSBT686A  JOB AKOOTEST,'DP2-JANOSSY',CLASS=E,MSGCLASS=X,
//   MSGLEVEL=(1,1),NOTIFY=BT05686
//*
//*     SIMPLE ONE-STEP JOB WITH BAD RETURN CODE EOJ CLEANUP
//*     THIS JCL = BT05686.SOURCE.CNTL(DEMOCOND)
//*
//********************************************************
//*                                                      *
//*     DELETE OLD SORT OUTPUT                     DEL    *
//*                                                      *
//********************************************************
//DELSTEP   EXEC  PGM=IEFBR14
//DEL1         DD   DSN=FS12.C05.SORTDATA,
//   UNIT=SYSDA,
//   DISP=(MOD,DELETE),
//   SPACE=(TRK,0)
//*
//********************************************************
//*                                                      *
//*     SORT THE DATA                              A      *
//*                                                      *
//********************************************************
//STEPA     EXEC  PGM=SORT
//SORTLIB      DD   DSN=SYS1.SORTLIB,DISP=SHR
//SORTIN       DD   DSN=FS12.C05.RAWDATA,
//   DISP=(OLD,KEEP)
//SORTOUT      DD   DSN=FS12.C05.SORTDATA,
//   UNIT=SYSDA,
//   DISP=(NEW,CATLG,DELETE),
//   DCB=(RECFM=FB,LRECL=50,BLKSIZE=6200),
//   SPACE=(6200,(40,8),RLSE)
//SYSOUT       DD   SYSOUT=*
//SYSUDUMP     DD   SYSOUT=A
//SORTWK01     DD   UNIT=SYSDA,SPACE=(CYL,2,,CONTIG)
//SORTWK02     DD   UNIT=SYSDA,SPACE=(CYL,2,,CONTIG)
//SYSIN        DD   *
     SORT FIELDS=(15,6,CH,A)
  /*
//********************************************************
//*                                                      *
//*     DELETE SORT OUTPUT IF BAD SORT           CLEANUP  *
//*                                                      *
//********************************************************
//CLEANUP   EXEC  PGM=IEFBR14,COND=(0,EQ,STEPA)
//DEL1         DD   DSN=FS12.C05.SORTDATA,
//   UNIT=SYSDA,
//   DISP=(MOD,DELETE),
//   SPACE=(TRK,0)
//
```

FIGURE 14.1. Production-oriented handling of sort using condition code checking to detect failures and clean up for recovery

be equal to the return code. Therefore the //CLEANUP step will be skipped.

- If the sort encounters an error and posts a user return code greater than zero, the COND test will not be true; 0 will not be equal to the return code. Therefore in this instance the //CLEANUP step will not be skipped; it will execute, which means that the DD statement coded for it will be processed and the sort output data set, in whatever shape it is, will be deleted, thus preventing a job from attempting to use it.

Generalizing the "on Failure Only" Step Execution

All we can ever achieve with an individual COND test on an EXEC statement is a definition of one or more conditions that, if met, will cause the step to be skipped. COND has no ability to state "execute this step when these conditions are met." Beneath these outwardly simple statements is a hidden but crucially important fact. *COND does not make it possible to skip a step based on a combination of tests that must all be satisfied; there is no AND capability to compound the tests.* This means that we cannot code a COND that states "skip this cleanup step if *all* of the foregoing steps executed successfully." Given these circumstances, how do we accomplish cleanup of newly created data sets in an end-of-job step that we normally skip when all of several steps went well?

Our example job stream, which involved only one real "worker" step to sort a data set, is trivial. Its triviality allows the use of COND coding that, although workable, is not extendable to jobs that have more worker steps. Let's take a look at a situation that requires generalization by putting two more worker steps into the job stream.

In Figure 14.2 we see a job stream that performs three sorts. This is similar to our first example, but we now have three steps, //SORTA, //SORTB and //SORTC, each of which is in charge of sorting a different data set and creating a different sort output. //SORTA sorts a data set called FS12.C05.UADDTRAN, or "unsorted add transactions," creating an output named FS12.C05.SADDTRAN, or "sorted add transactions." //SORTB sorts FS12.C05.UCHGTRAN, "unsorted change transactions," creating FS12.C05.SCHGTRAN. //SORTC performs the same task for "auxiliary" transactions in a data set named FS12.C05.UAUXTRAN resulting in the creation of FS12.C05.SAUXTRAN. Our concern in handling this job is the same as before: we want to insure that a job we later submit to use the sorted transactions does not try to run with flawed data sets. If any one or more of the sorts fail, we wish to abandon the run and do it over again "from the top."

At the bottom of this job stream, however, we see not one //CLEANUP step but //CLEAN1 and //CLEAN2. We use these two steps to "reverse" the nature of the COND test and arrange for //CLEAN2 to be skipped just when *all* of the worker steps post return codes of zero. If we tried to accomplish this by having a single cleanup step and coding COND = (0,EQ) on it, we would also skip the cleanup if just one or two of the worker steps ran successfully. *NERTS: any are true, skip.* On the other hand, COND = (0,NE) would skip the cleanup if any step or steps had a problem but would allow the cleanup to execute when all steps had run well—the opposite of what we want.

The generalization of the cleanup mechanism may appear roundabout.

It relies on the fact that a step that does not execute does not post a return code. We might inadvertently make the assumption that a step that doesn't execute will post a return code of zero. This assumption is incorrect; the posting of a return code is accomplished by MVS only if it actually processes a step. When a step is skipped, even though it is acknowledged by MVS, it receives no services. A skipped step's DD statements are not acted on, the program is not loaded and given control, and no return code for it is stored.

//STEPA, //STEPB and //STEPC are each coded with COND=(0,LT) which means that they will be skipped if any prior step posted a return

```
//FSBT686A  JOB AK00TEST,'DP2-JANOSSY',CLASS=E,MSGCLASS=X,
//  MSGLEVEL=(1,1),NOTIFY=BT05686
//*
//*     THREE "WORKER STEPS" WITH GENERALIZED BAD EOJ
//*     CLEANUP TO MAKE RERUN FROM TOP POSSIBLE
//*     THIS JCL = BT05686.SOURCE.CNTL(RETDEM02)
//*
//*************************************************************
//*                                                          *
//*     DELETE OLD SORT OUTPUT                          DEL   *
//*                                                          *
//*************************************************************
//DELSTEP  EXEC  PGM=IEFBR14
//DEL1      DD  DSN=FS12.C05.SADDTRAN,
//  UNIT=SYSDA,
//  DISP=(MOD,DELETE),
//  SPACE=(TRK,0)
//DEL2      DD  DSN=FS12.C05.SCHGTRAN,
//  UNIT=SYSDA,
//  DISP=(MOD,DELETE),
//  SPACE=(TRK,0)
//DEL3      DD  DSN=FS12.C05.SAUXTRAN,
//  UNIT=SYSDA,
//  DISP=(MOD,DELETE),
//  SPACE=(TRK,0)
//*
//*************************************************************
//*                                                          *
//*          SORT ADD TRANS                             A    *
//*                                                          *
//*************************************************************
//STEPA    EXEC  PGM=SORT,COND=(0,LT)
//SORTLIB   DD  DSN=SYS1.SORTLIB,DISP=SHR
//SORTIN    DD  DSN=FS12.C05.UADDTRAN,
//  DISP=(OLD,KEEP)
//SORTOUT   DD  DSN=FS12.C05.SADDTRAN,
//  UNIT=SYSDA,
//  DISP=(NEW,CATLG,DELETE),
//  DCB=(RECFM=FB,LRECL=50,BLKSIZE=6200),
//  SPACE=(6200,(80,16),RLSE)
//SYSOUT    DD  SYSOUT=*
//SYSUDUMP  DD  SYSOUT=A
//SORTWK01  DD  UNIT=SYSDA,SPACE=(CYL,2,,CONTIG)
//SORTWK02  DD  UNIT=SYSDA,SPACE=(CYL,2,,CONTIG)
//SYSIN     DD  *
    SORT FIELDS=(1,10,CH,A,21,2,CH,A,17,4,CH,A)
/*
//*
//*************************************************************
//*                                                          *
```

FIGURE 14.2.   Three-step, three-sort job stream with condition code testing and cleanup for "rerun from the top" recovery

```
//*        SORT CHG TRANS                              B    *
//*                                                         *
//************************************************************
//STEPB     EXEC  PGM=SORT,COND=(0,LT)
//SORTLIB   DD    DSN=SYS1.SORTLIB,DISP=SHR
//SORTIN    DD    DSN=FS12.C05.UCHGTRAN,
//  DISP=(OLD,KEEP)
//SORTOUT   DD    DSN=FS12.C05.SCHGTRAN,
//  UNIT=SYSDA,
//  DISP=(NEW,CATLG,DELETE),
//  DCB=(RECFM=FB,LRECL=142,BLKSIZE=6106),
//  SPACE=(6106,(110,22),RLSE)
//SYSOUT    DD    SYSOUT=*
//SYSUDUMP  DD    SYSOUT=A
//SORTWK01  DD    UNIT=SYSDA,SPACE=(CYL,2,,CONTIG)
//SORTWK02  DD    UNIT=SYSDA,SPACE=(CYL,2,,CONTIG)
//SYSIN     DD    *
   SORT FIELDS=(1,10,CH,A,29,3,PD,A)
/*
//*
//************************************************************
//*                                                         *
//*        SORT AUX TRANS                               C    *
//*                                                         *
//************************************************************
//STEPC     EXEC  PGM=SORT,COND=(0,LT)
//SORTLIB   DD    DSN=SYS1.SORTLIB,DISP=SHR
//SORTIN    DD    DSN=FS12.C05.UAUXTRAN,
//  DISP=(OLD,KEEP)
//SORTOUT   DD    DSN=FS12.C05.SAUXTRAN,
//  UNIT=SYSDA,
//  DISP=(NEW,CATLG,DELETE),
//  DCB=(RECFM=FB,LRECL=70,BLKSIZE=6230),
//  SPACE=(6230,(50,10),RLSE)
//SYSOUT    DD    SYSOUT=A
//SYSUDUMP  DD    SYSOUT=A
//SORTWK01  DD    UNIT=SYSDA,SPACE=(CYL,2,,CONTIG)
//SORTWK02  DD    UNIT=SYSDA,SPACE=(CYL,2,,CONTIG)
//SYSIN     DD    *
   SORT FIELDS=(5,7,PD,A,44,3,CH,D)
/*
//*
//************************************************************
//*                                                         *
//*    0000 RET CODE IF OK, ELSE NO CODE          CLEAN1 *
//*                                                         *
//************************************************************
//CLEAN1    EXEC  PGM=IEFBR14,COND=(0,LT)
/*
//************************************************************
//*                                                         *
//*    DO EOJ CLEANUP IF CLEAN1 WAS SKIPPED       CLEAN2 *
//*                                                         *
//************************************************************
//CLEAN2    EXEC  PGM=IEFBR14,COND=(EVEN,(0,EQ,CLEAN1))
//*
//DEL1      DD    DSN=FS12.C05.SADDTRAN,
//  UNIT=SYSDA,
//  DISP=(MOD,DELETE),
//  SPACE=(TRK,0)
//DEL2      DD    DSN=FS12.C05.SCHGTRAN,
//  UNIT=SYSDA,
//  DISP=(MOD,DELETE),
//  SPACE=(TRK,0)
//DEL3      DD    DSN=FS12.C05.SAUXTRAN,
//  UNIT=SYSDA,
//  DISP=(MOD,DELETE),
//  SPACE=(TRK,0)
//
```

FIGURE 14.2.   (con't.)

code greater than zero. //DELSTEP has no COND parameter because COND on the first step of a job stream is meaningless. Under normal conditions step //CLEAN1 controls the end-of-job cleanup. A zero return code will be received by //CLEAN2 from //CLEAN1 if everything above it went well; no return code at all will be received by //CLEAN2 from //CLEAN1 if anything above it went wrong. There are no DD statements coded on //CLEAN1. There is no requirement to code even one DD statement for a step and none are needed here. The only purpose of step //CLEAN1 is to post or not post its zero return code.

Step //CLEAN2 is our customary end-of-job cleanup step. We desire to skip execution of it if all the steps above it executed successfully. What test can tell us if everything above went well? *A COND test involving a return code from a step that was skipped is ignored.* COND = (0,EQ,CLEAN1) loses its ability to cause //CLEAN2 to be skipped when step //CLEAN1 does not execute. The execution of //CLEAN2 results in its DD statements being processed, and the end-status-normal dispositions of each cause the deletion of any of the data sets that may have been fully or partially created. Thus we are protected from having any jobs that run subsequently attempt to operate with flawed or missing data. This may seem confusing—COND has the capability of being *very* confusing. The examples that follow clarify this discussion but you may wish to review Figure 14.2 if this seems at all unclear.

In the production environment job streams are submitted and run by an operations crew, not the program authors or composers of the JCL. If a job fails it cannot leave incomplete or flawed data sets lying around for processing by subsequent jobs. The failed job must clean up after itself to the maximum extent possible. The job must be "recovered" and its successful execution achieved. This is especially true if a job is working with data sets that will be accessed on the next business day by a teleprocessing system. Return code testing plays a major role in initiating job stream recovery.

There is something else on the COND parameter on the //CLEAN2 EXEC statement, something that has not yet been discussed. The word "EVEN" is coded within COND, just ahead of the actual (0,EQ,CLEAN1) test. This word, although appearing as another condition of COND, was in a sense misplaced in the scheme of things when the designers of JCL "tacked it onto" the COND syntax. EVEN, and an opposite-sounding but not opposite in effect "ONLY," deals with the treatment accorded to the step in the event that a prior step has abended. The presence of EVEN here means that MVS will render more attention to //CLEAN2 than it would otherwise have done if a step above had such a catastrophically bad time of it that the serial execution of steps was preempted. EVEN and ONLY are discussed in connection with the additional issues below.

System actions at Job Step Failure

Up to this point only the handling of a job stream in which steps execute and remain in control have been addressed. Merely posting a nonzero user return code does not cause anything special to be done by MVS. In fact, if a COND test of the nonzero return code does not follow somewhere in the job stream, its only effect is to print the value in the system allocation/deallocation report; it does not even appear in the job log.

The handling of control assumes a different nature, however, if a program executing at a job step loses control. A program loses control when it attempts to do something that cannot be accomplished. Situations in which this may occur include attempting arithmetic on nonarithmetic data, dividing by zero or a quantity that is too small and accessing a memory address outside the authorized limits of the program. When an event of this kind occurs, MVS intervenes not only in the operation of the program but it switches the handling of the entire job stream into the "abend in progress" or "system termination" mode. In this mode of treatment the following actions are taken by MVS:

- A system completion code is constructed and posted for the offending step. If a user return code has been set, it is discarded; the user return code is printed as 0000 but does not actually exist. *Any following COND test of the user return code from the failed step is ignored.*

- The step in process is wrapped up with an "indicative dump" written to //SYSUDUMP if a DD statement by this name has been coded at the step. Abend wrapup includes file close actions, although they are not so complete as they would be for a normal file close; low-values (hexadecimal 00) or other characters may be written into the last block of data.

- The data sets for which DD statements are coded on the failing step are accorded the end-status-abend processing indicated. If no end-status-abend is coded, end-status-normal dictates the disposition processing to be rendered for the abend. Note that this holds only for the DD statements for the step that failed, not for the DD statements of prior steps that were completed successfully. *The disposition for data sets involved solely in steps already concluded is not affected by the abend.*

- All remaining steps are skipped with the message "STEP NOT EXECUTED" on the job log and on the allocation/deallocation report unless explicit instructions have been coded on a step-by-step basis to request attention for the step even in the system termination mode. EVEN and ONLY are the two subparameters that request this extraordinary attention.

Simply put, a job stream has no second chance. If one of its steps "blows up," the treatment given the job stream after that point is far different from that which occurs under ordinary circumstances.

Two Classes of System Termination Processing

There are two ways that a job stream "offends" MVS and causes system termination mode to be invoked. Unfortunately only one category of system termination mode invocation is susceptible to EVEN or ONLY catching the attention of MVS thereafter. To understand why this is so, it is necessary to understand how MVS and MVS/XA actually process the JCL that makes up a job stream.

When a job stream is received by MVS, it checks all JCL syntax and the job is "queued" for execution if it is syntactically acceptable. If it has syntax errors, the job stream never enters real processing but is quickly rejected. It still receives a job number but it never causes any devices to be allocated to it.

As each step of a syntactically correct job stream starts, device and resource allocation actions for the step are performed. These actions are undertaken before the program to be executed in the step assumes control in a process called "scheduling." It is possible for failures to occur during scheduling. Some are classified as "JCL errors" because they appear as inconsistencies between the type of device indicated in the JCL and that indicated for a data set in the catalog. Others appear as space problems because enough disk space is not available to satisfy the requirements of a step at the time the devices it requires are being assigned. Space problems can develop not only in initial step scheduling but at times when secondary allocations are being sought, when the program in execution in a step has temporarily relinquished control to MVS modules in charge of securing the additional space.

When a job fails during step scheduling actions, there is no way at all to dissuade MVS from skipping all remaining steps. The remaining steps are completely ignored and are not even acknowledged on the job log to exist. Nothing can be done in terms of COND coding to change this action. EVEN and ONLY have no effect on it; the end-of-job cleanup arrangement is not effective for it. This is unfortunate, but a fact of life. This type of failure always requires manual attention to correct. Data sets created in prior steps may have to be manually deleted if a complete rerun of the failed job is to be made.

When a job fails after a program being executed assumes control, termination mode processing is more orderly. MVS wraps up the failed step and begins to "acknowledge" each of the remaining job steps. Its acknowledgement of each remaining step includes determining if either EVEN or ONLY has been coded on a COND statement for the step. If neither is coded, the step is skipped. If one or the other has been coded, MVS accords customary treatment to the step, which begins by determining if there is any other basis for skipping the step; namely, MVS poses the question, "Is there any COND test present that is satisfied?" If no COND test is present or tests are present but are not satisfied, the step is executed even though an earlier step abended and initiation of system termination processing began.

EVEN and ONLY Subparameters

EVEN and ONLY, although syntactically an optional part of the COND parameter, are actually not of the same ilk as COND tests. "Any are true, skip" has no relevance to EVEN and ONLY. In addition, EVEN and ONLY have nothing to do with testing the user return code from prior steps. *Neither EVEN or ONLY can be coded as a condition applicable to a specific prior step.* Both serve just to catch the attention of MVS for a step when some prior step or steps have failed and the job stream is undergoing system termination mode processing. As illustrated in Figure 14.3, when a job stream is progressing normally, EVEN and ONLY have different effects:

- EVEN is the "wide open" specifier. When EVEN is coded by itself, it means "process this step EVEN when a system termination is underway." *It also means that the step will be accorded customary processing when the job is progressing normally.* "Process" does not mean unequivocal execution. If other COND tests are present along with EVEN, "process" means "consider them." If any one or more of those tests are satisfied, the step is skipped.
- ONLY is the "limiting" specifier. It means "process this step only if system termination is underway." If the job stream is progressing normally, ONLY tells MVS to skip it unconditionally; in this case, any other COND tests coded on the step are superfluous. If the job stream is in system termination mode, it is processed."Processed" does not necessarily mean executed. If other COND tests are present along with ONLY, "process" means "consider them." If any one or more of those tests are satisfied, the step is skipped.

From the foregoing discussion it should also be apparent that *EVEN and ONLY are effective only if system termination of the job stream is underway because of an abend that occurred when a program had control.* This is the type of system termination during which MVS acknowledges the presence of job steps following the step that abended. If the system termination is underway due to an error that was detected in step scheduling actions caused by device or space problems, then no COND pa-

	Normal processing	Abnormal termination mode processing
No COND code or COND return code tests only	Step is processed; return code tests can cause step to be skipped	Step is acknowledged but not processed
COND=EVEN	Step is processed; return code tests can cause step to be skipped	Step is processed; return code tests can cause step to be skipped
COND=ONLY	Step is acknowledged but not processed	Step is processed; return code tests can cause step to be skipped

FIGURE 14.3. Summary of EVEN and ONLY effect on job step execution

rameter, EVEN and ONLY included, is effective. For the latter type of system termination there is no way to force MVS to recognize any aspects of the steps remaining after the step that failed.

End-of-Job Cleanup Use of EVEN

We can now direct attention to the use of the EVEN subparameter on the final step in Figure 14.2:

```
//CLEAN2    EXEC   PGM=IEFBR14,COND=(EVEN,(0,EQ,CLEAN1))
```

EVEN is coded here because we wish to have the //CLEAN2 step processed by MVS when a system termination is underway, as well as when a step has posted a problem return code value.

EVEN secures MVS consideration when a prior step has abended under program control. When an abend is underway, //CLEAN1, the prior step, will have been skipped and the (0,EQ,CLEAN1) test at //CLEAN2 will be ignored; EVEN secures MVS attention and because nothing is blocking the execution of //CLEAN2 it will run. Note that coding ONLY instead of EVEN would not accomplish what we have set out to achieve.

True, ONLY, like EVEN, will cause the step to be processed during system termination, but ONLY will not allow the cleanup step to process when the problem was just an unacceptably high user return code value.

It is possible to confront three possible types of job failure:

- Failure in purely the application program sense in that a program posted a user return code regarded as indicative of a problem. This is caught by the COND test on //CLEAN1, the skipping of which causes //CLEAN2 to execute and delete all outputs from the job.

- System termination mode processing developing from an abend that occurred under program control. No user return code is retained from the failing step and MVS constructs a system completion code for it. //CLEAN1 is skipped by MVS termination actions. EVEN on //CLEAN2 catches MVS attention and causes the step to be processed. Because (0,EQ,CLEAN1), the COND test coded on it, is ignored when //CLEAN1 is skipped, //CLEAN2 executes and deletes all outputs from the job. A rerun from the top is possible with no manual data set cleanup.

- System termination mode processing developing from an abend that occurs during MVS resource scheduling actions, not under program control.

The end-of-job failure cleanup catches and cleans up after the first two of the three types of situation we may confront. End-of-job cleanup cannot aid in "clearing the decks" for a rerun in the third case. Nothing available in the syntax of JCL provides the means of catching the attention of MVS to process a step when an abend is prompted by job step scheduling activities.

Multiple Abends in a Job

It is somewhat unusual but possible for multiple steps to abend in one job. MVS termination mode processing normally precludes this occurrence, but if the EVEN or ONLY subparameter is coded and no other COND tests exist or are satisfied, a subsequent step can be executed and abend. There need be no connection between the abends; a step executed because of EVEN or ONLY is not "tainted" by the fact that it is being processed under system termination mode conditions.

If multiple step abends are encountered in a run, each receives its own system completion code. The individual system completion codes are printed on the job log and in the allocation/deallocation reports. Because each is separate, each must be diagnosed on its own by using the system completion code value and the indicative dump produced for each abending program.

Time Limit: The Overriding Factor

As if there were not enough stipulations connected with COND tests and the use of EVEN and ONLY, it is necessary to be aware of one additional factor that takes precedence over all others. It is possible for a job to fail and enter system termination mode processing because it has used enough processing time—not "wall time," which is the duration of execution—to have exceeded the time limit established for it.[4] If this happens, the step underway "times out" with a system completion code of 322.

When a job times out, there is no time left for it to process any steps that remain, even if they have EVEN or ONLY coded on COND parameters. This fact makes such a run another of the type over which EVEN and ONLY have no control.

UPGRADING THE SEQUENTIAL UPDATE JOB STREAM

Recovery Considerations

Figure 14.4 illustrates the programmer's test sequential update job stream developed in Chapter 3 and upgraded in intervening chapters. The //CLEAN1 and //CLEAN2 steps have now been added to the end of the job stream to perform generation data group data set elimination actions necessary to rerun the job from the beginning if a failure occurs. For this scope of job stream, the rerunning of the first step, or two of three steps, is preferable to trying to anticipate potential failures step by step and documenting individual recovery actions for each instance. The trade-off is in people resources, training, and the potential for data set and recovery error, as opposed to the amount of machine time that will be expended only infrequently to redo steps before the point of failure.

In this job stream any return code value greater than zero, posted by any step, is regarded as grounds for cleanup actions. This will catch a potential 0016 or 0020 return code posted by the sort utility or an 0008 that is possible with IEBGENER, as indicated in Appendix E. No manual actions would be needed to resubmit the job because the cleanup steps would eliminate any and all (+1) generations created during the run, regardless of the point at which the job failed.

In Figure 14.4 the disposition of DISP = (MOD,DELETE) is coded in the //CLEAN2 deletion DD statements, as is the DCB parameter that carries the GDG model data set label. Therefore, even if no (+1) generation had been written for one or more of the GDG data sets, //CLEAN2 would operate properly. Because of the nature of DISP = (MOD,DELETE), a data set is created, then deleted, when it does not exist and no specific VOL

```
//FSBT686A  JOB AK00TEST,'DP2-JANOSSY',CLASS=T,MSGCLASS=X,
//  MSGLEVEL=(1,1),NOTIFY=BT05686
//*
//*     TEST RUN OF SEQUENTIAL UPDATE FSBT3708 -- VER 6B
//*     JCL NOW INCLUDES COND CODE TESTS AND DATA SET
//*     CLEANUP STEPS. RERUN FROM TOP POSSIBLE IN CASE
//*     OF JOB FAILURE AT ANY POINT, WITHOUT MANUAL DATA
//*     DELETION ACTIONS.
//*
//*     THIS JCL = BT05686.SOURCE.CNTL(BT3708V6)
//*
//*************************************************************
//*                                                          *
//*     SORT TRANS FILE                              A       *
//*                                                          *
//*************************************************************
//STEPA     EXEC  PGM=SORT
//SORTLIB   DD  DSN=SYS1.SORTLIB,
//  DISP=SHR
//*
//SORTIN    DD  DSN=AK00.C99.TRANSIN,
//  UNIT=(TAPE,,DEFER),
//  DISP=(OLD,KEEP),
//  DCB=(RECFM=FB,LRECL=71,BLKSIZE=1420,DEN=3,OPTCD=Q),
//  VOL=SER=HXR452,
//  LABEL=(1,NL,EXPDT=98000)                 'EXPDT ONLY FOR
//*                                          'UCC-1 TMS
//SORTOUT   DD  DSN=&&TRANSORT,
//  UNIT=SYSDA,
//  DISP=(NEW,PASS,DELETE),
//  DCB=(RECFM=FB,LRECL=71,BLKSIZE=6177),
//  SPACE=(6177,(32,7),RLSE)                 '2800 TRANS
//SYSOUT    DD  SYSOUT=*
//SYSUDUMP  DD  SYSOUT=*
//SORTWK01  DD  UNIT=SYSDA,SPACE=(CYL,2,,CONTIG)
//SORTWK02  DD  UNIT=SYSDA,SPACE=(CYL,2,,CONTIG)
//SYSIN     DD  *
    SORT FIELDS=(1,4,CH,A,9,2,CH,A,5,4,CH,A,14,1,CH,D)
/*
//*
//*************************************************************
//*                                                          *
//*     UPDATE MASTER FILE                           B       *
//*                                                          *
//*************************************************************
//STEPB     EXEC  PGM=FSBT3708,REGION=2048K,COND=(0,LT)
//STEPLIB   DD  DSN=BT05686.TEST.LOADMODS,
//  DISP=SHR
//BT3708E1  DD  DSN=&&TRANSORT,
//  DISP=(OLD,DELETE)
//*
//BT3708E2  DD  DSN=AK00.C99.TELMAST(0),
//  UNIT=(TAPE,,DEFER),
//  DISP=(OLD,KEEP)
//*
//BT3708E3  DD  DSN=AK00.C99.AREAREF,
//  DISP=SHR
//*
//BT3708U1  DD  DSN=AK00.C99.BT3708U1(+1),
//  UNIT=SYSDA,
//  DISP=(NEW,CATLG,DELETE),
//  DCB=(XX90.A00.DUMMYLBL,RECFM=FBA,LRECL=133,BLKSIZE=9044),
//  SPACE=(9044,(45,20),RLSE)
//*
//BT3708U2  DD  DSN=AK00.C99.TELMAST(+1),
//  UNIT=(TAPE,,DEFER),
//  DISP=(NEW,CATLG,DELETE),
//  DCB=(XX90.A00.DUMMYLBL,RECFM=FB,LRECL=314,BLKSIZE=32656),
//  LABEL=RETPD=30
//*
//BT3708U3  DD  DSN=&&TRANSFIN,
```

FIGURE 14.4. The sequential update job stream using COND code testing and cleanup for "rerun from the top" recovery

```
//    UNIT=SYSDA,
//    DISP=(NEW,PASS,DELETE),
//    DCB=(RECFM=FB,LRECL=102,BLKSIZE=6222),    '2800 TRANS
//    SPACE=(6222,(46,9),RLSE)
//*
//SYSOUT     DD  SYSOUT=*
//SYSUDUMP   DD  SYSOUT=*
//**********************************************************
//*                                                        *
//*      PRODUCE TRAN REPORT (INTERNAL SORT)         C     *
//*                                                        *
//**********************************************************
//STEPC    EXEC  PGM=FSBT3719,REGION=2048K,COND=(0,LT)
//STEPLIB    DD  DSN=BT05686.TEST.LOADMODS,
//    DISP=SHR
//SORTLIB    DD  DSN=SYS1.SORTLIB,
//    DISP=SHR
//BT3719E1   DD  DSN=&&TRANSFIN,
//    DISP=(OLD,DELETE)
//*
//BT3719U1   DD  DSN=AK00.C99.BT3719U1(+1),
//    UNIT=SYSDA,
//    DISP=(NEW,CATLG,DELETE),
//    DCB=(XX90.A00.DUMMYLBL,RECFM=FBA,LRECL=133,BLKSIZE=9044),
//    SPACE=(9044,(45,20),RLSE)
//*
//BT3719U2   DD  DSN=AK00.C99.BT3719U2(+1),
//    UNIT=SYSDA,
//    DISP=(NEW,CATLG,DELETE),
//    DCB=(XX90.A00.DUMMYLBL,RECFM=FBA,LRECL=133,BLKSIZE=9044),
//    SPACE=(9044,(45,20),RLSE)
//*
//SORTWK01   DD  UNIT=SYSDA,SPACE=(CYL,2,,CONTIG)
//SORTWK02   DD  UNIT=SYSDA,SPACE=(CYL,2,,CONTIG)
//BT3719SM   DD  SYSOUT=*
//SYSOUT     DD  SYSOUT=*
//SYSUDUMP   DD  SYSOUT=*
//*
//**********************************************************
//*                                                        *
//*      PRINT THE REPORT OUTPUTS                    D     *
//*                                                        *
//**********************************************************
//STEPD    EXEC  PGM=IEBGENER,COND=(0,LT)
//*
//SYSUT1     DD  DSN=AK00.C99.BT3708U1(+1),DISP=SHR
//           DD  DSN=AK00.C99.BT3719U1(+1),DISP=SHR
//           DD  DSN=AK00.C99.BT3719U2(+1),DISP=SHR
//*
//SYSUT2     DD  SYSOUT=A,
//    DCB=(RECFM=FBA,LRECL=133,BLKSIZE=9044)
//SYSIN      DD  DUMMY
//SYSPRINT   DD  SYSOUT=*
//SYSUDUMP   DD  SYSOUT=*
//*
//**********************************************************
//*                                                        *
//*      0000 RET CODE IF OK, ELSE NO CODE        CLEAN1   *
//*                                                        *
//**********************************************************
//CLEAN1   EXEC  PGM=IEFBR14,COND=(0,LT)
/*
//**********************************************************
//*                                                        *
//*      DO EOJ CLEANUP IF CLEAN1 WAS SKIPPED     CLEAN2   *
//*                                                        *
//**********************************************************
//CLEAN2   EXEC  PGM=IEFBR14,COND=(EVEN,(0,EQ,CLEAN1))
//*
//DEL1       DD  DSN=AK00.C99.TELMAST(+1),
//    UNIT=(TAPE,,DEFER),
```

FIGURE 14.4. *(con't.)*

270

```
//   DISP=(MOD,DELETE),
//   DCB=(XX90.A00.DUMMYLBL,RECFM=FB,LRECL=314,BLKSIZE=32656)
//*
//DEL2         DD   DSN=AK00.C99.BT3708U1(+1),
//   UNIT=SYSDA,
//   DISP=(MOD,DELETE),
//   DCB=(XX90.A00.DUMMYLBL,RECFM=FBA,LRECL=133,BLKSIZE=9044),
//   SPACE=(TRK,0)
//*
//DEL3         DD   DSN=AK00.C99.BT3719U1(+1),
//   UNIT=SYSDA,
//   DISP=(MOD,DELETE),
//   DCB=(XX90.A00.DUMMYLBL,RECFM=FBA,LRECL=133,BLKSIZE=9044),
//   SPACE=(TRK,0)
//*
//DEL4         DD   DSN=AK00.C99.BT3719U2(+1),
//   UNIT=SYSDA,
//   DISP=(MOD,DELETE),
//   DCB=(XX90.A00.DUMMYLBL,RECFM=FBA,LRECL=133,BLKSIZE=9044),
//   SPACE=(TRK,0)
//
```

FIGURE 14.4. (con't.)

is coded. The DCB is necessary for GDG data sets when this is desired, because MOD requires the model data set label to create the dummy data set. If non-GDG data sets were being cleaned up in this manner, DCB would not have to be coded. If the printline data sets were being written to tape instead of disk, the AFF specification would be coded in the second and subsequent tape data set deletion DD statements in //CLEAN2 to minimize tape drive assignment to the step, limiting it to one drive.

A Production Forced Abort Routine

Program FSBT9999 is typical of a production forced abort routine usually employed in place of IEFBR14 at the //CLEAN2 step. It was developed in COBOL, but in some installations a module such as this is written in assembler. FSBT9999 performs the following actions when executed:

- It accepts as a parameter value from the EXEC statement a character string that is printed "three up" on 50 double-spaced lines, prefaced by the date and time.
- It intentionally abends by calling COBOL abend service module ILBOABN0 with a very noticeable user return code of 999. The abend is posted on the system console and focuses operator attention on the failed job.

The source code for FSBT9999 is provided in Figure 14.5 and is available on diskette as described at the end of Appendix D. Although it is written in COBOL, it can serve as the forced abort step in job streams that execute FORTRAN, PL/I, or assembler programs. At a minimum, a step invoking

```
000010 IDENTIFICATION DIVISION.
000020 PROGRAM-ID.     FSBT9999.
000030 AUTHOR.         J JANOSSY.
000040 DATE-WRITTEN.   JUNE 1986.
000050 DATE-COMPILED.
000060 ENVIRONMENT DIVISION.
000070 CONFIGURATION SECTION.
000080 SOURCE-COMPUTER.  IBM-4381.
000090 OBJECT-COMPUTER.  IBM-4381.
000100 INPUT-OUTPUT SECTION.
000110 FILE-CONTROL.
000120     SELECT OUTFILE  ASSIGN TO UT-S-ABORTMSG.
000130 DATA DIVISION.
000140*
000150 FILE SECTION.
000160 FD  OUTFILE
000170     LABEL RECORDS ARE STANDARD
000180     BLOCK CONTAINS 0 RECORDS
000190     RECORD CONTAINS 133 CHARACTERS.
000200 01  OUTFILE-REC         PIC X(133).
000210*
000220 WORKING-STORAGE SECTION.
000230*
000240*    NOTE: THE COBOL MODULE TO CALL FOR A STRAIGHT ABORT IS
000250*    SPELLED I-L-B-OH-A-B-N-ZERO AS CODED BELOW:
000260*
000270 01  WS-ABORT-MODULE     PIC X(8)   VALUE 'ILBOABNO'.
000280 01  WS-FAILURE-CODE     PIC S9(3) COMP.
000290*
000300 01  OUTREC-AREA.
000310     12 FILLER           PIC X(1).
000320     12 OR-DATE          PIC X(8).
000330     12 FILLER           PIC X(2)   VALUE SPACES.
000340     12 OR-TIME-HRS      PIC X(2).
000350     12 FILLER           PIC X(1)   VALUE ':'.
000360     12 OR-TIME-MIN      PIC X(2).
000370     12 FILLER           PIC X(1)   VALUE ':'.
000380     12 OR-TIME-SEC      PIC X(2).
000390     12 FILLER           PIC X(1)   VALUE ':'.
000400     12 OR-TIME-HUN      PIC X(2).
000410     12 FILLER           PIC X(3)   VALUE SPACES.
000420     12 OR-TEXT1         PIC X(36).
000430     12 OR-TEXT2         PIC X(36).
000440     12 OR-TEXT3         PIC X(36).
000450*
000460 01  WS-TIME             PIC 9(8).
000470 01  WS-TIME-BY-PARTS  REDEFINES  WS-TIME.
000480     12 WS-HRS           PIC X(2).
000490     12 WS-MIN           PIC X(2).
000500     12 WS-SEC           PIC X(2).
000510     12 WS-HUN           PIC X(2).
000520*
000530 LINKAGE SECTION.
000540 01  USER-PARM.
000550     05 UP-LENGTH        PIC S9(4) COMP.
000560     05 UP-MSG           PIC X(100).
000570*
000580 PROCEDURE DIVISION USING USER-PARM.
000590 0000-MAINLINE.
000600     MOVE CURRENT-DATE TO OR-DATE.
000610     ACCEPT WS-TIME FROM TIME.
000620     MOVE WS-HRS TO OR-TIME-HRS.
```

FIGURE 14.5. COBOL source code for forced-abort utility program (*continues next page*)

272

```
000630        MOVE WS-MIN TO OR-TIME-MIN.
000640        MOVE WS-SEC TO OR-TIME-SEC.
000650        MOVE WS-HUN TO OR-TIME-HUN.
000660        OPEN OUTPUT OUTFILE.
000670        IF UP-LENGTH GREATER +0
000680            MOVE UP-MSG
000690                TO OR-TEXT1  OR-TEXT2  OR-TEXT3
000700                    INSPECT OUTREC-AREA REPLACING ALL LOW-VALUES BY ' '
000710          ELSE
000720            MOVE '*** JOB ABENDED, CHECK ALL OUTPUT!! '
000730                TO OR-TEXT1  OR-TEXT2  OR-TEXT3.
000740        PERFORM 1000-WRITE-MSG 60 TIMES.
000750        CLOSE OUTFILE.
000760        MOVE +999 TO WS-FAILURE-CODE.
000770        CALL WS-ABORT-MODULE USING WS-FAILURE-CODE.
000780        STOP RUN.
000790*
000800 1000-WRITE-MSG.
000810        WRITE OUTFILE-REC FROM OUTREC-AREA
000820            AFTER ADVANCING 2 LINES.
```

FIGURE 14.5.   (con't.)

it must provide a DD statement that carries the name //ABORTMSG because that is where the report issued by the program emerges. It can be
assigned to SYSOUT = A or X or any other print destination.

DD statements can be coded at the forced abort step and will be processed if the step is executed, just as with IEFBR14. Whether or not DD
statements other than //ABORTMSG are coded depends on the data set
cleanup needed for a given job and the step at which the job will be
restarted. In Chapter 16 FSBT9999 is used in making the example sequential update job stream into a production caliber cataloged procedure.

JOB STEP COMMUNICATION VIA RETURN CODES

On rare occasions it is necessary to have one "worker" job step control
the execution of another worker step as a normal function. For example,
a program that reads one or more data sets and produces a data set that
will subsequently be sorted may encounter a run in which no records
exist to be output for sorting. It may be desirable to allow such a program
to tell the sort step that follows, or any other steps that follow and expect
to use the data, not to execute.

The COND parameter was designed to address this type of forward
interstep communication. Its contemporary use for this purpose, however, is much less intensive than originally thought necessary. Skipping
the execution of reporting programs for which no data existed in a run
was a common notion in the 1960s but is no longer in vogue.[5] COND
coding to cause step invocation or skipping, except to handle job failure
conditions, is now generally avoided.

Nevertheless, for those occasions on which purely normal forward interstep communication is needed it can be implemented easily if the basic elements of COND testing are kept in mind. This communication is possible with and without the type of end-of-job failure cleanup illustrated earlier. Because the use of forward interstep communication in conjunction with end-of-job failure handling is the more general case, we will use it to illustrate this aspect of COND coding.

Figure 14.6 is a diagram of a nine-step job stream involving five COBOL application programs, the sort utility, and three steps using IEFBR14. Although several data sets are illustrated, only those shown with names in this illustration are of concern for housekeeping and cleanup purposes because they are being created by the job stream. Five different reports are shown, labeled R-1, R-2, R-3, R-4, and R-5. Let's see what the worker steps of this job do:

- //STEPA reads two data sets and merges them to create two others that will be retained after the run.

- //STEPB reads two data sets; one has not been processed in the job stream and one is produced by FSBT3201 in //STEPA. //STEPB produces a report and a data set fed to the next sort step. It may have no data to put into the data set because of the nature of the processing it does. It sets a return code of 0000 if it places data into FS09.C01.MERGE03. If it has written this data set as an empty one, however, with no records in it, there is no need to do the sort.[6] In this case FSBT3202 sets a return code of 0004. This does not mean that there is an error that should cause the run to be abandoned; it is just communication telling //STEPC and //STEPD not to run.

- //STEPC is the sort utility; when FS09.C01.MERGE03 is created with no records in it, the sort should not run.

- //STEPD is program FSBT3203; it should execute only if data set FS09.C01.SRECPT01 exists. This data set will not exist if the sort did not run as a result of communication from //STEPB, the 0004 return code.

- //STEPE is program FSBT3204, which reads an existing data set and produces a report and a data set used in the next step. Its execution does not depend on whether or not FSBT3202 produced any data; //STEPE should always execute unless some problem return code, greater than 5, is posted above.

- //STEPF is program FSBT3205, which reads two data sets not previously processed, and FS09.C01.MATCHTR produced in //STEPE. This program merges the data to produce a report. Its execution does not depend on the presence of absence of data from //STEPB.

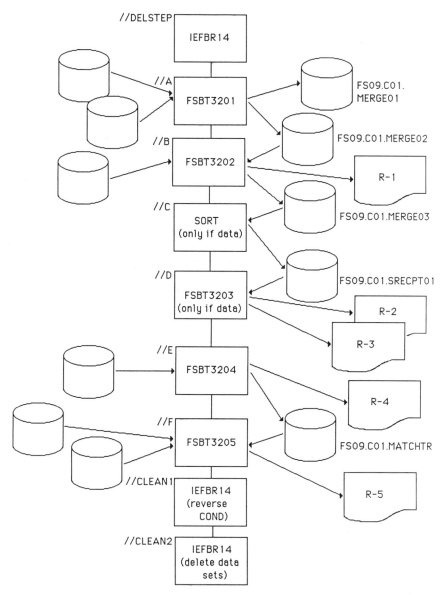

FIGURE 14.6. Job stream diagram of nine-step job stream performing several tasks

The initial step in the job is //DELSTEP; it uncatalogs and deletes the existing copies of the five data sets created in this run. These are shown as ordinary sequential data sets here; if they were generation data group data sets, there would be no housekeeping //DELSTEP at the start. At the bottom of the job stream //CLEAN1 and //CLEAN2 perform the same functions that they did in our prior example.

This much simplified listing of the JCL for the job stream shows only the EXEC statements for each step and the data sets involved in the housekeeping and cleanup steps:

```
//DELSTEP   EXEC   PGM=IEFBR14
     delete FS09.C01.MERGE01
     delete FS09.C01.MERGE02
     delete FS09.C01.MERGE03
     delete FS09.C01.SRECPT01
     delete FS09.C01.MATCHTR
   -
//STEPA     EXEC   PGM=FSBT3201
   -
//STEPB     EXEC   PGM=FSBT3202,COND=(5,LT)
   -
//STEPC     EXEC   PGM=SORT,COND=((5,LT),(4,EQ,STEPB))
   -
//STEPD     EXEC   PGM=FSBT3203,COND=((5,LT),(4,EQ,STEPB))
   -
//STEPE     EXEC   PGM=FSBT3204,COND=(5,LT)
   -
//STEPF     EXEC   PGM=FSBT3205,COND=(5,LT)
   -
//CLEAN1    EXEC   PGM=IEFBR14,COND=(5,LT)
   -
//CLEAN2    EXEC   PGM=IEFBR14,COND=(EVEN,(0,EQ,CLEAN1))
     delete FS09.C01.MERGE01
     delete FS09.C01.MERGE02
     delete FS09.C01.MERGE03
     delete FS09.C01.SRECPT01
     delete FS09.C01.MATCHTR
```

The DD statements for this JCL are not shown because they are not relevant to this discussion.

In our earlier example any nonzero return code from any step was regarded as indicative of a problem warranting abandonment of the job stream and invocation of end-of-job cleanup actions. In the majority of cases this is valid for production job streams. In this case, because of the forward interstep communication that occurs between //STEPB and the two steps that follow it, we must "leave room" in the range of possible return codes regarded as no problem values. In keeping with IBM's tradition for "no problem" values, FSBT3202 uses a return code of 0000 for completely normal program end and 0004 for successful end with no data written to FS09.C01.MERGE03. Therefore we cannot regard 0004 as a return code that should cause abandonment of the job. We'll regard return codes of 0005 and under, including 0005, as "OK" and codes of

0006 and higher as indicative of a serious problem that should invoke end-of-job cleanup.

The only difference in the overall pattern is that instead of coding the cleanup COND test as (0,LT) we now code it consistently as (5,LT). This test appears in every step after //STEPA, the first real worker step, and it means "skip this step if 5 is less than the return code of any prior step." Note, however, that an additional test is coded for //STEPC and //STEPD. Each of these steps carries an additional opportunity to be skipped.

At //STEPC and //STEPD we wish to see skipping occur when the return code from //STEPB is equal to 0004. We state that test as (4,EQ,STEPB) on the EXEC statement for each of these steps in combination with the overall end-of-job cleanup COND test. The two COND tests on each step are treated independently and the *satisfaction of either one will cause the step to be skipped*. "NERTS" means "any are true, skip." If the overall end-of-job cleanup arrangement is not being used, then the (5,LT) COND test will be missing from each step and //STEPC and //STEPD will carry just the (4,EQ,STEPB) test.

In actual practice it is unusual for COND tests more complicated than this to be employed in spite of the *ab ovo* examples contained in JCL manuals. Little need is encountered for skip control more involved than this; the need to insure data set cleanup in case of program failure overwhelmingly predominates in contemporary use of COND.[7]

REVIEW QUESTIONS AND (*)EXERCISES

1. What is the system completion code, what range of values can it assume, and what is responsible for posting it?

2. What is the user return code, what range of values can it assume, and how is it posted?

3. The COND parameter of the EXEC statement allows subsequent actions to be based on the relationship between a literal value and what other value?

4. COND = ((0,EQ,STEPB),COND = (0,EQ)) is coded on an EXEC statement at the end of a multistep job stream. Explain its effect and code it in an alternative way to accomplish the same thing.

5. What is the return code posted by a step that is not executed?

6. A job stream has four steps: //STEPA, //STEPB, //STEPC, and //STEPD. What is the effect of coding COND = (0,EQ,STEPB) on the third step?

*7. With the job stream described in item 6 code EXEC statements to execute //STEPD only if //STEPA, //STEPB, and //STEPC all execute with return codes of zero.

*8. With the job stream described in item 6 code EXEC statements to skip //STEPD only if //STEPA, //STEPB, and //STEPC all execute with return codes of zero.

*9. Code a trivial program in COBOL, FORTRAN, PL/I, or assembler named RETCODE4 that simply sets a return code of 0004 and ends execution. Copy it and create two additional programs, one named RETCODE0 which sets a return code of 0000 and one named RETCODE8 which sets a return code of 0008. Then build and run a job stream that executes them in this sequence:

```
//STEPA        RETCODE0
//STEPB        RETCODE8
//STEPC        RETCODE4
//STEPD        RETCODE0
//STEPE        RETCODE4
```

Identify the system completion codes and return codes from each step in the MVS allocation/deallocation report.

*10. Using the programs and job stream in item 9, code appropriate COND parameters to skip //STEPD if the return code from any prior step is greater than 6, and run the job stream to test your coding.

*11. Using the programs and job stream in item 9, code appropriate COND parameters to arrange for //STEPE to execute when any step preceding it posts a return code greater than 5, and run the job stream to test your coding.

*12. Build on the job stream in item 9 and add an IEFBR14 step at its start to allocate a data set. Code cleanup steps that carry DD statements with appropriate DISP = (MOD,DELETE) parameters for the allocated data set and for one that does not exist at all. Arrange for the last step of the job stream to delete both data sets if any step in the job stream posts a return code greater than 5. Note: You must use the MOD disposition for this purpose, not OLD or NEW.

NOTES

1. Successfully compiled COBOL programs may encounter logical errors in VSAM I/O, dynamic/nondynamic callable modules, and other areas that the compiler is

prepared to intercept and for which it can give notice. See the end of Appendix F for detailed information on COBOL compiler-specific user return codes.

2. Imprecision in terminology extends into the IBM system completion code error message manuals as well. In the message manuals the abbreviation rc is often used to denote a one to three position number that may be printed after the system completion code as a further indication of the basis for receipt of the error code. Manuals variously refer to rc as "return code" or "reason code." Reason code is correct; return code in the context of error message explanation is a reflection of the assembler-language mentality of the manuals. The inconsistency results from the sheer volume of technical writing needed to create and maintain the manuals, the number of personnel who contribute to the effort, and the extended time span involved.

   The rc value documented in the manuals is, in fact, a return code from lower level assembler system software modules to those of higher levels, the modules being the myriad that constitute the subsystems of MVS and MVS/XA. But rc had better stand for reason code for contemporary applications programming personnel or the message manuals serve little purpose for them. Under MVS/XA an additional message labeled REASON = 00000000 appears on the job log output associated with abend reporting. This message is an extension of abend message reporting intended for eventual use and is not inherently related to the reason codes associated with error message manuals.

   The issue is even more muddled if one considers that the field starting in bits 34 and 35 of the program status word, on which assembler language logical branch tests are made, is also called the "condition code." Happily, this field is entirely invisible to higher level language programmers.

3. The meaning of the 0016 and 0020 return codes from the DFSORT utility is explained in Appendix E, which lists the return codes for all commonly used IBM utility programs.

4. The time limit for a job is established by the TIME parameter on the JOB card or for a step on its EXEC statement. When these parameters are absent, an installation default applies to a given job, tied to the job class if a class structure is being used. The TIME parameter is discussed in Appendix A.

5. Printing a report with a message that states "no records to print" or something similar is a matter of good system design. It provides an end-user with assurance that a system actually ran and that reports have not simply been misplaced. This is in the same vein as printing a zero value as 0.00 on an accounting document instead of printing blanks—it indicates affirmatively that a null quantity is intended. IBM's famous "this page intentionally left blank," inserted into manuals as necessary as text modified, is an example of the same practice.

6. Why open and close a data set to which no records will be written? When generation data group data sets are used, it is often desirable to coordinate the generations of different data sets within an application system. If GDGs are holding report printlines or application data, it would be customary to create an empty generation of a data set rather than not create one at all, or it may appear that something malfunctioned and a program did not execute.

7. The author wishes to thank Craig Happel and Tom Vari, colleagues who provided valuable and perceptive insights in connection with the COND parameter.

═══ 15 ═══

PARM: Passing Parameters into Programs

In this chapter we examine the JCL PARM feature, which provides the means of passing controlling information to a program at the time it is invoked. PARM is accessible to any application program written in COBOL, PL/I, or assembler under MVS.

EXTERNAL CONTROL OF PROGRAMS

On many occasions it is necessary for the operation of a program to vary from one execution to the next; that is, to control some aspect of its operation externally. A program that performs reporting may have to be limited in a given run to report only those items that pertain to a specific date range. It may be necessary for an end-user to be able to control which of the several types of financial postings a program handles in a run. Another example is a program that copies stored print images to the print queue and must be controllable in regard to the starting page and quantity of pages from that point it will copy and print.

The three ways in which controlling parameters can be introduced into a program from an outside source are:

- They can be contained in the input data itself as records preceding the actual data input.
- They can be housed in a separate data set or "control file," placed there prior to the run using TSO, an online application system, or a separate job.
- They can be handed to the program at execution time by the JCL PARM facility.

The first method, under which run-controlling parameters are placed as a preface to input data, is a carryover from punched cards days. End-users provided input data on punched cards and it was convenient for them to place one or more controlling cards in front of their input. Nowadays, this is not convenient at all because most input data to production programs are supplied by key-to-disk equipment that produces tapes, by remote job entry transmission, or by data already on the mainframe as a result of teleprocessing actions.

The second external controlling method, that of using a separate data set to house controlling fields of information, is appropriate when this information has substantial bulk. In most cases, however, program-controlling information is small. For example, to specify plainly the date range for which records are to be selected for reporting only 13 bytes must be supplied to the program: the starting date, a separator character, and the ending date:

```
031588-101988
```

In this manner we might express the Gregorian (MMDDYY) date-controlling parameters for a reporting program to select only those records that are dated March 15 through October 19, 1988. If we created a control file as a sequential data set to be read by the program and used it to house this parameter, we would use up one whole track of disk space for it because one track is the minimum data set size under MVS.

The control file method has drawbacks much more serious than disk space waste. If the end-user is to supply the controlling information and enter it into a data set, the user must be supplied with some form of access to the control file. This may be provided by a teleprocessing system if it is designed to support this batch-oriented aspect of operation.

If this is not available, the end-user will probably have to be provided with a terminal capable of accessing TSO and be trained in using it to edit the contents of the control data set. Not all users need access to TSO; its provision and training on it is a high price to pay to provide an end-user with controlling capability for a batch job.

A major hidden problem in the control file approach is the fact that once a control file is set up for a run it cannot be changed until the run actually takes place. It is not possible to arrange the contents of the control file as should be for a run, submit the run, and then change the control file contents and submit another run. Until the first run executes, which may not be until the evening hours, it does not access the control file. When it executes, it will access and use the contents of the control file *as of that time*. If we did what is described here, both runs would execute with the controlling parameters set up for the second run.

THE JCL PARM FACILITY

PARM Coding on the EXEC Statement

MVS provides the facility to pass parameters to a program at the time of its execution via a special feature of the EXEC statement. You have undoubtedly already used this feature, called the PARM for PARaMeter, in your program compilations. It is normally used to pass controlling information to the compiler, in its "PARM options."

The compiler, a large assembler program, is written in a manner that allows it to receive customizing directives using the PARM facility. Notice in the JCL for the compile, shown in the //COB step of Figure 1.2 and reproduced here, how the EXEC statement is coded with a PARM:

```
//COB      EXEC  IKFCBL00,PARM=('SXR,DMA,CLI,APOST',
//    'NOSEQ,NOADV,LIB,DYN')
```

The information between the apostrophes after PARM= is really one character string that contains values the compiler is programmed to interpret. The commas are there because that's the way the compiler was set up to "see" the different values in the PARM. Except for the last comma on the first line, which shows a normal JCL continuation, those embedded commas have nothing to do with the JCL syntax.

Because compilers are rather special programs, it may appear that PARaMeters are something special. Not so. COBOL, PL/I, and assembler programs can be written to receive parameters and even to handle the situation gracefully when a PARM is expected but not received. Using PARMs is the easiest way to handle the passage of a run-specific date range, controlling code string, or other such item to a program. For example, passing a date range to a program set to receive it as a PARM could be done with an EXEC statement in this form:

```
//STEPF   EXEC PGM=FSBT3765,PARM='031586-101986'
```

If a COND parameter were also needed on the EXEC statement, it could take this form

```
//STEPF   EXEC PGM=FSTB3765,PARM='031586-101986',COND=(5,LT,STEPE)
```

or if line length were too great for one statement because of the PARM value the EXEC statement could be continued to another line:

```
//STEPF      EXEC  PGM=FSBT3765,COND=(5,LT,STEPE),
//  PARM='031586-101986'
```

There is no required order in the EXEC statement for the PARM parameter and other parameters such as COND.

The value for the PARM can be supplied by a symbolic parameter when the JCL is housed as a cataloged or instream procedure as illustrated at step //FS37651B in Chapter 16, Figure 16.3. Thus it is possible to feed PARM information into a program by simply changing a readily accessed item on the execution JCL for a production job. This PARM can be supplied by an end-user on the document employed to initiate a production batch run, and operations personnel who normally submit the execution JCL can set up the run by entering the parameters from the document into the execution JCL. This job set up is possible with cards but is now customarily done by the operations group using TSO-stored and edited images of the execution JCL. Many production batch runs handle day-in, day-out processing task variations in this manner.

A PARM enters the mainframe on the copy of JCL placed in the input queue by job submission. PARM values for a given job are set on submission of the job. The same JCL can be edited, the PARM value changed, and another job submission made immediately. The same program can also be executed more than once in a given job stream, each time with a different PARM value. This overcomes one of the most serious problems of control files, which cannot be changed until the first run using such a file executes.

How a COBOL Program Receives a PARM

A COBOL program coded to receive a PARM obtains it in exactly the same way that a CALLed program or subroutine obtains its linkage area.

COBOL CALLed programs are not necessarily one of the most familiar of items; this being so, the PARM mechanism is sometimes also miscast as esoteric. But it is not really complex at all.

When a PARM is coded on an EXEC statement, MVS takes the information in the PARM parameter and places it in memory. It prefaces this fragment of memory with two bytes in which it puts a signed, pure binary number to indicate the number of bytes of PARM data stored.[1] This number is described in COBOL as PIC S9(4) COMP and is aligned on a word boundary, where the first item under an 01 level is always located.

MVS passes the address of the two-byte PARM length field to the program being executed. That program can gain access to this already-established memory by coding a description for it in a LINKAGE SECTION. The program cannot code this description in its WORKING-STORAGE SECTION because working storage for a program is newly allocated to the program when MVS loads it for execution. The program "owns" its own working storage. MVS, as a program CALLing the program being EXECuted, "owns" the PARM memory area.

A COBOL program that receives a PARM is coded in exactly the same way that it would be if it were being called by another application program. It contains the description of the expected PARM data as an 01 item in a linkage section, the first field of which must be the PARM length PIC S9(4) COMP value. The maximum length of PARM that MVS will pass is 100 bytes beyond the two-byte length field. MVS is not concerned with the nature of this up to 100 bytes. The program's linkage section description of the PARM must identify the fields within it. The program must have logic in it to determine if the parameter fields are valid for its purposes and what effect they should have on program operation.

The relevant portions of COBOL coding for a program that is to receive the date range PARM used in the foregoing examples could appear as

```
WORKING-STORAGE SECTION.
   -
   -
   -
LINKAGE SECTION.
01   DATE-PARAMETER-VALUE.
     12 DATE-PARM-LENGTH            PIC S9(4) COMP.
     12 DATE-PARM-START.
        15 DP-START-MO              PIC X(2).
        15 DP-START-DA              PIC X(2).
        15 DP-START-YR              PIC X(2).
     12 FILLER                      PIC X(1).
     12 DATE-PARM-END.
        15 DP-END-MO                PIC X(2).
        15 DP-END-DA                PIC X(2).
        15 DP-END-YR                PIC X(2).
```

and any names can be used for the PARM fields. The critical factor is that the definition of the received fields matches the actual nature of the PARM string to be received. If numeric data other than the parameter string length received from MVS are to be received via the PARM, it is essential to perform numeric validation on the applicable fields before attempting arithmetic operations or comparisons, because human errors can occur in the entry of the PARM field on the EXEC statement when setting up the run.

How a COBOL Program Uses a PARM

When a program contains a linkage section, its mere presence does not mean that it is used by the program. For the linkage area to be recognized by the logic within the procedure division of a COBOL program the division heading must be coded with the USING phrase:

```
PROCEDURE DIVISION USING . . . .
```

The items named after the USING phrase must include the name of the PARM linkage area. With the establishment of the linkage area and the coding of the USING phrase in the procedure division heading, the program can receive the parameter string at the start of its execution and operate on it.

A prudent first step in the use of PARM is for the program to determine if a PARM was received at all. If the EXEC statement invoking the program did not have a PARM parameter coded, then no parameter string was supplied. In this case MVS will have placed a value of zero in the PARM length field. In a beginning-of-job action the program that receives the date range PARM could determine whether DATE-PARM-LENGTH is equal to zero; if so, no date range PARM was supplied. Perhaps in this case we wish the program to default to processing the entire input file rather than selecting records from a date range. On the other hand, perhaps we want the lack of PARM to be regarded as a fatal error and include logic in the program to set its return code to a value that the job stream detects and uses as the basis for a job-stream abort, as discussed in Chapter 14.

Extended PARM validations are usually performed. In the case of a date range PARM one meaningful validation consists of checking to see if the program has received a parameter string with a length of exactly 13 bytes. The pair of Gregorian dates expected, separated by a filler byte for legibility, must equal this length. The program might then check the validity of both dates, perhaps using an installation-provided date validation callable routine; a program that receives a PARM can CALL another program as usual. The program could convert the two dates in the range to Julian format for comparison purposes; if the second is less than the first, the program could abort for the error. If the values provided by the PARM passed all of these tests, the program could proceed to compare the date on each record being processed to this range, for possible inclusion in processing.[2]

How a PL/I Program Receives and Uses a PARM

A PL/I program receives a PARM somewhat differently than a COBOL program, and examination of the two-byte binary length field supplied by MVS is not necessary. PL/I receives the PARM data as a 100-byte string that can be manipulated by substring functions. The following PL/I source code fragment illustrates a means of receiving a date range PARM from an EXEC statement and performing preliminary edits on it.[3]

```
    PROCEDURE(INPARM) OPTIONS(MAIN);
         DECLARE INPARM CHAR(100) VARYING;
         DECLARE N FIXED BINARY(31),(DATE_START,DATE_END) CHAR(6);
         DECLARE PARM_FLAG BIT(1) INITIAL('0'B);
      -
      -

    GET_PARM: PROCEDURE;
    PUT LIST INPARM:                             /* ECHO THE PARM */
    IF LEN(INPARM) ^= 13 THEN DO;
         PUT LIST 'MISSING OR INVALID PARM ON EXEC STATEMENT';
         PUT LIST 'PROGRAM STOPPED WITH RETURN CODE 0008';
         EOF = '1'B;
         CALL IEHSARC(8);
         END;
     ELSE
    IF INDEX(INPARM,'-') ^= 7 THEN DO;
         PUT LIST 'MISSING DATE SEPARATOR IN DATE RANGE PARM';
         PUT LIST 'PROGRAM STOPPED WITH RETURN CODE 0012';
         EOF = '1'B;
         CALL IEHSARC(12);
         END;
     ELSE DO;
         N = INDEX(INPARM,'-');
         DATE_START = SUBSTR(INPARM,1,N-1);
         DATE_END = SUBSTR(INPARM,N+1,(LEN(INPARM)-LEN(DATE_START)-1));
         END;
    /*  AT THIS POINT DATE_START AND DATE_END CAN BE FURTHER EDITED. */
    /*  LOGIC INVOKING GET_PARM SHOULD TEST PARM_FLAG TO SEE IF THE  */
    /*  PARMS RECEIVED WERE ACCEPTABLE OR NOT, '0'B MEANS OK.        */
      -
      -

    RETURN;
    END GET_INPARM;
```

TYPICAL PARM USES

The uses and applications of the PARM feature are many and varied. The examples listed here are only a few of the many processes that benefit from this capability.

Processing Option Control

A parameter can be used to decide whether an update program edits, updates, and reports or just edits and reports on transactions. This allows an end-user to do "trial before doing it for real" reporting runs at his or her option.

Multiple-use Reporting Program

A general purpose listing routine can exist within an application system to handle several different selection report outputs stemming from the same data set. The PARM may consist of a three-byte value that indicates the types of records to be selected for a given execution of the program and the next 50 bytes of the PARM could carry the report title to be applied to the output for the run. The EXEC statement could appear as:

```
//STEPF     EXEC  PGM=FSBT3772,COND=(0,LT),
// PARM='ACT,LIST OF ACTIVE ANNUITANTS'
```

or

```
//STEPF     EXEC  PGM=FSBT3772,COND=(0,LT),PARM=('ACT',
// 'LIST OF ACTIVE ANNUITANT')
```

Another invocation of the same listing routine that will output a different selection of items from the same or another data set might be arranged with:

```
//STEPF     EXEC  PGM=FSBT3772,COND=(0,LT),
// PARM='6MO,ANNUITANT CANDIDATES FOR NEXT 6 MONTHS'
```

or

```
//STEPF     EXEC  PGM=FSBT3772,COND=(0,LT),PARM=('6MO',
// 'ANNUITANT CANDIDATES FOR NEXT 6 MONTHS')
```

The linkage section for this PARM could be coded as

```
LINKAGE SECTION.
01   PARM-FOR-RUN.
     12 PFR-PARM-LENGTH-IN              PIC S9(4) COMP.
     12 PFR-CONTROL-CODE                PIC X(3).
     12 FILLER                          PIC X(1).
     12 PFR-TITLE.
        15 PFR-TITLE-BYTE    PIC X(1)   OCCURS 50 TIMES.
```

where byte 4 of the PARM string will be received as a comma in both
EXEC examples; MVS unavoidably supplies a comma in the PARM string
at the point at which it is *continued* to another JCL line. The program
could employ logic to take only the length of PARM actually submitted
and create a centered page heading. This PARM may be coded as a symbolic parameter on different execution JCL decks that invoke the same
job stream. Thus an end-user could initiate what might appear to be
different runs, all of which really invoke the same underlying cataloged
procedure and program.

Foreign Tape id Input "Stamping"

A program handling unlabeled data entry tapes may need to "stamp"
every incoming record with the six position volume serial number on
the external paper reel label for audit trail purposes. The production
JCL is stored as a cataloged procedure. The external tape label identifier
enters the job as a symbolic parameter to be supplied to the DD statement
for the program reading and copying the tape. The same symbolic parameter, however, is also coded as the PARM for the program and is
made available to the program to be inserted into a field in each record
conveyed on the tape. This establishes an audit trail by providing in
each record the identity of the tape on which the record was conveyed,
as illustrated in the proc in Figure 16.3.

Customized Message from Forced Abort Routine

An installation will customarily use a forced abort routine that can be
executed at a step to abort job stream processing when an error affecting
job integrity has occurred. Program FSBT9999, whose source code is
illustrated in Figure 14.5, is an example of such a routine. It provides
the means of outputting a default job failure message or a message specific to the step or process that failed. The PARM mechanism is used
in FSBT9999 to receive the short message optionally coded on the EXEC
statement. The message is repeated across a few pages of output opposite
the system date and time as an aid in drawing operator attention to a
job failure.

Hints

A few potential problems may arise in connection with the use of PARMs:

- If you forget to code the USING phrase after the procedure division heading in a COBOL program but code the linkage section and manipulate its fields in logic, your program will not operate properly because it will not access the PARM field. USING is what allows your program to receive the address of the parameter string from MVS. Check first for an omission of this phrase if you encounter a problem in a new program using a PARM.

- There is no guarantee that the party completing the EXEC statement or execution JCL will do it correctly. Validate the PARM data before you attempt to use it, especially if any part of the parameter string is arithmetic. The portion of the 100-byte parameter string beyond the length of data supplied on the EXEC statement will contain low-values (hexadecimal 00).

- PARM data is not saved by MVS after a run; there is no readily accessible evidence of what PARM values entered a program without such echoing.[4] Echo the PARM received onto the start of printed output or onto a second status report. It can even be made a part of a report page heading so that it appears on each page of output, an especially informative technique for date range selection reporting. If a run has a problem and there is a question as to why it functioned the way it did, the echoed PARM values will be of considerable assistance.

- It is possible to encounter a situation in which you believe you are supplying appropriate controlling information to a program but have specified the wrong program and the intended results are not produced. If a PARM is supplied on the EXEC statement for a program that is not coded to receive it, no system error will occur. Check the program in such a case—you may not have installed the PARM-receiving logic.

REVIEW QUESTIONS AND (*)EXERCISES

1. Identify the three ways that a program can receive run tailoring or control information at the time it begins execution and cite the advantages and limitations of each method.

2. Why are language compiler EXEC statements usually associated with PARMs?

3. A controlling string to be passed to a program consists of 110 bytes of information. What syntax or other issues dictate the method to be used to pass this information to the program at execution time?

4. Throughout the business day an online system is employed by end-users to update data sets. Each update causes the current date to be written into a field in the records affected. At 6:00 PM each day a batch job is run, listing each of the records updated that day. Contrast the use of a PARM that carries a date to allow this program to make its reporting selection as opposed to a "print me today" flag that could be carried in the record and set on each time a record was updated.

5. A program is coded to receive a PARM value but no PARM parameter was coded on the EXEC statement invoking the program. Will the job step fail as a result? Why or why not?

6. Cite three typical uses of the PARM feature for production business data processing programs.

*7. Code a program in a language of your choice to receive a 38-byte character string as a PARM value. Arrange for the program to verify that it received a PARM value and if it did, to use it in the page heading for a report. If no PARM was received, the program is to use the centered literals "** NO TITLE **" in the title area.

*8. A date range selection PARM is to be received by a program called FSBT1533. The job step at which the program is invoked is //STEPF of a 12-step job. //STEPF is to execute only if //STEPC posted a return code of 7 or less. Code the EXEC statement for //STEPF.

*9. Using JCL such as that found in item 1 of Chapter 17, compile a small program with the debugging options of an appropriate compiler by overriding the PARM options of the compile and linkage edit proc. Make at least three runs and vary the placement of at least 10 compiler parameter options across four or more lines of JCL in which the PARM is split between lines. It is likely that because of the unusual syntax of continued PARMs you will receive one or more JCL syntax errors before succeeding. Analyze and highlight the MVS error messages and your successful run.

*10. Code a program in the language of your choice to receive a PARM that consists of an eight-digit number and a two-digit number, such as:

The program is to develop a printline that contains the first number in leading zero suppressed, imbedded comma format. It is to print this line, single-spaced, the number of times indicated by the second PARM-specified number. The program should use good business data processing practices and echo the PARM, validating it as necessary and reporting any errors it detects, without abending. Execute the program eight times, first using the foregoing PARM, and then once for each of the following PARM values, some of which contain intentional errors:

```
12345678-XX
0987X654-10
ABCD1234-YZ
00021812-00
00000000-30
006597-45
0003678-111
```

NOTES

1. The PARM information supplied to the program by MVS can occupy a maximum of 102 bytes of memory. The first two bytes are the signed binary length field. The value here indicates how many bytes of PARM string data were coded on the EXEC statement. *This value does not include the two bytes that it uses itself; in other words, the maximum value the length field will ever contain is 100.*

2. If records are being tested for a date that falls within a date range and the date is stored in Gregorian format, it is not essential to convert the dates to Julian format. Instead, a workable solution is to create a work field in memory for each of the three dates by moving the year to the high-order position:

```
        01   WS-RANGE-START-DATE.
             12 WS-RANGE START-YR      PIC X(2).
             12 WS-RANGE-START-MO      PIC X(2).
             12 WS-RANGE-START-DA      PIC X(2).
    *
        01   WS-END-DATE.
             12 WS-RANGE-END-YR        PIC X(2).
             12 WS-RANGE-END-MO        PIC X(2).
             12 WS-RANGE-END-DA        PIC X(2).
    *
        01   WS-RECORD-DATE.
             12 WS-RECORD-YR           PIC X(2).
             12 WS-RECORD-MO           PIC X(2).
             12 WS-RECORD-DA           PIC X(2).
```

After validation of the PARM-supplied date range, the year, month, and day fields from those dates are moved into WS-RANGE-START-DATE and WS-RANGE-END-

DATE. Each time a record is read for processing the year, month, and day fields within it are moved to WS-RECORD-DATE. Then this type of test can be made:

```
IF WS RECORD-DATE NOT LESS THAN WS-RANGE-START-DATE
   AND WS-RECORD-DATE NOT GREATER THAN WS-RANGE-END-DATE
      MOVE 'Y' TO F2-GET-FLAG.
```

This type of range test is discussed on page 154 of *Commercial Software Engineering: For Productive Program Design*, James G. Janossy, ISBN 0-471-81576-4, John Wiley and Sons, Inc., 1985. The generic model for selection logic is discussed in Chapter 9 of that book.

3. The author wishes to thank Ron Stevens and Wayne Bannister for their assistance in developing this PL/I PARM example.

4. Echoing user-supplied PARMs on a report is often the only way an end-user would be able to see the PARM values actually supplied to a production run. Although the PARM appears in the system allocation/deallocation reports, those reports demand a knowledge of JCL to interpret and end-users typically do not receive them.

16

PROC: Instream and Cataloged Procedures

If you took a course in COBOL or PL/I taught on a mainframe, you were provided with a few lines of JCL to perform a compile, linkage edit, and go. When you ran the jobs to process source code, you got back several pages solid with cryptic-looking JCL that seemed to materialize from nowhere. That JCL came from a cataloged procedure. Using procedures or "procs" is fairly easy. Building them is more involved, but it is a definite part of business data processing because jobs run repetitively are housed as procs.

WHAT IS A PROC?

A procedure is raw JCL in which the JOB statement is replaced by a PROC statement and the null // statement at the end is removed. Certain standard procs are provided by IBM to perform assemblies, compiles, linkage edits, and a variety of systems support functions. There is nothing sacred about those procs; some of them are, in fact, quite dated and of a primitive JCL style and format. Installations normally take the IBM procs for standard processes and modify them to suit local requirements. Locally composed JCL is made into procs to perform the production work of the installation.

The "cataloged" in "cataloged procedure" is not related to the system catalog, it means that the proc has been placed in a partitioned data set identified to MVS as a procedure library or "proc lib." Each member of this PDS, which is a normal, 80-byte card image PDS just like any CNTL data set, is a proc and each proc is known by its member name. The procedure library is usually named SYS1.PROCLIB. It may be, but usually is not, accessible to applications programmers for the writing of new members; normally an installation requires that new production procs be given to an installation librarian who alone is authorized to made additions or replacements in SYS1.PROCLIB. Procedures can be invoked "instream" without installation in a procedure library and are usually tested in this manner.

Procs provide the means to package the JCL to accomplish a specified series of application program executions. This makes it possible to initiate all processing by specifying just the name—the SYS1.PROCLIB member name—of the proc. Procs make it possible to hide the raw JCL from view, protect it, keep it standardized, and invoke it easily and reliably. Procs are much like a word processor's "bring in the boilerplate" function, or the compiler's COPY compiler directive. By citing a proc on an EXEC statement in execution JCL all JCL stored in the proc is brought in at that point. Just as in word processing slight modifications may be needed in the standard item to suit a given circumstance. Procs provide two means of altering the contents of the "canned" JCL when it is invoked. The invoking JCL can override items in the proc or symbolic parameters can be designed into the proc to be given values by the execution JCL.

A minor clarification in terminology is helpful. Raw JCL means JCL that is submitted with a JOB statement. When we talk of a proc, we are referring to JCL that has been stripped of its JOB statement and ending null statement. Execution JCL—also called a "run deck" or "go deck"—is JCL that includes EXEC statements to invoke procs. EXEC statements that take the form

```
//STEPA  EXEC  PGM=FSBT3708
```

execute a program. This EXEC can be raw JCL or a statement in a proc. To invoke a proc the EXEC statement appears a little differently

```
//STEPD   EXEC   BT3765P1
```

since PGM= is not coded. The omission of PGM= or the explicit coding
of PROC= indicates that what follows—BT3765P1 in this case—is a
cataloged procedure: JCL stored in a member of this name in
SYS1.PROCLIB, to be brought in at this step and executed. A proc may
have many steps of its own; one step of execution JCL may and usually
does explode to many steps of the proc. The execution JCL step is referred
to as the "stepname"; in other words, //STEPD is a stepname. Each step
within a proc is called a "procstepname." Because it is confusing to
have the same stepnames and procstepnames appear in jobs being executed, installations normally impose a standard naming convention on
procstepnames and a different convention for stepnames of the JCL invoking procs. *Procs cannot invoke other procs;* therefore the naming
convention need not be complicated.

A Compile, Linkage Edit, and "Go" Proc

In Chapter 1, raw JCL for compiling, linkage editing, and running a program was illustrated and dissected as a means of introducing JCL and
mainframe program execution. Figure 1.2 provided the full-length raw
JCL to accomplish the three steps in this process. The stepnames for the
three steps were //COB, //LKED, and //GO, representing COBOL compile,
linkage edit, and "go run the new program." Each of the three steps
executed a program; the compiler and linkage editor are just programs
as far as MVS is concerned.

The JCL in Figure 1.2 can be made into a proc, as illustrated in Figure
16.1. This figure is literally Figure 1.2 with the job statement and front
comments deleted and the ending null // statement dropped off. The line
numbers at the right remain the same as in Figure 1.2 so that you can
readily compare the two and see changes:

- Line 00060000 was formerly a comment; it is now the PROC statement. The name immediately following the two slashes is the name
  of the proc, the name under which it should be stored in the proc
  library.[1]
- //SYSIN under the //COB step has been omitted. This names the data
  set and member that contains the source code. We supply that in the
  execution JCL because it will change from compile to compile.
- //INDATA1 and //OTREPT1 have been omitted from the //GO step.
  These are DDnames particular to the program processed in Figure
  1.2. We supply DD statements required for a given program in the
  execution JCL so that the proc can be used to process any COBOL
  source code.

Suppose the JCL in Figure 1.2 were slimmed down and generalized as in Figure 16.1, and installed in a procedure library. To perform the same compile, linkage edit, and go as in Chapter 1 we could now submit this execution JCL:

```
//FSBT686A  JOB AK00COMP,'DP2-JANOSSY',CLASS=E,MSGCLASS=X,
//  MSGLEVEL=(1,1),NOTIFY=BT05686
//*
//* BT05686.SOURCE.CNTL(CLGEXAM1)  EXEC CLG PROC
//*
//STEPA    EXEC  CLGCOBOL
//COB.SYSIN  DD  DSN=BT05686.SOURCE.COBOL(PSD183),
//  DISP=SHR
//GO.INDATA1 DD  DSN=BT05686.SOURCE.CNTL(STATEDAT),
//  DISP=SHR
//GO.OTREPT1 DD  SYSOUT=*
//
```

The basis for the shortness of IBM's chosen names for the compile and go stepnames, here procstepnames, becomes apparent. The three DD statements we are supplying in the execution JCL "add" DD statements to the proc that do not exist within it. In order for the DD statements we supply in the execution JCL to be matched up with the intended procstep we must preface the DDnames with the procstepname and a period. If the procstepnames are long, it becomes more awkward to do so.

A Business Data Processing Compile and Linkage Edit Proc

Compile, linkage edit, and go is fine for learning a language, but it is customary to compile and linkage edit only and to retain the load module in a library. A series of compiled program load modules is then executed in a job stream. A compile and linkage edit proc, as illustrated in Figure 16.2, is a staple in every installation. The name of the proc is VSCOBCL. This rendition illustrates typical enhancements. Other procs, called VSCOBC, VSCOBCLG, and VSCOBCG, are also supplied by IBM and may be enhanced locally.

Symbolic Parameters

When raw JCL is converted into a procedure, various items within the JCL must be generalized because they will vary from one invocation of the proc to another. It is possible to handle many such situations with overrides or additions to DD statements. A more elegant and concise means is provided by symbolic parameters.

```
//CLGCOBOL PROC                                                    00060000
//****************************************************************** 00070000
//*                                                               *  00080000
//*      EXECUTE COBOL COMPILER                            COB     *  00090000
//*                                                               *  00100000
//****************************************************************** 00110000
//COB       EXEC  PGM=IKFCBL00,PARM=('SXR,DMA,CLI,APOST',             00120000
//  'NOSEQ,NOADV,LIB,DYN')                                            00130000
//SYSLIB    DD  DSN=SYS1.COPYLIB,                '"COPY" SOURCE       00140000
//  DISP=SHR                                                         00150000
//SYSIN     DD  DSN=BT05686.SOURCE.COBOL(PSD183),  'SOURCE CODE       00160000
//  DISP=SHR                                                         00170000
//SYSUT1    DD  UNIT=SYSDA,SPACE=(460,(700,100))  'WORK SPACE         00180000
//SYSUT2    DD  UNIT=SYSDA,SPACE=(460,(700,100))  'WORK SPACE         00190000
//SYSUT3    DD  UNIT=SYSDA,SPACE=(460,(700,100))  'WORK SPACE         00200000
//SYSUT4    DD  UNIT=SYSDA,SPACE=(460,(700,100))  'WORK SPACE         00210000
//SYSPRINT  DD  SYSOUT=*                                              00220000
//SYSUDUMP  DD  SYSOUT=*                                              00230000
//SYSLIN    DD  DSN=&&LOADSET,                   'OBJECT FILE OUT      00240000
//  UNIT=SYSDA,                                                      00250000
//  DISP=(NEW,PASS,DELETE),                                          00260000
//  SPACE=(3200,(500,100))                                           00270000
//*                                                                  00280000
//****************************************************************** 00290000
//*                                                               *  00300000
//*      EXECUTE THE LINKAGE EDITOR                       LKED     *  00310000
//*                                                               *  00320000
//****************************************************************** 00330000
//LKED      EXEC  PGM=IEWL,PARM='LIST,XREF,LET',COND=(5,LT)           00340000
//SYSLIN    DD  DSN=&&LOADSET,                                        00350000
//  DISP=(OLD,DELETE)                            'OBJECT FILE IN       00360000
//SYSLMOD   DD  DSN=&&GOSET(GO),                                      00370000
//  UNIT=SYSDA,                                  'LOAD MODULE OUT      00380000
//  DISP=(NEW,PASS,DELETE),                                          00390000
//  SPACE=(TRK,(2,2,1),RLSE)                                         00400000
//SYSLIB    DD  DSN=SYS1.VSCOBLIB,               'SERVICE ROUTINES     00410000
//  DISP=SHR                                                         00420000
//SYSUT1    DD  UNIT=SYSDA,SPACE=(1024,(50,20))  'WORK FILE           00430000
//SYSPRINT  DD  SYSOUT=*                         'MESSAGES            00440000
//SYSUDUMP  DD  SYSOUT=*                         'ABEND DUMP          00450000
//*                                                                  00460000
//****************************************************************** 00470000
//*                                                               *  00480000
//*      EXECUTE THE NEW PROGRAM (GO RUN IT)                GO     *  00490000
//*                                                               *  00500000
//****************************************************************** 00510000
//GO        EXEC  PGM=GO,COND=(5,LT)                                  00520000
//STEPLIB   DD  DSN=&&GOSET,                     'LOAD MODULE LIB      00530000
//  DISP=(OLD,DELETE)                                                00540000
//SYSOUT    DD  SYSOUT=*                         'DISPLAY MESSAGES     00580000
//SYSUDUMP  DD  SYSOUT=*                         'ABEND DUMP          00590000
//* NOTE THERE IS NO ENDING "//" NULL STATEMENT ON A PROC!            00600000
```

FIGURE 16.1. Chapter 1 "compile, link and go" JCL made into a cataloged procedure

Any DD subparameter or even a portion of it within JCL can be replaced by a symbolic parameter; the program name on the EXEC statement is the only item that cannot be coded as a symbolic parameter. A unique name of up to **seven** characters, prefaced with a single ampersand, is coded in place of the item in the proc JCL. A total of 11 items have been replaced with symbolic parameters in the VSCOBCL proc and all are given default values at the top of the proc. There is nothing special about symbolic parameter names; they can be composed of any seven letters, or even of JCL parameter names. Those illustrated in VSCOBCL are typical. This may seem like quite a few items on which to anticipate

changes at run time.[2] More likely than not, few sets of execution JCL
for this proc will carry values for these items. They have been coded as
symbolic parameters as a convenience so that they can be changed readily by the installation by altering the default value coded for each item
in the proc statement. All symbolic parameters must be satisfied or nullified by defaults or execution JCL.

*The same symbolic parameter can be used within the JCL of the proc
at any number of places.* For example, &PRINT is coded at two places,
so that both the //SYSPRINT source code listing and the //SYSUDUMP
compiler dump output, if produced, go to the same place. The same
value, &WORK, is plugged in for all four of the compiler's work data
set device specifications. The same value, symbolically named
&CSPACE, is used for all four work data set space allocations. Symbolic
parameters are just place holders in the JCL for which default or run-
time provided values are substituted by MVS before job execution. A
given item can even be broken up into more than one symbolic parameter
and have two "&names" coded for it. The two &names, when coded in
the form of

```
//    UNIT=&DEVTYPE&DEVSUF,
```

would become one concatenated character string after substitution. If
the proc default or execution JCL supplied, for example, DEV-
TYPE=TAPE and DEVSUF=HI, this parameter would be

```
//    UNIT=TAPEHI,
```

after MVS substitution processing. Concatenation on the DSN parameter
poses a slight exception to this, as described subsequently.

Symbolic Parameter Defaults

Default values for any or all symbolic parameters can be coded within
a proc by specifying the symbolic name, without the ampersand, and
the value in the PROC statement. The values can be stated in any order;
they are separated from one another by commas. In the VSCOBCL proc
in Figure 16.2 all symbolic parameters are assigned default values. The
execution JCL need not be concerned with them, but the values can be
set by the execution JCL if necessary, overriding defaults.

A few critical points:

- *Symbolic parameter default values are optional.* There is no requirement to code any default values on the PROC statement. If no defaults
  are to be coded, the PROC statement itself is not needed on a cataloged
  proc.

```
//*****************************************************************
//*    VSCOBOL COMPILE AND LINK PROC        LAST CHANGE 03-19-87   *
//*****************************************************************
//VSCOBCL  PROC PRINT='A',                        'SYSOUT CLASS
//   OPTIONS='SXR,DMA,CLI,APOST,NOSEQ,NOADV,LIB,DYN', 'COMPILER PARMS
//   LOADLIB='SYS1.TESTLIB',                      'TEST LOAD LIB
//   LMODNAM='********',                          'LOAD MOD NAME
//    CSPACE='700,100',                           'COMPILER SPACE
//    OBSBLK='3200',                              'OBJECT BLOCKING
//   OBSPACE='500,100',                           'OBJECT SPACE
//     LPARM='LIST,XREF,LET',                     'LINKER PARMS
//    LSPACE='50,20',                             'LINKER SPACE
//   LKEDLIB='SYS1.COBLIB',                       'COBOL SERV RTNS
//      WORK='SYSDA'                              'COMPILER SPACE
//*
//COB      EXEC  PGM=IKFCBLOO,PARM='&OPTIONS'
//*****************************************************************
//*    COMPILE WITH VSCOBOL                                        *
//*****************************************************************
//SYSLIB      DD   DSN=SYS1.COPYLIB,DISP=SHR
//SYSIN       DD   DDNAME=SOURCE
//SYSUT1      DD   UNIT=&WORK,SPACE=(460,(&CSPACE))
//SYSUT2      DD   UNIT=&WORK,SPACE=(460,(&CSPACE))
//SYSUT3      DD   UNIT=&WORK,SPACE=(460,(&CSPACE))
//SYSUT4      DD   UNIT=&WORK,SPACE=(460,(&CSPACE))
//SYSLIN      DD   DSN=&LOADSET,                   'OBJECT DECK OUT
//   UNIT=&WORK,
//   DISP=(NEW,PASS,DELETE),
//   SPACE=(&OBSBLK,(&OBSPACE))
//SYSPRINT    DD   SYSOUT=&PRINT
//SYSUDUMP    DD   SYSOUT=&PRINT
//*
//LKED     EXEC  PGM=IEWL,PARM='&LPARM',COND=(5,LT)
//*****************************************************************
//*    LINKAGE EDIT                                                *
//*****************************************************************
//SYSLIN      DD   DSN=&LOADSET,                   'OBJECT DECK IN
//   DISP=(OLD,DELETE)
//            DD   DDNAME=LKEDCTL
//SYSLMOD     DD   DSN=&LOADLIB(&LMODNAM),         'LOAD MODULE OUT
//   DISP=SHR
//SYSLIB      DD   DSN=&LKEDLIB,DISP=SHR
//            DD   DSN=&LOADLIB,DISP=SHR
//SYSUT1      DD   UNIT=&WORK,
//   SPACE=(1024,(&LSPACE))
//SYSPRINT    DD   SYSOUT=&PRINT
//SYSUDUMP    DD   SYSOUT=&PRINT
```

FIGURE 16.2. Typical customized VSCOBCL "compile and link" proc with symbolic parameters

- *The first symbolic parameter default follows the word PROC after a space, with no intervening comma. This is a quirk of JCL syntax. It is easy to place a comma erroneously after PROC and before the first default value, thus causing a syntax error. This error is commonly made by the majority of personnel who compose procs when they are introduced to the subject.*

- *A symbolic parameter default value with embedded "special characters" such as periods must be surrounded by apostrophes. This* includes data set names and is precisely *opposite* to the way in which DSN is coded in JCL. There is no harm in coding every default symbolic value and every run time supplied symbolic parameter value surrounded by apostrophes. It is easier to do so than to try to remember when apostrophes are optional here and when they are mandatory. The apostrophes never hurt in this area—they do *not* as in programming languages, distinguish a character literal from a numeric one.

- *A symbolic parameter can be given a default value that completely eliminates it by coding only an equal sign after it.*[3] The exception to nullification by the equal sign is DSN on output data sets because DSN in this case is actually optional; if not coded, MVS composes its own name for this data set. To nullify DSN the symbolic parameter value for it is given the value NULLFILE. Nullifying the DSN nullifies all other DCB parameters coded on the DD statement. These will still be checked for correct syntax but will otherwise be ignored.

The DDNAME Parameter

In two places in the VSCOBCL proc DDNAME is coded in JCL. DDNAME is a carryover from punched card days. It offers a means of deferring the definition of input. An example from that time illustrates its major intended use.

When source code was really keyed on punched cards, combined with JCL keyed on punched cards, and read into a physical card reader, immediate data, namely, the source code deck, was input at the compiler's //SYSIN DD statement by coding it //SYSIN DD * and inserting the whole source code deck at that point. The end of the deck was denoted by a card carrying only /* in the first two positions. Placing the large source code deck into the correct point in the small JCL deck required separating some of the JCL cards and getting the whole stack together in the right order, a process prone to error. The same potential for disaster was present when data being input to a program in a multistep job stream were presented on cards.

To make the process of punched-card source code and data submission easier, the DDNAME parameter was created. DDNAME says "look for this material somewhere below under the DDname specified." The word following DDNAME is the DDname that will appear somewhere later; for example, at the end of the card deck.

DDNAME allowed the packaging of a card deck job without the physical splitting of JCL cards for the insertion of the source code. The compiler's //SYSIN DD statement was ordinarily coded with it; therefore the source code being input to the compiler could be placed at the physical end of the JCL deck, following a deferred immediate input statement. For example, if this code appeared for the //COB step compiler's //SYSIN

```
//SYSIN    DD  DDNAME=SOURCE
```

then this could be the DD statement on which the source code was input at the very end of the JCL deck:

```
//COB.SOURCE  DD  *
```

Much of the basis for this use of the DDNAME parameter became obsolete along with punched cards.

DDNAME is now little used, except in isolated instances when it is desirable to change the apparent DDname on which an input is to be supplied. For example, some fourth generation software to be accessed by end-users may have awkward DDnames associated with inputs. An installation can code the JCL to be used with such a product with a DDNAME parameter and make it possible for an end-user to work with JCL that has a friendlier or more locally familiar DDname. The version of the VSCOBCL proc shown here uses DDNAME partly to illustrate what you might see in JCL as a carryover from the old days and partly to equate the compiler's //SYSIN to the slightly more meaningful //SOURCE.

Execution JCL

This is the typical way a programmer would invoke the rendition of VSCOBCL illustrated in Figure 16.2:

```
//FSBT686A  JOB AK00COMP,'DP2-JANOSSY',CLASS=E,MSGCLASS=A,
//  MSGLEVEL=(1,1),NOTIFY=BT05686
//*
//* BT05686.SOURCE.CNTL(VSCOBCL1)  EXEC COMPILE & LINK
//*
//STEPA    EXEC VSCOBCL,
//  PRINT='*',
//  LOADLIB='BT05686.TEST.LOADMODS',
//  LMODNAM='PSD183'
//COB.SOURCE  DD  DSN=BT05686.SOURCE.COBOL(PSD183),
//  DISP=SHR
//
```

Three symbolic parameters are supplied in this execution JCL. The source code to be compiled and linkage edited is input at the //SOURCE DDname that results from the proc's DDNAME parameter; this is a full DD statement, not a symbolic parameter, and the DISP parameter must be coded. In this case the source code has been stored under the same member name as the load module. This is not necessary but it is common practice. The coding of the procstepname can be omitted optionally if the DDNAME occurs in the first step of the proc, as it does here.

Symbolic parameters supplied in execution JCL are coded on the EXEC statement very much like defaults are coded on the PROC statement. Unlike the case with the PROC statement, a comma *must* follow the proc name on the EXEC. If this comma is not coded, symbolic parameters coded on the same line as EXEC appear to MVS to be comments; symbolic parameter values coded on continuation lines of the EXEC appear as spurious statements. This subtle syntax difference between PROC and EXEC can be troublesome and the source of much frustration.

Any symbolic parameter values supplied on the EXEC statement of the execution JCL take precedence over the default values contained in the proc itself. Between the EXEC statement supplied values and the PROC default values all symbolic parameter values must be assigned values or the job will fail for a JCL error.

A few minor rules exist in connection with EXEC statement symbolic parameter value assignments:

- Value assignments can be coded in any order; they do not need to be stated in the order in which symbolic parameters appear in the proc.
- If the same symbolic parameter is given a value more than once on an EXEC statement or in a PROC statement, the *first* value stated is used,[4]
- *A given EXEC statement symbolic parameter value assignment can't be split between lines of execution JCL.*
- If the item in the proc JCL is a concatenation of two or more symbolic parameters, the full character string built up of the concatenated parameters can be no longer than 120 characters.

LOADLIB in Figure 16.2 is the symbolic parameter for the name of the load module library, a partitioned data set. The default value within the proc names the installation-standard common test load module library, in this case SYS1.TESTLIB. Our execution JCL specifies a different LOADLIB and overrides the default. LMODNAM specifies the load module name under which the executable program will be stored. The new or replacement load module that results from the submission of this execution JCL will become member PSD183 of the partitioned data set BT05686.TEST.LOADMODS or, stated as a JCL DSN parameter, BT05686.TEST.LOADMODS(PSD183).

In many installations programming teams use a developmental copylib to work directly with record descriptions and refine them as programming of an application system progresses. When an application is to be put into production, the members in the developmental copylib are placed in the installation's production copylib. Production compilations of the source code are then performed by an installation librarian. If a developmental copylib is part of the local *modus operandi* it should be given priority and searched first to satisfy COPY directives of a program under development because it will contain the most recent version of copylib items. Copylibs such as standard linkage records not found there should be sought in the installation's production copylib. This execution JCL illustrates the overriding of the VSCOBCL proc //COB step //SYSLIB DDname, at which the compiler seeks copylib items:

```
//FSBT686A   JOB AK00COMP,'DP2-JANOSSY',CLASS=E,MSGCLASS=X,
//   MSGLEVEL=(1,1),NOTIFY=BT05686
//*
//* BT05686.SOURCE.CNTL(VSCOBCL2)   EXEC COMPILE & LINK
//*
//STEPA      EXEC  VSCOBCL,
//   PRINT='*',
//   LOADLIB='BT05686.TEST.LOADMODS',
//   LMODNAM='PSD183'
//*
//COB.SYSLIB  DD   DSN=BT05686.DEVCOPY.COBOL,DISP=SHR
//           DD   DSN=SYS1.COPYLIB,DISP=SHR
//*
//COB.SOURCE  DD   DSN=BT05686.SOURCE.COBOL(PSD183),
//   DISP=SHR
//
```

and the concatenation of a developmental copylib and a production copylib. This override does not use a symbolic parameter, it is a full DD statement in itself, and therefore DISP must be coded on it.

This is how VSCOBCL could be invoked if honest-to-goodness punched cards were used and all proc defaults except load module name were to apply:

```
//FSBT686A   JOB  AK00COMP,'DP2-JANOSSY',CLASS=E,MSGCLASS=A
//STEPA      EXEC  VSCOBCL,LMODNAM='PSD183',
//SOURCE     DD  *
       (source code punched card deck here)
/*
//
```

No NOTIFY parameter is carried on the JOB statement because TSO is not used to submit this JCL and an immediate DD * specification on the

//SOURCE DD statement is followed by the punched card source code. This source code is ended with a /* statement and the execution JCL deck itself is ended with the null // statement.

Results of Proc Execution

When a cataloged procedure is executed, a copy of it is brought into the job stream by MVS. The EXEC statement and proc default symbolic parameter values are substituted in a manner that the EXEC statement values, if present, take precedence. The leading // characters are changed by MVS to XX to denote that the lines came from a cataloged proc. The JCL is then processed as if it had all been submitted in raw form.

Both MVS and MVS/XA provide indications of the substitutions for symbolic parameters in the system allocation/deallocation reports. Under MVS the substitutions are grouped and listed after the JCL of the proc, referenced by the JCL statement number. Comparison of the substitution information with the JCL statement involves looking in two places that may be a few pages apart. MVS/XA provides greater convenience in examining the substitutions: it prints the proc's coding, then the line as it appears after all the substitutions that affect it. This is one of the lines of the VSCOBCL proc

```
//SYSUT1    DD   UNIT=&WORK,SPACE=(460,(&CSPACE))
```

and below is how the substitution information for it is presented in the allocation/deallocation reports when the proc defaults prevail:

```
IEF653I SUBSTITUTION JCL - UNIT=SYSDA,SPACE=(460,(700,100))
```

All symbolic parameters in a proc must be satisfied by values coded on the EXEC statement that invokes the proc or by proc-coded defaults. The default chosen for LMODNAM, '********', is patently invalid. The basis for this default is a matter of safety: it forces the execution JCL to supply this symbolic parameter or the job will fail. No execution JCL should attempt to compile and linkage-edit a program without supplying an explicit name for the load module because the linkage editor will create a "catch all" name of "TEMPNAME" in such a case.

Inputting Linkage Editor Control Statements

In the VSCOBCL proc in Figure 16.2 there is a DDNAME parameter on the linkage editor's //SYSLIN DD statement named LKEDCTL. This stands for "linkage editor control" and provides a way of supplying optional control statements to the linkage editor. When supplied, such control statements can enter it via the same DDname as does the object file from the compiler. Both the object file, which is sometimes called the object deck, and the control statements for the linkage editor are 80-byte-card image records. In the oldest of the old days the object deck really was a deck of.cards punched out by the compiler.

There is little need in the MVS environment to use linkage editor control statements for most application programs. MVS supports dynamically loaded subroutine modules, a facility in effect when the DYN compiler parameter is used. This makes it possible for a program load module to omit the machine code for each CALLed program and to access the modules dynamically at run time. The practical benefit is that load modules are smaller and CALLed programs need not be individually hard linked to the calling program. Even for hard-linked, "NODYN" static callable modules it is not necessary to use linkage editor control statements if a load module of the compiled and linkage-edited CALLed routine resides in a library accessible to the linkage editor at its //SYSLIB DDname. //SYSLIB is associated with partitioned data set load module libraries in which the linkage editor searches for CALLed routine load modules as it resolves references to called routines.[5]

This is how one might use the DDNAME LKEDCTL to direct the forced linkage of the load modules for routines named DPDATECV, DPADDRF1, and DPSITEF1 with a new load module being created for a program that makes static CALLs to them:

```
//FSBT686A  JOB AK00COMP,'DP2-JANOSSY',CLASS=E,MSGCLASS=A,
//   MSGLEVEL=(1,1),NOTIFY=BT05686
//*
//* BT05686.SOURCE.CNTL(VSCOBCL3)  EXEC COMPILE & LINK
//*
//STEPA     EXEC  VSCOBCL,
//   PRINT='*',
//   LOADLIB='BT05686.TEST.LOADMODS',
//   LMODNAM='FSBT5501'
//*
//COB.SYSLIB    DD  DSN=BT05686.DEVCOPY.COBOL,DISP=SHR
//              DD  DSN=SYS1.COPYLIB,DISP=SHR
//*
//COB.SOURCE    DD  DSN=BT05686.SOURCE.COBOL(FSBT5501),
//   DISP=SHR
//LKED.LKEDCTL DD  *
    INCLUDE  XTRAMODS(DPDATECV,DPADDRF1,DPSITEF1)
/*
//LKED.XTRAMODS  DD  DSN=BT90000.LOAD.SPECIAL,DISP=SHR
//
```

The INCLUDE control statement names a DDname that is coded *following* and cites the partitioned data set in which the CALLed routine load modules reside. The inclusion of these modules in the new load module is unconditional; if modules that are not actually required are specified, they will be added anyway, thus making the new load module larger but serving no purpose.

Whenever a DDNAME parameter exists in a proc but is not referenced in the execution JCL, this message appears in the allocation/deallocation report for the job:

```
IEF686I DDNAME REFERRED TO ON DDNAME KEYWORD IN PRIOR STEP WAS NOT RESOLVED
```

This is only an informational message. It has no effect on the job and it should be disregarded; it is simply the consequence of inclusion in the proc of a DDNAME not used. For the version of the VSCOBCL proc shown it will normally be received as a result of not making use of LKEDCTL.

Overriding Compile Proc PARM Options

The IBM VSCOBOL, PL/I, and FORTRAN compilers provide a significant number of options that can be modified by programmers for given executions. When a compiler is invoked by a proc, the PARM options specified in that proc can be replaced even if no symbolic parameter for the PARM is provided by the proc. When this is done, the new PARM *completely replaces* the PARM coded in the proc itself. For this reason options that may be coded in the standard proc, such as SIZE for compiler memory allocation, must be reproduced in the replacement PARM. Overriding PARM within a proc has a useless but dangerous feature. If the procstepname is omitted from the PARM override in the execution JCL and is coded as:

```
//MYCOMP   EXEC  VSCOBCL,
//   PARM=('SIZE=1024K,SXR,LIB,DYN,DMA',        wrong: procstepname
//   'NOADV,APO,CLI,VERB',                      is missing from
//   'LANGLVL(2),COUNT,SYM',                    PARM
//   'ACE2,FLO=50')
```

then PARM, lacking specificity as to which step in the proc it applies, is applied to the first step. In this case, however, *all PARM values for all other steps in the proc's JCL are nullified*. This has the effect in the compile and link proc of still allowing the compile to work properly but shortchanging the linkage editor of the PARM values hardcoded for it in the proc. The "other step PARM nullification" does not occur when the PARM override is made specific to a step, as in this correct coding:

```
//MYCOMP   EXEC  VSCOBCL,
//    PARM.COB=('SIZE=1024K,SXR,LIB,DYN,DMA',   right: procstepname
//    'NOADV,APO,CLI,VERB',                      follows PARM
//    'LANGLVL(2),COUNT,SYM',
//    'ACE2,FLO=50')
```

TURNING THE SEQUENTIAL UPDATE JOB STREAM INTO A PROC

The first stage of creating a production proc from the sequential update job stream, last revised in Figure 14.4, involves the changing of step names from the informal ones to the standard names specified by an installation. In our earlier versions of this job stream we used names like //STEPA and //STEPB. The actual convention we need to implement involves these facts:

- The real production proc is named FS3765P1; it is one of a number of procs that support an application system named FS37.

- The installation requires that the procstepnames follow the pattern of the proc name with a trailing letter ascending for each step. The first step is //FS37651A, the second step, //FS37651B, and so on.

Next, we need to establish the items in the raw JCL that warrant generalization as symbolic parameters. There is only one item that may actually change from one run to the next: the volume serial number of the input transaction tape. This data set enters at the //SORTIN DD statement in the first step as input to the sort. We replace a hardcoded volume serial number at this VOL parameter with the symbolic parameter &VOLID, for volume id. We could have used VOLSER or any other name. The actual formation of the name is not overly constrained by MVS because the only "reserved words" to be avoided are the EXEC statement parameter keywords PGM, COND, PARM, and the others cited in Appendix A. Special characters are not allowed in a symbolic parameter name and the name must start with a letter or a national symbol such as @, #, or $.

&VOLID also exists in the proc at the PARM specification to program FSBT3708, which has been modified to accept it as described in Chapter 15, and stamps the tape identifier into each finished transaction record for audit trail purposes. Figure 3.2 illustrates the six byte field starting in position 72 that carries this value, which has not been mentioned until this point.

The JCL in Figure 16.3 shows four other symbolic parameters with defaults in the proc statement: HILEVEL, SORTCYL, TRSPACE, and PLSPACE. These are similar in nature to most of the symbolic parameters cited in the VSCOBCL proc in that they are not intended for regular execution JCL changes from run to run. Instead, they are needed for maintenance and testing convenience.

HILEVEL may appear to be unusual, but it is coded to increase the rapidity and reliability of testing the procedure. In the installation used here as an example production data sets are distinguished from test data sets by a naming convention. Any data set name starting with AK is a test data set; AK00, AK01, and so forth, are all nonproduction prefixes associated with data sets that will never enter into a production run. On the other hand, any data set with a name starting with FS or certain other letters is a production data set, one that can contain live data.

The default for HILEVEL in the proc is FS37, which makes all data sets names production. When the proc is invoked without mention of HILEVEL in the execution JCL, the default applies, and after MVS substitution all permanent data set names take the form:

```
FS37.C99.TRANSIN
```

For proc testing purposes the execution JCL can carry the HILEVEL symbolic parameter and assign it the value of AK00 so that in one simple action all data sets used by the run carry test data set names.

Coding a symbolic parameter for DSN for HILEVEL presents a slightly unusual appearance because of the need to follow the symbolic name with a period. Because a period normally separates the qualifiers of the data set name, this results in proc coding with two periods between the symbolic name and the middle portion of the data set name. This is not a typographical error; two periods really do appear in the proc, but only one will be there after the symbolic parameter value substitution is made by MVS.

SORTCYL is coded as a symbolic parameter to simplify changing the space allocation for the sort work data sets. In our earlier JCL we specified this as two cylinders divided between two disk units. The proc being developed carries the same space allocation but arrives at it via the SORTCYL symbolic parameter. We can adjust the sort space on all of the many sort work DD statements in the proc just by changing the default. Execution JCL for a job that is known to have an unusually large input data set can specify this symbolic parameter to avoid an "out of space" error by increasing the allocation for only that run.

TRSPACE is the symbolic parameter that conveys primary and sec-

```
//FSBT686A   JOB AK00TEST,'DP2-JANOSSY',CLASS=T,MSGCLASS=X,
//   MSGLEVEL=(1,1),NOTIFY=BT05686
//*
//*      EXECUTE PROC FS3765P1 INSTREAM
//*      (PROC VERSION OF FIGURE 14.4  V7B)
//*      THIS JCL = BT05686.SOURCE.CNTL(BT3708V7)
//*
//* - - - - - - - - - - - - - - - - - - - - - - - - - - - -
//FS3765P1 PROC  VOLID='******',
//   HILEVEL='FS37',                  'PRODUCTION NAME PREFIX
//   SORTCYL='2',                     'SORT WORK CYLINDERS
//   TRSPACE='46,9',                  '61 TRANS/BLOCK
//   PLSPACE='45,20'                  '68 PRINTLINES/BLOCK
//******************************************************
//*                                                    *
//*      SORT TRANS FILE                          A    *
//*                                                    *
//******************************************************
//FS37651A EXEC  PGM=SORT
//SORTLIB    DD  DSN=SYS1.SORTLIB,
//   DISP=SHR
//*
//SORTIN     DD  DSN=&HILEVEL..C99.TRANSIN,
//   UNIT=(TAPE,,DEFER),
//   DISP=(OLD,KEEP),
//   DCB=(RECFM=FB,LRECL=71,BLKSIZE=1420,DEN=3,OPTCD=Q),
//   VOL=SER=&VOLID,
//   LABEL=(1,NL,EXPDT=98000)                'EXPDT ONLY FOR
//*                                          'UCC-1 TMS
//SORTOUT    DD  DSN=&&TRANSORT,
//   UNIT=SYSDA,
//   DISP=(NEW,PASS,DELETE),
//   DCB=(RECFM=FB,LRECL=71,BLKSIZE=6177),
//   SPACE=(6177,(&TRSPACE),RLSE)            '2800 TRANS
//SYSOUT     DD  SYSOUT=*
//SYSUDUMP   DD  SYSOUT=*
//SORTWK01   DD  UNIT=SYSDA,SPACE=(CYL,&SORTCYL,,CONTIG)
//SORTWK02   DD  UNIT=SYSDA,SPACE=(CYL,&SORTCYL,,CONTIG)
//SYSIN      DD  DSN=SYS1.CTLCARDS(FS3765AA),DISP=SHR
//*
//******************************************************
//*                                                    *
//*      UPDATE MASTER FILE                        B   *
//*                                                    *
//******************************************************
//FS37651B EXEC  PGM=FSBT3708,REGION=2048K,COND=(0,LT),
//   PARM='&VOLID'
//STEPLIB    DD  DSN=BT05686.TEST.LOADMODS,
//   DISP=SHR
//BT3708E1   DD  DSN=&&TRANSORT,
//   DISP=(OLD,DELETE)
//*
//BT3708E2   DD  DSN=&HILEVEL..C99.TELMAST(0),
//   UNIT=(TAPE,,DEFER),
//   DISP=(OLD,KEEP)
//*
//BT3708E3   DD  DSN=&HILEVEL..C99.AREAREF,
//   DISP=SHR
//*
//BT3708U1   DD  DSN=&HILEVEL..C99.BT3708U1(+1),
//   UNIT=SYSDA,
//   DISP=(NEW,CATLG,DELETE),
//   DCB=(XX90.A00.DUMMYLBL,RECFM=FBA,LRECL=133,BLKSIZE=9044),
//   SPACE=(9044,(&PLSPACE),RLSE)
//*
//BT3708U2   DD  DSN=&HILEVEL..C99.TELMAST(+1),
//   UNIT=(TAPE,,DEFER),
//   DISP=(NEW,CATLG,DELETE),
//   DCB=(XX90.A00.DUMMYLBL,RECFM=FB,LRECL=314,BLKSIZE=32656),
//   LABEL=RETPD=30
//*
//BT3708U3   DD  DSN=&&TRANSFIN,
//   UNIT=SYSDA,
```

FIGURE 16.3. The sequential update job stream as an "instream" proc with symbolic parameters

```
//    DISP=(NEW,PASS,DELETE),
//    DCB=(RECFM=FB,LRECL=102,BLKSIZE=6222),    '2800 TRANS
//    SPACE=(6222,(&TRSPACE),RLSE)
//*
//SYSOUT      DD   SYSOUT=*
//SYSUDUMP    DD   SYSOUT=*
//*********************************************************
//*                                                       *
//*      PRODUCE TRAN REPORT (INTERNAL SORT)          C   *
//*                                                       *
//*********************************************************
//FS37651C EXEC  PGM=FSBT3719,REGION=2048K,COND=(0,LT)
//STEPLIB     DD   DSN=BT05686.TEST.LOADMODS,
//    DISP=SHR
//SORTLIB     DD   DSN=SYS1.SORTLIB,
//    DISP=SHR
//BT3719E1    DD   DSN=&&TRANSFIN,
//    DISP=(OLD,DELETE)
//*
//BT3719U1    DD   DSN=&HILEVEL..C99.BT3719U1(+1),
//    UNIT=SYSDA,
//    DISP=(NEW,CATLG,DELETE),
//    DCB=(XX90.A00.DUMMYLBL,RECFM=FBA,LRECL=133,BLKSIZE=9044),
//    SPACE=(9044,(&PLSPACE),RLSE)
//*
//BT3719U2    DD   DSN=&HILEVEL..C99.BT3719U2(+1),
//    UNIT=SYSDA,

//    DISP=(NEW,CATLG,DELETE),
//    DCB=(XX90.A00.DUMMYLBL,RECFM=FBA,LRECL=133,BLKSIZE=9044),
//    SPACE=(9044,(&PLSPACE),RLSE)
//*
//SORTWK01    DD   UNIT=SYSDA,SPACE=(CYL,&SORTCYL,,CONTIG)
//SORTWK02    DD   UNIT=SYSDA,SPACE=(CYL,&SORTCYL,,CONTIG)
//BT3719SM    DD   SYSOUT=*
//SYSOUT      DD   SYSOUT=*
//SYSUDUMP    DD   SYSOUT=*
//*
//*********************************************************
//*                                                       *
//*      PRINT THE REPORT OUTPUTS                     D   *
//*                                                       *
//*********************************************************
//FS37651D EXEC  PGM=IEBGENER,COND=(0,LT)
//*
//SYSUT1      DD   DSN=&HILEVEL..C99.BT3708U1(+1),DISP=SHR
//            DD   DSN=&HILEVEL..C99.BT3719U1(+1),DISP=SHR
//            DD   DSN=&HILEVEL..C99.BT3719U2(+1),DISP=SHR
//*
//SYSUT2      DD   SYSOUT=A,
//    DCB=(RECFM=FBA,LRECL=133,BLKSIZE=9044)
//SYSIN       DD   DUMMY
//SYSPRINT    DD   SYSOUT=*
//SYSUDUMP    DD   SYSOUT=*
//*
//*********************************************************
//*                                                       *
//*      0000 RET CODE IF OK, ELSE NO CODE            E   *
//*                                                       *
//*********************************************************
//FS37651E EXEC  PGM=IEFBR14,COND=(0,LT)
/*
//*********************************************************
//*                                                       *
//*      DO EOJ CLEANUP IF FS37651E WAS SKIPPED       F   *
//*                                                       *
//*********************************************************
//FS37651F EXEC  PGM=FSBT9999,COND=(EVEN,(0,EQ,FS37651E)),
//    PARM='*** ATTENTION: FS3765P1 FAILED ***'
//*
//ABORTMSG    DD   SYSOUT=*
//*
//DEL1        DD   DSN=&HILEVEL..C99.TELMAST(+1),
```

FIGURE 16.3. (con't.)

```
//    UNIT=(TAPE,,DEFER),
//    DISP=(MOD,DELETE),
//    DCB=(XX90.A00.DUMMYLBL,RECFM=FB,LRECL=314,BLKSIZE=32656)
//*
//DEL2        DD  DSN=&HILEVEL..C99.BT3708U1(+1),
//    UNIT=SYSDA,
//    DISP=(MOD,DELETE),
//    DCB=(XX90.A00.DUMMYLBL,RECFM=FBA,LRECL=133,BLKSIZE=9044),
//    SPACE=(TRK,0)
//*
//DEL3        DD  DSN=&HILEVEL..C99.BT3719U1(+1),
//    UNIT=SYSDA,
//    DISP=(MOD,DELETE),
//    DCB=(XX90.A00.DUMMYLBL,RECFM=FBA,LRECL=133,BLKSIZE=9044),
//    SPACE=(TRK,0)
//*
//DEL4        DD  DSN=&HILEVEL..C99.BT3719U2(+1),
//    UNIT=SYSDA,
//    DISP=(MOD,DELETE),
//    DCB=(XX90.A00.DUMMYLBL,RECFM=FBA,LRECL=133,BLKSIZE=9044),
//    SPACE=(TRK,0)
//* - - - - - - - - - - - - - - - - - - - - - - - - - - - -
//    PEND
//STEPA       EXEC  FS3765P1,
//    VOLID='HXR452',
//    HILEVEL='AK00'
//
```

FIGURE 16.3. (con't.)

ondary space allocation in terms of data blocks for DD statements at which the update transactions are written to disk data sets. It appears twice in the proc: at //SORTOUT in the first step and at //FS3708U3 in the second. Because the size of the transaction records is greater in the second step, a value coded here that is adequate for that purpose is slightly too large for //SORTOUT. Separate symbolic parameters may be desirable for these space specifications but they are not accorded that treatment here.

PLSPACE conveys the primary and secondary space allocation in terms of data blocks for the three print image data sets. Like TRSPACE, the symbolic parameter is a compromise between convenience and specificity because the actual amount of space needed for each of the printline data sets may vary up to the amount coded. RLSE, coded on the SPACE parameters, releases any excess space allocated but not used. A combination symbolic parameter would be impractical if these three outputs were not all relatively small or approximately equal in bulk.

*Procs cannot handle immediate DD * data.* This means that items such as sort and utility control statements cannot be input in that manner. The sort control statement formerly coded within the JCL at the DDname //SYSIN in the first step has been placed in a "control card library" named SYS1.CTLCARDS. All installations have a library or multiple libraries to house these types of statements. They are partitioned data sets into which the card images constituting given control statements are placed as members. This DD statement in the proc now references member FS3765AA, a name formed according to another local naming convention.

The only other change between the raw JCL in Figure 14.4 and the instream proc in Figure 16.3 is that we have changed the name of the program executed in the forced abort step at the bottom of the job stream. Previously IEFBR14 had been coded at this point to provide for handling the DISP parameters that delete any data sets created by a failed run. The program now executed at this point is called FSBT9999, as discussed in Chapter 14. It is typical of installation-created forced abort routines that do reporting in addition to providing a place to code DD statements for DISP processing.

Running the Proc Instream

A new proc must be tested before installation. Figure 16.3 illustrates a way of testing a proc without installing it in SYS1.PROCLIB or any other installation procedure library. Everything between the horizontal lines of hyphens at the top and bottom constitutes the proc. By placing a job statement above the proc, a PEND—for "Proc END"—below it, and coding the execution JCL after the PEND statement we can execute the proc instream. The PEND statement can have an optional //name and, like any line of JCL, can have comments delimited by at least one space after the word PEND. Note that PEND *cannot* start immediately after the slashes; if the optional //name is not coded, as in this example, at least one space is still needed after the slashes and before PEND.

Instream execution of a proc is possible because the receipt of a PROC statement causes the MVS to temporarily store the statements that follow. This storage action stops when a PEND statement is encountered. The proc statements can then be drawn in as if they constituted an installed cataloged procedure. After the PEND statement, normal execution JCL is coded; an EXEC statement can specify the proc for execution by using the name coded after the slashes on the PROC statement.[1]

The execution JCL that follows the PEND statement in this example is quite simple. It merely supplies a volume serial number by using the VOLID symbolic parameter and specifies the test data set name prefix with the HILEVEL symbolic parameter.

Running a proc instream produces a large allocation/deallocation report because the proc is listed twice: first as it was read in and again as it appeared when drawn in by the execution JCL as a proc. When a cataloged procedure is invoked, the first of these renditions is omitted because the JCL submitted for processing is made up simply of the execution JCL. For an instream proc MVS replaces the slashes on the proc JCL statements with + + instead of XX, as it does when it lists cataloged procedure JCL statements on its allocation/deallocation report. This has no bearing on execution.

Instream proc execution is most often a stepping stone to the finalization of a production cataloged proc. It is convenient at times, however, when a programmer performs "one-shot" tasks. If several data files or groups of program source code have been conveyed as separate data sets on the same transmittal tape, an instream proc using IEBGENER with symbolic parameters for tape relative data set number and output data set name can be constructed. The proc can be executed instream with several steps coded after the PEND statement, each invoking the proc but supplying the next highest tape relative data set number and a different output data set name. An instream proc such as this is a tool, perhaps never intended to be placed into production but useful in its own right.

After Instream Proc Testing

When an instream proc is successfully tested, it is turned into an installable proc:

- The job statement ahead of the PROC statement is removed.
- The PEND statement and the lines of execution JCL that follow it are removed.
- SPACE allocation parameters, IDCAMS data set size allocation control statements, if any, and sort utility file size control parameters are increased from their small testing values to full production size.
- Program load modules are placed into the installation production program library and any references to a test load module library are removed.

The last two items—changing data set size specifications and eliminating reference to test load module libraries—are important because jobs may run for a period of time if these last two actions have not be taken. They will, however, ultimately encounter serious problems.

After placement in SYS1.PROCLIB or a similar library the proc can be submitted for a final test from the production proc library via TSO, using this JCL:

```
//FSBT686A  JOB AK00TEST,'DP2-JANOSSY',CLASS=T,MSGCLASS=X,
//   MSGLEVEL=(1,1),NOTIFY=BT05686
//*
//*     THIS JCL = BT05686.SOURCE.CNTL(FS3765T1)
//*
//STEPA    EXEC  FS3765P1,VOLID='HXR452',
//   HILEVEL='AK00'
//
```

This approximates the execution JCL that a production group would use. Aside from the job statement, just one other is needed to run the entire job stream and this statement, an EXEC, invokes the proc. It supplies the volume serial number of a tape that carries test transactions. Because this is still a test, it specifies the HILEVEL symbolic parameter that carries the testing data set name "front part." To make this into a "run deck" or "go deck" for an operations group it would be necessary only to eliminate the reference to HILEVEL, supply a production-oriented job statement, and place the execution JCL into a library that the operations group could access. An operations group would typically initiate this job at user request or on a schedule without any end-user terminal entry or the involvement of programming personnel.

Built-in Report Reprint with a Proc

Aside from default space quantities and coding of a test load module library the proc in Figure 16.3 is production caliber. Let's take a look, however, at a slightly different breakdown of the steps that addresses the need for a means to reprint end-user reports. Because we already have a GENER step developed to print from the printline GDG data sets, why not get double value out of it and let it be used for reprints as well?

Figure 16.4 is a variation of proc FS3765P1 with space quantity defaults set to production sizes, reference to a test load module library removed, and GENER to print step FS37651D removed.[6] The proc will now perform the update and produce system allocation/deallocation reports and the sort's normal technical reporting and create end-user report printlines. It will not, however, print the end-user reports. The customary forced abort housekeeping steps are still at the end of the proc, but they now follow the last COBOL program execution immediately.

Figure 16.5 shows where the "GENER to print" step went. We have now made it into a second proc, FS3765P2. This proc is rather simple: it consists only of the GENER step, followed by the forced abort steps. The final cleanup step that invokes the abort program FSBT9999 has no DDnames coded under it. There are no data sets to be deleted if IEBGENER encounters a problem; we are invoking FSBT9999 only to produce its attention-getting warning sheet and return code. The chances of FSBT9999 being executed in this proc are rather remote but we gain its benefits easily in this usage.

The symbolic parameters of the additional proc, FS3765P2, warrant mention. We no longer have VOLID, SORTCYL, TRSPACE, and PLSPACE defaults because these symbolic parameters do not exist in this proc. HILEVEL is still present. We have also added two more convenience defaults for two new symbolic parameters: GEN and COPIES.

```
//FS3765P1 PROC  VOLID='******',
//   HILEVEL='FS37',              'DATA SET NAME PREFIX
//   SORTCYL='8',                 'SORT WORK CYLINDERS
//   TRSPACE='1400,280'           '61 TRANS/BLOCK (40K TRANS)
//   PLSPACE='750,150'            '68 PRTLNS/BLOCK (51K LINES)
//*
//*     FULL PRODUCTION PROC WITH REPORT PRINT HANDLED
//*     SEPARATELY FOR CONVENIENCE AND REPRINTING
//*     REVISION 8B   LAST CHANGE DATE  03-19-87 JGJ
//*                        ORIGINAL DATE  12-15-86 JGJ
//*
//***********************************************************
//*                                                         *
//*      SORT TRANS FILE                            A   *
//*                                                         *
//***********************************************************
//FS37651A EXEC  PGM=SORT
//SORTLIB    DD  DSN=SYS1.SORTLIB,
//   DISP=SHR
//*
//SORTIN     DD  DSN=&HILEVEL..C99.TRANSIN,
//   UNIT=(TAPE,,DEFER),
//   DISP=(OLD,KEEP),
//   DCB=(RECFM=FB,LRECL=71,BLKSIZE=1420,DEN=3,OPTCD=Q),
//   VOL=SER=&VOLID,
//   LABEL=(1,NL,EXPDT=98000)                 'EXPDT ONLY FOR
//*                                            'UCC-1 TMS
//SORTOUT    DD  DSN=&&TRANSORT,
//   UNIT=SYSDA,
//   DISP=(NEW,PASS,DELETE),
//   DCB=(RECFM=FB,LRECL=71,BLKSIZE=6177),
//   SPACE=(6177,(&TRSPACE),RLSE)             '2800 TRANS
//SYSOUT     DD  SYSOUT=*
//SYSUDUMP   DD  SYSOUT=*
//SORTWK01   DD  UNIT=SYSDA,SPACE=(CYL,&SORTCYL,,CONTIG)
//SORTWK02   DD  UNIT=SYSDA,SPACE=(CYL,&SORTCYL,,CONTIG)
//SORTWK03   DD  UNIT=SYSDA,SPACE=(CYL,&SORTCYL,,CONTIG)
//SYSIN      DD  DSN=SYS1.CTLCARDS(FS3765AA),DISP=SHR
//*
//***********************************************************
//*                                                         *
//*      UPDATE MASTER FILE                         B   *
//*                                                         *
//***********************************************************
//FS37651B EXEC  PGM=FSBT3708,REGION=2048K,COND=(0,LT),
//   PARM='&VOLID'
//BT3708E1   DD  DSN=&&TRANSORT,
//   DISP=(OLD,DELETE)
//*
//BT3708E2   DD  DSN=&HILEVEL..C99.TELMAST(0),
//   UNIT=(TAPE,,DEFER),
//   DISP=(OLD,KEEP)
//*
//BT3708E3   DD  DSN=&HILEVEL..C99.AREAREF,
//   DISP=SHR
//*
//BT3708U1   DD  DSN=&HILEVEL..C99.BT3708U1(+1),
//   UNIT=SYSDA,
//   DISP=(NEW,CATLG,DELETE),
//   DCB=(XX90.A00.DUMMYLBL,RECFM=FBA,LRECL=133,BLKSIZE=9044),
//   SPACE=(9044,(&PLSPACE),RLSE)
//*
//BT3708U2   DD  DSN=&HILEVEL..C99.TELMAST(+1),
//   UNIT=(TAPE,,DEFER),
//   DISP=(NEW,CATLG,DELETE),
//   DCB=(XX90.A00.DUMMYLBL,RECFM=FB,LRECL=314,BLKSIZE=32656),
//   LABEL=RETPD=30
//*
//BT3708U3   DD  DSN=&&TRANSFIN,
//   UNIT=SYSDA,
//   DISP=(NEW,PASS,DELETE),
//   DCB=(RECFM=FB,LRECL=102,BLKSIZE=6222),    '2800 TRANS
//   SPACE=(6222,(&TRSPACE),RLSE)
```

FIGURE 16.4. Sequential update proc with "GENER to print" step removed

```
//*
//SYSOUT    DD  SYSOUT=*
//SYSUDUMP  DD  SYSOUT=*
//*********************************************************
//*                                                       *
//*     PRODUCE TRAN REPORT (INTERNAL SORT)          C    *
//*                                                       *
//*********************************************************
//FS37651C EXEC  PGM=FSBT3719,REGION=2048K,COND=(0,LT)
//SORTLIB   DD  DSN=SYS1.SORTLIB,
//  DISP=SHR
//BT3719E1  DD  DSN=&&TRANSFIN,
//  DISP=(OLD,DELETE)
//*
//BT3719U1  DD  DSN=&HILEVEL..C99.BT3719U1(+1),
//  UNIT=SYSDA,
//  DISP=(NEW,CATLG,DELETE),
//  DCB=(XX90.A00.DUMMYLBL,RECFM=FBA,LRECL=133,BLKSIZE=9044),
//  SPACE=(9044,(&PLSPACE),RLSE)
//*
//BT3719U2  DD  DSN=&HILEVEL..C99.BT3719U2(+1),
//  UNIT=SYSDA,
//  DISP=(NEW,CATLG,DELETE),
//  DCB=(XX90.A00.DUMMYLBL,RECFM=FBA,LRECL=133,BLKSIZE=9044),
//  SPACE=(9044,(&PLSPACE),RLSE)
//*
//SORTWK01  DD  UNIT=SYSDA,SPACE=(CYL,&SORTCYL,,CONTIG)
//SORTWK02  DD  UNIT=SYSDA,SPACE=(CYL,&SORTCYL,,CONTIG)
//SORTWK03  DD  UNIT=SYSDA,SPACE=(CYL,&SORTCYL,,CONTIG)
//BT3719SM  DD  SYSOUT=*
//SYSOUT    DD  SYSOUT=*
//SYSUDUMP  DD  SYSOUT=*
//*
//*********************************************************
//*                                                       *
//*     0000 RET CODE IF OK, ELSE NO CODE            D    *
//*                                                       *
//*********************************************************
//FS37651D EXEC  PGM=IEFBR14,COND=(0,LT)
/*
//*********************************************************
//*                                                       *
//*     DO EOJ CLEANUP IF FS37651D WAS SKIPPED       E    *
//*                                                       *
//*********************************************************
//FS37651E EXEC  PGM=FSBT9999,COND=(EVEN,(0,EQ,FS37651D)),
//  PARM='*** ATTENTION: FS3765P1 FAILED ***'
//*
//ABORTMSG  DD  SYSOUT=*
//*
//DEL1      DD  DSN=&HILEVEL..C99.TELMAST(+1),
//  UNIT=(TAPE,,DEFER),
//  DISP=(MOD,DELETE),
//  DCB=(XX90.A00.DUMMYLBL,RECFM=FB,LRECL=314,BLKSIZE=32656)
//*
//DEL2      DD  DSN=&HILEVEL..C99.BT3708U1(+1),
//  UNIT=SYSDA,
//  DISP=(MOD,DELETE),
//  DCB=(XX90.A00.DUMMYLBL,RECFM=FBA,LRECL=133,BLKSIZE=9044),
//  SPACE=(TRK,0)
//*
//DEL3      DD  DSN=&HILEVEL..C99.BT3719U1(+1),
//  UNIT=SYSDA,
//  DISP=(MOD,DELETE),
//  DCB=(XX90.A00.DUMMYLBL,RECFM=FBA,LRECL=133,BLKSIZE=9044),
//  SPACE=(TRK,0)
//*
//DEL4      DD  DSN=&HILEVEL..C99.BT3719U2(+1),
//  UNIT=SYSDA,
//  DISP=(MOD,DELETE),
//  DCB=(XX90.A00.DUMMYLBL,RECFM=FBA,LRECL=133,BLKSIZE=9044),
//  SPACE=(TRK,0)
```

FIGURE 16.4. (con't.)

```
//FS3765P2 PROC  GEN='(**)',
//  HILEVEL='FS37',
//  COPIES='1'
//*
//*     PRINT/REPRINT REPORTS FROM FS3765P1 RUN
//*     REVISION 8    LAST CHANGE DATE   03-19-87 JGJ
//*                       ORIGINAL DATE   12-15-86 JGJ
//*
//*********************************************************
//*                                                       *
//*     PRINT THE REPORT OUTPUTS                     A    *
//*                                                       *
//*********************************************************
//FS37652A EXEC  PGM=IEBGENER,COND=(0,LT)
//*
//SYSUT1     DD  DSN=&HILEVEL..C99.BT3708U1&GEN,DISP=SHR
//           DD  DSN=&HILEVEL..C99.BT3719U1&GEN,DISP=SHR
//           DD  DSN=&HILEVEL..C99.BT3719U2&GEN,DISP=SHR
//*
//SYSUT2     DD  SYSOUT=A,
//  DCB=(RECFM=FBA,LRECL=133,BLKSIZE=9044),
//  COPIES=&COPIES
//SYSIN      DD  DUMMY
//SYSPRINT   DD  SYSOUT=*
//SYSUDUMP   DD  SYSOUT=*
//*
//*********************************************************
//*                                                       *
//*     0000 RET CODE IF OK, ELSE NO CODE            B    *
//*                                                       *
//*********************************************************
//FS37652B EXEC  PGM=IEFBR14,COND=(0,LT)
/*
//*********************************************************
//*                                                       *
//*     DO EOJ CLEANUP IF FS37652B WAS SKIPPED       C    *
//*                                                       *
//*********************************************************
//FS37652C EXEC  PGM=FSBT9999,COND=(EVEN,(0,EQ,FS37652B)),
//  PARM='*** ATTENTION: FS3765P2 FAILED ***'
//*
//ABORTMSG   DD  SYSOUT=*
//*
```

FIGURE 16.5. "GENER to print" step housed as a separate proc

GEN allows us to set the relative generation number of the printline data sets to be printed or reprinted. COPIES lets us specify how many copies are to be produced.

The GEN symbolic parameter includes the parentheses that surround the relative generation number. Therefore, if the generation number is nullified, the parentheses are also eliminated. GEN is defaulted to an invalid value. The reason is that any execution JCL that invokes proc FS3765P2 must specify the generation of printlines to be printed. The current generation is different, depending on whether FS3765P2 is invoked separately or during the normal run.

COPIES is defaulted to provide one copy. The end-user temporarily desires two copies of the reports rather than one. The execution JCL is an appropriate place to specify this temporary change in requirements.

Invoking Multiple Procs in the Same Execution JCL

This production execution JCL is normally used to run procs FS3765P1 and FS3765P2:

```
//FS376501 JOB FSBT3799,'PROD-FINANCE',CLASS=P,
// MSGCLASS=A,MSGLEVEL=(1,1)
//*
//*     EXECUTION JCL FS376501
//*     RUN TELMAST UPDATE AND PRINT USER REPORTS
//*
//*     TSO SET UP REQUIRED AT VOLID
//*
//STEPA    EXEC FS3765P1,VOLID='******',    <=== set up
//STEPB    EXEC FS3765P2,
//  GEN='(+1)',
//  COPIES='2'
//
```

A brief comment is included for the benefit of operations personnel who will flash this execution JCL on a TSO/ISPF screen, set up the job by entering the volume serial number of the tape for the run, and submit it.

This execution JCL invokes both procs FS3765P1 and FS3765P2, one after another. *All of the work done under one job statement is one job.* It makes no difference to MVS that it draws in two or even more procs to construct the JCL that will constitute the job. The significance of this is that new generation data group data sets created by steps in proc FS3765P1 as the (+1) generation, remain the (+1) generation through the execution of proc FS3765P2. Our invocation of the second proc needs to have the "GENER to print" use the (+1) generation.

This is a separate set of execution JCL installed in production and ready to perform end-user report reprinting at any time:

```
//FS376591 JOB FSBT3799,'PROD-FINANCE',CLASS=E,MSGCLASS=A,
// MSGLEVEL=(1,1)
//*
//*     EXECUTION JCL FS376591
//*     REPRINT USER REPORTS
//*
//*     NO TSO SET UP UNLESS HISTORICAL REPRINT;
//*     TO GET ALL GENS CHANGE TO GEN=
//*
//STEPB    EXEC  FS3765P2,GEN='(-0)',
//  COPIES=2
//
```

This execution JCL carries a job name different from the update and invokes only the second proc, FS3765P2. This JCL would be submitted only if the end-user requested the reprinting of the latest report or a report from the last several days. If the current reports are requested, the GEN symbolic parameter specification is suitable as coded and no set up actions are required. If an older report is requested, a historical generation number, such as (-1) for yesterday's reports and (-2) for the day before yesterday, must be supplied. This assumes, of course, that the job is run daily; the generations are not tied to days but rather to runs or cycles of update job execution.

When the reprint execution JCL is submitted, it is its own job. The current generation of the update reports is the (0) generation, also codable as the (-0) generation. The current generation was $(+1)$ during the run that created it, but when that run ended MVS adjusted relative generation numbers and made it into the (0) generation, as described in Chapter 13. If the execution JCL nullifies the relative generation symbolic parameter by coding GEN= with nothing after the equal sign, *all* generations of the reports are reprinted in a retrieval of the existing generations en masse. This is sometimes the most convenient way to respond to a user who cannot indicate precisely which of the latest cycles of reporting must be reprinted, especially if the bulk of the reports is not overwhelming.

A Proc Cannot Invoke a Proc

Nesting of command lists is permitted on a DEC VAX under VMS with DCL .COM files, on many minicomputer operating systems, and with an MS-DOS .BAT file, but procs on an IBM mainframe under MVS cannot be nested. The JCL statements that make up a proc cannot include EXEC statements that refer to other procs; MVS procs are strictly limited to invoking programs. The execution JCL that is used to invoke one or more procs can, however, also include steps that invoke programs.

This limitation does not ordinarily pose a serious problem but it does create frustration among personnel who have performed ad hoc tasks such as sorting with an installation proc. When it becomes necessary to place a sort step into JCL intended to become a proc, one needs to bite the bullet: the sort proc has to be understood because parts of it must be coded in raw form in the proc under development to invoke the sort. The sort is the single most commonly used item for which ad hoc or end-user procs may exist and a utility of major use in production work. Chapter 17 and the sequential update job streams purposely provide several examples of sort JCL for use as models.

PROC OVERRIDES

Adding DD Statements to Procs

A proc is "canned" JCL. To make the canning worthwhile the JCL that is placed in the proc usually does something of general utility or something that must be repeated on a reliable basis. A compile, linkage edit, and go proc or a compile and link proc is the first type: it is general-purpose in nature and intended to be useful to many personnel. The CLGCOBOL proc illustrated in Figure 16.1 is such an item.

To be highly generalized JCL the compile, linkage edit, and go proc cannot specify two things: the source code to be compiled and DD statements particular to a given program. CLGCOBOL lacks both and the execution JCL that invokes it must add them. DD statements added to a proc carry a combination name after the two slashes. This name is made up of the procstepname—the name of the step within the proc that is to receive the added DD statement—and the DDname at that step. To execute the CLGCOBOL proc we can supply the source code at //COB.SYSIN and if we wish ignore the DDNAME parameter that equates //SYSIN to //SOURCE:

```
//COB.SYSIN  DD  DSN=BT05686.SOURCE.COBOL(PSD183),
//  DISP=SHR
```

MVS acts like a word processor and places this in the //COB step of the proc as it is drawn in.

In an execution of CLGCOBOL early in this chapter we used it to compile, linkage edit, and run a program named PSD183 that has an input INDATA1 and an output OTREPT1. As a generalized compile proc CLGCOBOL cannot carry anything but the ordinary //SYSOUT DD statement that is applicable to any COBOL program—it's where DISPLAYed items emerge—and a //SYSUDUMP DD statement for dump print. To provide DD statements for INDATA1 and OTREPT1 we added these DD statements to the proc via the execution JCL:

```
//GO.INDATA1  DD  DSN=BT05686.SOURCE.CNTL(STATEDAT),
//  DISP=SHR
//GO.OTREPT1  DD  SYSOUT=*
```

The following are the actual rules that apply to adding DD statements to a proc via execution JCL:

• Added DD statements preface the DDname with the procstepname.[7]

- Added DD statements must be *complete* DD statements.

- Added DD statements carry DDnames that *are not found in the step in which they are entered*—the definition of an added item.

- Added DD statements must be coded *after* any DD statement overrides also coded for the procstep. The overrides and adds for a given procstep are grouped together in the execution JCL but within the group the overrides for the procstep must come first, in DD statement order.[8] Both overrides and adds for a procstep are cited before overrides and adds for a subsequent procstep.

- Added DD statements do not become a permanent part of the proc and are effective only for a given run.

Statements from a cataloged procedure emerge from MVS processing with their starting // symbols replaced by XX in the final JCL. For instream procs + + is used by MVS instead of XX. In contrast, added DD statements appear in the allocation/deallocation report with their doubles slashes intact. Aside from using them in a compile proc, programmers only rarely find a need to add DD statements to a proc.

Overriding DD Statements in Procs

To examine the use of DD statement overrides let's reconsider the issue of test versus production data set names, addressed by the HILEVEL symbolic parameter in Figure 16.4. HILEVEL makes it easy to change the DSNs of all data sets from production to test names. We used this parameter to force DSNs to default to FS37 production prefixes; for testing purposes we were able to specify a symbolic parameter in the execution JCL that gave all prefixes the testing name AK00.

Let's suppose that we did not code the symbolic parameter &HILEVEL in the data set name and instead hardcoded DSNs with the FS37 prefix. To perform a test of test instead of production data sets, we still have to make the proc use the test DSN prefix. Although tedious and subject to greater error, DD statement overrides provide the means to accomplish this. If the proc shown in Figure 16.4 did not provide HILEVEL as a symbolic parameter, the execution JCL to override the FS37 data set names with AK00 names for test purposes would have to be coded in this manner:

```
//FSBT686A  JOB AK00TEST,'DP2-JANOSSY',CLASS=T,MSGCLASS=A,
//   MSGLEVEL=(1,1),NOTIFY=BT05686
//*
//*    EXECUTION JCL FS376501 FOR TEST
```

```
//*      RUN TELMAST UPDATE AND PRINT USER REPORTS
//*      THIS JCL = BT05686.SOURCE.CNTL(OVERRIDE)
//*
//STEPA     EXEC FS3765P1,VOLID='HXR452'
//FS37651B.BT3708E2  DD  DSN=AK00.C99.TELMAST(0)
//FS37651B.BT3708E3  DD  DSN=AK00.C99.AREAREF
//FS37651B.BT3708U1  DD  DSN=AK00.C99.BT3708U1(+1)
//FS37651B.BT3708U2  DD  DSN=AK00.C99.TELMAST(+1)
//FS37651C.BT3719U1  DD  DSN=AK00.C99.BT3719U1(+1)
//FS37651C.BT3719U2  DD  DSN=AK00.C99.BT3719U2(+1)
//*
//STEPB     EXEC FS3765P2,
//  GEN='(+1)'
//FS37652A.SYSUT1     DD  DSN=AK00.C99.BT3708U1(+1)
//                    DD  DSN=AK00.C99.BT3708U2(+1)
//                    DD  DSN=AK00.C99.BT3719U1(+1)
//
```

DD statement overrides are coded similarly to DD statement adds. The formal rules for DD statement overrides are:

- DD statement overrides preface the DDname with the procstepname.[7]
- DD statement overrides replace *individual JCL parameters only*. If an override carries a parameter present in the original DD statement, the parameter is replaced. If the override carries a parameter that is not on the original statement, the parameter is added. DCB, a parameter for which several subparameters may be coded, is an exception and is discussed below.
- DD statement overrides carry DDnames that *already exist* in the step they are to affect—the definition of an override.
- DD statement overrides must be coded in execution JCL physically *preceding* any added DD statements for the procstep.[8]
- DD statement overrides must be listed in the order in which the overridden DD statements occur in the proc.
- DD statement overrides do not become a permanent part of the proc but are effective only for a given run.

Overridden statements in a cataloged procedure carry X/ in their first two positions on MVS allocation/deallocation reports; they were in the JCL of the proc but were affected by execution JCL. For a proc being executed instream +/ is used by MVS instead of the X/ characters.

Overriding Proc DCB Parameters

The DCB parameter is treated unlike any other parameter in the DD statement as far as overrides are concerned. All other parameters are overridden completely, but *DCB is overridden subparameter by subparameter*. For example, if we wanted to override the LABEL parameter in step //FS37651A to specify a standard labeled rather than a nonlabeled tape, we would code this override.

```
//FS37651A.SORTIN    DD   LABEL=(1,SL,EXPDT=98000)
```

supplying the full LABEL parameter. When we wish to alter one portion of the DCB, we can specify just that subparameter and all the other DCB subparameters coded in the proc will still be in effect. Suppose that we wanted to change a different item at this DD statement by reading the input tape at 6,250 bpi instead of the 1,600 bpi coded in the proc. We would provide this override:

```
//FS37651A.SORTIN    DD   DCB=DEN=4
```

If we wanted to change the label and density and make the block size 16,000 bytes—three items—for this DD statement, we would code

```
//FS37651A.SORTIN    DD   LABEL=(1,SL,EXPDT=98000),
//   DCB=(DEN=4,BLKSIZE=16000)
```

or

```
//FS37651A.SORTIN    DD   DCB=(BLKSIZE=16000,DEN=4),
//   LABEL=(1,SL,EXPDT=98000)
```

because the order of the parameters within the override is of no consequence.[9]

Nullification of Proc Symbolic Parameters

It is possible to nullify parameters that exist in the proc by specifying the parameters, followed only by an equal sign, in the execution JCL override statement. This is the same syntax that exists in the default coding on the PROC statement when the default value for a symbolic parameter is its nullification. An entire DD statement can be nullified by overriding the DSN with NULLFILE. The coding of all parameters on the DD statement will still be checked by MVS for syntax errors but the parameters will otherwise be ignored.

USE OF PROC OVERRIDES IN BUSINESS DATA PROCESSING

Practically speaking, the use of proc overrides in business data processing falls into these distinct categories:

- Use of compiling procs
- Testing new procs
- Recovery from production failures by using an alternate data set in conjunction with a production run or running "temporary fixes" from a test load module library pending normal installation of revised programs
- Changing hardcoded devices that have failed or space allocations that temporarily require larger values

The first two categories have been discussed at length in this chapter. The last two categories are no different in terms of syntax or add/override rules, but some illustrations are helpful. Only the last two categories have any bearing on the work of the operations group of an organization; when proc overrides are mentioned, that group will typically call to mind only the latter situations.

Overrides in Recovering from Production Failures

If a production job abends, leaving some data sets in usable and others in unusable condition, an operations group may not be able to patch together the necessary fixes to restore an application system to operation. Programmer attention is then directed to filling this gap, which sometimes results in the need to recreate a transaction or master file data set required by the production run. If this data set is part of a recovery but carries a name other than the actual production data set name, an override can be inserted into the execution JCL for the proc to "point to" the data set for a given run.

Overrides to change space allocations for which no symbolic parameters have been provided are especially simple. The entire SPACE parameter for the affected DD statement is coded as an override that uses a DDname of the procstepname.DDname format. This is placed in the execution JCL before any DD statements added to the procstep.

Running Production from a Test Load Module Library

On occasion, it is not a data set but a program name that must be overridden because a production job failure was due to incorrect program logic. *The program name is the single parameter of a proc that cannot* be *overridden*. How then do you substitute one program load module for another, without yet installing the new load module into the real production load module library?

The answer is that the program name at a step is not overridden. Instead, the step is made to "execute from testlib" rather than from production. What is changed is the partitioned data set load module library for the step. The program is compiled and linkage-edited and the resulting load module is placed in a test load module library such as BT05686.TEST.LOADMODS. Then a DD statement is added to the execution JCL to create a //STEPLIB in the step for which load module substitution is to occur. For example, if proc FS3765P1 was in production but an emergency change was needed in program FSBT3708, invoked in the proc's second step, we could retrieve the source code, change it, compile, linkage edit and test it, and place its load module in BT05686.TEST.LOADMODS or a similar nonproduction load library. We would then add this statement at the bottom of the execution JCL for this proc:

```
//FS37651B.STEPLIB    DD   DSN=BT05686.TEST.LOADMODS,
//  DISP=SHR
```

This would allow the step to run from testlib instead of from the default production load module library. No //STEPLIB statement occurs in most production JCL because programs are normally sought from the installation's default production load module library. Therefore this is an execution JCL DD statement "added" for this step of the proc rather than an override.

This is execution JCL that runs production proc FS3765P1, takes program FSBT3708 from a test load module library, and uses a test data set for the FS37.C99.AREAREF reference file:

```
//FSBT686A   JOB AK00TEST,'DP2-JANOSSY',CLASS=T,MSGCLASS=A,
//  MSGLEVEL=(1,1),NOTIFY=BT05686
//*
//*     EXECUTION JCL BT05686.SOURCE.CNTL(TEST16)
//*     *** THIS IS PATCH UP JCL ***
//*
//STEPA    EXEC  FS3765P1,VOLID='HXR452'
//FS37651B.BT3708E3 DD  DSN=AK00.C99.AREAREF
//FS37651B.STEPLIB   DD  DSN=BT05686.TEST.LOADMODS,
//  DISP=SHR
//*
//STEPB    EXEC FS3765P2,
//  GEN='(+1)'
//
```

Note that the overrides and adds are coded immediately after the invocation of the proc within the execution JCL step that invokes it, not at the bottom of the whole set of execution JCL. Because of this localization of overrides and adds in the execution JCL, the same DDnames can be used in different procs and different add and/or overrides can be handled for each of them. The same proc can also be invoked several times in execution JCL with different adds and/or overrides local to each invocation.

Overriding Concatenated DD Statements

At times it is necessary to concatenate another data set to one coded within a proc, to override one data set name that exists in a concatenation list in a proc, or to terminate a concatenation list in a proc prematurely. The override coding for this is unique.

Earlier in this chapter the concatenation of copylibs was discussed in connection with the COBOL compiler DDname //SYSLIB. This DD statement is where the COBOL compiler seeks copylib members and SYS1.COPYLIB is a typical name for a production copylib. Suppose a programmer wants to use the compile, linkage edit, and go proc illustrated as CLGCOBOL in Figure 16.1 but wishes to draw in copylibs from a personal copy library if they are not located in the standard. This is the opposite of the situation discussed earlier, in which priority was to be given to the developmental copylib; the intention here is to take the copylib items from the production library if they are there, and if they are not to take them from a second PDS called BT05686.DEVCOPY.COBOL. This execution JCL accomplishes it:

```
//FSBT686A   JOB AK00COMP,'DP2-JANOSSY',CLASS=E,MSGCLASS=X,
//  MSGLEVEL=(1,1),NOTIFY=BT05686
//*
//* BT05686.SOURCE.CNTL(CONCAT)   EXEC CLG PROC
//* CONCATENATION OF DEVELOPMENTAL COPYLIB
//*
//STEPA      EXEC  CLGCOBOL
//*
//COB.SYSLIB   DD
//             DD  DSN=BT05686.DEVCOPY.COBOL,DISP=SHR
//*
//COB.SYSIN    DD  DSN=BT05686.SOURCE.COBOL(PSD183),
//  DISP=SHR
//GO.INDATA1   DD  DSN=BT05686.SOURCE.CNTL(STATEDAT),
//  DISP=SHR
//GO.OTREPTI   DD  SYSOUT=*
//
```

The first item in the //COB.SYSLIB concatenation list is blank. This is the way that execution JCL indicates that no change is to be made in the concatenation list *at that relative position*. This means that the proc's coding of SYS1.COPYLIB as the first data set at //COB.SYSLIB will remain as it is. A normal concatenation is then coded in the execution JCL stating the developmental copylib.

A NULLFILE or DUMMY data set name coded in a concatenation list terminates the list at that point. It is possible to force premature termination of concatenation of simple sequential data sets within a proc by coding empty DD statements in the execution JCL down to the position of the desired concatenation end. DSN=NULLFILE is coded at the position following the last position to remain. The proc will see the end of the concatenation list as the data set with the NULLFILE override. NULLFILE is not valid when the concatenation involves entire partitioned data sets like those at the //SYSLIB DD statement; it is appropriate when individual members of PDSs or simple sequential data sets are specified. If DUMMY is coded with a whole PDS library, an abend and system completion code of 013-64 will result.

REVIEW QUESTIONS AND (*) EXERCISES

1. Describe briefly what a JCL procedure is and how it differs from raw JCL.

2. How is an instream proc different from a cataloged procedure?

3. What is meant by generalizing a set of JCL as it is made into a cataloged procedure?

4. How is an item of JCL transformed into a symbolic parameter in a proc and how are names for symbolic parameters constrained?

5. A default value is not coded for a certain symbolic parameter on the PROC statement for a cataloged procedure. What must be done when invoking the proc to avoid a job failure?

*6. Examine the information in Appendix A that concerns the TYPRUN job statement subparameter. Submit a job to compile, linkage edit, and run a program by using your installation's standard proc for this process and specifying TYPRUN=SCAN on the JOB statement. Then submit another run of this job and code TYPRUN=COPY on the job statement. Compare the two sets of output and use Appendix A to explain why they are different. Note: No actual compile, linkage edit and run will occur in either case.

*7. Compile a program in the language of your choice by using your installation's standard compile-only procedure. Examine the listing of the proc that is returned in the MVS system reports and code raw JCL without any symbolic parameters to accomplish the same thing. Test the JCL by running it raw with your program to accomplish the same compile.

*8. Turn the JCL you composed and ran in item 7 into an instream proc with symbolic parameters for a compiler //SYSPRINT print class, the input source code data set name, and the compiler PARM string. Run the compile-only with values for these three symbolic parameters supplied by execution JCL, and identify the MVS substitutions made in the allocation/deallocation report.

*9. Find the business section of a newspaper and code 20 test data records in your CNTL data set, each listing the name of a stock on the New York Stock Exchange in a 25-byte field and its current selling price as a decimal number in a 7-byte field. Using the examples of sort JCL and the information in item 14 in Chapter 17, develop a two-step job stream that will sort the stock data into descending order of selling price, and list it. The first step is to output the data to a temporary data set called &&TEMPSORT. The second step is to list the sorted data with a descriptive column heading above each field, using IEBPTPCH. After running this job stream as raw JCL transform it into a proc with symbolic parameters for temporary file primary and secondary space, IEBPTPCH //SYSUT2 print class, and the number of COPIES of the list to be printed. Code the appropriate defaults on a PROC statement. Run the proc instream twice, once with no execution JCL symbolic parameters and the second time with execution JCL symbolic parameters different from the defaults. Note: Remember that procs cannot handle instream data.

*10. Code a program in the language of your choice to receive a 23-byte PARM, using the guidance provided in Chapter 15. This program simply prints this PARM value five times on paper, single-spaced. Compose JCL to execute the load module of the program, but build it to be an instream proc in which the PARM is coded as a symbolic parameter. Arrange a default in the proc for this symbolic parameter to be ** NO PARM SUBMITTED **. Run the proc instream with six invocations—six EXEC statements following the PEND statement named //STEPA, //STEPB, //STEPC, and so forth. The execution JCL is to supply these PARM values at each step:

```
//STEPA          THIS IS A TEST
//STEPB          HELLO HELLO #2
//STEPC                          (no PARM on the EXEC)
//STEPD          123-456,789.10
//STEPE          ** ** ** ** **
//STEPF          THE LAST OF THE PARMS
```

NOTES

1. If no symbolic parameter default values are coded, the proc statement is optional. The name coded on it after the slashes is not the proc name except in the case of procs being executed instream. The proc statement is usually coded in all cases to document the intended name of the proc.

2. The //SYSLIN object data set name in the //COB procstep, &LOADSET, is actually coded as a symbolic parameter as well, but a symbolic parameter for a DSN commands special treatment by MVS and has not been included in the list discussed. A symbolic parameter for a DSN acts in two capacities: as a normal symbolic parameter that can be supplied a value at run time or as a temporary data set name. Temporary data set names are usually coded with two ampersands. When coded with one ampersand, the DSN can be specified at run time by the execution JCL. If it is not, the & name is treated as if it were coded with the && of a temporary data set name.

3. When a symbolic parameter is nullified by coding it and an equal sign, the parameter is eliminated from the JCL for the run. However, leading and trailing commas or parentheses coded in the proc are not affected. It is often expedient to code changeable subparameters such as the VSCOBCL space allocations as shown, with the symbolic parameter supplying multiple JCL subparameters. This is possible because the characters supplied by the symbolic parameter are just that: characters and not numeric quantities. Only after MVS analyzes the JCL do the values like disk blocks, record size, and block size become numeric in storage format and treatment. The parentheses surrounding the relative generation number of a GDG data set in the latter figures of this chapter are included in the symbolic parameter and will be eliminated with nullification.

4. Coding a value assignment for the same symbolic parameter value more than once on an EXEC or PROC statement usually represents an unintentional error. If this is done the *first* value coded is used. This is opposite the treatment that occurs for a compiler PARM option coded more than once. In the case of duplicate coding of compiler PARMs the *last* value coded is the one that applies.

5. Both the COBOL compiler and the linkage editor have a DDname //SYSLIB, but the two inputs have nothing to do with one another. Copylib members are sought in //SYSLIB at the compiler. Load modules for CALLed routines to be hard linked for static CALLs are input at //SYSLIB at the linkage editor. "A foolish consistency is the hobgoblin of small minds." Here the hobgoblin manifests itself on persons other than the perpetrators of the consistency by introducing needless potential for confusion. There is absolutely no connection between these DDnames or the partitioned data sets associated with them.

6. It is projected that 85,000 transactions per run may be processed in this job. The amount of sort work space needed for production purposes was calculated by determining how many bytes of storage would be needed to house 85,000 of the 102-

byte records and then estimating how many cylinders of disk this would require. The space requirement is about 9 megabytes. On the 3350 disks to be used for the run, which have a cylinder capacity of about 0.57 megabytes, this requires about 16 cylinders. Because actual data storage on disk tracks depends on factors such as the size of sort key and the blocking computed by the sort utility, a margin of safety is gained by adding 30 to 50 percent to this value to produce a figure of 24 cylinders.

The sort requires enough space to completely house the data set spread across at least two disk units. With a data set that contains several thousand records, the use of more disk units can improve sort speed. Specification of SORTWK03 in each step that uses a sort was therefore made. This meant that 24 ÷ 3 or 8 cylinders would be appropriate for each of the three disk space allocations. It is also possible to use dynamic sort work space allocation for external and internal sorts, as shown in item 3 of Chapter 17. IBM's DFSORT utility can accommodate 32 sort work data sets but the use of more than eight is unusual.

7. If the proc's stepname is not prefaced on the DDname, the treatment of the added or overridden DD statement is "up for grabs." It will go to the same step to which a prior added DD statement went, if there was one, or to the first step in the proc. It is poor form to omit the proc's stepname on an added or overridden DD statement in execution JCL because of the doubt that ensues regarding the proc step intended to be affected.

8. An unusual mnemonic device helps to remember the order of proc overrides and adds. "OOT" means "Overrides On Top." Silly, but it works.

9. See *The sequential update job stream using tape* in Chapter 10 for an explanation of the EXPDT = 98000 subparameter, which may not be required in your installation.

17

JCL Tools: Compiler, Sort, VSAM, and Utility Examples

This chapter provides practical examples of JCL as used day-to-day on the job. These examples describe the types of tasks that a programmer is often called on to handle with JCL and utilities but that usually take research, trial and error, and frustration with syntax idiosynchrasies to accomplish. These JCL building blocks are useful in a wide variety of circumstances.

COMPILING WITH AND USING DEBUGGING OPTIONS

1. COBOL Compile and Link into a Load Library with Debugging Options

A compile, linkage edit, and go cataloged procedure is often used in program language training situations. CLG procs exist on the job, but programs are more often compiled and linkage edited separate from test runs. The result of invoking a CL proc like the VSCOBL proc discussed in Chapter 16 is the creation of a load module in a permanent load module library.

A compile and linkage edit proc may or may not provide by default the COBOL compiler PARM options for debugging purposes. Figure 17.1 is the JCL that executes the VSCOBCL proc in Chapter 16, overriding the //COB step compiler PARM with one that includes the SYM, FLOW, COUNT, and STATE debugging options. //SYSUT5 is a required DD statement when the SYM option is used. The .SYM data set should be allocated once as a partitioned data set, before the first compile, using the TSO 3.2 allocate option, or with this JCL:

```
//STEPA    EXEC   IEFBR14
//ALLOC1   DD   DSN=BT05686.TEST.SYM,
//   UNIT=SYSDA,
//   DISP=(NEW,CATLG,DELETE),
//   DCB=(RECFM=F,LRECL=512,BLKSIZE=512,DSORG=POU),
//   SPACE=(TRK,(30,30))
```

```
//FSBT686A  JOB AK00TEST,'DP2-JANOSSY',CLASS=E,MSGCLASS=X,
//   MSGLEVEL=(1,1),NOTIFY=BT05686
//*
//*    LOAD MODULE PREPARATION WITH DEBUG OPTIONS
//*    THIS JCL = BT05686.SOURCE.CNTL(JCL171)
//*
//***********************************************************
//*                                                         *
//*    COMPILE AND LINKAGE EDIT WITH DEBUG OPTIONS           *
//*                                                         *
//*    CAUTION: THIS RUN JCL IS INTENDED TO WORK             *
//*    WITH THE REVISED VSCOBCL PROC OF FIGURE 16.2.         *
//*    THE BARE IBM-SUPPLIED PROC NAMED VSCOBCL DOES         *
//*    NOT PROVIDE MANY OF SYMBOLIC PARAMETERS SHOWN.        *
//*    SEE CHAPTER 16 FOR ADDITIONAL INFORMATION.            *
//*                                                         *
//*    HELPFUL ADVICE: SYMBOLIC PARAMETER NAMES MUST         *
//*    BE NO LONGER THAN 7 CHARACTERS FOLLOWING THE          *
//*    AMPERSAND. IF YOU CODE EXECUTION JCL AND GET          *
//*    ANY JCL ERROR IEF642I:                                *
//*                                                         *
//*  "EXCESSIVE PARAMETER LENGTH IN SYMBOLIC PARAMETER"      *
//*                                                         *
//*    IT MEANS ONE OR MORE SYMBOLIC PARAMETER NAMES         *
//*    ARE MORE THAN SEVEN CHARACTERS LONG. FOR EXAMPLE      *
//*    IF YOU CODE "LMODNAM" BELOW AS "LMODNAME" THIS        *
//*    WILL OCCUR. THIS TYPE OF ERROR IS EASY TO MAKE        *
//*    BUT HARD TO CORRECT THE FIRST TIME EXPERIENCED        *
//*    BECAUSE THE MESSAGE MAKES IT SEEM A SYMBOLIC          *
//*    PARAMETER IS INVOLVED RATHER THAN SYNTAX.             *
//*                                                         *
//***********************************************************
//STEPA     EXEC  VSCOBCL,
//   PARM.COB=('SIZE=1024K,SXR,DMA,CLI,APOST',
//   'NOSEQ,NOADV,LIB,DYN',
//   'SYM,FLOW=99,COUNT,STA'),
//   PRINT='*',
//   LOADLIB='BT05686.TEST.LOADMODS',
//   LMODNAM='PSD183'
//*
//COB.SYSIN DD DSN=BT05686.SOURCE.COBOL,DISP=SHR
//COB.SYSUT5 DD DSN=BT05686.TEST.SYM(PSD183),DISP=SHR
//
```

FIGURE 17.1. Overriding compile PARM in a proc to specify debugging options

The SYM data set is unusual in that it is "unmovable" because the compiler places track-specific pointers in it for its own purposes. This is the reason that the DSORG for it carries the suffix "U". The data set member output by the compile as a member of this special PDS contains variable name references in coded form. *//SYSUT5, illustrated in Figure 17.2, is also named in the execution JCL for this program.*

Once a program tests successfully it is recompiled without the debugging options when it is placed in production. The debugging options carry a penalty in execution overhead that is not desirable in a production program.

2. Executing a Load Module with Debugging Options

A COBOL program load module compiled with debugging options requires special DD statements to which the compiler-supplied debugging logic sends information. Most of these options can be assigned to the printer, but //SYSUT5 must name a data set. Figure 17.2 illustrates the JCL that can be used to test a COBOL program load module compiled with the SYM, FLOW, COUNT, and STATE debugging options. FLOW and STATE use the //SYSDBOUT DD statement, COUNT uses the //SYSCOUNT DD statement, and SYM uses //SYSDTERM, //SYSDBOUT, and //SYSUT5.

The JCL shown here to execute the program is separate from any compile and linkage edit JCL. For a compile, linkage edit, and go or CLG proc the same debugging options are available; the proc itself may in-

```
//FSBT686A  JOB AK00TEST,'DP2-JANOSSY',CLASS=E,MSGCLASS=X,
//   MSGLEVEL=(1,1),NOTIFY=BT05686
//*
//*     LOAD MODULE EXECUTION WITH DEBUG OPTIONS
//*     THIS JCL = BT05686.SOURCE.CNTL(JCL172)
//*
//************************************************************
//*                                                          *
//*     EXECUTE LOAD MODULE WITH DEBUG                        *
//*                                                          *
//************************************************************
//STEPA     EXEC  PGM=PSD183
//STEPLIB    DD   DSN=BT05686.TEST.LOADMODS,
//   DISP=SHR
//INDATA1    DD   DSN=BT05686.SOURCE.CNTL(STATEDAT),
//   DISP=SHR
//OTREPT1    DD   SYSOUT=*
//SYSOUT     DD   SYSOUT=*
//SYSDTERM   DD   SYSOUT=*                        'DEBUG
//SYSDBOUT   DD   SYSOUT=*                        'DEBUG
//SYSCOUNT   DD   SYSOUT=*                        'DEBUG
//SYSUT5     DD   DSN=BT05686.TEST.SYM(PSD183),   'DEBUG
//   DISP=SHR
//
```

FIGURE 17.2. Executing a load module compiled with debugging options

clude the extra DD statements except for the SYM data set. When a program tests successfully, it is normally recompiled and linkage-edited into a load module without the debugging options for placement in production. The extra four DD statements should not be coded in a step that executes a production program. By definition, CLG procs are not production oriented.

THE SORT/MERGE UTILITY

3. Sorting with Dynamic Sort Work Space Allocation

The IBM DFSORT utility and sorts from non-IBM vendors provide access to the dynamic space allocation facilities of MVS. These facilities make it possible to avoid use of hardcoded space allocation parameters and //SORTWKnn DDnames, normally an item of JCL that can be troubling. Instead an estimate of the number of records to be sorted and the number of disk drives across which MVS can spread the sort work space can be indicated on the sort control statement. Figure 17.3a illustrates the use of this option.

It is also possible to use dynamic sort work space allocation under DFSORT when the sort is invoked by the SORT verb within a COBOL program that performs an internal sort. The JCL for this uses a DD statement named //SORTCNTL to carry the "extra" sort specifications for which there is no support in COBOL itself. Figure 17.3b shows how the JCL for //STEPC of the job stream in Figure 3.4 would appear when making use of dynamic sort work space allocation and not explicit //SORTWKnn data sets.

A complete synopsis of the DFSORT utility and its more subtle facilities is contained in Appendix A of *Commercial Software Engineering: For Productive Program Design*, James G. Janossy, ISBN 0-471-81576-4, John Wiley and Sons, Inc., 1985.

4. Merging Data Sets

In many applications a small quantity of new records is produced daily and added to a "pot" of like records that cover a given time period. The merging of daily output into a year-to-date data set is one example. This data set is usually stored in record key sequence by account number.

It would be possible to concatenate the current generation of the year-to-date data set and the data set produced daily into a sort and output the new year-to-date generation in this manner. As the year progressed, however, the time to perform the sort would grow. For an application that produces hundreds of thousands or millions of records a year sorting

```
//FSBT686A  JOB  AK0OTEST,'DP2-JANOSSY',CLASS=E,MSGCLASS=X,
//  MSGLEVEL=(1,1),NOTIFY=BT05686
//*
//*     THIS JCL = BT05686.SOURCE.CNTL(JCL173)
//*
//***********************************************************
//*                                                        *
//*     EXTERNAL SORT WITH DYNAMIC SORT WORK SPACE         *
//*                                                        *
//***********************************************************
//STEPA     EXEC  PGM=SORT
//SORTLIB    DD   DSN=SYS1.SORTLIB,DISP=SHR
//SYSOUT     DD   SYSOUT=*
//SYSUDUMP   DD   SYSOUT=A
//SORTIN     DD   DSN=FDS112.C52.WRTRANS,
//   UNIT=(TAPE,,DEFER),
//   DISP=(OLD,KEEP)
//SORTOUT    DD   DSN=FDS112.C52.WRSORT,
//   UNIT=SYSDA,
//   DISP=(NEW,CATLG,DELETE),
//   DCB=(RECFM=FB,LRECL=162,BLKSIZE=6156),
//   SPACE=(6156,(6000,1200),RLSE)
//SYSIN      DD   *
    SORT  FIELDS=(15,1,CH,A,16,4,CH,A,10,5,CH,A),
          FILSZ=E175000,DYNALLOC=(SYSDA,6)
/*
//
```

(a)

```
//***********************************************************
//*                                                        *
//*     PRODUCE TRAN REPORT (INTERNAL SORT)          C     *
//*                                                        *
//***********************************************************
//STEPC     EXEC  PGM=FSBT3719
//STEPLIB    DD   DSN=BT05686.TEST.LOADMODS,
//   DISP=SHR
//SORTLIB    DD   DSN=SYS1.SORTLIB,
//   DISP=SHR
//BT3719E1   DD   DSN=&&TRANSFIN,
//   DISP=(OLD,DELETE)
//BT3719U1   DD   SYSOUT=*
//BT3719U2   DD   SYSOUT=*
//SORTCNTL   DD   *                         'DYNAMIC
    OPTION  DYNALLOC=(SYSDA,3)FILSZ=E30000  'SORT WORK
/*                                          'SPACE
//BT3719SM   DD   SYSOUT=*
//SYSOUT     DD   SYSOUT=*
//SYSUDUMP   DD   SYSOUT=*
//
```

(b)

FIGURE 17.3. (a) A sort using dynamic sort work space instead of hardcoded SORTWKnn DD statements and (b) JCL for a COBOL program using internal sort and dynamic sort work space

the whole year-to-date data set to accomplish a merge is wasteful; it is necessary to sort only the day's new accumulation of records and then merge the daily and existing year-to-date data sets. The sort/merge utility provides a merge capability that allows two data sets, already sorted on the same field, to be combined. This results in reading both data sets and writing a third collating the records into one data set.

```
//FSBT686A  JOB AKOOTEST,'DP2-JANOSSY',CLASS=W,MSGCLASS=X,
//  MSGLEVEL=(1,1),NOTIFY=BT05686
//*
//*     THIS JCL = BT05686.SOURCE.CNTL(JCL174)
//*
//************************************************************
//*                                                         *
//*     MERGE PREVIOUSLY SORTED DATA SETS                   *
//*                                                         *
//************************************************************
//STEPA     EXEC  PGM=SORT
//SORTLIB   DD    DSN=SYS1.SORTLIB,DISP=SHR
//SYSOUT    DD    SYSOUT=*
//SYSUDUMP  DD    SYSOUT=A
//SORTINO1  DD    DSN=FS14.C99.DAILYTRN,
//  DISP=(OLD,KEEP)
//SORTINO2  DD    DSN=FS14.C99.YTDTRN(0),
//  DISP=(OLD,KEEP)
//SORTOUT   DD    DSN=FS14.C99.YTDTRN(+1),
//  UNIT=SYSDA,
//  DISP=(NEW,CATLG,DELETE),
//  DCB=(XX90.AO0.DUMMYLBL,RECFM=FB,LRECL=252,BLKSIZE=6048),
//  SPACE=(6048,(900,180),RLSE)
//SORTWK01  DD    UNIT=SYSDA,SPACE=(CYL,5,,CONTIG)
//SORTWK02  DD    UNIT=SYSDA,SPACE=(CYL,5,,CONTIG)
//SORTWK03  DD    UNIT=SYSDA,SPACE=(CYL,5,,CONTIG)
//SYSIN     DD    *
    MERGE  FIELDS=(1,15,CH,A)
/*
//
```

FIGURE 17.4. Using the sort/merge utility to collate two previously sorted data sets into one

Figure 17.4 shows how a merge is accomplished. The merge is accomplished by coding a slightly different control statement. The merge will succeed only if both input data sets are already sorted on the specified merge field or fields.

IDCAMS: USEFUL NON-VSAM AND VSAM FUNCTIONS

5. Creating a Test Sequential Data Set

Often a program being developed or modified deals with an existing data set that may contain hundreds of thousands of records. Testing this program usually includes running it with a subset of live data, perhaps doctored to reflect a wider variety of test cases. A utility to peel off a few thousand records from a main data set is a convenient tool.

IDCAMS, the multipurpose Access Method Services utility, can be used to take a subset of records from a sequential data set and copy them to a second sequential data set. Although IDCAMS is usually associated with VSAM, it was designed to provide a wider range of support. Figure 17.5 shows how to use the REPRO command with the COUNT option to designate how many records are to be copied. The SKIP option allows

```
//FSBT686A  JOB AK00TEST,'DP2-JANOSSY',CLASS=T,MSGCLASS=X,
//  MSGLEVEL=(1,1),NOTIFY=BT05686
//*
//*    THIS JCL = BT05686.SOURCE.CNTL(JCL175)
//*
//**********************************************************
//*                                                        *
//*    BUILD SUBSET TEST FILE AND DUMP IT                  *
//*                                                        *
//**********************************************************
//STEPA     EXEC  PGM=IDCAMS
//SYSPRINT  DD    SYSOUT=*
//DDIN      DD    DSN=FS23.C99.MILEARCH,
//  UNIT=(TAPE,,DEFER),
//  DISP=(OLD,KEEP)
//DDOUT     DD    DSN=AK00.C99.MILETEST,
//  UNIT=SYSDA,
//  DISP=(NEW,CATLG,DELETE),
//  DCB=(RECFM=FB,LRECL=204,BLKSIZE=6120),
//  SPACE=(6120,(35,7),RLSE)
//SYSIN     DD    *
      REPRO        INFILE(DDIN) -
                   OUTFILE(DDOUT) -
                   SKIP(15000) -
                   COUNT(1000)

      PRINT        INFILE(DDOUT) -
                   DUMP
/*
//
```

FIGURE 17.5.   IDCAMS control statements to copy and dump a subset of records from a sequential data set

skipping over a quantity of records before the copy process starts. The input data set is //DDIN and the output emerges at //DDOUT.

This JCL also shows invocation of the IDCAMS PRINT command to create a dump listing of the test data set in the same job. Figures 17.6*a,b,* and *c* indicate how to use the IDCAMS PRINT option freestanding. RE-PRO and PRINT are separate IDCAMS functions and need not be used together.

6. Using IDCAMS as a General Purpose hex Dump Utility

IDCAMS, although heavily used as the VSAM utility, was designed to handle a wide variety of tasks unrelated to VSAM data sets. The PRINT command provides the means of producing a character and hexadecimal dump of a sequential data set or PDS member.

Figure 17.6*a* indicates how to use IDCAMS to produce a dump of a data set. The COUNT option limits the dump to the stated number of records. The SKIP option, although not coded here, follows the format illustrated in Figure 17.5, and allows skipping over a quantity of records before the dump starts. The input data set need not be fixed blocked sequential; IDCAMS PRINT readily handles variable length records and VSAM data sets or alternate indexes as input to be dumped.

Selectively dumping samples of various record organizations such as

```
//FSBT686A  JOB AK00TEST,'DP2-JANOSSY',CLASS=E,MSGCLASS=X,
//  MSGLEVEL=(1,1),NOTIFY=BT05686
//*
//*     THIS JCL = BT05686.SOURCE.CNTL(JCL176A)
//*
//*************************************************************
//*                                                          *
//*      HEX & CHARACTER DUMP A FILE WITH IDCAMS             *
//*                                                          *
//*************************************************************
//STEPA     EXEC  PGM=IDCAMS
//SYSPRINT  DD    SYSOUT=*
//DD1       DD    DSN=AK00.C99.MILETEST,
//  DISP=SHR
//SYSIN     DD    *
     PRINT        INFILE(DD1) -
                  COUNT(50) -
                  DUMP
/*
//
```

(a)

```
//FSBT686A  JOB AK00TEST,'DP2-JANOSSY',CLASS=E,MSGCLASS=X,
//  MSGLEVEL=(1,1),NOTIFY=BT05686
//*
//*     THIS JCL = BT05686.SOURCE.CNTL(JCL176B)
//*
//*************************************************************
//*                                                          *
//*      DUMP VARIABLE LENGTH RECORDS WITH DEBLOCKING        *
//*                                                          *
//*************************************************************
//STEPA     EXEC  PGM=IDCAMS
//SYSPRINT  DD    SYSOUT=*
//DD1       DD    DSN=BT05686.SOURCE.CLIST(DISKINFO),
//  DISP=SHR
//SYSIN     DD    *
     PRINT        INFILE(DD1) -
                  DUMP
/*
//*
//*************************************************************
//*                                                          *
//*      DUMP VB RECORDS SEEING BLOCK/RECORD DESCRIPTORS     *
//*                                                          *
//*************************************************************
//STEPB     EXEC  PGM=IDCAMS
//SYSPRINT  DD    SYSOUT=*
//DD1       DD    DSN=BT05686.SOURCE.CLIST(DISKINFO),
//  DISP=SHR,
//  DCB=(RECFM=U,LRECL=6233)
//SYSIN     DD    *
     PRINT        INFILE(DD1) -
                  DUMP
/*
//
```

(b)

FIGURE 17.6. (*a*) IDCAMS control statements to dump sequential data set in character and hexadecimal, (*b*) IDCAMS control statements to dump variable length records as RECFM = U to see MVS-supplied block and record length control fields, and (*c*) IDCAMS control statements to dump a PDS directory block

```
//FSBT686A  JOB AKOOTEST,'DP2-JANOSSY',CLASS=E,MSGCLASS=X,
//   MSGLEVEL=(1,1),NOTIFY=BT05686
//*
//*     THIS JCL = BT05686.SOURCE.CNTL(JCL176C)
//*
//**********************************************************
//*                                                        *
//*     DUMP A PDS DIRECTORY TO ANALYZE IT                 *
//*                                                        *
//**********************************************************
//STEPA     EXEC  PGM=IDCAMS
//SYSPRINT  DD    SYSOUT=*
//DD1       DD    DSN=BT05686.SOURCE.CNTL,
//   DISP=SHR,
//   DCB=(RECFM=U,LRECL=256,DSORG=PS)
//SYSIN     DD    *
     PRINT        INFILE(DD1) -
                  DUMP
/*
//*
```

(c)

FIGURE 17.6. *(con't.)*

VB variable length blocked records can be informative. If the JCL DCB parameter is used to override the data set label information for a variable length record data set, specifying RECFM = U and a block size arbitrarily large enough to house the largest record, you can see the MVS-written block length and record length binary fields of variable length records, the "block descriptor word" and "record descriptor word." Figure 17.6*b* illustrates this learning exercise by dumping a CLIST variable record length data set allowing MVS deblocking to occur and then dumping the same data set by overriding its data set label with JCL DCB subparameters so that the descriptor words that preface each record can be seen. Compare the second dump produced by such JCL with Figure 7.4 to see what variable length records really contain.

Figure 17.6*c* illustrates dumping the 256-byte records that make up the directory of a partitioned data set. These records contain a 12 to 42-byte entry for each member in the data set, with housekeeping information in COMP-3 packed decimal and COMP binary fields. The DCB parameter overrides the data set label and allows IDCAMS to access the directory records merely as records. This dump serves no production purpose but provides a means of exploring the internal workings of the PDS data set organization. See Chapter 2 for additional information on PDSs.

7. Renaming, Uncataloging, Cataloging, and Deleting Data Sets and PDS Members

Figure 17.7*a* illustrates the use of IDCAMS to perform common data set maintenance functions. IDCAMS is the replacement for IEHPROGM in

```
//FSBT686A  JOB AKOOTEST,'DP2-JANOSSY',CLASS=E,MSGCLASS=X,
//  MSGLEVEL=(1,1),NOTIFY=BT05686
//*
//*    THIS JCL = BT05686.SOURCE.CNTL(JCL177A)
//*
//************************************************************
//*                                                         *
//*    RENAME DATA SETS OR MEMBERS USING IDCAMS             *
//*                                                         *
//************************************************************
//STEPA     EXEC  PGM=IDCAMS
//SYSPRINT  DD  SYSOUT=*
//SYSIN     DD  *
     ALTER   AKOO.C99.RAWTRANS -                 /* RENAME A  */
             NEWNAME(AKOO.C99.OLDTRANS)          /* DATA SET  */

     ALTER   BT05686.TEST.LOADMODS -             /* RENAME A  */
             NEWNAME(BT05792.TEST.LOADMODS)      /* WHOLE PDS */

     ALTER   BT05686.SOURCE.COBOL(PSD183)        /* RENAME A    */
             NEWNAME(BT05686.SOURCE.COBOL(PSD100))  /* PDS MEMBER */
/*
//
```

(a)

```
//FSBT686A  JOB AKOOTEST,'DP2-JANOSSY',CLASS=E,MSGCLASS=X,
//  MSGLEVEL=(1,1),NOTIFY=BT05686
//*
//*    THIS JCL = BT05686.SOURCE.CNTL(JCL177B)
//*
//************************************************************
//*                                                         *
//*    DELETE DATA SETS OR MEMBERS USING IDCAMS             *
//*                                                         *
//************************************************************
//STEPA     EXEC  PGM=IDCAMS
//SYSPRINT  DD  SYSOUT=*
//SYSIN     DD  *
     DELETE  AKOO.C99.TESTDATA                   /* DELETE A   */
                                                 /* DATA SET   */

     DELETE  AKOO.C99.VEHMAST1 -                 /* DELETE AN  */
             PURGE                               /* UNEXPIRED  */
                                                 /* DATA SET   */

     DELETE  BT05686.SOURCE.COBOL(PSD189)        /* DELETE A    */
                                                 /* PDS MEMBER */
/*
//*
```

(b)

FIGURE 17.7. (a) IDCAMS data set and member rename control statements and (b) IDCAMS data set and member deletion control statements

addressing these tasks for sequential data sets and PDSs. The catalog structure of MVS has evolved since its earliest days and IEHPROGM can no longer be used for certain tasks; it will probably be eliminated by IBM entirely as MVS/XA continues to evolve.

IDCAMS performs renames in a more capable manner than IEH-PROGM. Specifying the uncataloging and recataloging actions for a data set that was renamed were once the responsibility of the programmer.

Now, when a data set is renamed by IDCAMS, the old name is automatically uncataloged and the data set is cataloged under the new name.

Figure 17.7*b* illustrates the use of IDCAMS to delete a disk data set, an unexpired disk data set and a member of a PDS.

8. VSAM Key Sequenced Data Set Definition and Loading, with Alternate Indexes

VSAM is the access method by which IBM currently supports indexed files. "Key sequenced data set," abbreviated "KSDS," is the formal VSAM term for an indexed file. Unlike ISAM files—IBM's earlier and now obsolete indexed file support—VSAM data sets cannot be created by using JCL specifications alone. Instead the several characteristics of a VSAM data set are stored in the system catalog and must be defined using IDCAMS, the Access Method Services utility. IDCAMS provides a multitude of control statements in a unique language syntax of its own.

Figure 17.8*a* is a graphic layout of the records to be loaded to a VSAM key sequenced data set. These records contain a primary key field named Account Number, a nonunique alternate key based on address, and an alternate key based on customer name. While the customer name alternate key by itself would not be unique, the placement of this field in front of the primary key makes it possible to include the primary key at the end of the customer name alternate key, forcing it to be fully unique in all cases. Both alternate keys will be used for online "browse" access, not direct full key single record access. Figure 17.8*b* illustrates the JCL step in which the data will be loaded to the KSDS. Several IDCAMS processes are involved in this example:

DELETE	data set, indexes, paths
DEFINE, REPRO	data set, primary index, load
DEFINE, BLDAIX	create first alternate index
DEFINE	create 'path' between data set and first alternate index
DEFINE, BLDAIX	create second alternate index
DEFINE	create 'path' between data set and second alternate index
LISTCAT	print data set information

The initial delete action is performed to eliminate completely the existing VSAM data set of the intended name, should one exist, and its defined parameters. This is analogous to a housekeeping IEFBR14 step with sequential data sets. The data set definition of IDCAMS coding is lengthy because it creates the catalog entries for all of the data set attributes. REPRO is the general purpose IDCAMS copy, analogous to IEBGENER,

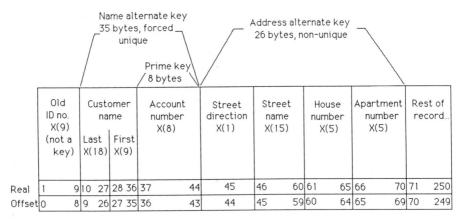

	Old ID no. X(9) (not a key)	Customer name		Account number X(8)	Street direction X(1)	Street name X(15)	House number X(5)	Apartment number X(5)	Rest of record...
		Last X(18)	First X(9)						
Real	1 9	10 27	28 36	37 44	45	46 60	61 65	66 70	71 250
Offset	0 8	9 26	27 35	36 43	44	45 59	60 64	65 69	70 249

Name alternate key 35 bytes, forced unique

Prime key 8 bytes

Address alternate key 26 bytes, non-unique

(a)

```
//FSBT686A  JOB AK00TEST,'DP2-JANOSSY',CLASS=T,MSGCLASS=X,
//  MSGLEVEL=(1,1),NOTIFY=BT05686
//*
//*     THIS JCL = BT05686.SOURCE.CNTL(JCL178B)   REV. C
//*
//***********************************************************
//*                                                         *
//*     DEFINE AND LOAD/RELOAD VSAM DATA SET                *
//*     WITH TWO ALTERNATE INDEXES                          *
//*                                                         *
//***********************************************************
//STEPA     EXEC  PGM=IDCAMS
//SYSPRINT   DD   SYSOUT=*
//SYSUDUMP   DD   SYSOUT=A
//MASTIN     DD   DSN=AK00.C98.CUSTBKUP(0),
//  UNIT=(TAPE,,DEFER),
//  DISP=(OLD,KEEP)
//WORKSRT1  DD   DSN=AK00.C98.IDCUT1,
//  UNIT=SYSDA,                      'AIX IDCAMS WORKFILE;
//  DISP=OLD,                        'VSAM REQUIRES DISP=OLD
//  AMP='AMORG',                     'EVEN THOUGH DOES NOT
//  VOL=SER=FSDC03                   'EXIST PRIOR TO USE!
//WORKSRT2  DD   DSN=AK00.C98.IDCUT2,
//  UNIT=SYSDA,                      'AIX IDCAMS WORKFILE;
//  DISP=OLD,                        'VSAM REQUIRES DISP=OLD
//  AMP='AMORG',                     'EVEN THOUGH DOES NOT
//  VOL=SER=FSDC03                   'EXIST PRIOR TO USE!
//SYSIN      DD   *
                                     /* HOUSEKEEPING DELETES */
       DELETE     AK00.C98.CUSTMAST -
                  CLUSTER

                  AK00.C98.IDCUT1  -
                  PURGE

                  AK00.C98.IDCUT2  -
                  PURGE

       SET LASTCC=0                  /* SOME ABOVE MAY NOT BE  */
       SET MAXCC=0                   /* FOUND; GET RID OF RC=8 */
```

(b)

FIGURE 17.8. (a) Graphic layout of record used in VSAM KSDS definition and load JCL and (b) IDCAMS definition and loading of VSAM key sequenced data set with two alternate indexes

```
/* - - - - - - - - CREATE THE BASE CLUSTER AND PRIMARY INDEX- - */

    DEFINE -
      CLUSTER    (    NAME(AK00.C98.CUSTMAST) -
                      VOLUMES(FSDC14) -
                      RECORDSIZE(250 250) -
                      KEYS(8 36) -
                      SHAREOPTIONS(2 3) -
                      SPEED                              ) -
                      -
      DATA       (    NAME(AK00.C98.CUSTMAST.BASE.DATA) -
                      CONTROLINTERVALSIZE(4096) -
                      CYLINDERS(1 1) -
                      FREESPACE(18 1)                    ) -
                      -
      INDEX      (    NAME(AK00.C98.CUSTMAST.BASE.INDEX)  )

/* - - - - - - - - IF CREATION SUCCESSFUL LOAD THE KSDS - - - - */

IF LASTCC = 0 -
THEN -
    REPRO         INFILE(MASTIN) -
                  OUTDATASET(AK00.C98.CUSTMAST)

/* FIRST AIX - - - CREATE THE NONUNIQUE ADDRESS ALTERNATE INDEX */

    DEFINE -
      AIX        (    NAME(AK00.C98.CUSTMAST.ADDRAIX) -
                      RELATE(AK00.C98.CUSTMAST) -
                      VOLUMES(FSDC14) -
                      RECORDSIZE(47 79) -      /* MAX 6 OCCURRENCES SO   */
                      KEYS(26 44) -            /* 5 + AIX + (N x PRIME) */
                      NONUNIQUEKEY -           /* GIVES 5+26+(2x8)=47    */
                      SHAREOPTIONS(2 3) -      /* AND   5+26+(6x8)=79    */
                      UNIQUE -
                      UPGRADE -
                      SPEED                              ) -
                      -
      DATA       (    NAME(AK00.C98.CUSTMAST.ADDRAIX.DATA)  -
                      CONTROLINTERVALSIZE(4096) -
                      CYLINDERS(1 1) -
                      FREESPACE(15 15)                   ) -
                      -
      INDEX      (    NAME(AK00.C98.CUSTMAST.ADDRAIX.INDEX) )

    BLDINDEX      INDATASET(AK00.C98.CUSTMAST) -
                  OUTDATASET(AK00.C98.CUSTMAST.ADDRAIX) -
                  WORKFILES(WORKSRT1 WORKSRT2)

    DEFINE -
      PATH       (    NAME(AK00.C98.CUSTMAST.ADDRAIX.PATH) -
                      PATHENTRY(AK00.C98.CUSTMAST.ADDRAIX)   )

/* SECOND AIX - - -CREATE THE FORCED UNIQUE NAME ALTERNATE INDEX */

    DEFINE -
      AIX        (    NAME(AK00.C98.CUSTMAST.NAMEAIX) -
                      RELATE(AK00.C98.CUSTMAST) -
                      VOLUMES(FSDC14) -
                      RECORDSIZE(48 48) -        /* 5 + AIX + PRIME */
                      KEYS(35 9) -               /* GIVES 5+35+8=48 */
                      UNIQUEKEY -
                      SHAREOPTIONS(2 3) -
                      UNIQUE -
                      UPGRADE -
                      SPEED                              ) -
                      -
      DATA       (    NAME(AK00.C98.CUSTMAST.NAMEAIX.DATA)  -
                      CONTROLINTERVALSIZE(4096) -
                      CYLINDERS(1 1) -
                      FREESPACE(15 15)                   ) -
```

(b) continued

345

```
        INDEX     (    NAME(AK00.C98.CUSTMAST.NAMEAIX.INDEX) )

    BLDINDEX    INDATASET(AK00.C98.CUSTMAST) -
                OUTDATASET(AK00.C98.CUSTMAST.NAMEAIX) -
                WORKFILES(WORKSRT1 WORKSRT2)

    DEFINE -
      PATH      (    NAME(AK00.C98.CUSTMAST.NAMEAIX.PATH) -
                     PATHENTRY(AK00.C98.CUSTMAST.NAMEAIX)  )

 /* - - - - LIST CATALOG TO SEE INFO ON THE DATA SET AND INDEXES */

    LISTCAT -
      ENTRIES   (    AK00.C98.CUSTMAST -
                     AK00.C98.CUSTMAST.ADDRAIX -
                     AK00.C98.CUSTMAST.NAMEAIX    ) -
                ALL
 /*
 //
```

(b)

FIGURE 17.8.   *(b)*   *(con't.)*

and it copies the records from the load file into the newly defined VSAM data set. As the REPRO of this coding is performed, IDCAMS builds the tree and primary index structure that constitute the VSAM KSDS. When the data loading of the VSAM data set concludes, the KSDS and its primary index will exist.

The creation of an alternate index requires a separate DEFINE command to establish the characteristics of the data set that houses it. The BLDAIX command then reads the KSDS and builds the alternate index, a process that requires two special sort work files. These work files are named IDCUT1 and IDCUT2 by default but can be identified by other names; the names used here incorporate IDCUT1 and IDCUT2 within them just to associate them visually, although it is not necessary to do so. Alternate indexes are not created during the data loading of the RE-PRO but are built after the KSDS already exists. When more than one alternate index is to exist, separate DEFINE, BLDAIX, and DEFINE PATH operations are needed for each. These are shown as entirely separate actions here but the could be grouped so that, for example, both alternate index paths are defined at the same point.

DEFINE PATH establishes an entry in the system catalog by which access to an alternate index is arranged. The alternate index definition itself points to the KSDS with which it is associated. Nothing is contained in the path itself; it exists to provide an item that refers to the alternate index. The JCL for batch programs that access a KSDS with an alternate index is somewhat unusual because of the existence of the path, as discussed in item 10.

Figure 17.8b is a workable guide to IDCAMS coding that can be used as a pattern for experimentation, syntax verification, and learning. However, the development of efficient choices for each of the many VSAM KSDS parameter settings for a production VSAM data set that contains thousands or millions of records requires considerable knowledge of VSAM itself. The level of VSAM knowledge needed for real VSAM work is far higher than can be treated in a book about JCL. For comprehensive background and guidance, extended examples, reference materials, and automated computational aids critical to the rapid design of efficient VSAM key sequenced data sets see *Practical VSAM For Today's Programmers*, James G. Janossy and Richard E. Guzik, John Wiley and Sons, Inc., 1987, and the distribution diskette described at the end of Appendix D in *Practical MVS JCL*.

9. VSAM Key Sequenced Data Set Backup Using REPRO; Reorganization

Creating a backup copy of the data in a VSAM key sequenced data set—an indexed file—involves executing IDCAMS using the REPRO command. REPRO copies the data to a sequential file. The records in the output data set may be accessed with any other software, such as utilities or COBOL programs. It is customary to create backups by using REPRO for all VSAM data sets updated online. These backups, usually created as generation data group or GDG data sets, serve as production and end-user accessible copies of the data and can be used to restore the VSAM data sets if they become damaged by equipment failure or corruption. Figure 17.9 shows the JCL needed to REPRO a VSAM KSDS to tape, making use of extra buffers to speed processing.

Reorganizing a VSAM data set is accomplished by running a REPRO and then a delete, definition, and loading job stream, as discussed in item 8, using the current generation of the REPRO backup tape as input. This is the same JCL that can restore a VSAM data set from a backup tape. The reorganized data set will reflect any changes that might have been made in the IDCAMS control statements to expand or shrink allocated space and control interval or control area size.

10. Batch Processing a VSAM KSDS with Alternate Indexes

The JCL for a COBOL program accessing a VSAM key sequenced data set is unusual in that there are more DD statements for the KSDS than SELECT/ASSIGN statements. MVS requires that a DD statement exist for the *base cluster* or data/primary index of the data set and separate DD statements for each alternate index *path*. But VSCOBOL provides no way of coding more than one DDname for a data set; therefore MVS

```
//FSBT686A  JOB AK00TEST,'DP2-JANOSSY',CLASS=T,MSGCLASS=X,
//  MSGLEVEL=(1,1),NOTIFY=BT05686
//*
//*     THIS JCL = BT05686.SOURCE.CNTL(JCL179)
//*
//************************************************************
//*                                                          *
//*     REPRO CUSTOMER MASTER FILE TO GENERATION             *
//*     DATA GROUP TAPE FOR BACKUP, USING EXTRA              *
//*     VSAM KSDS BUFFERS TO BOOST EFFICIENCY                *
//*                                                          *
//************************************************************
//STEPA      EXEC  PGM=IDCAMS,REGION=2048K
//SYSPRINT   DD   SYSOUT=*
//SYSUDUMP   DD   SYSOUT=A
//DD1        DD   DSN=AK00.C98.CUSTMAST,
//  AMP=('BUFND=12,BUFNI=5'),
//  DISP=(OLD,KEEP)
//DD2        DD   DSN=AK00.C98.CUSTBKUP(+1),
//  UNIT=(TAPE,,DEFER),
//  DISP=(NEW,CATLG,DELETE),
//  DCB=(RECFM=FB,LRECL=250,BLKSIZE=32750),
//  LABEL=(1,SL,RETPD=90)
//SYSIN      DD   *
    REPRO          INFILE(DD1) -
                   OUTFILE(DD2)
 /*
 //
```

FIGURE 17.9.   IDCAMS REPRO backup of key sequenced data set with increased buffers for efficiency

concocts the DDnames for the alternate indexes using a simple convention.

COBOL program FSBT1522 performs batch START/READ NEXT browse access to a VSAM KSDS named AK00.C98.CUSTMAST.BASE. Within the program the data set is known as CUST-MASTER; the SELECT/ASSIGN statement for the data set equates CUST-MASTER to the DDname //B1522CSM:

```
SELECT CUST-MASTER ASSIGN TO B1522CSM
       ORGANIZATION IS INDEXED
       ACCESS MODE IS DYNAMIC
       RECORD KEY IS CM-CUST-ID-PRIMKEY
       ALTERNATE RECORD KEY IS CM-ADDR-AIXKEY
           WITH DUPLICATES
       ALTERNATE RECORD KEY IS CM-NAME-AIXKEY
       FILE STATUS IS WS-SM-VSAMSTAT.
```

This data set has two alternate indexes—a situation ordinarily avoided, for efficiency reasons—the names of which are AK00.C98.-

CUSTMAST.ADDRAIX and AK00.C98.CUSTMAST.NAMEAIX. The name of the path to the first alternate index is AK00.C98.CUSTMAST.-ADDRAIX.PATH. The name of the path to the second alternate index is AK00.C98.CUSTMAST.NAMEAIX.PATH. These names were purposely chosen according to a convention that helps keep the several names in order. Without a convention it is possible to choose names poorly and make it much more difficult to deal with a KSDS with multiple indexes.

MVS requires that the JCL for the step executing this program carry DDname //B1522CSM stating the base cluster of the KSDS, the actual data set. But MVS concocts other DDnames for DD statements that must state the alternate index paths. It does so by appending or replacing the last character in the SELECT/ASSIGN DDname with a digit; therefore it expects to find a DD statement named //B1522CS1 associated with the step that points to the path of the ADDR alternate index, the first alternate index cited in the SELECT/ASSIGN statement. The JCL for this step is coded in Figure 17.10. If the stated DDname has seven or fewer characters, MVS appends the "1" otherwise it overlays the eighth character of that name. For the second alternate index MVS concocts the DDname for the path with a "2" as the appended or replacement character, making this alternate index path DD statement carry DDname //B1522CS2.

```
//FSBT686A  JOB AK00TEST,'DP2-JANOSSY',CLASS=W,MSGCLASS=X,
//  MSGLEVEL=(1,1),NOTIFY=BT05686
//*
//*     THIS JCL = BT05686.SOURCE.CNTL(JCL1710)
//*
//********************************************************
//*                                                      *
//*     EXECUTE PROGRAM DOING BATCH DYNAMIC ACCESS        *
//*     TO VSAM DATA SET USING BOTH ALTERNATE KEYS        *
//*                                                      *
//********************************************************
//STEPA     EXEC  PGM=FSBT1522
//SYSOUT     DD   SYSOUT=*
//SYSUDUMP   DD   SYSOUT=A
//BT1522E1   DD   DSN=AK00.C99.DRVTRANS,
//  DISP=SHR
//B1522CSM   DD   DSN=AK00.C98.CUSTMAST,              'VSAM DATA SET
//  DISP=OLD
//B1522CS1   DD   DSN=AK00.C98.CUSTMAST.ADDRAIX.PATH, 'ADDR ALT INDEX
//  DISP=OLD
//B1522CS2   DD   DSN=AK00.C98.CUSTMAST.NAMEAIX.PATH, 'NAME ALT INDEX
//  DISP=OLD
//BT1522U1   DD   SYSOUT=*                            'REPORT
//
```

FIGURE 17.10. JCL for batch COBOL program accessing VSAM KSDS with alternate indexes

IEBCOMPR: COMPARING TWO DATA SETS

11. Comparing Data Sets Record by Record

The IEBCOMPR utility was provided in the 1960s to allow a comparison of punched card data sets and tape or disk copies to insure that conversion from cards was being accomplished accurately. It can compare whole PDSs as well. The utility has two inputs, //SYSUT1 and //SYSUT2, and it merely compares records between the two to produce a report at //SYSPRINT. Its //SYSIN input accepts just a few controlling specifications.

The original use of IEBCOMPR became moot many years ago. The usefulness of IEBCOMPR, however, has once again increased in connection with a thoroughly modern development. IBM and several other vendors have recognized the need for tools to upgrade portions of the vast installed base of COBOL source code that constitutes the bulk of the business data processing investment in automation. Many installations run and maintain COBOL programs written several years ago, when programming style was not structured. The systems composed of these programs are often vital to the installation and will continue to be run, but they have become difficult to maintain. The solution? Automated recoding of the routines with software that employs artificial intelligence.

Several vendors offer products that read and understand what old, unstructured COBOL code is attempting to accomplish and then generate new, structured code to accomplish the same thing. IBM's COBOL Structuring Facility or "COBOL/SF" performs this process, as does the RECODER product of Language Technology Corporation, and PATHVU/ Structured Retrofit of Peat Marwick Mitchell. The basic function of each of these products is similar. They read 80-character card image old source code and produce new, restructured and reengineered COBOL source code as another set of 80-character card images. The new source code in many cases is guaranteed to compile correctly and produce exactly the same processing results as the old, unstructured code when compiled, linkage edited, and executed.

Prudence dictates that the operation of reengineered code be tested and verified before turning a recoded program loose in production. IEBCOMPR can readily be used to perform this testing. The comparison of machine-readable outputs comes to mind first. It is also possible, however, to compare reports produced by old and new code for the same input data by treating the printlines produced by the programs as 133-byte records and storing them on disk or tape. Thus IEBCOMPR can almost totally automate the process of comparing old and new program operation. Testing recoded programs involves taking a copy of the production JCL that normally invokes the program, and creating a parallel test executing the recoded program using a quantity of representative production data.

The JCL to invoke IEBCOMPR is illustrated in Figure 17.11. This includes two IEBGENER steps to overcome the fact that the utility talks in terms of records and blocks. That is, if it detects a difference between the input data sets it identifies the block and record in which the difference occurred. This is not convenient when a printline or data set comparison is being made for recoded programs; instead reporting by record number or printline line number is desirable.

The IEBGENER steps ahead of the IEBCOMPR read the blocked input data sets and copy them to unblocked, temporary data sets. IEBCOMPR still reports by records and blocks, but they are now synonymous. *Note, however, that such GENERs to unblocked data sets are suitable only when the quantity of records being compared is small.* When more than a few thousand records are involved, the I/O associated with an unblocked data set is absolutely prohibitive and time consuming. For large data set comparisons omit the IEBGENER steps and use a calculator to compute displayed record numbers, using the block number and blocking factor on the IEBCOMPR report, if any differences are detected.

IEBCOMPR will provide a hexadecimal rendition of records from both inputs when it detects a difference. If differences are detected in 10 consecutive records, IEBCOMPR quits, assuming that grossly different inputs are present.

A few hints:

- When comparing the printline image outputs of old and recoded programs, keep in mind that the outputs should be produced on the same date. Differences in report date within printlines will, of course, be detected by IEBCOMPR and reported.
- The plain hex rendition that IEBCOMPR provides of records with differences are best supplemented by a hex/character dump for analysis. Run the IEBCOMPR first; if differences are detected, also run an IDCAMS or other dump on the data sets to see more easily what the differing records contain.

IEBCOMPR provides a minimal number of control statement options at the //SYSIN DDname. One is

```
COMPARE   TYPORG=xx
```

where xx can be PS for a sequential data set or PO for a partitioned data set. If //SYSIN is dummied out, TYPORG defaults to PS. If a member of

```
//FSBT686A  JOB AK00TEST,'DP2-JANOSSY',CLASS=E,MSGCLASS=X,
//  MSGLEVEL=(1,1),NOTIFY=BT05686
//*
//*     COMPARE TWO DATA SETS USING IEBCOMPR UTILITY
//*     THIS JCL = BT05686.SOURCE.CNTL(JCL1711)
//*
//***********************************************************
//*                                                         *
//*     GENER ONE DATA SET TO DEBLOCKED DATA SET            *
//*                                                         *
//***********************************************************
//STEPA     EXEC  PGM=IEBGENER
//SYSPRINT  DD    SYSOUT=*
//SYSUT1    DD    DSN=AK00.C99.ORIGREPT,
//  DISP=SHR
//SYSUT2    DD    DSN=&&TEMPOLD,
//  UNIT=SYSDA,
//  DISP=(NEW,PASS,DELETE),
//  DCB=(RECFM=F,LRECL=133,BLKSIZE=133),
//  SPACE=(133,(3000,600),RLSE)
//SYSIN     DD    DUMMY
//*
//***********************************************************
//*                                                         *
//*     GENER SECOND DATA SET TO DEBLOCKED DATA SET         *
//*                                                         *
//***********************************************************
//STEPB     EXEC  PGM=IEBGENER
//SYSPRINT  DD    SYSOUT=*
//SYSUT1    DD    DSN=AK00.C99.NEWREPT,
//  DISP=SHR
//SYSUT2    DD    DSN=&&TEMPNEW,
//  UNIT=SYSDA,
//  DISP=(NEW,PASS,DELETE),
//  DCB=(RECFM=F,LRECL=133,BLKSIZE=133),
//  SPACE=(133,(3000,600),RLSE)
//SYSIN     DD    DUMMY
//*
//***********************************************************
//*                                                         *
//*     COMPARE THE DEBLOCKED DATA SETS                     *
//*                                                         *
//***********************************************************
//STEPC     EXEC  PGM=IEBCOMPR
//SYSPRINT  DD    SYSOUT=*
//SYSUT1    DD    DSN=&&TEMPOLD,
//  DISP=(OLD,DELETE)
//SYSUT2    DD    DSN=&&TEMPNEW,
//  DISP=(OLD,DELETE)
//SYSIN     DD    *
   COMPARE  TYPORG=PS
/*
//
```

FIGURE 17.11. Comparing two data sets using IEBCOMPR

a PDS is being compared with another data set and the member is named on the //SYSUT1 or //SYSUT2 DD statements in parentheses, *do not* code this control statement with PO. TYPORG = PO should be coded only when the input data sets being compared are both PDSs and comparison of the entire partitioned data sets is desired. In such a case neither //SYSUT1 or //SYSUT2 will carry member names.

IEBGENER: THE COPY AND REFORMAT UTILITY

12. Concatenation of Inputs in JCL

MVS JCL provides powerful facilities for concatenation of inputs on DD statements. Figure 17.12 shows how several different data sets can be stated under the same input DDname and processed as if they were one data set. All named data sets will be received by the program as if it were reading one continuous data set; MVS handles the opening and closing of the different data sets and the program cannot discern when one of the data sets has reached its end and the reading of the next has begun.

Different sequential data set references can be intermixed. This ex-

```
//FSBT686A  JOB AK00TEST,'DP2-JANOSSY',CLASS=E,MSGCLASS=X,
//   MSGLEVEL=(1,1),NOTIFY=BT05686
//*
//*     THIS JCL = BT05686.SOURCE.CNTL(JCL1712)
//*
//************************************************************
//*                                                         *
//*     GENER SEVERAL DATA SETS WITH LIKE RECORD            *
//*     CHARACTERISTICS INTO ONE                            *
//*                                                         *
//************************************************************
//STEPA      EXEC  PGM=IEBGENER
//SYSPRINT   DD    SYSOUT=*
//*
//SYSUT1     DD    DSN=AK00.C99.TESTTRAN,DISP=SHR
//           DD    DSN=BT05686.SOURCE.CNTL(TRANDATA),DISP=SHR
//           DD    DSN=AK00.C99.TESTDATA(0),DISP=SHR
//           DD    DSN=AK00.C99.TRANS003,DISP=SHR
//*
//SYSUT2     DD    DSN=AK00.C99.NEWDATA,
//   UNIT=SYSDA,
//   DISP=(NEW,CATLG,DELETE),
//   DCB=(RECFM=FB,LRECL=80,BLKSIZE=6160),
//   SPACE=(6160,(200,40),RLSE)
//SYSIN      DD    DUMMY
//
```

FIGURE 17.12. Concatenating data sets at a DD statement

ample shows sequential data sets, members of partitioned data sets, and generation data group data sets in the concatenation list at the IEBGENER //SYSUT1 DDname. Note that the DD statements concatenated at //SYSUT1 are actually separate; each carries a "DD" and unlike "continued" DD statements no commas exist between them. IEBGENER is a simple copy utility and the output at //SYSUT2 will be one sequential data set that contains all inputs.

Concatenated data sets must have the same characteristics and reside on the same type of device; disk and tape data sets cannot be concatenated. The block size need not be the same, but record lengths for fixed length or fixed length blocked data sets must be. If different block sizes are involved, the data set with the largest block size must be listed first to obtain buffers of sufficient size. When tape data sets are concatenated the AFF feature of the UNIT parameter is usually coded at the second and subsequent data sets in order to minimize the number of tape drives allocated to the step, as discussed in *Unit Affinity Specification AFF* of Chapter 5.

13. Copying and Reformatting Records

IEBGENER is commonly used to copy sequential data sets or partitioned data set members from one place to another. In such simple uses its //SYSIN DD statement carries only the null specification of DUMMY. Control statements can be input at //SYSIN to reformat the input data and create output records that are longer, shorter, have fields in different positions, or create new fields in output records that contain literal values. Fields can also be converted to and from COMP-3 "packed decimal" format, allowing test data to be entered in character form—zoned decimal—and quickly transformed into a format often required for program testing.[1]

Figure 17.13a displays the layout of a data record created by TSO. Figure 17.13b illustrates a desired test data record, reformatted and containing packed decimal fields. Figure 17.13c presents the IEBGENER coding needed to reformat and convert the TSO-entered record into the desired form. Figure 17.13d is a TSO/ISPF screen that shows the hexadecimal rendition of the resultant 60-byte records; "ABCDE" is just a string of literals added to indicate how literals may be inserted in a record using IEBGENER. The packed fields will take half the number of bytes of space as the original field, plus one byte, if the original field is an even number of bytes long. If the original field is an odd number of bytes in length, the packed version will take half the number of bytes rounded up to the next whole number.

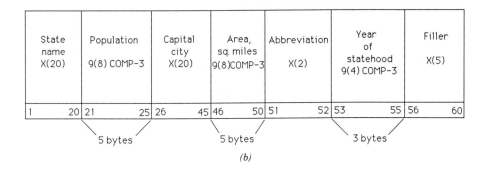

(a)

State name X(20)	Population 9(8)	Capital city X(20)	Area, sq. miles 9(8)	Abbreviation X(2)	Year of statehood 9(4)	Filler X(18)
1 — 20	21 — 28	29 — 48	49 — 56	57 — 58	59 — 62	63 — 80

(b)

State name X(20)	Population 9(8) COMP-3	Capital city X(20)	Area, sq. miles 9(8)COMP-3	Abbreviation X(2)	Year of statehood 9(4) COMP-3	Filler X(5)
1 — 20	21 — 25	26 — 45	46 — 50	51 — 52	53 — 55	56 — 60

5 bytes   5 bytes   3 bytes

```
//FSBT686A  JOB AK00TEST,'DP2-JANOSSY',CLASS=E,MSGCLASS=X,
// MSGLEVEL=(1,1),NOTIFY=BT05686
//*
//*     THIS JCL = BT05686.SOURCE.CNTL(JCL1713C)
//*
//***********************************************************
//*                                                         *
//*     CONVERT TSO-KEYED TEST DATA INTO PACKED             *
//*     DECIMAL FORMAT                                      *
//*                                                         *
//***********************************************************
//STEPA     EXEC   PGM=IEBGENER
//SYSPRINT   DD    SYSOUT=*
//*
//SYSUT1     DD    DSN=BT05686.SOURCE.CNTL(STATEDAT),
//  DISP=SHR
//*
//SYSUT2     DD    DSN=AK00.C99.STATEDAT.PACKED,
//  UNIT=SYSDA,
//  DISP=(NEW,CATLG,DELETE),
//  DCB=(RECFM=FB,LRECL=60,BLKSIZE=6180),
//  SPACE=(6180,(1,1),RLSE)
//SYSIN      DD    *
    GENERATE  MAXFLDS=99,MAXLITS=80
      RECORD  FIELD=(20,1,,1),
              FIELD=(8,21,ZP,21),
              FIELD=(20,29,,26),
              FIELD=(8,49,ZP,46),
              FIELD=(2,57,,51),
              FIELD=(4,59,ZP,53),
              FIELD=(5,'ABCDE',,56)
/*
//
```

(c)

FIGURE 17.13. (*a*) Graphic layout of TSO-entered test data set records, (*b*) Format of desired test data record with packed decimal (COMP-3) fields and reduced literal filler, (*c*) Use of IEBGENER to copy and reformat input at //SYSUT1 to //SYSUT2, and (*d*) TSO/ISPF split-screen displaying original and reformatted records with HEX mode

```
BROWSE - BT05686.SOURCE.CNTL(STATEDAT) -------------- LINE 000001 COL   001 072
COMMAND === >                                          SCROLL ===> HALF
----+----1----+----2----+----3----+----4----+----5----+----6----+----7----+----8
ALABAMA                03891000MONTGOMERY           00051609AL1819
CDCCCDC4444444444444FFFFFFFFDDDECDDCDE4444444444FFFFFFFFFCDFFFF444444444444444444
1312141000000000000000389100046537645980000000000000516091318190000000000000000
--------------------------------------------------------------------------------
ALABAMA                00400000JUNEAU              00586412AK1959
CDCEDC4444444444444FFFFFFFFFDEDCCE4444444444444FFFFFFFFFCDFFFF4444444444444444444
1312210000000000000004000001455140000000000000005864121219590000000000000000000

  . . . . . . . . . . . . . . . . . . . . . . . . . . . . . . . . . . . . . . .

BROWSE - AK00.C99.STATEDAT.PACKED -------------------- LINE 000001 COL   001 060
COMMAND ===>  HEX ON                                   SCROLL ===> HALF
----+----1----+----2----+----3----+----4----+----5----+----6----+----7----+----8
ALABAMA           ..j..MONTGOMERY           ...-.AL.a.ABCDE
CDCCCDC44444444444444403900FFFDDDECDDCDE444444400569CD089CCCCC
1312141000000000000008810F00046537645980000000010F1311F12345
--------------------------------------------------------------------------------
ALASKA            .....JUNEAU              ..f..AK.n.ABCDE
CDCEDC4444444444444400000FFFDEDCCE4444444444400842CD099CCCCC
1312210000000000000400F0001455140000000000000561F1215F12345
--------------------------------------------------------------------------------
```

(d)

FIGURE 17.13.   *(con't.)*

IEBPTPCH: THE LISTING UTILITY

14. "PTPCH" Short Course: Listing Records with Titles

IEBPTPCH is an original OS utility that employs a number of cryptic
control statements to produce simple data listings. The output of
"PTPCH" or "print-punch," as it is called, is always intended to be directed to the printer or card punch; it was one of the first easy to use
listing tools. The "punch" part of print-punch is obsolete in most places
because card punches are now gone.

IEBPTPCH can be put to good use if one knows its strong points and
ignores those that are weak and dated. Although other more capable
data listing utilities abound, not all installations have such items of third-
party software. IEBPTPCH, on the other hand, comes with MVS and
every MVS shop has it. PTPCH provides packed-to-zoned decimal and
hex conversion options that allow experimention with and display of
COMP-3 packed decimal storage.

Figure 17.13a describes the layout of a record entered by TSO. Figure
17.14a illustrates a desired print layout for this record, which includes
column headings. Figure 17.14b shows IEBPTPCH coding that can be

```
STATE NAME          ABBREV   POP      AREA         CAPITAL              YEAR
<------------------>  --   <------>  <------>  <------------------>  <-->

XXXXXXXXXXXXXXXXXXXX  XX   XXXXXXXX  XXXXXXXX  XXXXXXXXXXXXXXXXXXXX  XXXX
XXXXXXXXXXXXXXXXXXXX  XX   XXXXXXXX  XXXXXXXX  XXXXXXXXXXXXXXXXXXXX  XXXX
```

(a)

```
//FSBT686A  JOB AKOOTEST,'DP2-JANOSSY',CLASS=E,MSGCLASS=X,
//  MSGLEVEL=(1,1),NOTIFY=BT05686
//*
//*    THIS JCL = BT05686.SOURCE.CNTL(JCL1714B)
//*
//***********************************************************
//*                                                         *
//*     PRODUCE LISTING OF CHARACTER DATA,                  *
//*     PROVIDING COLUMN HEADINGS                           *
//*                                                         *
//***********************************************************
//STEPA     EXEC  PGM=IEBPTPCH
//SYSPRINT  DD    SYSOUT=*
//SYSUT1    DD    DSN=BT05686.SOURCE.CNTL(STATEDAT),
//  DISP=SHR
//SYSUT2    DD    SYSOUT=*
//SYSIN     DD    *
     PRINT    MAXFLDS=99,MAXLINE=55,CNTRL=2
     RECORD   FIELD=(20,1,,1),
              FIELD=(8,21,,30),
              FIELD=(20,29,,52),
              FIELD=(8,49,,41),
              FIELD=(2,57,,25),
              FIELD=(4,59,,75)
     TITLE    ITEM=('     STATE NAME          ABBREV      POP     ',1),
              ITEM=(' AREA           CAPITAL              YEAR    ',41),
              ITEM=('                                             ',81)
     TITLE    ITEM=('<------------------>    --    <------>       ',1),
              ITEM=('<------>   <------------------>    <-->      ',41),
              ITEM=('                                             ',81)
/*
//
```

(b)

FIGURE 17.14. (a) Desired print layout for listing of records shown in Figure 17.13(a), (b) IEBPTPCH control statements to produce listing from input of Figure 17.13(a), (c) Sample of listing produced by IEBPTPCH from plain character input fields, and (d) IEBPTPCH control statements for input of Figure 17.13(b) with COMP-3 packed decimal fields

357

```
      STATE NAME        ABBREV    POP      AREA       CAPITAL            YEAR

<------------------->     --    <------>  <------>  <------------------->  <-->

ALABAMA                   AL    03891000  00051609  MONTGOMERY             1819

ALASKA                    AK    00400000  00586412  JUNEAU                 1959

ARIZONA                   AZ    02718000  00113909  PHOENIX                1912

ARKANSAS                  AR    02285000  00053104  LITTLE ROCK            1836

CALIFORNIA                CA    23669000  00158693  SACRAMENTO             1850

COLORADO                  CO    02890000  00104247  DENVER                 1876

CONNECTICUT               CN    03107000  00005009  HARTFORD               1788

DELAWARE                  DE    00596000  00002057  DOVER                  1787

FLORIDA                   FL    09739000  00058560  TALLAHASSEE            1845
```

(c)

```
//FSBT686A  JOB AK00TEST,'DP2-JANOSSY',CLASS=E,MSGCLASS=X,
//   MSGLEVEL=(1,1),NOTIFY=BT05686
//*
//*    THIS JCL = BT05686.SOURCE.CNTL(JCL1714D)
//*
//************************************************************
//*                                                          *
//*     PRODUCE LISTING OF DATA WITH PACKED DECIMAL          *
//*     FIELDS, PROVIDING COLUMN HEADINGS                    *
//*                                                          *
//************************************************************
//STEPA     EXEC  PGM=IEBPTPCH
//SYSPRINT  DD   SYSOUT=*
//SYSUT1    DD   DSN=BT05686.SOURCE.CNTL(STATEDAT),
//  DISP=SHR
//SYSUT2    DD   SYSOUT=A
//SYSIN     DD   *
     PRINT    MAXFLDS=99,MAXLINE=55,CNTRL=2
     RECORD   FIELD=(20,1,,1),
              FIELD=(5,21,PZ,30),
              FIELD=(20,26,,52),
              FIELD=(5,46,PZ,41),
              FIELD=(2,51,,25),
              FIELD=(3,53,PZ,75),
              FIELD=(5,56,,88)
     TITLE    ITEM=('      STATE NAME        ABBREV     POP   ',1),
              ITEM=('  AREA             CAPITAL          YEAR ',41),
              ITEM=('    FILLER (JUNK)                        ',81)
     TITLE    ITEM=('<------------------->     --    <------> ',1),
              ITEM=('<------>   <------------------->   <-->  ',41),
              ITEM=('      <--->                              ',81)
/*
//
```

(d)

FIGURE 17.14.   (con't.)

used to produce the simple listing of the data set illustrated in Figure 17.14c. If the input to IEBPTPCH were to be the format illustrated in Figure 17.13b, containing packed decimal fields, the listing could be produced by using the IEBPTPCH code shown in Figure 17.14d. Packed decimal forces one additional leading zero if the nonpacked version of the field has an even number of positions. IEBPTPCH displays all leading zeros. It also displays the sign of the packed decimal number as a trailing + or − character. *The output of IEBPTPCH is a maximum of 120 printable positions wide.* This must be kept in mind because confusing error messages will be issued if the printline or title lines are composed with more than 120 print positions.

There are seven control statements for IEBPTPCH: PRINT, PUNCH, TITLE, EXITS, MEMBER, RECORD, and LABELS. Only four of the seven are useful in contemporary times: *PRINT, RECORD, TITLE,* and occasionally, *MEMBER.* Each statement has a different set of options, but *PRINT, RECORD,* and *TITLE* work together to define how the printing of an input data set is to be done, what input fields are placed into a printline, and where, how, and what, if anything, the optional title lines for the listing will be.

PRINT *Control Statement:* A total of 13 specifications exist for PRINT. Only eight of these are normally useful, and even then only a handful is necessary in any given case:

CNTRL = 2 Allows print to be double spaced. The values after the equal sign can be 1 or 3 as well. If not specified, the default is 1.

STRTAFT = n
"Start after" is a value identical to the SKIP specification of the IDCAMS PRINT function. The "n" is limited to the range 1 to 32,767 and represents the number of records to be bypassed before printing starts, coded without comma.

STOPAFT = n
"Stop after" indicates the same thing that COUNT does on the IDCAMS PRINT function; this is the number of records to print. In PTPCH, however, this value cannot exceed 32,767, coded without comma.

SKIP = n Unlike the SKIP in the IDCAMS PRINT function, this indicates a *repeated skip* within print. For example, SKIP = 2 indicates print every second record and SKIP = 3 indicates print every third record, and so forth. See item 15 for an example of the use of SKIP.

MAXLINE = n

> The number of lines written to a page is set by MAX-LINE. This defaults to 60 if not coded. It can be set to a maximum value of 99 if a laser printer is used to receive the output and a small, high density print font is used.

TYPORG = PO

> Input at //SYSUT1 can be a sequential data set or a member of a partitioned data set and TYPORG is not needed. If, however, //SYSUT1 is a partitioned data set and the member name is not coded at the //SYSUT1 DD statement, it can be specified with a MEMBER statement. This allows the processing of several members from the same PDS at one time. To make the MEMBER statement acceptable TYPORG = PO must be coded as an option on the PRINT specification, as illustrated in item 17.

MAXFLDS = 99

> IEBPTPCH originated when machine memory was limited. "Maximum fields" ties in with the FIELD specification of RECORD and indicates the maximum number of FIELD specifications. If MAXFLDS is set too low, the PTPCH step fails. This usually results in frustration when an old PTPCH run has been copied and changed to perform a different listing that involves more fields. Memory is no problem now and MAXFLDS should be coded as 99 and never changed. This minimizes the chance of failure.

RECORD Control Statement: This statement defines the format in which records will be printed. It can be omitted but the result is a useless grouping of characters in sets of eight, which has relevance only for a raw memory dump. One or more FIELD specifications follow the RECORD statement; each describes one field on the printline to be produced. The number of FIELD specifications must be no greater than the value specified in MAXFLDS on the PRINT control statement. Leave MAXFLDS at 99 and you are not likely to have a problem.

Every FIELD specification carries four positional items:

```
FIELD=(in-length,in-position,convert,out-position)
```

The first two items, input field length and input field starting position, are placed exactly opposite to the way that the sort utility FIELD spec-

ification is coded. This inconsistency is the source of much frustration because programmers usually have more contact with the sort than with PTPCH. Problems in this area are common when one tries to do a "quick little job" with IEBPTPCH or IEBGENER—*GENER coding, like that of PTPCH, is the reverse of the sort.*

> **In-length** is the actual number of bytes that the input field occupies in the input record. When the input field is packed decimal, it is not the same as the length of the field as printed because packed decimal format stores numbers two digits to the byte.[1]
>
> **In-position** is the starting position of the input field within the input record; the first byte of the record is counted as 1.
>
> **Convert** is a conversion specification. If omitted, no conversion of the input is made, and it prints, byte-for-byte. If coded, conversion functions in one of two ways. This can be "PZ" or "HE" and the conversion differs for each case:
>
> PZ. This means "packed to zoned decimal." This indicates that the input field is in COMP-3 form and is to be rendered as zoned decimal, which is equivalent to plain text character format. This is specified when a packed decimal field is carried on the input and is to be printed in a meaningful form. *The print field will be twice as long as the input* and will show a trailing + or − sign. Nonnumeric input causes errors.
>
> HE. This means that the input data is alphanumeric—it can be anything at all, including packed decimal—and is to be printed in hexadecimal, two characters for each individual input byte. *The print field will be twice as long as the input.*
>
> **Out-position** is the position in the printline in which the field will start to print.

A typical FIELD specification is

```
FIELD=(18,5,,31)
```

which indicates that the input field is 18 bytes long, starts in position 5 of the input record, and no conversion services are desired. The field is to begin printing in position 31 of the printline and will print through position 48. When no conversion services are desired, the comma is coded after the empty positional slot to denote its absence. A FIELD specification with packed-to-plain text conversion for a PIC 9(5)V99 COMP-3 field appears as

```
FIELD=(4,45,PZ,16)
```

which indicates that the packed field occupies four bytes in the input record—it is found in positions 45 through 48 of the input record—packed-to-zoned decimal conversion is requested, and the printline field will start printing in column 16 of the printline. The printline field will take twice the length, in bytes, of the input packed field. It will be eight print positions long and will occupy positions 16 through 23 of the printline.

TITLE Control Statement. Two lines of title can optionally be applied to a listing. Each can be a full 120 bytes, but the specification for the title composition is made with multiple "ITEMs" that individually can be no more than 40 bytes long. The number following the literals in a given ITEM indicates the position at which these literals start in the printline; if this number is omitted, position one is assumed. The TITLE/ITEM specifications in Figure 17.14*b* produce the column heading line in the output as shown. The continuation lines that carry just the ITEM coding must start in columns 4 to 16 of the card image. Manuals indicate a nonblank character in column 72 to serve as a continuation indicator, but it is not actually necessary; the commas after the first two ITEMs in each TITLE also suffice for continuation.

```
//FSBT686A  JOB AK00TEST,'DP2-JANOSSY',CLASS=E,MSGCLASS=X,
//  MSGLEVEL=(1,1),NOTIFY=BT05686
//*
//*      THIS JCL = BT05686.SOURCE.CNTL(JCL1715)
//*
//***********************************************************
//*                                                         *
//*      PRODUCE SKIP-DUMP LISTING OF DATA WITH PACKED      *
//*      DECIMAL FIELDS (NO COLUMN HEADINGS)                *
//*                                                         *
//***********************************************************
//STEPA     EXEC  PGM=IEBPTPCH
//SYSPRINT  DD    SYSOUT=*
//SYSUT1    DD    DSN=BT05686.SOURCE.CNTL(STATEDAT),
//  DISP=SHR
//SYSUT2    DD    SYSOUT=*
//SYSIN     DD    *
     PRINT    MAXFLDS=99,MAXLINE=55,CNTRL=2,
              STRTAFT=10,
              STOPAFT=6,
              SKIP=3
     RECORD   FIELD=(20,1,,1),
              FIELD=(5,21,PZ,30),
              FIELD=(20,26,,52),
              FIELD=(5,46,PZ,41),
              FIELD=(2,51,,25),
              FIELD=(3,53,PZ,75),
              FIELD=(5,56,,88)
  /*
  //
```

FIGURE 17.15.   IEBPTPCH coding to produce "skip dump" sampling of a data set

15. "Skip Dump" Partial Data Set Analysis Listing

Occasionally it is desirable to produce a data set listing for purposes of analysis, but the number of records in the data set makes it unappealing to list them all. The first few hundred records, however, or even a few hundred records from somewhere within it, would not necessarily be representative of the contents of the data set. It is possible to use some of the specifications of IEBPTPCH to do a partial "skip dump" of the data set. This means starting somewhere within it, listing every nth record, and quitting after some specific quantity of records has been listed.

Figure 17.15 shows an IEBPTPCH run similar to that of Figure 17.14d, except that the STRTAFT, STOPAFT, and SKIP specifications have also been used. If a skip dump of the entire data set is desired, STRTAFT and STOPAFT could be omitted. STRTAFT indicates the number of records to bypass before starting the listing, whereas STOPAFT indicates the number of records to list before stopping—*not* the sequential record number in the data set at which to stop. Purely for illustrative variety, the column headings have been dropped from this example.

16. Printing All Members of a Partitioned Data Set

It is possible to specify the //SYSUT1 input to IEBPTPCH as a partitioned data set without a specific member name. When TYPORG = PO is specified on the PRINT statement and no specified PDS member is named—

```
//FSBT686A  JOB AKOOTEST,'DP2-JANOSSY',CLASS=E,MSGCLASS=X,
//  MSGLEVEL=(1,1),NOTIFY=BT05686
//*
//*    THIS JCL = BT05686.SOURCE.CNTL(JCL1716)
//*
//**********************************************************
//*                                                        *
//*      PRINT ALL MEMBERS OF A PDS                        *
//*                                                        *
//**********************************************************
//STEPA      EXEC  PGM=IEBPTPCH
//SYSPRINT   DD    SYSOUT=*
//SYSUT1     DD    DSN=BT05686.SOURCE.COBOL,
//  DISP=SHR
//SYSUT2     DD    SYSOUT=A
//SYSIN      DD    *
     PRINT    TYPORG=PO,MAXFLDS=1
     RECORD   FIELD=(80,1,,1)
/*
//
```

FIGURE 17.16. Listing all members of a partitioned data set using IEBPTPCH

only a RECORD statement is coded, as shown in Figure 17.16—
IEBPTPCH will list every member in the PDS. IEBPTPCH will not make
any use of the PDS directory but instead will list the active members
in the PDS as it encounters them in the PDS data area. Members exist in the data area in the order in which they were stored after their
last modification. Thus an IEBPTPCH listing of all PDS members
will not necessarily be in alphabetical order by member name. If you
wish to obtain a listing of all members in alphabetical order by member name, use TSO function 3.1, option L, which accesses the PDS
directory.

17. Printing Selected Members of a Partitioned Data Set

MEMBER control statements can be added to the IEBPTPCH control
statements in Figure 17.16 to select only certain members for listing.
Each MEMBER statement has the obligation to carry its own RECORD
statement with one or more FIELD specifications on it. Figure 17.17
shows how three members from a partitioned data set can be selected
for printing. When one or more MEMBER statements are coded, the wide
open, list all members action of IEBPTPCH is abandoned.

18. Printing One Member of a PDS Without MEMBER

A member of a PDS, when specified by PDS name and member name
in a DD statement, is treated exactly as if it were a sequential data set.
Although this is true no matter what program is reading the member,
the point is well illustrated by the IEBPTPCH code in Figure 17.18. In
this case a single member of a PDS is specified at the //SYSUT1 DD
statement. Note that TYPORG = PO is *not* coded on the PRINT statement
and *no* MEMBER statement is coded.

The Basic Partitioned Access Method, "BPAM," handles completely
the task of extracting a member from a partitioned data set when its
name is specified in parentheses after the PDS name. When this is coded,
the data set being input at the DD statement is, to the program being
executed, indistinguishable from a simple data set. It would even be
possible to concatenate several different members of the same or different
PDSs at IEBPTPCH's //SYSUT1, as long as each PDS contained the same
format of records and the records were of the same length. In this case,
however, IEBPTPCH would not see each member as distinct and would
not provide its default member name page heading as each new member
started.

```
//FSBT686A  JOB AKOOTEST,'DP2-JANOSSY',CLASS=E,MSGCLASS=X,
//  MSGLEVEL=(1,1),NOTIFY=BT05686
//*
//*     THIS JCL = BT05686.SOURCE.CNTL(JCL1717)
//*
//*********************************************************
//*                                                       *
//*     PRINT SELECTED MEMBERS OF A PDS                   *
//*                                                       *
//*********************************************************
//STEPA     EXEC  PGM=IEBPTPCH
//SYSPRINT  DD    SYSOUT=*
//SYSUT1    DD    DSN=BT05686.SOURCE.COBOL,
//  DISP=SHR
//SYSUT2    DD    SYSOUT=A
//SYSIN     DD    *
    PRINT   TYPORG=PO,MAXFLDS=1,MAXNAME=99
    MEMBER  NAME=PSD183
    RECORD  FIELD=(80,1,,1)
    MEMBER  NAME=FSBT3708
    RECORD  FIELD=(80,1,,1)
    MEMBER  NAME=FSBT9999
    RECORD  FIELD=(80,1,,1)
/*
//
```

FIGURE 17.17. Listing selected members of a partitioned data set using IEBPTPCH and the "MEMBER" statement

```
//FSBT686A  JOB AKOOTEST,'DP2-JANOSSY',CLASS=E,MSGCLASS=X,
//  MSGLEVEL=(1,1),NOTIFY=BT05686
//*
//*     THIS JCL = BT05686.SOURCE.CNTL(JCL1718)
//*
//*********************************************************
//*                                                       *
//*     PRINT A MEMBER OF A PDS WITHOUT THE               *
//*     "MEMBER" SPECIFICATION                            *
//*                                                       *
//*********************************************************
//STEPA     EXEC  PGM=IEBPTPCH
//SYSPRINT  DD    SYSOUT=*
//SYSUT1    DD    DSN=BT05686.SOURCE.COBOL(FSBT3708),
//  DISP=SHR
//SYSUT2    DD    SYSOUT=A
//SYSIN     DD    *
    PRINT   TYPORG=PS,MAXFLDS=1
    RECORD  FIELD=(80,1,,1)
/*
//
```

FIGURE 17.18. Listing one member of a partitioned data set using IEBPTPCH without the "MEMBER" statement

```
//FSBT686A  JOB AK00TEST,'DP2-JANOSSY',CLASS=E,MSGCLASS=X,
//  MSGLEVEL=(1,1),NOTIFY=BT05686
//*
//*     THIS JCL = BT05686.SOURCE.CNTL(JCL1719)
//*
//****************************************************************
//*                                                             *
//*     PRINT A PDS MEMBER LIST FROM THE PDS DIRECTORY           *
//*     USING THE IEHLIST UTILITY                                *
//*                                                             *
//****************************************************************
//STEPA      EXEC   PGM=IEHLIST
//SYSPRINT   DD     SYSOUT=*
//DISK       DD     UNIT=3380,
//   DISP=SHR,
//   VOL=SER=FSDC03
//SYSIN      DD  *
     LISTPDS       DSNAME=BT05686.SOURCE.COBOL,VOL=3380=FSDC03
/*
//
```

FIGURE 17.19. Using IEHLIST to print a partitioned data set member list

IEHLIST: PDS AND VTOC LISTING UTILITY

19. Printing a Partitioned Data Set Member List

The IEHLIST utility originally provided three main functions: listing partitioned data set contents, listing a disk volume table of contents or "VTOC," and performing catalog displays from OS catalog "CVOL" control volumes. As MVS moved ahead into VSAM catalogs and the ICF catalog structure, IEHLIST lost ground to IDCAMS in regard to catalog displays, which it can no longer perform. IEHLIST now functions as a poor second to TSO for ordinary PDS content lists. But anyone interested in the technical nature of a PDS directory or disk volume table of contents finds IEHLIST entertaining.

Figure 17.19 illustrates the JCL to obtain a member list of a partitioned data set. The DD statement named //DISK can be anything at all, a rather unusual circumstance but true because IEHLIST meddles in MVS control blocks and scans its DD statements without regard to name. The control statement that enters the utility at //SYSIN carries a redundant-appearing VOL specification that is *not* the same as a JCL parameter of the same name.

20. Printing a Formatted Disk Volume Table of Contents (VTOC) Listing

The disk volume table of contents carries the names of all data sets on the disk. Although TSO function 3.7 provides a one line per data set

```
//FSBT686A  JOB AK00TEST,'DP2-JANOSSY',CLASS=E,MSGCLASS=X,
//  MSGLEVEL=(1,1),NOTIFY=BT05686
//*
//*     THIS JCL = BT05686.SOURCE.CNTL(JCL1720)
//*
//********************************************************
//*                                                      *
//*     PRINT A FORMATTED LISTING OF DISK VOLUME         *
//*     TABLE OF CONTENTS (VTOC)                         *
//*                                                      *
//********************************************************
//STEPA     EXEC  PGM=IEHLIST
//SYSPRINT  DD    SYSOUT=*
//DISK      DD    UNIT=3380,
//  DISP=SHR,
//  VOL=SER=FSDC03
//SYSIN     DD    *
    LISTVTOC   FORMAT,VOL=3380=FSDC03
/*
//
```

FIGURE 17.20. Using IEHLIST to produce a formatted list of a disk volume table of contents (VTOC)

display, IEHLIST can produce a printed display of all the various formats of the data set control block or "DSCB" records in the VTOC for all data sets as well as "free space" records in the VTOC. The coding that produces such a listing is shown in Figure 17.20. If the control word FORMAT is changed to DUMP, a hexadecimal printline dump rendition of the VTOC records is produced with printlines 121 bytes in length. The format of VTOC records, also known as data set control block or DSCB records, is described in an IBM reference publication titled *System/360 Control Blocks, GC28-6628.* Caution: A VTOC listing in either format can be voluminous. If produced, it is best viewed on a computer terminal using the TSO 3.8 outlist function or SDSF rather than printed immediately.

IEHPROGM: MAINTAINING DATA SET PASSWORDS

21. Creating, Changing, and Deleting OS Passwords

IEHPROGM is a multipurpose utility, most of the functions of which have been stripped away by IDCAMS. IEHPROGM is no longer used to create generation data group indexes, now called "bases" under the VSAM and ICF catalog structures. IDCAMS is also now the preferred utility to rename, force delete, catalog and uncatalog data sets, and delete PDS members, as illustrated in item 7.

The one area in which IEHPROGM is still used is in the maintenance of OS passwords. Even an installation that has a modern access security system like IBM's RACF or ACF2 by SKK, Inc., has a small amount of OS password maintenance to perform in connection with certain MVS system data sets. OS passwords are words of up to eight characters associated with a data set. An entry for every password is contained in a special password data set that must be located on the system residence volume, a permanently mounted disk on which many MVS system data sets reside. IEHPROGM modifies entries in the password data set when used as described here. OS passwords are separate from VSAM passwords, which are maintained by IDCAMS.

OS passwords provide two levels or modes of security beyond no security at all. Read/write protection means that the password for the data set must be provided by the computer console operator at the time any job wants to read from or write to the data set. Read-without-password protection allows jobs to read a data set without the use of a password but makes operator provision of the password necessary when a job attempts to write to the data set.

A data set protected by an OS password carries an indication of this fact in its data set label. The indication is a signal to MVS to request entry of the password by the operator when the data set is accessed; in response to this indication MVS knows to check the system password data set for the access. The password flag is activated differently, depending on whether the data set is housed on tape or disk. For tape the PASSWORD/NOPWREAD subparameter of the label parameter is used. PASSWORD sets read/write protection; NOPWREAD is an acronym for "no password read" and sets the label indicator to read-without-password security. To use PASSWORD/NOPWREAD with a tape data set IEHPROGM is first used to place the password into the password data set. For disk data sets MVS has access to the data set label, and the data set security indicator in it is altered automatically when passwords are added to or deleted from the password data set using IEHPROGM.

The first password supplied for a data set is called the "control password." Additional passwords called "secondary" passwords can also be associated with the data set. The password entry in the password data set provides several fields: password, protection mode, an access counter, and 77 bytes of free form user data. In addition to other password manipulations, IEHPROGM can be used to list the contents of the password data set entry for a data set.

IEHPROGM uses three command specifications for password operations:

ADD   to create a new control or secondary password for a
      data set

REPLACE   to change a password

DELETEP   to delete password

For disk data sets these commands alter the security indicator in the data set label to conform to the desired security level. For tape data sets IEHPROGM cannot alter the label and the security level established at the time the tape data set is created remains in effect. Five detailed subspecifications exist and are used with the three commands in various combinations:

DSNAME =   the full name of the data set

PASWORD1 = the current password

PASWORD2 = the new password

CPASWORD = the control password

```
//FSBT686A  JOB AKOOTEST,'DP2-JANOSSY',CLASS=E,MSGCLASS=X,
//  MSGLEVEL=(1,1),NOTIFY=BT05686
//*
//*     THIS JCL = BT05686.SOURCE.CNTL(JCL1721)
//*
//************************************************************
//*                                                          *
//*     OS PASSWORD MAINTENANCE USING IEHPROGM               *
//*     (FOR SECURITY PARM='NOPRINT' AT THE EXEC             *
//*     SUPPRESSES PRINTING OF IEHPROGM MESSAGES)            *
//*                                                          *
//************************************************************
//STEPA     EXEC  PGM=IEHPROGM,PARM='NOPRINT'
//SYSPRINT   DD   SYSOUT=*
//DISK       DD   UNIT=SYSDA,
//  VOL=REF=SYS1.SVCLIB,
//  DISP=OLD
//SYSIN      DD   *
      ADD    DSNAME=FS10.C99.AUDIT87A,
             PASWORD2=KK39VL7,
             TYPE=1,
             DATA='DETAIL TRANS FOR YEAR-END AUDIT PER ARW'
   REPLACE   DSNAME=FS24.C99.RATETABL,
             PASWORD1=CYF194P,
             PASWORD2=BR7D312
     LIST    DSNAME=FS15.C99.EMPLYMST,
             PASWORD1=A167RPW
/*
//
```

FIGURE 17.21. IEHPROGM control statements to create a control password, replace a password, and list characteristics of a password entry

TYPE=   1   means that the password allows read and write access, but for a control password and a disk data set read/write protection mode is indicated in the data set label

         2   means that the password allows only read access, but for a control password and a disk data set read/write protection mode is indicated in the data set label

         3   means that the password allows read and write access, but for a control password and a disk data set read-without-password protection mode is indicated in the data set label

VOL=   the disk volume that contains the data set affected; it is not needed if the data set is cataloged

DATA=   up to 77 bytes of user data, surrounded by apostrophes

Figure 17.21 illustrates the use of IEHPROGM to create the control password for a new tape data set, the replacement of the existing control password for a cataloged disk data set, and the listing of the password entry for a third data set. Continuation of a control statement is indicated by an X in column 72 in addition to the comma on a line.

NOTE

1. Packed decimal storage of numeric quantities relies on the fact that the hexadecimal representation of each number symbol 0-9 differs only in the last four bits of each byte, as shown in the EBCDIC/ASCII collation sequence chart in Appendix C. Only half of each byte is necessary to carry the information represented by a given digit. COMP-3 stores numbers two digits to a byte by carrying only these low-order four bits for each position. The conversion from zoned decimal PIC 9 storage to PIC 9 COMP-3, and vice versa, is handled automatically by COBOL when a MOVE statement transfers data from a field of one type to a field of the other.

    For a complete discussion of packed decimal format and the space occupied by the digits and sign see pages 137–38 and page 236 of *Commercial Software Engineering: For Productive Program Design*, ISBN 0-471-81576-4, John Wiley and Sons, Inc., 1985.

JOB and EXEC Statement Parameters

The JOB statement flags the start of a new series of JCL statements that constitute a unit of work for MVS. Every job starts with a JOB statement and ends with a null // statement or with the JOB statement for the next job in the input queue. The JOB statement provides 19 different parameters that:

- Name the job and identify the party submitting it.
- Allow resource utilization for the job to be recorded for accounting purposes.
- Specify the handling of the job by MVS, including the priority the job will be accorded in relation to other jobs.

Only nine of the parameters are commonly useful and in any given instance only a few are coded. The remaining parameters serve special purposes for systems programmers and IBM's RACF security system or are added temporarily in job-failure recovery actions.

COMMONLY USED JOB STATEMENT PARAMETERS

A typical JOB statement is similar to

```
//FSBT686A   JOB WCWC13DT,'DP2-JANOSSY',CLASS=E,
//   MSGCLASS=X,MSGLEVEL=(1,1),TYPRUN=SCAN,NOTIFY=BT05686
```

or

```
//FS379211   JOB 1,'BIN-47',CLASS=T,MSGCLASS=A,TIME=(5,15)
```

but the precise content varies from installation to installation. The commonly used JOB statement parameters are:

//FSBT686A *job name; mandatory:* The one to eight letters following the slashes are printed in large block letters on the paper output separator pages. If the job were submitted via TSO, this name is coded as the TSO logon identifier; a final distinguishing letter can be coded or supplied at a TSO prompt when a job is submitted.

JOB *JCL statement type; mandatory:* These literals distinguish the statement as a JOB statement.

WCWC13DT *account; MVS optional, usually required:* Composition unique to an installation, this field is picked up by MVS and used within the System Management Facility or "SMF" records that constitute the log and system performance measurement data set. The account field can be made up of one to several positions and the maximum overall length can be 142 bytes. Account is an optional positional parameter on the JOB statement but it also exists as an optional keyword parameter on the EXEC statement. An installation documents its own use of this parameter and informs its programmers of the format.

'DP2-JANOSSY' *recipient name; MVS optional, often needed:* This will appear in separator page lines and indicate the recipient or output routing. Local standards apply to its content. The value between the apostrophes is free form but local conventions may require it to be coded uniformly.

CLASS=E *job class; MVS optional, usually required:* A single character that indicates a job initiation category. Installations generally create different job classes for job by type, depending on the kind and amount of resources used. Short jobs using only disk and producing few printlines are usually given initiation preference. If job class is not used by an installation, all work is handled as if it were coded for job class A and CLASS is not coded.

The job class of a job on the system input queue is examined by MVS "nanny programs" called initiators. As many as 15 or more initiators may be active at a time, each "holding hands" or seeking to hold hands with one program at a time. Each initiator is governed by a reconfigurable list of job classes from which it picks jobs preferentially from the input queue and ushers through execution. The console operator can reconfigure the job class list for each initiator, allowing it to favor or discriminate against jobs of different classes. If no initiator carries a given job class in its selection list, a job in the input queue coded with that job class will not be picked for execution. Jobs within a class are picked for execution in descending order of their PRIORITY, another job statement parameter.

The operator is provided with MVS console commands that can change the class of a job before its initiation. If a job is to be given very special treatment, the operator will change it to a job class that is coded at the beginning of the picking list for several initiators, thus guaranteeing that the job will be picked up quickly. Programmers do not usually have access to or even knowledge of the system console commands that can perform these actions.

MSGCLASS = A   *message class; MVS optional, often used:* The output print class in which the MVS job log and allocation/deallocation outputs will be printed. The standard convention is MSGCLASS = A for the printer and MSGCLASS = X for the held queue for TSO viewing.

MSGLEVEL = (a,b)   *message level; MVS optional, local defaults:* The first number specifies what JCL *statements* are to be listed and the second number indicates what types of allocation/deallocation *messages* are to be printed.

a = JCL statements

> 0 Print only the JOB statement.
> 1 Print JOB statement, JCL, and invoked proc JCL.
> 2 Print JOB statement and JCL only, no invoked proc JCL.

b = system messages

> 0 Print allocation/deallocation messages only if the job abends.
> 1 Always print all messages.

A value of (1,1) produces maximum print. If not specified, these default to installation-defined values. Just the "statements" value can be specified by coding MSGLEVEL = 1.

TYPRUN = SCAN   *type of run; optional:* The run can be held and not processed, a purely syntax-checking scan can be requested, or the JCL can be copied out to the SYSOUT class coded in MSGCLASS. Omission of TYPRUN is the norm.

> HOLD   JCL syntax is checked and rejected if in error, but if syntactically correct the job execution is delayed until the operator releases the job for processing.

> JCLHOLD   JCL syntax is not checked and execution is delayed until the operator releases the job for processing. Syntax checks performed at the time the job is released may cause it to fail.

> SCAN   Syntax checking only is performed.

> COPY   Execution JCL is copied out to the specified SYSOUT class.

HOLD is often used when a special resource, such as a custom impact printer form, foreign tape, or dedicated printer is needed for a job. SCAN is ideal for initial JCL syntax checkout and for obtaining a listing of the JCL within a proc because the contents of procs invoked are listed. COPY is of less utility because it only copies to print the execution JCL; procs invoked by the JCL are not brought in and listed. Note that the statements field of MSGLEVEL will limit the amount of JCL listed even when SCAN is specified. SCAN with MSGLEVEL = (0,0) checks syntax and will produce any JCL error messages but will not list the JCL; this is normally inconsistent with the output desired of SCAN.

NOTIFY = BT05686   *send message to tso user; optional:* The value coded after NOTIFY is a TSO identifier. This tells MVS to send a message when the job finishes and is commonly requested on programmer-submitted compiles and test runs. MVS uses the TSO "SEND" facility to transmit the message. The MVS "SE" abbreviated send command for the message is visible in the system log.

TIME = (5,15)   *processor time limit for job; optional:* This establishes a time limit for the entire job. This is central processor time, not "wall" or elapsed time, which can be much longer because of the slow pace of I/O operations and the sharing of the processor with other jobs. The first value is minutes and the last value is seconds. To establish a time limit less than a minute the value can be coded as TIME = (,n) which sets "n" seconds as the limit. The limit is approximate because

MVS checks accumulated CPU time used at 10.5-second intervals. TIME can also be coded on individual steps. Exceeding the allowed job time anywhere within the job results in termination. An inactive job in a wait state performing no activity will be timed out with a system completion code of 522 after 30 minutes or after another installation-defined limit. If the JOB time parameter is coded TIME = 1440, a full day, then all time checking, including for wait-state inactivity, is abandoned.

LESSER USED JOB STATEMENT FEATURES

The following parameters are used infrequently in JOB statements because they serve specialized purposes:

ADDRSPC = VIRT or ADDRSPC = REAL   This parameter requests either virtual memory or real memory. The default is virtual memory and is applicable in nearly all cases. Use of REAL is usually prohibited to all but critical support software.

COND = (0,LT)   Blanket condition code tests can be specified on the JOB statement and are applied to each step of the job in advance of the COND testing coded on the steps. COND is more typically used with individual EXEC statements. COND on the JOB statement requires the execution JCL to be intimately involved with recovery mechanisms within invoked procs but different procs may require different internal recovery mechanisms.

GROUP =   This parameter specifies a security group under IBM's RACF security system; it is meaningful only if the installation uses RACF.

PASSWORD =   This instruction specifies a RACF security system password; it is meaningful only for non-TSO submitted batch jobs and only if the installation uses RACF.

PERFORM = nnn   This value, stated as 1 to 999, places the job in a specified "performance group." Performance groups allow segregation of work and may be established by an installation to balance the workload of the system. This parameter is usually left to the locally defined default.

PRTY = n   Priority dictates the sequence in which jobs are stacked in their job classes in the input queue. This value ranges from 0 to 15; 15 is at the immediate attention end of the spectrum for initiation, whereas 0 is given attention only after all other jobs with the same CLASS, carrying higher priorities, have been initiated. In some installations priority is assigned by default or by a "reader exit" that intercepts submitted JCL, and programmers cannot specify it. When it can be specified, local rules govern the priority to be coded for a given job.

RD = R or RD = RNC or RD = NC or RD = NR   RD means "restart definition" and defines actions to be taken automatically to restart the job if a failure occurs. The use of this parameter is defined by the local manner of handling job restarts. RD may not be used in an installation if special-purpose, non-IBM software such as a job scheduling and recovery system has been installed.

The four possible values for restart definition are the following:

R   Restart. Automatic step restart is permitted. Automatic does not mean that MVS takes complete control; the console operator must initiate the recovery action. MVS uses a job journal, which must be active, and checkpoints are taken during processing to resume processing at a point prior to failure.

RNC   Restart, no checkpoint. Automatic step restart is permitted but automatic and deferred checkpoint restart are not.

NC   No checkpoint. Automatic step restart, automatic checkpoint restart, and deferred checkpoint restart are not permitted.

NR   No automatic restart. Checkpointing according to the CHKPT macro instruction is permitted but automatic restart is not. This coding allows resubmission of the job with the RESTART parameter on the job statement to specify at what checkpoint the job is to resume.

See *OS/VS2 MVS Checkpoint Restart*, GC26-3877, for a concise description of MVS restart facilities associated with this job statement specification.

REGION = 1024K   Memory allocation for job, optional. Each step in a job is allocated an installation-defined default amount of virtual memory, in kilobytes, such as 512K or 1024K. The number is always even. It is possible to specify the region size parameter to provide greater or lesser amounts of virtual storage. REGION, however, is more often specified on individual EXEC statements instead, where it applies more precisely to given programs. *If REGION is specified on the JOB statement, it overrides REGION parameters coded on EXECs and applies for each step.*

RESTART =   Deferred restart of job, a production restart. A parameter used only to recover from a failed job, RESTART is typically well known to operations groups and much less so to applications programmers, who do not normally run production jobs. On the *JOB statement for production execution JCL, which invokes one or more cataloged procedures to perform its work*—in other words, on the run deck job card—coding similar to this is added only for a special restart run and then removed

```
,RESTART=STEPC.FS44873H
```

where STEPC is the name of an execution JCL step that invokes a proc and FS44873H is a step name within that proc. For this coding the restart would begin at the start of step //FS44873H within the proc being invoked. The name of the proc itself, which is established in this example at //STEPC, is *not* coded in the restart parameter. The run deck for this restart could appear as

```
//FS448731   JOB FSBTCP99,'PROD-BIN AK',CLASS=P,MSGCLASS=A,
//   MSGCLASS=(1,1),RESTART=STEPC.FS44873H
//*
//STEPA      EXEC FS4487P1
//STEPB      EXEC FS4487P2
//STEPC      EXEC FS4487P3
//STEPD      EXEC FS4487P4
//
```

according to the naming conventions discussed in Chapter 16. After the restart run submission the RESTART parameter is removed from the execution JCL; it is only a temporary appendage to remedy an unusual situation.

Restarting a failed job is not a task to be undertaken lightly. *To restart a failed job successfully several items must be resolved, and some may require altering the proc JCL, either directly or with special overrides.* All backward references that point to steps before the point of restart must be eliminated; this may involve PGM references but much more likely VOL=REF. The COND parameters on EXEC statements remaining to be processed will be ignored if they refer to steps before the point of restart. The sliding of generation data group generation numbers that normally occurs did so in the failed job for steps processed before failure. Any steps remaining to be executed that reference the (+1) or higher generation must be changed to refer to (0) generation prior to the restart; the highest number +n generation created became (0) at the time the job ended. Passed data sets, created by the steps executed before the point of failure, will not be present.

It is also possible to restart a job at a point that is coded directly in the JCL; that is, when the restart point does not occur within a proc. In this case the syntax of the RESTART parameter involves only the stepname. "Raw JCL" production jobs are distinctly atypical and restart coding is not common. If attempted, resolution of backward references, COND coding, GDG generation numbers, and passed data sets must be treated like an execution JCL/proc restart.

It is also possible to specify a restart at a checkpoint taken within a step. The use of checkpoint restart is sufficiently complex to warrant detailed documentation within an installation. It requires the use of a special //SYSCHK DD statement on the execution JCL for the job to be restarted and must cite the checkpoint data set to which the run wrote checkpointing information up to the point of failure. Checkpoint restart is ordinarily applied only to lengthy jobs that are normally designed to minimize the awkwardness of restart considerations and rely on coding of a second subparameter on the RESTART specification that names the checkpoint at which the restart is to begin. See *OS/VS2 MVS Checkpoint Restart*, GC26-3877, for a concise description of MVS restart facilities associated with this job statement specification.

USER=xxxxxxx   identifies a RACF "userid" and is applicable only if an installation uses IBM's Resource Acquisition Control Facility security system.

COMMONLY USED EXEC STATEMENT PARAMETERS

One EXEC statement is coded for each step of a job stream. A total of 13 EXEC statement parameters exist, of which seven are commonly useful. In testing JCL, a job step often resembles

```
//STEPA     EXEC   PGM=FSBT3758
or
//STEPA     EXEC   PGM=FSBT3758,TIME=(1,40)
```

but a more fully loaded EXEC used in production JCL could take the form

```
//FS56162C   EXEC   PGM=FSBT3758,COND=(0,LT),
//    PARM='031586-071586'
```

and additional parameters could be specified. These EXEC parameters serve general purposes:

//FS56162C   *name of step; optional but rarely omitted:* Without a name, the documentation of JCL would be unwieldy and other steps cannot refer to the step in referbacks.

PGM=   *program to be executed; mandatory unless a proc is being
            invoked;* see "PROC" following. Names the program to be executed.
            This can be coded literally or can be a referback to the program load
            module output in a prior step *within* a proc or raw JCL:

```
PGM=*.LKED.SYSLMOD
```

It can also be a referback to a load module output in a step within a
proc *invoked earlier in the execution JCL:*

```
PGM=*.STEPB.LKED.SYSLMOD
```

In the preceding case the JCL would have invoked a compile and linkage edit procedure at its //STEPB; LKED is a step name within that
proc and SYSLMOD is the DDname at which the load module is produced. IBM's convention for discussing program referbacks is, re-
spectively:

```
PGM=*.stepname.ddname
PGM=*.stepname.procstepname.ddname
```

This referback, however, is not at all common.

PROC=   *procedure to be executed: optional:* Not often used, PROC
            is the explicit way to specify that a procedure, and not a program, is
            to be invoked. It is not usually coded because the EXECution defaults
            to a proc if PGM is not coded. These two statements are identical in
            meaning:

```
EXEC   PROC=FS5616P1
EXEC   FS5616P1
```

COND=(0,LT)   *condition code test; optional:* This test attempts to
            skip the execution of the step if the test or tests coded are satisfied.
            A test coded (0,LT) says "skip this step if zero is less than the user
            return code of any prior step." If coded (6,EQ,FS56163B) it reads "skip
            this step if 6 is equal to the user return code of //FS56163B." Chapter
            14 is devoted entirely to the application of this parameter. COND is
            widely used to trigger job stream recovery actions in case of program
            abends or I/O failure.

PARM='ABC'   *program parameter; optional:* Indicates that a pa-
            rameter string follows and is to be passed by MVS to the program
            being executed. Often used with the compiler, it is a general capability
            available to any program. Chapter 15 is devoted entirely to the EXEC
            statement's PARM parameter.

REGION = 1024K   *memory allocation for step; optional:*   Each step
is allocated an installation-defined default amount of virtual memory,
in kilobytes, such as 512K or 1024K. The number is always even. It
is possible to specify the region parameter on a step to provide greater
or lesser amounts of virtual storage. REGION coded on the JOB statement, however, overrides any REGION coded on a step. REGION is
an EXEC statement parameter that had much more relevance in the
days of OS, prior to virtual memory operating system techniques.
REGION is normally not specified now unless a particular step uses
especially large I/O buffers due to large block sizes, specifies several
buffers via the DCB BUFNO subparameter, or requests numerous
VSAM data set buffers via the AMP BUFND and/or BUFNI subparameters. Large application programs or the sort utility may require or
run better with a region size greater than the installation default.

TIME = (1,30)   *processor time limit for step; optional:*   This establishes a time limit for the step and is actually central processor time,
not "wall" or elapsed time, which can be much longer because of the
slow pace of I/O operations and the sharing of the processor with
other jobs. The first value is minutes and the last value is seconds.
To establish a time limit less than a minute, the value can be coded
as TIME = (,6) which sets 6 seconds as the step limit. The limit is only
approximate; MVS checks CPU time accumulated in the step at 10.5
second intervals. Exceeding the allowed time in a step causes job termination. If the time parameter is coded TIME = 1440 then all time
checking for the step, including for wait state inactivity, is abandoned.

LESSER USED EXEC STATEMENT FEATURES

ACCOUNT = 'xxx...xxx'   This is optional accounting information that
identifies the party or records-keeping entity to be charged for the
resources used by the step. An EXEC statement keyword parameter,
ACCOUNT, is also a *positional* parameter on the JOB statement. If
ACCOUNT appears on an EXEC statement *both job and step accounting information is recorded.* The composition of the account field is
specified by an installation and it can have up to 142 characters. If a
step in execution JCL carries an ACCOUNT parameter and invokes a
proc that has ACCOUNT information coded on its steps, the execution
JCL's ACCOUNT parameter overrides the proc's coding.

ADDRSPC = VIRT or ADDRSPC = REAL   This requests either virtual
memory or real memory for the step. The default is virtual memory
and is applicable in nearly all cases. Use of VIRT is usually prohibited
to all but critical support software.

DPRTY = (x,y)   dispatch priority; this specification contains two
fields, each of which can be a value of 0 through 15. DPRTY allows
making a step have higher or lower priority than the job as a whole.
Dispatch priority is coded even less frequently than PRTY. Applications programmers are typically precluded from specifying it because the balancing of workload across the system is the responsibility
of the operations group. It is not a programming responsibility.

DYNAMNBR   dynamic number; an obsolete specifier that accomplishes for the step what the obsolete DD DYNAM parameter does for
a DD statement. It would hold a resource if it could to allow other
steps in the job to use it more readily. DD DYNAM and DYNAMNBR
are unnecessary now because MVS attempts to hold onto resources
for a job in all cases. Although ignored, DD DYNAM and DYNAMNBR
are still accepted within the syntax of MVS JCL.

PERFORM = nnn   This is a value of 1 to 999 that places the step into
a specified performance group. Performance groups allow segregation
of work underway and may be established by an installation to balance
the workload of the system. This parameter is usually left to the locally
defined default. It can appear in the JOB statement as well; if coded
there, it supersedes any EXEC statement PERFORM.

RD = R or RD = RNC or RD = NC or RD = NR   These restart definition
options define actions to be taken to restart the job if a failure occurs.
The use of this parameter is dictated and defined by an individual
installation according to the local manner of handling job restarts. See
the RD parameter discussed for the JOB statement for information on
the meaning of the four possible values of this parameter.

Partitioned Data Set Batch Reorganization JCL

The JCL provided here performs partitioned data set reorganization in a batch manner and allows respecification of PDS space and secondary allocations, directory size, and blocking. It requires no control card use, provides safeguards against data set loss by interruption or failure, and as a cataloged procedure can be invoked by anyone with a simple one-line EXEC statement. The job stream does not require the party submitting it to know the disk volume on which the PDS resides, but the PDS is always written back automatically to this same disk volume, thus precluding unintended migration of the PDS to other volumes. The proc itself illustrates many JCL details and techniques that make it a learning device as well as a useful tool.

This JCL can be entered from the listing, but it is one of several items also available on diskette for uploading to a mainframe by a suitably equipped PC, as described at the end of Appendix D. It has also been placed on several major microcomputer based bulletin boards in the United States and Europe for convenient downloading. You are welcome to copy it, use it, and pass it on intact and unmodified—it is "shareware" original to this book.

BACKGROUND

TSO libraries are partitioned data sets; every individual program or set of JCL is a PDS member. A programmer usually has at least two PDSs: one with the last part of the name COBOL, PLI, ASM, or FORT, for source code statements and one with a final name portion of CNTL to house JCL statements.

When a given program or JCL member is updated by TSO and subsequently saved at the end of the edit session, it is written back into its PDS library in toto. It is not written back into the space it had occupied; that copy of the information remains but is dead and no longer accessible. The updated member is automatically written to new, unused space at the end of the present PDS members by using, if necessary, secondary allocation of disk space if defined as a characteristic of the PDS when established. BPAM, the Basic Partitioned Access Method within MVS, updates the PDS directory entry for the member to refer to its new position in the PDS. When a member is deleted, the space it occupies is not reusable by any other member; it, too, becomes dead space.

A PDS will eventually become filled with members and dead space. Reclaiming the dead space occupied by superseded members is often called compressing a PDS because, at least conceptually, it appears afterward that the members have been squeezed upward to eliminate the dead space and leave all unused space available at the tail end of the PDS. Although the online TSO compression function may appear to be appealing, it is time consuming, especially for large data sets, and it demands that the terminal that invokes it remain inactive during the time it is operating. Online compress also carries the potential of corrupting a data set if an interruption occurs during the operation. TSO online compress does not release secondary space allocations that the PDS may have acquired as it grew.

USING THE PDS REORGANIZATION PROC

The JCL for the reorganization proc is listed in Figure B.1. This should be entered in a CNTL PDS. The JCL uses only the standard IBM utilities IEFBR14 and IEBCOPY, which are present as MVS operating system software.

```
//PDSREORG  PROC PDS='***',
//  RECFORM='FB',
//     QREC='80',
//     QBLK='3840',          'USE 3600 FOR 3350 DISK, 3840 FOR 3380 DISK
//    ALLOC='TRK',
//    QPRIM='50',
//     QSEC='30',
//  QDIRBLK='40'
//*
//*     PROC TO REALLOCATE AND REORGANIZE A PARTITIONED DATA SET.
//*     ORIG  10-15-85 J JANOSSY    LAST CHANGE  10-27-85 J JANOSSY
//*
//****************************************************************
//*                                                              *
//*      FIND ORIGINAL PDS TO BE REORGANIZED                  A  *
//*                                                              *
//****************************************************************
//STEPA     EXEC  PGM=IEFBR14
//FIND1      DD   DSN=&PDS,
//  DISP=(OLD,KEEP)
//*
//****************************************************************
//*                                                              *
//*     COPY PDS TO ANOTHER, SAME NAME BUT .NEWCOPY APPENDED      *
//*     NOTE: THERE IS NO IEFBR14 OF THE .NEWCOPY DATA SET        *
//*     AHEAD OF THIS BECAUSE .NEWCOPY IF PRESENT WHEN THIS    B  *
//*     STARTS INDICATES A PROBLEM WITH A PRIOR REORG THAT        *
//*     SHOULD BE CORRECTED WITH RECOVERY ACTIONS                 *
//*                                                              *
//****************************************************************
//STEPB     EXEC  PGM=IEBCOPY,COND=(0,LT)
//SYSPRINT   DD   DUMMY,DCB=BLKSIZE=121
//SYSUDUMP   DD   SYSOUT=A
//SYSUT1     DD   DSN=&PDS,
//  DISP=(OLD,KEEP)
//SYSUT2     DD   DSN=&PDS..NEWCOPY,
//  UNIT=SYSDA,
//  DISP=(NEW,CATLG,DELETE),
//  DCB=(RECFM=&RECFORM,LRECL=&QREC,BLKSIZE=&QBLK),
//  SPACE=(&ALLOC,(&QPRIM,&QSEC,&QDIRBLK)),
//  VOL=REF=*.STEPA.FIND1
//SYSUT3     DD   UNIT=SYSDA,SPACE=(CYL,(1,1))
//SYSUT4     DD   UNIT=SYSDA,SPACE=(CYL,(1,1))
//SYSIN      DD   DUMMY
//*
//****************************************************************
//*                                                              *
//*     DELETE ORIGINAL PDS SINCE COPY WAS MADE OK            C  *
//*                                                              *
//****************************************************************
//STEPC     EXEC  PGM=IEFBR14,COND=(0,LT)
//DEL1       DD   DSN=&PDS,
//  DISP=(MOD,DELETE),
//   SPACE=(TRK,0)
//*
//****************************************************************
//*                                                              *
//*     COPY .NEWCOPY BACK TO ORIGINAL PDS NAME              D  *
//*                                                              *
//****************************************************************
//STEPD     EXEC  PGM=IEBCOPY,COND=(0,LT)
//SYSPRINT   DD   SYSOUT=*
//SYSUDUMP   DD   SYSOUT=A
//SYSUT1     DD   DSN=&PDS..NEWCOPY,
//  DISP=(OLD,KEEP)
//SYSUT2     DD   DSN=&PDS,
//  UNIT=SYSDA,
//  DISP=(NEW,CATLG,DELETE),
//  DCB=(RECFM=&RECFORM,LRECL=&QREC,BLKSIZE=&QBLK),
//  SPACE=(&ALLOC,(&QPRIM,&QSEC,&QDIRBLK)),
//  VOL=REF=*.STEPA.FIND1
//SYSUT3     DD   UNIT=SYSDA,SPACE=(CYL,(1,1))
```

FIGURE B.1.   JCL to perform a batch reorganization of a partitioned data set with options to change block size and number of directory blocks (*continues next page*)

```
//SYSUT4     DD  UNIT=SYSDA,SPACE=(CYL,(1,1))
//SYSIN      DD  DUMMY
//*
//*****************************************************************
//*                                                              *
//*    IF ALL OK, DELETE THE .NEWCOPY                          E *
//*                                                              *
//*****************************************************************
//STEPE     EXEC  PGM=IEFBR14,COND=(0,LT)
//DEL1         DD  DSN=&PDS..NEWCOPY,
//   DISP=(MOD,DELETE),
//   SPACE=(TRK,0)
```

FIGURE B.1.   (con't.)

To invoke this as an instream procedure place your normal job statement at the front of the JCL, a // PEND statement after the last line of the JCL, and follow with the invocation of the procedure that names the PDS to be reorganized:

```
//RUNIT    EXEC  PDSREORG,DSN='BT05686.SOURCE.COBOL'
//
```

To invoke the reorganization as a cataloged procedure enter it into a PDS, have it transferred into SYS1.PROCLIB or the designated proc library in your installation, and invoke it with only a JOB statement and the EXEC statement.

The procedure was written with symbolic parameters for the PDS characteristics that are likely to differ between common library types and data sets. Typical default values are provided for all but the PDS name symbolic parameters in the procedure itself. An installation can make these defaults appropriate to local customs and conventions; personnel can then invoke the procedure specifying only the PDS name. COND tests built into the JCL skip processing if an abnormal condition is encountered.

EXPLANATION OF THE PROC

//STEPA of this JCL accomplishes no data set manipulation action at all; it uses the IEFBR14 null program as an excuse to have MVS act on the //FIND1 DD statement. This step causes MVS to look for the data set in the system catalog, find the volume on which it resides, and insure that exclusive use of the data set is possible. Because of this step, subsequent steps can use a referback to //FIND1 to supply the volume serial number of the disk on which the reorganized PDS is to be placed. The party running the job therefore does not have to know or specify this volume serial number.

The job uses IEBCOPY to copy the PDS to another data set, named similarly to the original but with .NEWCOPY appended to the data set name. A data set by this name should not exist on the disk if prior runs of the reorganization ended successfully; therefore we intentionally provide no housekeeping IEFBR14 to delete a data set of the .NEWCOPY name. The .NEWCOPY data set will be written with the same space specification that is intended to apply to the final reorganized data set; if this space allocation cannot be made, the job will stop without doing anything to the original PDS.

Once the .NEWCOPY has been successfully created the original PDS is deleted at //STEPC. In //STEPD the .NEWCOPY is copied back to a PDS of the original name. The same symbolic parameters for data set space are employed here as in the first copy. Finally, if everything goes as planned, the .NEWCOPY data set is deleted.

IEBCOPY, often demonstrated in connection with //SYSIN control cards pointing to an input and output data set, readily works without control cards. This utility accepts input at //SYSUT1 and directs its output to //SYSUT2. No control cards are required for this method of operation and the //SYSIN DD statement is assigned to DUMMY status. The entire procedure may therefore be packaged as a fully self-contained proc. The //SYSPRINT output of the initial IEBCOPY is assigned to dummy status to avoid duplication of member listings. The //SYSPRINT listing from the second IEBCOPY is assigned to print and is a useful inventory of the members in the data set.

REBLOCKING A PDS CHANGING THE SPACE OR DIRECTORY ALLOCATION

If a change in PDS blocking, space allocation, or directory size is desired, it can be done at the time of reorganization by specifying the items in the EXEC statement, overriding the default values. For example, to invoke the procedure to change blocking to 3,840 bytes, a more efficient value than 3,120 bytes for the IBM 3380 disk, PDSREORG can be invoked in this way:

```
//RUNIT     EXEC   PDSREORG,DSN='BT05686.SOURCE.COBOL',
//   QBLK=3840
//
```

If the primary and secondary space allocations are to be changed, but the default blocking is to prevail, the invocation can be done as:

```
//RUNIT     EXEC   PDSREORG,DSN='BT05686.SOURCE.COBOL',
//   QPRIM=90,
//   QSEC=50
//
```

Similarly, the number of directory blocks can be changed in the course of the reorganization

```
//RUNIT    EXEC  PDSREORG,DSN='BT05686.SOURCE.COBOL',
//  QDIRBLK=60
//
```

or all of the defaults can be overridden at one time.

To use the procedure to reorganize a load module library JCL can execute it:

```
//RUNIT    EXEC  PSDREORG,DSN='BT05686.TEST.LOADMODS',
//  RECFORM=U,
//  QREC=0,
//  QBLK=23476    'FOR IBM 3380
//
```

The value for QBLK in this case should be track size; 23,476 allows two blocks to fit on the 47,476-byte tracks of the IBM 3380. For the IBM 3350 disk drive a value of 19,069 can be used and for the IBM 3330-II, 13,030. The values for primary and secondary allocation and directory blocks can also be specified to match or modify the nature of the existing load module library.

WHAT TO DO IF THE REORGANIZATION RUN FAILS

The reorganization procedure will fail if space is not available to house the .NEWCOPY copy of the data set. In this case, try the run again. This type of abend causes no change in the name or status of the original data set.

If the run fails after //STEPB, the .NEWCOPY of the PDS will exist. Depending on whether the run failed during or after //STEPC, the original PDS may or may not exist or it may exist but be incomplete as a result of interruption in //STEPD. To recover from the failure rename the original PDS by using the TSO 3.2 function, manually allocate a new PDS with the desired characteristics under the original name, and use TSO 3.3 or a JCL invocation of IEBCOPY to copy the .NEWCOPY data set back to the newly allocated original. Verify that the new data set of the original name is intact. Then use TSO function 3.2 to delete the renamed and .NEWCOPY versions of it.

EBCDIC, ASCII, Hexadecimal, Binary, Decimal Code Translation Table

This chart indicates the decimal, binary, hexadecimal and octal representations for all possible bit patterns in an eight-bit byte. In addition, it indicates the interpretation of each bit pattern in the EBCDIC (Extended Binary Coded Decimal Interchange Code) of IBM mainframes and in the ASCII (American Standard Code for Information Interchange) code schemes. The "CTL" column shows what combinations of the control key and symbol keys produce the bit pattern on a standard ASCII terminal device.

DECIMAL	BINARY	HEX	NIBBLES	EBCDIC	ASCII	CTL	OCTAL	CRUMBLES
0	00000000	00	0000 0000	NUL	NUL	sp	000	00 000 000
1	00000001	01	0000 0001	SOH	SOH	A	001	00 000 001
2	00000010	02	0000 0010	STX	STX	B	002	00 000 010
3	00000011	03	0000 0011	ETX	ETX	C	003	00 000 011
4	00000100	04	0000 0100	PF	EOT	D	004	00 000 100
5	00000101	05	0000 0101	HT	ENQ	E	005	00 000 101
6	00000110	06	0000 0110	LC	ACK	F	006	00 000 110
7	00000111	07	0000 0111	DEL	BEL	G	007	00 000 111
8	00001000	08	0000 1000	GE	BS	H	010	00 001 000
9	00001001	09	0000 1001	RLF	HT	I	011	00 001 001
10	00001010	0A	0000 1010	SMM	LF	J	012	00 001 010
11	00001011	0B	0000 1011	VT	VT	K	013	00 001 011
12	00001100	0C	0000 1100	FF	FF	L	014	00 001 100
13	00001101	0D	0000 1101	CR	CR	M	015	00 001 101
14	00001110	0E	0000 1110	SO	SO	N	016	00 001 110
15	00001111	0F	0000 1111	SI	SI	O	017	00 001 111
16	00010000	10	0001 0000	DLE	DLE	P	020	00 010 000
17	00010001	11	0001 0001	DC1	DC1	Q	021	00 010 001
18	00010010	12	0001 0010	DC2	DC2	R	022	00 010 010
19	00010011	13	0001 0011	TM	DC3	S	023	00 010 011
20	00010100	14	0001 0100	RES	DC4	T	024	00 010 100
21	00010101	15	0001 0101	NL	NAK	U	025	00 010 101
22	00010110	16	0001 0110	BS	SYN	V	026	00 010 110
23	00010111	17	0001 0111	IL	ETB	W	027	00 010 111
24	00011000	18	0001 1000	CAN	CAN	X	030	00 011 000
25	00011001	19	0001 1001	EM	EM	Y	031	00 011 001
26	00011010	1A	0001 1010	CC	SUB	Z	032	00 011 010
27	00011011	1B	0001 1011	CU1	ESC	[	033	00 011 011
28	00011100	1C	0001 1100	IFS	FS	\	034	00 011 100
29	00011101	1D	0001 1101	IGS	GS	]	035	00 011 101
30	00011110	1E	0001 1110	IRS	RS	~	036	00 011 110
31	00011111	1F	0001 1111	IUS	US	?	037	00 011 111
32	00100000	20	0010 0000	DS	sp		040	00 100 000
33	00100001	21	0010 0001	SOS	!		041	00 100 001
34	00100010	22	0010 0010	FS	"		042	00 100 010
35	00100011	23	0010 0011		#		043	00 100 011
36	00100100	24	0010 0100	BYP	$		044	00 100 100
37	00100101	25	0010 0101	LF	%		045	00 100 101
38	00100110	26	0010 0110	ETB	&		046	00 100 110
39	00100111	27	0010 0111	ESC	'		047	00 100 111
40	00101000	28	0010 1000		(		050	00 101 000
41	00101001	29	0010 1001		)		051	00 101 001
42	00101010	2A	0010 1010	SM	*		052	00 101 010
43	00101011	2B	0010 1011	CU2	+		053	00 101 011
44	00101100	2C	0010 1100		,		054	00 101 100
45	00101101	2D	0010 1101	ENQ	-		055	00 101 101
46	00101110	2E	0010 1110	ACK	.		056	00 101 110
47	00101111	2F	0010 1111	BEL	/		057	00 101 111
48	00110000	30	0011 0000		0		060	00 110 000
49	00110001	31	0011 0001		1		061	00 110 001
50	00110010	32	0011 0010	SYN	2		062	00 110 010
51	00110011	33	0011 0011		3		063	00 110 011
52	00110100	34	0011 0100	PN	4		064	00 110 100
53	00110101	35	0011 0101	RS	5		065	00 110 101
54	00110110	36	0011 0110	UC	6		066	00 110 110
55	00110111	37	0011 0111	EOT	7		067	00 110 111

DECIMAL	BINARY	HEX	NIBBLES	EBCDIC	ASCII	CTL	OCTAL	CRUMBLES
56	00111000	38	0011 1000		8		070	00 111 000
57	00111001	39	0011 1001		9		071	00 111 001
58	00111010	3A	0011 1010		:		072	00 111 010
59	00111011	3B	0011 1011	CU3	;		073	00 111 011
60	00111100	3C	0011 1100	DC4	<		074	00 111 100
61	00111101	3D	0011 1101	NAK	=		075	00 111 101
62	00111110	3E	0011 1110		>		076	00 111 110
63	00111111	3F	0011 1111	SUB	?		077	00 111 111
64	01000000	40	0100 0000	sp	@		100	01 000 000
65	01000001	41	0100 0001		A		101	01 000 001
66	01000010	42	0100 0010		B		102	01 000 010
67	01000011	43	0100 0011		C		103	01 000 011
68	01000100	44	0100 0100		D		104	01 000 100
69	01000101	45	0100 0101		E		105	01 000 101
70	01000110	46	0100 0110		F		106	01 000 110
71	01000111	47	0100 0111		G		107	01 000 111
72	01001000	48	0100 1000		H		110	01 001 000
73	01001001	49	0100 1001		I		111	01 001 001
74	01001010	4A	0100 1010	¢	J		112	01 001 010
75	01001011	4B	0100 1011	.	K		113	01 001 011
76	01001100	4C	0100 1100	<	L		114	01 001 100
77	01001101	4D	0100 1101	(	M		115	01 001 101
78	01001110	4E	0100 1110	+	N		116	01 001 110
79	01001111	4F	0100 1111	|	O		117	01 001 111
80	01010000	50	0101 0000	&	P		120	01 010 000
81	01010001	51	0101 0001		Q		121	01 010 001
82	01010010	52	0101 0010		R		122	01 010 010
83	01010011	53	0101 0011		S		123	01 010 011
84	01010100	54	0101 0100		T		124	01 010 100
85	01010101	55	0101 0101		U		125	01 010 101
86	01010110	56	0101 0110		V		126	01 010 110
87	01010111	57	0101 0111		W		127	01 010 111
88	01011000	58	0101 1000		X		130	01 011 000
89	01011001	59	0101 1001		Y		131	01 011 001
90	01011010	5A	0101 1010	!	Z		132	01 011 010
91	01011011	5B	0101 1011	$	[		133	01 011 011
92	01011100	5C	0101 1100	*	\		134	01 011 100
93	01011101	5D	0101 1101	)	]		135	01 011 101
94	01011110	5E	0101 1110	;	^		136	01 011 110
95	01011111	5F	0101 1111	¬	_		137	01 011 111
96	01100000	60	0110 0000	-			140	01 100 000
97	01100001	61	0110 0001	/	a		141	01 100 001
98	01100010	62	0110 0010		b		142	01 100 010
99	01100011	63	0110 0011		c		143	01 100 011
100	01100100	64	0110 0100		d		144	01 100 100
101	01100101	65	0110 0101		e		145	01 100 101
102	01100110	66	0110 0110		f		146	01 100 110
103	01100111	67	0110 0111		g		147	01 100 111
104	01101000	68	0110 1000		h		150	01 101 000
105	01101001	69	0110 1001		i		151	01 101 001
106	01101010	6A	0110 1010	¦	j		152	01 101 010
107	01101011	6B	0110 1011	,	k		153	01 101 011
108	01101100	6C	0110 1100	%	l		154	01 101 100
109	01101101	6D	0110 1101	_	m		155	01 101 101
110	01101110	6E	0110 1110	>	n		156	01 101 110
111	01101111	6F	0110 1111	?	o		157	01 101 111

DECIMAL	BINARY	HEX	NIBBLES	EBCDIC	ASCII	CTL	OCTAL	CRUMBLES
112	01110000	70	0111 0000		p		160	01 110 000
113	01110001	71	0111 0001		q		161	01 110 001
114	01110010	72	0111 0010		r		162	01 110 010
115	01110011	73	0111 0011		s		163	01 110 011
116	01110100	74	0111 0100		t		164	01 110 100
117	01110101	75	0111 0101		u		165	01 110 101
118	01110110	76	0111 0110		v		166	01 110 110
119	01110111	77	0111 0111		w		167	01 110 111
120	01111000	78	0111 1000		x		170	01 111 000
121	01111001	79	0111 1001	`	y		171	01 111 001
122	01111010	7A	0111 1010	:	z		172	01 111 010
123	01111011	7B	0111 1011	#	{		173	01 111 011
124	01111100	7C	0111 1100	@	|		174	01 111 100
125	01111101	7D	0111 1101	'	}		175	01 111 101
126	01111110	7E	0111 1110	=	~		176	01 111 110
127	01111111	7F	0111 1111	"	DEL		177	01 111 111
128	10000000	80	1000 0000				200	10 000 000
129	10000001	81	1000 0001	a			201	10 000 001
130	10000010	82	1000 0010	b			202	10 000 010
131	10000011	83	1000 0011	c			203	10 000 011
132	10000100	84	1000 0100	d			204	10 000 100
133	10000101	85	1000 0101	e			205	10 000 101
134	10000110	86	1000 0110	f			206	10 000 110
135	10000111	87	1000 0111	g			207	10 000 111
136	10001000	88	1000 1000	h			210	10 001 000
137	10001001	89	1000 1001	i			211	10 001 001
138	10001010	8A	1000 1010				212	10 001 010
139	10001011	8B	1000 1011				213	10 001 011
140	10001100	8C	1000 1100				214	10 001 100
141	10001101	8D	1000 1101				215	10 001 101
142	10001110	8E	1000 1110				216	10 001 110
143	10001111	8F	1000 1111				217	10 001 111
144	10010000	90	1001 0000				220	10 010 000
145	10010001	91	1001 0001	j			221	10 010 001
146	10010010	92	1001 0010	k			222	10 010 010
147	10010011	93	1001 0011	l			223	10 010 011
148	10010100	94	1001 0100	m			224	10 010 100
149	10010101	95	1001 0101	n			225	10 010 101
150	10010110	96	1001 0110	o			226	10 010 110
151	10010111	97	1001 0111	p			227	10 010 111
152	10011000	98	1001 1000	q			230	10 011 000
153	10011001	99	1001 1001	r			231	10 011 001
154	10011010	9A	1001 1010				232	10 011 010
155	10011011	9B	1001 1011				233	10 011 011
156	10011100	9C	1001 1100				234	10 011 100
157	10011101	9D	1001 1101				235	10 011 101
158	10011110	9E	1001 1110				236	10 011 110
159	10011111	9F	1001 1111				237	10 011 111
160	10100000	A0	1010 0000				240	10 100 000
161	10100001	A1	1010 0001	~			241	10 100 001
162	10100010	A2	1010 0010	s			242	10 100 010
163	10100011	A3	1010 0011	t			243	10 100 011
164	10100100	A4	1010 0100	u			244	10 100 100
165	10100101	A5	1010 0101	v			245	10 100 101
166	10100110	A6	1010 0110	w			246	10 100 110
167	10100111	A7	1010 0111	x			247	10 100 111

DECIMAL	BINARY	HEX	NIBBLES	EBCDIC	ASCII	CTL	OCTAL	CRUMBLES
168	10101000	A8	1010 1000	y			250	10 101 000
169	10101001	A9	1010 1001	z			251	10 101 001
170	10101010	AA	1010 1010				252	10 101 010
171	10101011	AB	1010 1011				253	10 101 011
172	10101100	AC	1010 1100				254	10 101 100
173	10101101	AD	1010 1101				255	10 101 101
174	10101110	AE	1010 1110				256	10 101 110
175	10101111	AF	1010 1111				257	10 101 111
176	10110000	B0	1011 0000				260	10 110 000
177	10110001	B1	1011 0001				261	10 110 001
178	10110010	B2	1011 0010				262	10 110 010
179	10110011	B3	1011 0011				263	10 110 011
180	10110100	B4	1011 0100				264	10 110 100
181	10110101	B5	1011 0101				265	10 110 101
182	10110110	B6	1011 0110				266	10 110 110
183	10110111	B7	1011 0111				267	10 110 111
184	10111000	B8	1011 1000				270	10 111 000
185	10111001	B9	1011 1001				271	10 111 001
186	10111010	BA	1011 1010				272	10 111 010
187	10111011	BB	1011 1011				273	10 111 011
188	10111100	BC	1011 1100				274	10 111 100
189	10111101	BD	1011 1101				275	10 111 101
190	10111110	BE	1011 1110				276	10 111 110
191	10111111	BF	1011 1111				277	10 111 111
192	11000000	C0	1100 0000	{			300	11 000 000
193	11000001	C1	1100 0001	A			301	11 000 001
194	11000010	C2	1100 0010	B			302	11 000 010
195	11000011	C3	1100 0011	C			303	11 000 011
196	11000100	C4	1100 0100	D			304	11 000 100
197	11000101	C5	1100 0101	E			305	11 000 101
198	11000110	C6	1100 0110	F			306	11 000 110
199	11000111	C7	1100 0111	G			307	11 000 111
200	11001000	C8	1100 1000	H			310	11 001 000
201	11001001	C9	1100 1001	I			311	11 001 001
202	11001010	CA	1100 1010				312	11 001 010
203	11001011	CB	1100 1011				313	11 001 011
204	11001100	CC	1100 1100				314	11 001 100
205	11001101	CD	1100 1101				315	11 001 101
206	11001110	CE	1100 1110				316	11 001 110
207	11001111	CF	1100 1111				317	11 001 111
208	11010000	D0	1101 0000	}			320	11 010 000
209	11010001	D1	1101 0001	J			321	11 010 001
210	11010010	D2	1101 0010	K			322	11 010 010
211	11010011	D3	1101 0011	L			323	11 010 011
212	11010100	D4	1101 0100	M			324	11 010 100
213	11010101	D5	1101 0101	N			325	11 010 101
214	11010110	D6	1101 0110	O			326	11 010 110
215	11010111	D7	1101 0111	P			327	11 010 111
216	11011000	D8	1101 1000	Q			330	11 011 000
217	11011001	D9	1101 1001	R			331	11 011 001
218	11011010	DA	1101 1010				332	11 011 010
219	11011011	DB	1101 1011				333	11 011 011
220	11011100	DC	1101 1100				334	11 011 100
221	11011101	DD	1101 1101				335	11 011 101
222	11011110	DE	1101 1110				336	11 011 110
223	11011111	DF	1101 1111				337	11 011 111

DECIMAL	BINARY	HEX	NIBBLES	EBCDIC	ASCII	CTL	OCTAL	CRUMBLES
224	11100000	E0	1110 0000	\			340	11 100 000
225	11100001	E1	1110 0001				341	11 100 001
226	11100010	E2	1110 0010	S			342	11 100 010
227	11100011	E3	1110 0011	T			343	11 100 011
228	11100100	E4	1110 0100	U			344	11 100 100
229	11100101	E5	1110 0101	V			345	11 100 101
230	11100110	E6	1110 0110	W			346	11 100 110
231	11100111	E7	1110 0111	X			347	11 100 111
232	11101000	E8	1110 1000	Y			350	11 101 000
233	11101001	E9	1110 1001	Z			351	11 101 001
234	11101010	EA	1110 1010				352	11 101 010
235	11101011	EB	1110 1011				353	11 101 011
236	11101100	EC	1110 1100				354	11 101 100
237	11101101	ED	1110 1101				355	11 101 101
238	11101110	EE	1110 1110				356	11 101 110
239	11101111	EF	1110 1111				357	11 101 111
240	11110000	F0	1111 0000	0			360	11 110 000
241	11110001	F1	1111 0001	1			361	11 110 001
242	11110010	F2	1111 0010	2			362	11 110 010
243	11110011	F3	1111 0011	3			363	11 110 011
244	11110100	F4	1111 0100	4			364	11 110 100
245	11110101	F5	1111 0101	5			365	11 110 101
246	11110110	F6	1111 0110	6			366	11 110 110
247	11110111	F7	1111 0111	7			367	11 110 111
248	11111000	F8	1111 1000	8			370	11 111 000
249	11111001	F9	1111 1001	9			371	11 111 001
250	11111010	FA	1111 1010				372	11 111 010
251	11111011	FB	1111 1011				373	11 111 011
252	11111100	FC	1111 1100				374	11 111 100
253	11111101	FD	1111 1101				375	11 111 101
254	11111110	FE	1111 1110				376	11 111 110
255	11111111	FF	1111 1111				377	11 111 111

The author is indebted to Ron Stevens, who wrote the clever program that generated this multipurpose chart. The program was written in Microsoft BASIC and run on an IBM PC. The grouping of the binary values for hexadecimal and octal best demonstrates the nature of these representational schemes. The chart was originally entitled "So What's a Byte?" explaining the origin of "nibbles" and "crumbles."

APPENDIX D

TSO CLISTs for Block Size and SPACE Calculation

Three TSO CLISTS are provided here to help develop efficient block sizes for fixed length records without keys. The source code for these command lists can be entered into a CLIST library. It is also obtainable on diskette for uploading to a mainframe via a suitably equipped PC, as described at the end of this appendix.

TAPEINFO, listed in Figure D.1, prompts for the length of records to be written to a tape data set and returns with the largest block size that will fit into the maximum block length limitation of 32,760 bytes. It also composes and presents the actual JCL DCB parameter needed.

DISKINFO, shown in Figure D.2, is a comprehensive CLIST that prompts first for the type of disk to which a new data set will be written—the IBM 3330, 3350, 3380, or a mixture of these—and then for the size of fixed length records that will be written to a data set. DISKINFO com-

```
          /* CLIST 'TAPEINFO'      J JANOSSY   2-24-86 */
/*--+----1----+----2----+----3----+----4----+----5----+----6----+----7----+----8
          WRITENR *** TAPEINFO CLIST AT &SYSTIME ON &SYSDATE; +
             RECORD LENGTH?
          READ &RECLEN
          SET &BLKCNT = 32760 / &RECLEN
          SET &BLKSIZ = &BLKCNT * &RECLEN
          WRITE *** BEST BLOCKING IS &BLKCNT RECORDS PER BLOCK; JCL IS:
          WRITE     // DCB=(RECFM=FB,LRECL=&RECLEN,BLKSIZE=&BLKSIZ)
```

FIGURE D.1.   TAPEINFO TSO command list for tape data set block size computation

putes the most efficient block size and asks for an estimate of the number of records to be housed. It composes the DCB and SPACE statements using a primary allocation large enough to house the estimated number of records and allowing an amount equal to 20% of the primary amount for each secondary allocation. It also computes and displays the efficiency of disk storage on the device specified; in the case of the compromise blocking of 6,233 bytes, effective for a mixture of 3330, 3350, and 3380 disk units, it provides a comparison of efficiency on all three units. This CLIST requires several terminal screen lines and is best invoked from TSO/ISPF function 6 or TSO READY mode.

DISKJCL, listed in Figure D.3, is a stripped down version of DISKINFO that uses a single line prompt for disk type, record length, and estimate of records to be housed. It generates the DCB and SPACE statements that meet the requirements, and an indication of efficiency on the type of unit specified. DISKJCL is the most convenient to invoke using the TSO passthrough feature on the command line when actually composing JCL. Its interactions are limited to the few extended message overlay lines at the bottom of the screen, and it does not produce a "***" bottom of screen prompt until it finishes execution.

The TSO 3.2 allocate function or an IEFBR14 step in a batch run can be used to allocate a CLIST data set. Common characteristics are RECFM = VB for variable length blocked records and LRECL = 255 for a maximum size TSO-editable line. Block size is specified as 6,233, track size on the disk to be used, or 23,476 on the IBM 3380 disk. The invocation of a CLIST can be assigned to a PF key, thus making it especially easy to use from any point in TSO/ISPF.

A distribution diskette with the CLIST source code also carries versions of these computational aids in a form directly executable on IBM PCs or compatibles, and other items from this book. The diskette is available postpaid for $6.00 (US) from:

Practical MVS JCL Diskette
P.O.Box 46078
Chicago, Illinois 60646

```
          /* CLIST 'DISKINFO'      J JANOSSY   8-24-86 */
/*--+----1----+----2----+----3----+----4----+----5----+----6----+----7----+*/
          SET &SECFRAC = 5        /* THIS IS 20% FOR SECONDARY ALLOCATION */
          WRITE *** DISKINFO CLIST FOR DATA SET SPACE AT &SYSTIME +
          ON &SYSDATE
     MENU: -
          WRITE            1 - IBM 3330
          WRITE            2 - IBM 3350
          WRITE            3 - IBM 3380
          WRITE            4 - COMPROMISE BLOCKING, OK FOR 3330/50/80
          WRITENR    COMPUTATION OPTION?
     SELECT: -
          READ &OPT
          IF &OPT EQ 1 THEN DO
             SET &DISK = 3330
             SET &BLK  = 13030
             SET &TCAP = 13030
             GOTO OPTOK
             END
          IF &OPT EQ 2 THEN DO
             SET &DISK = 3350
             SET &BLK  = 19069
             SET &TCAP = 19069
             GOTO OPTOK
             END
          IF &OPT EQ 3 THEN DO
             SET &DISK = 3380
             SET &BLK  = 23476     /* CAN'T USE 47,476 SINCE 32,767 I/O LIMIT */
                                   /* SO WE SETTLE FOR TWO BLOCKS/TRK MAX     */
             SET &TCAP = 47476
             GOTO OPTOK
             END
          IF &OPT EQ 4 THEN DO
             SET &DISK = COMPROMISE
             SET &BLK  = 6233
             GOTO OPTOK
             END
     OPTBAD: DO
          WRITE *** INVALID SELECTION
          WRITE
          GOTO MENU
          END
     OPTOK: DO
          IF &DISK = COMPROMISE THEN -
             WRITENR *** COMPROMISE TARGET OF &BLK USED, REC LEN? (NO COMMAS)
          ELSE -
             WRITENR *** TRACK SIZE TARGET OF &BLK USED, REC LEN? (NO COMMAS)
          END
     GETLEN: -
          READ &RECLEN
          IF &RECLEN GT &BLK THEN DO
             WRITE >>> RECORD LENGTH EXCEEDS &BLK
             WRITE      RECHECK YOUR FIGURES AND START OVER
             WRITE      NOTE: TRACK OVERFLOW IS NOT DESIRABLE
             EXIT
             END
     COMPUTE: -
          SET &RECPBLK = &BLK / &RECLEN
          SET &BLKSIZ = &RECPBLK * &RECLEN
          WRITE      BLOCK SIZE IS &BLKSIZ, WITH &RECPBLK RECORDS PER BLOCK
     JCLHELP: -
          WRITENR *** ESTIMATED RECORDS IN DATA SET? (NO COMMAS)
          READ &RECNO
```

FIGURE D.2. DISKINFO TSO command list for disk data set block size and DCB/SPACE JCL composition (*continues next page*)

```
        SET &BLKNEED = ( &RECNO / &RECPBLK ) + 1
        SET &SECNEED = ( &BLKNEED / &SECFRAC ) + 1
        WRITE    DATA SET SHOULD BE ALLOCATED WITH AT LEAST &BLKNEED BLOCKS
        WRITE *** WORKABLE JCL FOR THIS IS:
        WRITE    // DCB=(RECFM=FB,LRECL=&RECLEN,BLKSIZE=&BLKSIZ),
        WRITE    // SPACE=(&BLKSIZ,(&BLKNEED,&SECNEED),RLSE)
STATS: -
    IF &DISK = 3330 OR &DISK = COMPROMISE THEN DO
        SET &BLKPTRK = 0
        IF &BLKSIZ LE 13030 THEN SET &BLKPTRK = &BLKPTRK + 1
        IF &BLKSIZ LE  6447 THEN SET &BLKPTRK = &BLKPTRK + 1
        IF &BLKSIZ LE  4253 THEN SET &BLKPTRK = &BLKPTRK + 1
        IF &BLKSIZ LE  3156 THEN SET &BLKPTRK = &BLKPTRK + 1
        IF &BLKSIZ LE  2498 THEN SET &BLKPTRK = &BLKPTRK + 1   /* NEVER */
        SET &BPT3330 = &BLKPTRK
        END
    IF &DISK = 3350 OR &DISK = COMPROMISE THEN DO
        SET &BLKPTRK = 0
        IF &BLKSIZ LE 19069 THEN SET &BLKPTRK = &BLKPTRK + 1
        IF &BLKSIZ LE  9442 THEN SET &BLKPTRK = &BLKPTRK + 1
        IF &BLKSIZ LE  6233 THEN SET &BLKPTRK = &BLKPTRK + 1
        IF &BLKSIZ LE  4628 THEN SET &BLKPTRK = &BLKPTRK + 1
        IF &BLKSIZ LE  3665 THEN SET &BLKPTRK = &BLKPTRK + 1
        IF &BLKSIZ LE  3024 THEN SET &BLKPTRK = &BLKPTRK + 1   /* NEVER */
        SET &BPT3350 = &BLKPTRK
        END
    IF &DISK = 3380 OR &DISK = COMPROMISE THEN DO
        SET &BLKPTRK = 0
        IF &BLKSIZ LE 23476 THEN SET &BLKPTRK = &BLKPTRK + 2   /* 2/TRK */
        IF &BLKSIZ LE 14476 THEN SET &BLKPTRK = &BLKPTRK + 1
        IF &BLKSIZ LE 11476 THEN SET &BLKPTRK = &BLKPTRK + 1
        IF &BLKSIZ LE  9076 THEN SET &BLKPTRK = &BLKPTRK + 1
        IF &BLKSIZ LE  7476 THEN SET &BLKPTRK = &BLKPTRK + 1
        IF &BLKSIZ LE  6356 THEN SET &BLKPTRK = &BLKPTRK + 1
        IF &BLKSIZ LE  5492 THEN SET &BLKPTRK = &BLKPTRK + 1
        IF &BLKSIZ LE  4820 THEN SET &BLKPTRK = &BLKPTRK + 1
        IF &BLKSIZ LE  4276 THEN SET &BLKPTRK = &BLKPTRK + 1
        IF &BLKSIZ LE  3860 THEN SET &BLKPTRK = &BLKPTRK + 1
        IF &BLKSIZ LE  3476 THEN SET &BLKPTRK = &BLKPTRK + 1
        IF &BLKSIZ LE  3188 THEN SET &BLKPTRK = &BLKPTRK + 1
        IF &BLKSIZ LE  2932 THEN SET &BLKPTRK = &BLKPTRK + 1   /* NEVER */
        SET &BPT3380 = &BLKPTRK
        END
    IF &DISK = COMPROMISE THEN DO
        SET &EFF3330 = ( &BPT3330 * &BLKSIZ * 100 ) / 13030
        SET &TRT3330 = ( &BLKNEED / &BPT3330 ) + 1
/* */
        SET &EFF3350 = ( &BPT3350 * &BLKSIZ * 100 ) / 19069
        SET &TRT3350 = ( &BLKNEED / &BPT3350 ) + 1
/* */
        SET &EFF3380 = ( &BPT3380 * &BLKSIZ * 100 ) / 46476
        SET &TRT3380 = ( &BLKNEED / &BPT3380 ) + 1
/* */
        WRITE    EFFICIENCY STATISTICS FOR &RECNO RECORDS +
            USING &BLKSIZ BLOCKSIZE:
        WRITE    3330: &EFF3330%       3350: &EFF3350%        3380: &EFF3380%
        WRITE    TRKS: &TRT3330    TRKS: &TRT3350    TRKS: &TRT3380
        END
    ELSE DO
        SET &EFF = ( &BLKPTRK * &BLKSIZ * 100 ) / &TCAP
        SET &TRTOT = ( &BLKNEED / &BLKPTRK ) + 1
        WRITE    THIS IS &EFF% EFFICIENT DISK UTILIZATION AND
        WRITE    A TOTAL OF &TRTOT TRACKS WILL BE REQUIRED
        END
    END /*END OF CLIST*/
```

FIGURE D.2. (*last part*)

```
        /* CLIST 'DISKJCL'        J JANOSSY   2-24-86 */
/*--+----1----+----2----+----3----+----4----+----5----+----6----+----7----+*/
        SET &SECFRAC = 5          /* THIS IS 20% FOR SECONDARY ALLOCATION */
    MENU: -
    WRITENR ENTER DISK OR "ANY", LRECL, #RECS, EG., 3350 80 1000 ===>
    SELECT: -
        READ &OPT, &RECLEN, &RECNO
        IF &OPT EQ 3330 THEN DO
            SET &DISK = 3330
            SET &BLK  = 13030
            SET &TCAP = 13030
            GOTO GETLEN
            END
        IF &OPT EQ 3350 THEN DO
            SET &DISK = 3350
            SET &BLK  = 19069
            SET &TCAP = 19069
            GOTO GETLEN
            END
        IF &OPT EQ 3380 THEN DO
            SET &DISK = 3380
            SET &BLK  = 23476   /* CAN'T USE 47,476 SINCE 32,767 I/O LIMIT */
                                /* SO WE SETTLE FOR TWO BLOCKS/TRK MAX     */
            SET &TCAP = 47476
            GOTO GETLEN
            END
        IF &OPT EQ ANY THEN DO
            SET &DISK = COMPROMISE
            SET &BLK  = 6233
            GOTO GETLEN
            END
    OPTBAD: DO
        WRITE *** INVALID ENTRY, MUST BE 3330, 3350, 3380, OR WORD "ANY"
        GOTO MENU
        END
    GETLEN: -
        IF &RECLEN GT &BLK THEN DO
            WRITE >>> RECORD LENGTH EXCEEDS &BLK, CHECK VALUES, START OVER
            EXIT
            END
    COMPUTE: -
        SET &RECPBLK = &BLK / &RECLEN
        SET &BLKSIZ = &RECPBLK * &RECLEN
        SET &BLKNEED = ( &RECNO / &RECPBLK ) + 1
        SET &SECNEED = ( &BLKNEED / &SECFRAC ) + 1
        WRITE      // DCB=(RECFM=FB,LRECL=&RECLEN,BLKSIZE=&BLKSIZ),
        WRITE      // SPACE=(&BLKSIZ,(&BLKNEED,&SECNEED),RLSE)
        END  /*END OF CLIST*/
```

FIGURE D.3. DISKJCL TSO command list for disk data set for DCB/SPACE JCL composition

===== APPENDIX **E** =====

IBM Utility Return Code Summary

IBM utility programs customarily post a user return code of 0000 if execution is entirely successful. The various utilities post return codes of 0004, 0008, 0012 and higher, in increments of 4, when problems or unusual conditions have been encountered. *Different utilities confer different meanings on return code values,* as summarized in Figure E.1.

Utility	Purpose	Return codes and their meaning
DFSORT	General purpose sort/merge utility	0000 Successful execution 0004 (Not used) 0008 (Not used) 0012 (Not used) 0016 I/O error or sequence error; terminated 0020 //SYSOUT DDname or message DDname missing
IDCAMS	Multipurpose Access Method Services utility to copy, print, dump, catalog, uncatalog, rename data sets, delete unexpired data sets and PDS members, define, alter and delete VSAM data sets, list catalog entries; create, alter, and delete generation data groups bases.	0000 Successful execution 0004 Problem in a non-critical function 0008 Error in requested function, bypassed 0012 Serious logical error, function abandoned 0016 Severe error, command processing terminated
IEBCOMPR	Compare records or whole PDSs	0000 Successful completion 0004 (Not used) 0008 Unequal comparison, processing continue 0012 Unrecoverable error, terminated 0016 User routine passed 0016 (rarely used)
IEBCOPY	Copy or merge partitioned data sets, select members	0000 Successful completion 0004 Recoverable error; investigate 0008 Unrecoverable error, terminated
IEBDG	Create test data in patterns using control statement coding that is tedious and fussy; output created is of limited variability.	0000 Successful completion 0004 User routine passed 0016 (rarely used) 0008 Error in control statements; continues 0012 Error during I/O, terminated 0016 Unrecoverable error, terminated

FIGURE E.1. IBM utility program usage and return code meanings (*continues on several pages*)

Utility	Description	Code	Meaning
IEBEDIT	Manipulate JCL statements in batch mode	0000	Successful completion
		0004	Error, output may not be usable
		0008	Unrecoverable I/O or control statement error
		0012	(Not used)
		0016	(Not used)
IEBGENER	Copy and reformat records	0000	Successful completion
		0004	Warning error
		0008	User requested label processing only
		0012	Unrecoverable error, terminated
		0016	User routine passed 0016 (rarely used)
IEBIMAGE	Create and maintain forms control buffer (FCB) modules in SYS1.IMAGELIB control data set, electronically replacing physical carriage control tapes for printers; also create or modify printer character tables for certain laser printers, also housed in SYS1.IMAGELIB.	0000	Successful completion
		0004	Operations performed, exceptions encountered
		0008	Something not performed, investigate messages
		0012	Severe errors, possible termination
		0016	Catastrophic exception, execution terminated
		0020	//SYSPRINT data set can't be opened, terminated
		0024	Control statement/parameter error, terminated
IEBISAM	Copy ISAM data set to sequential data set	0000	Successful completion
		0004	User routine passed 0004 or 0012
		0008	Error terminated the operation
		0012	User routine passed value not 00, 04, 08, or 12
		0016	Error terminated the operation
IEBPTPCH	Produce formatted print from records	0000	Successful completion
		0004	Data set empty or PDS specified has no members
		0008	PDS member specified does not exist
		0012	Fatal error or flawed user routine return code
		0016	User routine passed 0016 (rarely used)
IEBUPDTE	Modify lines in sequential or partitioned data set in batch mode.	0000	Successful completion
		0004	Incorrect syntax or use of control statement
		0008	(Not used)
		0012	Unrecoverable error, step terminated
		0016	User routine passed 0016 (rarely used)

FIGURE E.1. (con't.)

IEHATLAS	Recover data from damaged disk volume; done by operations personnel.	0000 Successful completion, alternate track assigned
		0004 Device does not have software-assignable tracks
		0008 All alternate tracks are in use
		0012 Requested main memory not available
		0016 I/O error in alternate track assignment
		0020 Error, not data check or missing address marker
		0024 Error in VTOC Format 4 DSCB record
		0028 Alternate track information not reliable
		0032 Error in count field of last record on track
		0036 Errors in home address or in record zero
		0040 Errors even after alternate track assignment
		0044 (Not used)
		0048 No error found and no alternate assigned
		0052 I/O error, cannot reexecute the EXCP for it
		0056 System does not support track overflow
		0060 Track address does not belong to data set
IEHDASDR	Initialize disk volumes, assign alternate tracks for defective ones, dump or restore disk contents (done by operations personnel).	0000 Successful completion
		0004 Unusual condition but result satisfactory
		0008 Operation did not complete successfully
		0012 (Not used)
		0016 Error invoking, or opening input or //SYSPRINT
IEHINITT	Apply volume label and tape mark to a tape (done by operations personnel).	0000 Successful and //SYSPRINT present
		0004 Successful but //SYSPRINT DDname missing
		0008 Errors, reported at //SYSPRINT
		0012 Errors, but //SYSPRINT DDname missing
		0016 Error in reading control statement or data set

FIGURE E.1. (con't.)

404

IEHLIST	List PDS members, disk VTOC	0000	Successful completion
		0004	(Not used)
		0008	Error encountered, request bypassed, continues
		0012	Permanent I/O error encountered, terminated
		0016	Unrecoverable read error, terminated
IEHMOVE	Move or copy data sets including OS catalogs but not ISAM or VSAM data sets, renaming or replacing specified PDS members.	0000	Successful completion
		0004	Specified function not completed, continues
		0008	Abnormal condition but recovery completed
		0012	Unrecoverable error, terminated
		0016	Impossible to open //SYSIN or //SYSPRINT
IEHPROGM	Create, modify, and delete OS passwords (other functions now handled by IDCAMS).	0000	Successful completion
		0004	Syntax error in control statement name field or in PARM field of the EXEC statement
		0008	Incorrect control statement or invalid request
		0012	I/O error on disk VTOC, //SYSIN, or //SYSPRINT
		0016	Unrecoverable error, terminated

FIGURE E.1. *(last part)*

APPENDIX F

System Completion Codes and Subcodes

This appendix provides independent coverage of the meaning of MVS system completion codes and corrective measures to remedy the errors with which they are associated. The listings here are more extensive than those found in manuals and have been developed for an audience that is familiar with higher level languages rather than IBM assembler.

The frequently encountered program exception codes 0C1, 0C2, 0C3, 0C4, 0C5, 0C6, 0C7, and 0C8 through 0CF are simply 15 of the system completion codes. Extended explanations of these codes and suggestions for resolution of errors that produce them begin on page 412.

MVS and MVS/XA communicate the basis for job failures via a three-position hexadecimal value known as the system completion code. This values appears as 000 when a job step has completed successfully and is not generated at all when execution of a step is skipped. When a step abnormally ends, the system completion code appears on the job log in this form:

```
MVS:          Snnn

MVS/XA:       ABEND CODE SYSTEM=nnn
```

The system completion code is also contained in error message lines within the body of the system allocation/deallocation report. Figure F.1 describes the fields typically found in error message lines to aid in identifying the nature of a problem.

The range of 001-FFF constitutes 4095 values, but MVS uses only approximately 480 system completion code values, some of which deal with obsolete access methods and system software. Some of the still-current values are followed by a one to three position hexadecimal reason code, "rc." Certain software such as fourth generation languages, security systems, and tape management systems generate other values in the system completion code field.

The COBOL compiler can cause to be issued one of 10 special user return codes that function like system completion codes. Although they are not system completion codes, these user return codes are generated by successfully compiled and executing programs in response to internal problems. This summary includes VSCOBOL compiler initiated code values, such as 0519, with an individual depth of treatment governed by the applicability of a code to an application programmer. These four position values occur in the user return code field, not in the system completion code field.

The IBM reference manuals dealing with system completion codes and error messages are:

MVS/370 Message Library: System Codes, GC38-1008. Full listing of all MVS and MVS/XA system completion codes.

MVS/370 Message Library: System Messages
Volume 1   Messages prefixed by AHL thru IEB, GC28-1374
Volume 2   Messages prefixed by IEC thru ISG, GC28-1375

The messages contained in the last two volumes are referenced directly by the prefix and message number that appears on job log and allocation/deallocation lines. These message identifiers take the form "IECnnnI."

001   RECORD LENGTH/BLOCK SIZE DISCREPANCY OR I/O ERROR

-0   A discrepancy exists between the record length and block size specified in the program or JCL and these values in the data set label. Examine and correct the JCL or program. This can occur in a subtle way in COBOL if the "BLOCK

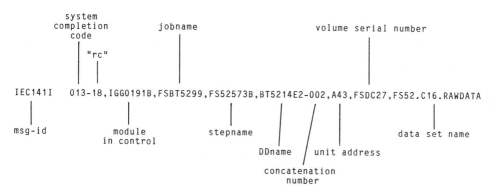

FIGURE F.1.   MVS error message line content and meaning

CONTAINS 0 RECORDS" statement is omitted from the FD for a file that is blocked. This phrase, when present, indicates that blocking is specified externally in JCL. The blocking defaults to *one record per block* if the phrase is omitted, which conflicts with the actual blocking of the data set if it is blocked.

-1   A write was attempted for a data set opened for input, a read was attempted for a data set opened for output, data set concatenation was attempted for data sets of unlike blocking factor or other attributes, a read was attempted after end of file was reached, or for format U (undefined) type data sets the logical record length was not specified. Concatenation of data sets of the same type but different record lengths is possible if they are arranged in descending order of block size in the concatenation.

-2   Error detected in closing the data set.

-3   Queued sequential access method (QSAM) error which could not be resolved.

-4   An error occurred and the operating system was attempting to follow the dictates of the EROPT parameter of the DCB, normally used by the job stream designer to specify a customized error handling routine. The EROPT value was in its default state of ABE (for ABEnd) or contained an invalid value. This can have the unfortunate effect of masking the rc value which might otherwise have been presented. *See the note for value 1.*

-5   Additional I/O was attempted after end of file was reached.

The specific diagnostic messages associated with the rc values are typical of the low-level specificity of system completion codes. For code 001 the basis for the abend is usually rather simple. The problem lies in damaged tape or disk media, a hardware error on a tape or disk drive, conflicting record or block size specifications in the program or JCL, or incorrect logic attempting to read after end of data set has been reached. Incorrectly created tapes lacking an end of file marker can also cause this problem, especially when the input tape was created on a key-to-disk system on which the creating program itself had to write the end of file mark explicitly. With unlabeled tapes, such as those often used to convey data from key-to-disk entry operations, there is no internal tape identification that MVS can use to verify that a tape mounted for the job was actually the one specified. An incorrect tape that carries unrelated data may have been mounted for the job; the record length or blocking of the tape does not match that of the required tape.

If there is an IEA000I message associated with the 001 completion code, a hardware error is the problem; notify computer operations or resubmit the job. If no IEA000I message is present and the I/O medium is tape, the tape may be dirty; having it cleaned and resubmitting the job may resolve the problem. Examine JCL and program logic to make sure no discrepancy in record and block size exists and that reading after end of file is not inadvertently attempted. If the input tape is not labeled, verify that the correct tape was mounted for the job.

013 CONFLICTING DCB PARAMETERS WHEN OPENING DATA SET

-04 ASCII processing not available on the system.

-0C Dynamic buffering requires nonzero buffer length.

-10 Null (dummy) data set needs buffer space; specify BLKSIZE or BUFL greater than zero.

-14 DCB must specify a partitioned data set; code DSORG as PO or POU or imply PDS organization by use of directory block parameter in SPACE specification.

-18 Specified member is not found in the partitioned data set.

-1C I/O error while searching directory of partitioned data set.

-20 Block size is not a multiple of record length or is incorrect for variable length records.

Ordinarily this occurs because of an inconsistency in the JCL DCB parameter between LRECL and BLKSIZE. It can develop in a subtle way in a COBOL program in which the AFTER ADVANCING phrase is used erroneously in connection with records written to a data set rather than printed. If the ADV compiler PARM option is in effect, printlines are coded at 132 bytes, not 133 bytes, in the FD. The compiler, however, prefaces each record output with the AFTER ADVANCING option with the additional carriage control byte, thus making the records emerging from the program 133 bytes in length. *For ADV the records written with the AFTER ADVANCING phrase are actually one byte longer than coded in the FD.* In this case if the BLKSIZE specified in JCL is a multiple of 132 instead of 133, it will conflict because the program's record length specification will take precedence over the record length coded in JCL. The AFTER ADVANCING phrase should be used only with printlines being written out, but the real culprit in this subtle error is the ADV compiler parm option.

Ifthe "NOADV" option is in effect, COBOL does not add the carriage control byte to the coded record length; instead the carriage control character is inserted by the compiler into the first byte of the record.

-34 Record length versus block size is inconsistent or null output data set needs buffer space. Note that requirements for record length and block size depend on the specific file organization being used.

-4C DCB is corrupted, buffer is too short for the record length specified in JCL in the DCB; block size specification is invalid.

-50 Attempt to open a printer for other than output.

-60 Block size is not equal to record length for unblocked data set.

-64 Null data set (DUMMY or NULLFILE) must be specified as sequential (PS), either BSAM or QSAM.

-68 Block size cannot be greater than 32,760.

-6C Track overflow was requested with RECFM = T in the DCB but the device used does not support it.

-70 Inconsistent DCB specifications for data set; tape recording technique cannot be specified for 9 track tapes, ASCII and EBCDIC tape options cannot be mixed, and OPTCD = Q to convert ASCII to EBCDIC can be indicated only on tape data sets. Can also be experienced if trying to read an ISAM data set with the sort utility.

-8C RECFM must be specified for BDAM data set.

-A4 SYSIN or SYSOUT data sets must be physical sequential data set (PS) organization.

-A8 Invalid record format for SYSIN or SYSOUT data set.

-B4 Conflict between DCB and OPEN macro parameters.

-BC Repositioning or updating a spooled data set such as SYSIN or SYSOUT is not permitted; DCBs for these data sets carry invalid options.

-C0 SYSIN or SYSOUT data set could not be opened. Under JES2 this happens when a subsystem JCL facility (SJF) incurs an error. Under JES3 it is experienced when a DD statement specifies a reserved DDname.

-CC Open of IBM 3800 printing subsystem failed; message IEC162I also issued. See SETPRT macro instruction information in *OS/VS2 Data Management Macro Instructions*, GC26-3873.

-D0 Partitioned data set (PDS) cannot carry record format of FBS or FS.

-E4 Number of concatenated partitioned data sets (PDS) exceeds the limit of 16.

The actions to resolve a completion code of 013 depend on the specific reason code value received. Check the relevant part of the DCB parameter in JCL and the OPEN, FD, and SELECT/ASSIGN statements in the program itself. *The problem may lie not in the JCL but in the lack of presence of a data set on the system, as with reason code 18.*

Note.   The error detection occurs *after* the "dcb merge" and therefore the error may be due to specifications contained in the program, the JCL DCB parameter, the data set label, or the installation-defined default for them. The foregoing information is stated in the same form as DCB is referenced in IBM manuals. Most of the references to DCB do not mean the JCL DCB parameter but rather the actual data control block formed in memory by MVS or the assembler DCB macro instruction. The traditional imprecision in terms in this area, dating from days when assembler application programs that used the DCB macro instruction were commonplace, can and does lead to confusion.

04E DB2 INTERNAL ERROR

A connected user task or a task internal to the DB2 database has been terminated because MVS has detected an internal DB2 error. Information may be displayed at the user's terminal and in a record written to SYS1.LOGREC, the system error log data set. Refer to *IBM DATABASE 2 Messages and Codes*, SC26-4113 for problem resolution suggestions.

04F DB2 INTERNAL ERROR OR SYSTEM ERROR

This message may be received after one or more error messages have been issued. It may indicate an internal problem in DATABASE 2 logic or failure in an MVS subsystem. A message may have been written to SYS1.LOGREC for analysis and message DSNV086E may appear on the system console. This problem requires system programmer attention that involves the use of an SVC dump, system termination dump, examination of the Common Service Area (CSA) used by MVS, and reference to *IBM DATABASE 2 Messages and Codes*, SC26-4113.

0C1 OPERATION EXCEPTION

At the point of abend the machine is being directed to perform a machine language instruction that is not valid or that hasn't been implemented on the particular model of computer. This can occur as a result of a variety of different situations, all of which lead to an erroneous sequence of control flow within the machine language load module representing the program.

A DD statement may be missing or the DDname spelled differently than in the program. Extra DD statements in the JCL for a step are not regarded by MVS as an error, but a DD statement needed but not present is a fatal error. Subtle ways in which this can occur include the following:

- Use of DISPLAY, TRACE, or EXHIBIT in a COBOL program directs output to a DDname SYSOUT. Check to see if this DDname is present in your JCL for the step. The DD statement is required even if the verb is present but not executed.
- The SORT verb may cause an 0C1 if the sort was not able to complete normally. This may occur if the sort output procedure was exited before all of the records in the sort work area had been RETURNed to the program.
- Use of the SORTMSG option with the SORT verb requires placement of an associated DD statement in the JCL for the step. If SORTMSG is not used, the SORT verb writes its messages out to SYSOUT, which must then be present as a DD name.
- The value after the AFTER ADVANCING phrase in a COBOL WRITE statement is outside the range of zero to 99.
- A subscript value that exceeds the bounds of the table with which it is associated causes access to an incorrect memory location.
- A data set not open when an I/O was directed on it.
- Files have not been closed before a STOP RUN is executed.

Check diagnostic messages that may indicate a missing DD statement. If a message is not present, check file operations in program logic; if the problem is not there, determine the instruction on which the failure occurred by using installation dump analysis aids or raw dump analysis techniques and debug the program statement on which the failure is indicated. See also 0C5.

0C2 PRIVILEGED OPERATION EXCEPTION

The program has attempted to invoke a machine language operation available only to specially authorized programs. This can occur if:

- a DD statement is missing or incorrect;
- a data set was not open at the time an I/O was directed on it;
- a subscript is uninitialized or carrying a value out of bounds for the table with which it is associated;
- in assembler, an explicit attempt is made to invoke a privileged instruction.

Examine JCL first, then program logic if necessary. An 0C2 may develop in circumstances similar to an 0C1; the origin of both is the erroneous interpretation of a portion of program content as a machine instruction. See also 0C5.

0C3 EXECUTE EXCEPTION

In the machine code that results from the compile/link edit process one execute instruction is attempting to invoke another execute instruction. This results from seriously incorrect program logic that must be corrected and may occur in circumstances similar to those resulting in an 0C1 or 0C2.

0C4 PROTECTION EXCEPTION

The program is attempting to access a memory address that is not within the memory area that the program is authorized to use. The example in which this can occur include those involving:

- an incorrect or missing DD statement;
- a subscript or index that is not initialized or has taken on a value outside the bounds of the table with which it is associated;
- an attempt to read an unopened file;
- the block size and record size incorrectly specified as the same for variable length records;
- a missing SELECT statement in a COBOL program;
- an incorrect COBOL ASSIGN clause system name;
- omission of the USING phrase after the procedure division heading in a called module.

Check JCL first; then if necessary perform an intensive analysis of program logic. An 0C4 can be a particularly tedious abend to analyze. Its incidence can be minimized with good program design. Older "bowl of spaghetti" programs undergoing maintenance present especially high potential for 0C4s if they make heavy use of multiple-subscripted tables. See also 0C5.

0C5   ADDRESSING EXCEPTION

The program is attempting to access a memory location which is outside the bounds of available real storage on the machine. This can be caused by

- a missing or incorrect DD statement or erroneous DCB values;
- a data set not being open at the time an I/O was directed on it;
- reference to record fields in the file section of a COBOL program before an output file is opened, before reading the first record from an input file, or after execution of the AT END option for an input file;
- a subscript or index out of bounds for the table with which it is associated;
- an uninitialized subscript or index;
- an attempt to close a data set a second time;
- improper exit from a performed paragraph, which can occur when logic within the paragraph does a GO TO exit but the paragraph had not been performed through the exit;
- incorrect CALLed module parameters or coding.

Check the JCL for the failed program first. If this is correct, examine the program for appropriate file open and close logic. If the problem is not resolved by these actions, perform an intensive review of logic within the program that affects subscript and/or index manipulations and within called modules.

0C6   SPECIFICATION EXCEPTION

This exception indicates a problem with the alignment of a data field on an appropriate word boundary. The IBM 360/370/43xx/308x/3090/9370 architecture provides single-byte orientation and data accessibility, but certain operations require operands to be placed at the boundaries of four-byte words; for example, binary (COMP) fields must be aligned on word boundaries. This is accomplished in COBOL by placing the fields at the 01 level or specifying the SYNC working storage option for a field. An 0C6 can arise when the following applies:

- COMP fields are used for record storage, as opposed to use for internal program values only, and they are positioned without regard to forcing alignment on word boundaries. If used in records, COMP fields require special techniques such as positioning with unused slack bytes or definition as PIC X quantities with decoding done by special actions using working storage fields.
- Inconsistent usage of linkage area fields exists between a calling program and a called program, involving COMP fields.
- The multiplier or divisor in a decimal arithmetic operation is larger than 15 digits and a sign.
- In assembler a floating-point register other than 0, 2, 4, or 6 was specified.
- A subscript takes on a value outside the bounds of the table with which it is associated.
- An improper exit was made from a performed paragraph; this can occur when logic within the paragraph does a GO TO exit but the paragraph had not been performed through the exit.
- A missing or incorrect DD statement.

Check the working storage definition of binary fields. It is also possible to encounter this completion code because of an incorrect or missing DD statement in JCL or because of a subscript value out of appropriate bounds. These errors may lead to incorrect processing that will attempt to involve a data field in an arithmetic operation that requires special address alignment.

0C7   DATA EXCEPTION

The single most commonly experienced abend code, an 0C7 indicates an attempt to perform an arithmetic operation on nonnumeric data. In low-level terms the machine has been directed to perform processing that results in the involvement of inappropriate data in a decimal operation. Decimal in this context is synonomous with COBOL's COMP-3 packed decimal format and the fixed decimal specification of PL/I.

Decimal operations are inherent to arithmetic and the formatted presentation of numbers with COBOL print "pictures," even if COMP-3 format is not involved, because arithmetic and formatted print invokes compiler-generated steps that involve conversion to decimal format. 0C7s can also result from incorrect input data to a program that is not performing sufficient numeric testing on it before attempting arithmetic. More subtle causal factors include a subscript value out of bounds, an invalid index value, or uninitialized working storage fields. *The movement of nonnumeric data to a COBOL formatted output picture such as $ZZZ,ZZZ.99 is a common cause of an 0C7.* Program logic is at fault and must be corrected or enhanced with additional input data validation.

0C8   OVERFLOW EXCEPTION, FIXED POINT

A computed value is too large to be accommodated by the indicated receiving field. This can be caused by division by a value that is too small, repeated computation involving the same fields within a loop, or multiplication of numbers that are too large. COBOL normally traps this interruption and truncates a result rather than, in the case of PIC 9 and COMP-3 fields, allowing it to cause an abend. Field sizes within the program should be expanded.

0C9   DIVIDE EXCEPTION, FIXED POINT

A value that results from a division is too large to be accommodated by the indicated receiving field. This is usually caused by division by zero but can also be triggered by division by a value that is too small or repeated computation involving the same fields within a loop. A logic test may be warranted before a division operation to identify the occurrence of a zero divisor, and the division not made if a zero divisor is detected.

0CA   OVERFLOW EXCEPTION, DECIMAL

A computed value is too large to be accommodated by the indicated receiving field. This can be caused by division by a value that is too small, repeated computation involving the same fields within a loop, or multiplication of numbers that are too large. COBOL normally traps this interruption and truncates a result rather than, in the case of PIC 9 and COMP-3 fields, allowing it to cause an abend. Field sizes within the program should be expanded.

0CB   DIVIDE EXCEPTION, DECIMAL

A value that results from a division is too large to be accommodated by the indicated receiving field. This is usually caused by division by zero but can also be triggered by division by a value that is too small or by repeated computation involving the same fields within a loop. A logic test may be warranted before a division operation to identify the occurrence of a zero divisor, and the division not made if a zero divisor is detected.

0CC   OVERFLOW EXCEPTION, EXPONENT

A value resulting from a floating point computation is too large to be accommodated by the receiving field. This can be caused by division by a value that is too small, repeated computation involving the same fields within a loop, or multiplication of numbers that are too large. Program logic must be corrected.

0CD   UNDERFLOW EXCEPTION, EXPONENT

The result of a floating point (COMP-1 or COMP-2) computation is so small that it cannot be represented. This may occur in multiplication by too small a number, division by too large a number, or a program loop involving repeated computation with the same quantities. Program logic must be corrected. COMP-1 and COMP-2 data types are associated with scientific notation and are rarely used in the business environment.

0CE   SIGNIFICANCE EXCEPTION

A computation involving floating point COMP-1 or COMP-2 data resulted in an absolute zero quantity, one possessing an all zero fraction. Program logic must be corrected. COMP-1 and COMP-2 data types are associated with scientific notation and are rarely used in the business environment.

0CF   DIVIDE EXCEPTION, FLOATING POINT

Division by a floating point number with a zero fraction has been attempted. Program logic must be corrected to avoid division when a divisor is zero. Insert logic to test the divisor for a zero value before the division is done; if the divisor is zero, do not execute the division.

106   LINK, LOAD, ATTACH, OR XCTL PROGRAM IS NOT LOADABLE

-0B   A FETCH processing error.
-0C   Not enough memory available for FETCH to do GETMAIN for the module or control blocks.
-0D   Invalid record type in load module.
-0E   Invalid address in load module.
-0F   I/O error or load module PDS is corrupted.

For reason code -0C the region size is most likely too small. For TSO use the SIZE(2000) option or a greater value. For batch jobs use a larger region on the JOB card, such as REGION=2048K. For other rc values recreate the load module.

117   CLOSE I/O ERROR ON BSAM DATA SET, SVC 23

-04   An error in writing the file mark occurred on the direct access device.

-08, -10, -14, -1C, -20, -24, -28, -2C, -30:   an I/O error occurred during tape positioning.

-34   The extent number in the data control block indicates a value higher than the number of extents in the data set and the location to write the file mark could not be determined.

A defective device or volume is likely to be the cause of the 117 except with reason code 34, for which corruption of the data control block is indicated. If the reason code is not 34, rerun the job and specify a different device or volume. For reason code 34 correct your assembler code.

122   THE OPERATOR CANCELLED THE JOB AND REQUESTED A DUMP; YOU MUST ASK THE OPERATOR WHY.

* The program was producing an abnormal number of error messages.
* A higher priority job had to be scheduled and needed resources the job was holding.
* The program needed a resource that was not available.
* The program appeared to be stalled in a wait state.
* The program was in an apparent loop, not outputting or producing a large amount of I/O.
* An operator error.

The message line in the job log for the run contains a place for an operator comment. Check it and the program logic and/or contact operations personnel about the cancellation.

137   I/O ERROR ON LAST TAPE DATA SET LABELS READ

-04   An I/O error occurred in writing the end-of-volume label or tape mark.

-08   An I/O error occurred while positioning the tape for label processing.

-0C   An I/O error occurred in reading the trailer label.

-10   An I/O error occurred while positioning the tape at the end of the data set.

-14   An I/O error occurred while reading the header labels for a data set opened INPUT or IN/OUT or while reading the trailer labels for a data set being read backward.

-18   An I/O error occurred in positioning the tape for the first data record in the data set.

-1C   An invalid trailer label appeared during end-of-volume processing; use IEBGENER to copy the tape in an attempt to salvage the data. IEBGENER will copy a tape data set successfully with flawed trailer labels and merely post a return code of 0008.

-20　An invalid header label appeared during end-of-volume processing of a tape being read backward; use IEBGENER in an attempt to salvage the data. IEBGENER will copy a tape data set successfully with flawed last-read labels and merely post a return code of 0008.

Note.　In regard to 137-1C and 137-20 errors some editions of the manuals incorrectly suggest using IEBPTPCH to copy a tape that exhibits I/O errors on trailer labels. This is a typographical error; IEBGENER is the utility intended.

-24　The first data set on the second tape volume mounted as a scratch tape carries an expiration date that has not been reached. MVS prompted the operator for confirmation that the data set could be overwritten but the response was negative. Do not request a specific series of volumes for output—let MVS call for scratch tapes by omitting the VOL parameter—or specify a volume that is known to contain only expired data sets.

-28　An operator responded negatively to an MVS request to write a VOL1 label record on the tape to be used for output.

-2C　The tape being read contains an ASCII label format that is not processed by MVS.

-30　A tape label violation of the standard for that label.

System completion code 137 usually results from flawed media or a malfunctioning device. It can also result from an error that occurred in trailer label writing that escaped detection at the time it happened. Before recreating a data set that cannot be processed try different devices to access it. See the suggested use of IEBGENER under reason codes 1C and 20. Cleaning a tape may restore it to readability.

0187, 0203　SEE COBOL USER COMPLETION CODES AT THE END OF APPENDIX

213　OPEN COULD NOT BE EXECUTED ON DIRECT ACCESS DEVICE

-04, -0C　An I/O error occurred in reading the data set label, the format 1 data set control block or DSCB in the disk volume table of contents, the VTOC. Alternatively, no such item could be associated with the stated data set name. Check the spelling of the DSN and for correct VOL = SER.

-08　The data set is password-protected but the password data set cannot be located on the MVS system residence volume.

-18　An I/O error occurred in writing the format-1 DSCB disk data set label. An I/O error in a disk VTOC is a serious matter and must be reported to the operations group.

-20　The data set contains more than 16 extents; MVS cannot process. It is likely to be a mainframe DOS data set that must be recreated.

-24　A data set has a type of split cylinder allocation not supported by MVS. It is likely to be a mainframe DOS data set that must be recreated.

-28　The data set was assigned to a disk unit that already had 127 active users, the maximum number. Rerun the job; it may have no error.

-2C　The MVS module that handles reason codes 04 and 0C experienced an internal problem. Inform the operating system support group.

A 213 is usually caused by an illogical DD statement and MVS cannot process a data set it has been asked to access. Check JCL for incorrect DSN and VOL = SER and check to see if the data set does, in fact, exist.

214   CLOSE HAD TAPE I/O ERROR

-04   An error occurred in reading a user label.

-08   An error occurred in positioning the tape.

It is likely that a hardware or tape media error exists or that a tape mark is missing after the data. Have the tape cleaned and/or retry the operation on a different tape drive. If these actions fail, recreate the data set.

222   THE OPERATOR CANCELLED THE JOB AND DID NOT REQUEST A DUMP; ASK THE OPERATOR WHY. SEE COMPLETION CODE 122.

237   INVALID BLOCK COUNT OR DATA SET NAME

-04   The block count in the data control block does not match the block count in the trailer label. A block of data has probably been missed or skipped because of a hardware error.

-08   The data set name on the second or a subsequent volume of a tape data set is not correct.

A 237 error stems from a failure in label verification processing. If the data set is not cataloged, an incorrect VOL = SER may have been specified. Check the JCL associated with the job. If the VOL = SER is correct, have the tape cleaned and attempt to process it. If these steps do not resolve the problem, the data set must be recreated.

0295   SEE COBOL USER COMPLETION CODES AT THE END OF APPENDIX

2F3   SYSTEM FAILURE OCCURRED DURING A RUN; RESUBMIT IT.

0303,   0304: SEE COBOL USER COMPLETION CODES AT THE END OF APPENDIX

313   AN I/O ERROR OCCURRED READING VTOC

Only one reason code, 04, is associated with this completion code. It indicates that an I/O error has occurred in attempting to read a format 2 or a format 3 data set control block record, or DSCB, in the disk volume table of contents. A format 2 DSCB supports ISAM organization. Format 3 houses information on the last 13 of the 16 possible data set extents for sequential and partitioned data sets. VTOC errors are serious; inform the operations group. The data set very likely must be recreated.

314   CLOSE HAD A DISK I/O ERROR ON THE VTOC

-04   An I/O error occurred on the volume table of contents or VTOC, or the data set control block accessed for the data set was not a format 1 data set label as expected.

-08   An I/O error occurred on VTOC, as for reason code 04, but user labels were also specified. User labels are allocated an entire track.

A defective volume or device may be involved. Because volumes are no longer demountable on contemporary large disk drives, it is not possible to try the same volume mounted on a different device. Notify your operations group of this occurrence.

317   CLOSE VTOC I/O ERROR CLOSING DATA SET

-04   An I/O error occurred on the volume table of contents or VTOC during the reading of the format 1 DSCB, the disk data set label.

-08   An I/O error or invalid contents of format 1 or format 4 DSCB occurred when reading the VTOC. Format 1 data set control block records constitute the disk data set label and the format 4 record is the master VTOC record that contains summary volume table of contents information.

A defective volume or device may be involved. Because volumes are no longer demountable on contemporary large disk drives, it is not possible to try the same volume mounted on a different device. Notify operations of this occurrence.

322   THE JOB, STEP, OR PROCEDURE EXCEEDED THE TIME LIMIT; THE JOB WAS CANCELLED.

The TIME parameter on the job card, or on the EXEC for the step executing when cancelled, did not allow enough time for completion. If the TIME parameter was not used, the default for the job class did not provide the required time. Check the program for logic loops. If the program has been run successfully on larger equipment and is now being run on older models, it may require more time. If logic is correct the volume of work to be done may require more time; check the installation job class structure for a class that will provide it.

413   OPEN COULD NOT BE EXECUTED

-04   No device was available for the data set or the device was allocated but is now unavailable. Specify another device in the UNIT parameter.

-08   An I/O error occurred while a tape was being positioned.

-0C   An I/O error occurred while reading the tape label.

-10   I/O error occurred while the tape mark was being written.

-18   The data set is to be opened for input but the volume serial number is not specified and the data set is not cataloged.

-1C   The volume sequence number subparameter of VOL in the DD statement is higher than the number of volumes on which the data set resides.

-20   An I/O error occurred while reading the disk volume label; the label was invalid. An I/O error on the format 4 DSCB VTOC; master record may have invalid format. Inform the operations group immediately.

-24   The tape density parameter DEN coded in DCB is not consistent with the density capabilities of the device allocated.

-28   A system error occurred in the module that opens direct data sets.

-2C   A mass storage system (MSS) operation error.

-30   MSS mounted the incorrect volume.

-34   A tape data set other than 1 was specified but no specific volume was indicated.

A system completion code of 413 usually means that an illogical DD statement is present or that MVS cannot locate a specified tape data set. The data set may not have been created in a prior step as assumed. At the root of this situation may be a JCL and data set label conflict.

414, 417   CLOSE HAD AN ERROR IN WRITING A VTOC ENTRY; INFORM THE OPERATIONS GROUP IMMEDIATELY.

422   THE JOB IS TOO LARGE FOR THE CURRENT INSTALLATION STANDARDS; TOO MANY STEPS OR TOO MANY DD STATEMENTS.

The space allocated by the installation for tables, control blocks, and system messages cannot accommodate the length of the JCL that makes up the job. The job stream must be broken down into separate, smaller jobs. This is an older system completion code that deals with limits that do not apply to contemporary versions of MVS.

513   OPEN ERROR FOR THE TAPE DATA SET

-04   OPEN was attempted for a data set already open.

-08   The label format is invalid for the standard describing that label.

-0C   The label on the tape being read is not version 1 or 3 ASCII, or attempted processing for the ASCII label is not supported.

The problem may occur if an attempt is made to open more than one data set on the same tape at the same time.

0519   SEE THE COBOL USER COMPLETION CODES AT THE END OF APPENDIX

522   EXCESSIVE TIME WAS TAKEN IN THE WAIT STATE; THE TIME LIMIT WAS EXCEEDED.

The job step was in the wait state, having no activity for 30 minutes or more. The program may be awaiting resources it cannot receive or a higher priority program may be blocking this one from continuing. The 30-minute time limit can be overridden by coding TIME = 1440 on the JOB or EXEC statement but this removes completely any time limit on the job. Any TIME value less than 1440 does not avoid the 30-minute, wait-state cancellation. This type of cancellation is unusual and is often caused by program error or unavailable data sets.

A 522 can be received during a TSO session for lack of interaction with the host computer for longer than a few minutes; the exact length of time, in the range of 5 to 15 minutes, is specified by the installation. Cursor movement and full screen editing do not constitute host involvement because of the local memory nature of 3270s and their controllers. Only pressing the "enter" key or other PF keys triggers host interaction.

613   OPEN HAD AN I/O ERROR ON MAGNETIC TAPE

-04   An I/O error occurred while positioning the tape.

-08   An I/O error occurred during reading of the tape label.

-0C   An invalid label was read. The tape may have been positioned improperly
      as a result of a prior step that did not complete successfully. Unload it with
      a disposition of (OLD,KEEP) and cause it to be mounted again by attempting
      to access it.

-10   An I/O error occurred while writing a tape label.

-14   An I/O error occurred while writing the tape mark after the header labels.

The tape or drive may need cleaning. Tape cleaning may eliminate the error but
try also to use a different drive because hardware is often at the root of a 613
system completion code.

614   CLOSE ERRORS APPEAR ON THE DATA SET

-04   An I/O error occurred while writing a disk file mark.

-08   The extent number in the data control block indicates a value higher than
      the number of extents in the data set and the location to write the file mark
      could not be determined.

-0C   The MVS CLOSE subsystem was not operating.

-10   The spooled or subsystem data set could not be closed; the failing data
      control block could not be closed but others continued to be processed.

A defective volume or device may be involved. Because volumes are no longer
demountable on contemporary large disk drives, it is not possible to try the same
volume mounted on a different device. Notify operations of this occurrence to
allow media to be replaced or hardware maintenance initiated.

622   EXECUTION WAS ABANDONED FOR THE TASK ENTERED FROM TSO
TERMINAL; ATTN KEY PRESSED

637   AN EOV I/O ERROR OCCURRED IN CONCATENATION OR END OF TAPE

-04   An I/O error occurred in reading the tape label, writing the tape mark, or
      in positioning a tape.

-08   An I/O error occurred in positioning the tape after the user trailer label
      processing.

-0C   Data sets with with unlike characteristics were concatenated; this is not
      permitted.

-10, -14, -18, -1C, -38, -3C, -40, -4C   An I/O error occurred in positioning a tape.

-24, -2C: An I/O error occurred in rewinding a scratch tape.

-34   An I/O error occurred during end-of-volume processing while reading the
      volume label.

-44   An I/O error occurred in checking the sense byte to determine whether the
      write enable ring is on the tape.

Defective media or hardware are probably at fault. Have the tape and drive cleaned.
It may be necessary to recreate the data set on a different volume.

706   THE LINK, ATTACH, LOAD, OR XCTL MODULE IS MARKED "NOT EXECUTABLE"

The linkage editor marked the module "not executable" because of an error it detected or because of instructions that the compiler placed in the object module. Check the diagnostic messages from the linkage edit that created the load module. Note that these messages are relatively small and may be buried among the listing of module names that were used to form the final load module. The compile and/or linkage edit must be rerun correctly.

713   OPEN FOUND THAT THE EXPIRATION DATE OF A DATA SET HAD NOT BEEN REACHED

An attempt was made to overwrite or "MOD onto" and extend an existing data, the expiration date of which had not yet been reached. This can happen if DISP=OLD is specified to overwrite an existing data set or DISP=MOD is specified to extend a data set. The system seeks permission from the operator to take this action, and in most cases operators are under directions *not* to "reply U," which is the console code for "use the data set." Disk data sets are not usually given expiration dates, but tape data sets are in order to secure their retention. FORTRAN programs may require use of the VOL "IN" subparameter because this language opens data sets for both input and output processing depending on the way in which the data set is first accessed.

714, 717.   CLOSE HAD AN ERROR IN WRITING THE TRAILER LABEL OR TAPE MARK

-04, -08, -0C   An I/O error occured in writing the trailer label or tape mark.

The hardware or media are probably defective, or the media and/or tape drive need cleaning. Notify the operations group and rerun the job with a different scratch volume and drive. If the tape has physical damage such as a crimp or tear, it may be necessary to recreate the data set.

722   OUTLIM OR JOBPARM SPECIFICATION IS EXCEEDED

Printline output limits coded in the OUTLIM subparameter of the SYSOUT parameter or the cards or lines limit of the JOBPARM statement have been exceeded. In the JES3 environment limits coded on the STANDARDS or JES3 MAIN statement have been exceeded. Modify the limits and rerun the job if the outputs do not appear to be excessive.

737   I/O ERROR AT END OF DISK DATA SET OR IN SECONDARY ALLOCATION

-04   An I/O error occurred while reading the format 1 DSCB record for the disk data set or the format 1 DSCB record could not be found in the volume table of contents, or VTOC, of the disk volume specified in the DD statement. *This data set control block is the disk data set label.* Check the DSN and VOL=SER parameters of the DD statement for the DDname indicated.

-08   An I/O error occurred while reading the disk volume label, the format 4 DSCB record in the VTOC.

-0C   An I/O error occurred while reading VTOC entries for a concatenated partitioned data set.

-10   An I/O error occurred while writing a file mark on disk.

-14   An I/O error occurred while reading a VTOC entry in preparation for writing data set trailer labels.

-1C   An I/O error occurred while reading a format 3 DSCB, a disk volume table of contents, or VTOC, entry that documents the fourth through sixteenth disk extents for a data set.

-24   A missing PDS member name was detected. The member was named in JCL in concatenation with other data sets. The error message indicates the number of the data set in the concatenated data set list in the DD statement. Check the JCL for an incorrectly spelled member name.

-28   A functional or logical error occurred in a JES3 subsystem; inform systems programming personnel.

-2C   An error occurred while attempting to write the file mark at the end of a disk data set. The number of disk extents that the data set includes, located in the DCBFDAD field of the data control block, is higher than the actual number of extents. Check the assembler logic dealing with the data control block.

-3C   The error routine that handles a "format 1 DSCB record not found" error has itself failed. The format 1 data set control block in the disk volume table of contents, or VTOC, is the data set label and may have an I/O error or be missing. Inform systems programming personnel.

804   GETMAIN COULD NOT FIND ENOUGH VIRTUAL MEMORY. SEE 80A.

806   A LINK, XCTL, ATTACH, OR LOAD PROGRAM OR SVC NOT FOUND

A requested program module could not be found and loaded on request. This may be a program named on an EXEC statement and housed in other than the default load library, but a //STEPLIB DD statement that names the library was omitted from the step or a //JOBLIB DD statement was omitted from the job stream. This can also occur when a dynamically called module cannot be located when called during a program run. Most likely the program name has been misspelled on the EXEC statement or in a source code CALL. It is also possible that the load module was deleted or never created or that an I/O error occurred while searching the directory of the load module partitioned data set. Correct the JCL or replace the load module in the appropriate load library.

80A   R-GETMAIN COULD NOT FIND ENOUGH VIRTUAL MEMORY

Check the REGION value on the JOB or EXEC statement. It may need to be increased, especially if tape blocks as large as 32K or multiple data buffers for sequential VSAM access are being used to increase processing efficiency. The installation default for REGION may not have been updated to take advantage of larger memory sizes, in which case the REGION parameter may need to be coded on most jobs. SIZE is an option with some programs, such as compilers, that if increased causes an increase in required memory resources. System completion code 804 is similar to 80A. See EXEC statement REGION parameter in Appendix A.

813 OPEN FOUND THAT THE DATA SET NAME IN THE LABEL DID NOT MATCH THE SPECIFICATIONS

-04 The DSN parameter and volume serial number are not consistent with the information contained in the tape data set label. Check the spelling of the data set name in JCL and the volume serial number specified. If the tape is cataloged and the volume serial number is not explicitly coded, check to see if the data set may have been deleted but not uncataloged.

If data set access is being attempted by an explicit VOL = SER specification, it may be that the data set was written to the stated volume but has expired and the tape has been reused as scratch to receive another data set. Check the JCL that created the data set for correct use of the LABEL RETPD/EXPDT subparameter. If possible, dump the data set label to see the actual data set name on the tape.

822 A MEMORY REGION REQUESTED COULD NOT BE ALLOCATED

837 AN EOV ERROR OCCURRED AT THE END OF THE VOLUME

-08 All space on the specified volume was used and no additional volumes were specified. More space is needed to house the data set being written. It is necessary to specify more volume serial numbers explicitly or code the VOL parameter to indicate a larger volume count.

-0C The tape volume indicated was mounted but another data set on the volume is currently in use.

878 GETMAIN COULD NOT FIND ENOUGH VIRTUAL MEMORY. SEE 80A.

913 ERROR IN OPENING DATA SET DUE TO A SECURITY PROBLEM

A total of 22 rc values pinpoint the problem as the result of RACF, password, or step catalog omission. Message IEC301A may have been transmitted to the console operator to request entry of a password and the entry made was unsatisfactory to continuation of the job. Correcting this problem involves resolving the local authorization and password protection arrangement for the data set in question.

It is possible to incur a 913 error immediately after an error such as 613-10, which indicates a problem in writing a tape label. Security systems are usually geared to authorization checking by data set name. When an I/O error prevents writing a correct tape label, including the data set name, the security system naturally detects a discrepancy between the data set name qualifiers the job is authorized to access and the potentially corrupted data set name that resides in the tape label as a result of the I/O error.

922 THE JOB WAS CANCELLED BECAUSE OF MACHINE OR SYSTEM FAILURE

Actual processing of the job had begun under the control of an initiator program but an abend was experienced, the console restart key was pressed, or some other machine problem occurred that forced this job and most likely all others to be cancelled. MVS attempts to write a record to SYS1.LOGREC to document the occurrence. There is most likely no error in the program or run; resubmit it.

937   CHECKPOINT DATA SET SECURITY ERROR

A total of 14 rc values pinpoint the problem. This completion code results when a checkpoint data set carries optional security. In connection with access to the data set, the system has issued message IEC254D, IEC255D, or IEC256A to the computer console operator, asking for verification that a given media volume can be used for the checkpoint data set or is no longer secure as a volume for this data set. An unsatisfactory operator response to this prompt can generate this completion code. Check the specific meaning of the rc value in the full *MVS/370 System Messages*, GC38-1008, and determine the basis for the operator's response.

A13   AN OPEN COULD NOT FIND THE TAPE DATA SET REQUESTED

     -04   An unexpected load point was encountered. This can occur in nonlabeled tape processing if there is an error in the file sequence number or if the tape was demounted between processing different files on a multidata set tape.

 -08, -0C   The requested file sequence number is less than the file sequence number of the first file on a standard IBM or ASCII labeled tape. There is probably an error in specifying the volume serial number of a multivolume tape. The operation underway was an open to the start of the file.

-10, -14, -18   A multidata set volume ends well before the desired file. Check to see that the job that wrote the tape actually wrote any or all of the files intended, or whether the file sequence number desired is correct. The job creating the tape may not have completed its operation. Check the volume serial number in the JCL to make sure that the correct tape was specified.

A14   CLOSE HAD AN ERROR RELEASING DISK SPACE

The rc value in this case is superfluous because there is only one possible value for it, namely, 04. A defective media volume or device probably exists. It may be possible to overcome the problem by specifying a different scratch volume or requesting a different device on the DD statement; the device is identified in the job log message that carries the A14 completion code. Installation management should be made aware of this occurrence to focus attention on potentially defective hardware.

A22   AN OPERATOR FORCED CANCELLATION OF THE JOB

The job was killed with a bigger gun than is ordinarily necessary; the operator may have tried to cancel the job with the regular cancel operator command and had not been able to do so. An unusual situation may have developed in which this job was deadlocked with another, each awaiting a needed resource held by the other. It is also possible that an installation standard was violated. No program logic may be in error. Check with the operator and determine why the job was canceled and why the use of the FORCE command was necessary.

A37 AN EOV OPEN DCB WAS CORRUPTED OR CLOSED PRIOR TO USE

-04   SVC 55 was invoked to perform end-of-volume processing but the required data control block was not open.

-08   The data extent block (DEB) is corrupted and does not correctly point to a DCB.

This can occur if a program failure resulted in overlaying the memory occupied by the data control block or if the program closed it. It is also possible that an earlier end-of-volume error triggered data control block closure but did not abend the job because of the specification of "ignore" for that error. This occurs in assembler programs in which the program itself has access to memory areas and manipulations usually not available in higher level languages. Program logic must be examined by using the reason codes as a guide and logic corrections must be made before rerunning the job.

B13 AN ERROR OCCURRED IN OPENING A 1403 PRINTING DEVICE

See message IEC152I, which cites several reason codes that identify various problems that may have occurred with the universal character set (UCS) feature, the forms control buffer (FCB), or dataset SYS1.IMAGELIB in which FCBs reside.

B14 CLOSE FAILED ON A PDS OPENED FOR OUTPUT TO A MEMBER

-04   A duplicate member name.

-0C   The PDS directory is full.

-10   An I/O error occurred while writing the PDS directory.

-14   A DCB inconsistency exists in the program or JCL and the PDS and directory.

-18   There is insufficient memory for a close; increase the REGION size.

Except for a reason code of 18, the PDS probably requires reorganization before the failed program can be rerun. It may be necessary to allocate more directory blocks for the PDS by copying it to a new PDS using IEBCOPY with an appropriate application of the SPACE parameter on the DD statement for the new data set. The deletion of existing members of the PDS and its reorganization may also resolve the problem. See Appendix B for reorganization JCL.

If an error is experienced under TSO in which the B14-0C "PDS directory is full" message is received, a trick is possible to complete the "save" of the data set at the expense of TSO statistics. TSO normally carries 42 bytes for every member entry in the directory but only 12 bytes are needed for PDS operation; the extra 30 bytes carry the statistics that appears for each member when a member list is presented. The statistics are optional and can be removed. If this is done, many more member entries will fit into the same number of directory blocks.

Place the cursor in midscreen and press PF2 to enter split screen mode. Use the TSO/ISPF 3.5 function to remove statistics from the data set that you are editing on the top portion of the screen. This may take a few minutes if you have several members in the data set. When the function finishes, press PF3 to end the split screen and you will be able to save the data set you were editing. Then reorganize the data set.

This cure to a full directory in a TSO editing session causes the loss of the user statistics for the data set. If TSO function 3.5 is then used to reset statistics for the members in the PDS, all statistics will reflect the current date and time. Information on the last update date and time of each member will have been lost but fresh statistics will begin to accrue from this point on.

B37   DISK VOLUME IS OUT OF SPACE, CANNOT WRITE OUTPUT

-04   All space requested by the program on the disk volume has been used; MVS wants to mount another volume for the data set but cannot do so because the present disk is permanently mounted or is in use for other data sets of the failing job or other jobs. It is possible that space exists on the volume but that the volume table of contents, or VTOC, is filled. For a tape volume B37-04 indicates that no more records can be written to the tape for physical reasons or that this is the last of the 255 possible reels to which a single data set can spread.

-08   Overlapping disk extent or inappropriate split cylinder allocations exist; these are technical problems in space allocation on the volume typical of mainframe DOS-created disk volumes. The data set must be recreated in a format that MVS can process.

-0C   The disk unit to which the data set was assigned already has 127 jobs associated with it, which is the maximum that can be handled at one time. Rerun the job.

A B37 usually means an incorrect space allocation, specification of a particular disk volume that is reserved, or a program logic loop involving a WRITE statement. You received all the primary space you requested and as much of the secondary space as MVS could provide, but this was still not enough. For rc 04 check the program logic and JCL space specifications first. For codes 08 and 0C see message IEC030I which prescribes corrective actions. The UNIT count subparameter, ordinarily not coded and therefore defaulted to 1, can be coded as 2 or greater to provide secondary allocations on additional disk volumes for a sequential data set. See *VOL and UNIT Parameter Interplay* in Chapter 9, page 155.

C13   OPEN ERROR ON CONCATENATED PDS OR A PDS NOT ON THE DISK DEVICE

-10   Output to a concatenated PDS is attempted. PDSs cannot be concatenated for output.

-18   An open for input has been attempted for concatenated PDSs but one or more of the PDSs are not on disk. Concatenated PDSs must have like attributes, including being on disk, not tape.

It is also possible to encounter completion code C13 on certain types of I/O errors affecting graphics devices or the VTOC of a disk volume. If the rc items do not appear relevant, check the device open logic and/or consult with operations personnel to see if a hardware problem exists with the disk device.

C37 DOS-CREATED DATA SET CANNOT BE READ BY MVS; RECREATE IT

-04   The next volume of the data set contained more than the 16 allowable extents.

-08   The next volume of the data set exhibits a nonallowable form of split cylinder space allocation.

D37 PRIMARY DISK SPACE WAS EXCEEDED AND NO SECONDARY SPACE ALLOCATION WAS SPECIFIED

There is only one rc, 04, associated with a system completion code of D37. In writing a data set to a disk device, JCL specified only a primary disk space allocation, which was exceeded. Change the DD statement associated with the data set in JCL to specify more primary space or provide a secondary allocation of space. Before rerun it may be necessary to delete and uncatalog the partly written data set created by the failed run.

E37 PRIMARY AND SECONDARY SPACE ALLOCATIONS WERE FILLED

-04   Not enough storage volumes were specified, a PDS was being written and filled the volume, a PDS being written used its maximum 16 extents, or the disk volume table of contents, or VTOC, is full. A PDS can reside on only one disk volume; it cannot extend across volumes even if more than one volume is provided with the VOL or UNIT parameters. E37-04 can be received even when the disk has free space if the VTOC is allocated too little space when it is established by the installation.

-08   The next volume of a multivolume disk data set is not capable of receiving the data set because of a duplicate data set name or lack of space.

-0C   Installation procedures prevent the extension of the data set.

An E37 indicates a lack of appropriate disk resources to receive output. For a batch program check the logic for a loop involving a write statement. If the reason code is 0C, confirm the installation standards that prevent data set extension and change the space allocation parameters in the JCL to a larger value; then rerun the job.

An E37 will be experienced under TSO when a TSO library partitioned data set is depleted of free space and needs to be reorganized. When ending the edit of a member, TSO saves the member. It is at this point that the E37 will be encountered. To end the edit enter CANCEL on the command line, abandoning the edit. Some of the most recent updates will be lost. Then submit the batch PDS reorganization JCL listed in Appendix B. Note that if the PDS is underallocated in terms of primary or secondary space you can use the symbolic parameters in the PDS reorganization JCL to implement more appropriate space values. A part of TSO housekeeping chores is to keep a watch on PDS status via TSO/ISPF function 3.2 and submit PDS reorganizations ahead of complete free space depletion, to avoid receiving an E37.

It is also possible to compress a PDS as it is being edited by using the compress data set option of TSO function 3.1. Initiate split screen mode with the cursor high on the screen and use the bottom portion of the screen to enter function 3.1. Perform an online compress on the PDS in which the member being edited resides. When the compress completes, end split screen and then end the edit on the member. This alternative is available only if your installation provides the online compress. Ordinarily online compress is avoided. For larger PDSs or work on a heavily loaded system online compress can take a long time to complete, and during its operation data set integrity can be lost if the terminal is disturbed or the system interrupted. The batch reorganization runs faster and can be submitted for unattended operation but it cannot run when a data set is being edited. Even if submitted from split screen operation the batch reorganization will not execute until after the data set is released from the edit.

An E37-04 can also indicate that the disk VTOC is full. There is no recovery possible from this condition. If it is encountered during an attempt to save the results of a TSO edit, the changes are lost. Notify installation management immediately.

F13   INCORRECT ABEND CODE ON FAILED OPEN

Opening of a device has failed, but the termination code passed to the system's problem determination routine by the OPEN macro instruction is not recognizable. Register 12 contains this code. A problem in system support programming is hiding the underlying application problem. Check the associated DCBs for consistency and errors associated with system completion codes ending with 13.

F14   INCORRECT ABEND CODE ON FAILED CLOSE

Closing of a device has failed, but the termination code passed to the system's problem determination routine by the CLOSE macro instruction is not recognizable. Register 12 contains this code. A problem in system support programming is hiding the underlying application problem. Check for errors associated with system completions codes ending with 14.

F15   INCORRECT ABEND CODE ON FAILED CLOSE OF PDS

Closing of a device has failed, but the termination code passed to the system's problem determination routine by the STOW macro instruction, which updates the partitioned data set directory, is not recognizable. Register 12 contains this code. A problem in system support programming is hiding the underlying application problem. Check for errors documented with system completion codes 115, 215, and 315.

F37   INCORRECT ABEND CODE ON FAILED EOV TASK

Closing of a device has failed, but the termination code passed to the system's problem determination routine by the EOV macro instruction is not recognizable. Register 12 contains this code. A problem in system support programming is hiding the underlying application problem. Check for circumstances that would otherwise result in the receipt of system completion codes ending with 37.

Fxx   INVALID SUPERVISOR CALL (SVC); xx = HEXADECIMAL VALUE

A call was made to an invalid supervisor call number. The SVC number may be entirely nonexistent or may simply not be installed on a given computer system. The SVC number is expressed in hexadecimal in the last two positions of the completion code; this may be confusing because SVCs are specified in assembler code as decimal numbers. For example, SVC 223 is typically not assigned. Use of SVC 223 results in the receipt of system completion code FDF because the decimal value 223 is DF in hexadecimal.

COBOL USER RETURN CODES

In certain circumstances COBOL programs that have been successfully compiled will post an unusual user return code. This happens because, unseen by the programmer, the COBOL compiler builds into the object deck and the resultant load module the logic to post relatively unusual return codes as an indication of specialized execution-time errors. These code values are documented in Appendix K of the *IBM OS/VS COBOL Compiler and Library Programmer's Guide*, SC28-6483, but they are easy to overlook.

The COBOL return codes are user return codes, not system completion codes. When they are posted, they appear as four-digit decimal numbers, not in hexadecimal, and they are prefaced by U or USER. The information here is placed with the system completion codes because, in a manner of speaking, these are COBOL completion codes in intent, even though they are referred to as user abends.

0187   INCORRECT COMPILER-GENERATED VERB TABLE

If this error occurs, it is caused by an internal problem in the compiler itself and results from an invalid entry in the table that the compiler built to count verb occurrences. IBM software support personnel must be notified to correct the compiler.

0203   DIVIDE BY ZERO

Normally a system completion code of 0CB results when an attempt is made to divide by zero or by so small a quantity that the result is too large to be stored. COBOL support module ILBOXDI also intercepts this error and may issue this return code if it occurs. The error can be avoided by using the ON SIZE ERROR option or by checking explicitly before dividing to make sure that the divisor is not zero or a small quantity less than one.

0295   RETURN CODE HAS BEEN CHANGED FROM POSITIVE TO NEGATIVE

Issued by a COBOL service routine, this may appear after a message to a terminal in an interactive compile mode on TSO.

0303 VSAM DATA SET CATALOG SYNCHRONIZATION ERROR

A VSAM data set being processed appears to be out of synchronization with its catalog entry as far as its last closure time stamp. This may also be detected by IDCAMS when it is invoked to perform a VERIFY on the data set. Checking file status after the OPEN of the data set detects this error in a more customary manner.

0304 VSAM DATA SET INDEX SYNCHRONIZATION ERROR

A VSAM data set being processed is out of synchronization with its index. The time stamps on the base cluster and index do not match, indicating that one has been updated independently as a result of prior system interruption or incorrect restoration of items to disk. Checking file status after OPEN of the data set detects this error in a more customary manner.

0519 AN ERROR IN LOGIC FLOW, OFTEN IN CALLABLE MODULES

COBOL user abend 0519 is the most commonly encountered of these codes and is usually the result of inconsistent use of the DYN or RES compiler PARM options. The underlying error is that the next instruction to be executed is not identifiable. The error can also result in a CICS program if it issues a GOBACK statement instead of EXEC CICS RETURN. Although a routine CALLed by a CICS program must issue a GOBACK to return control to its caller, no CICS program itself can issue GOBACK.

If an 0519 user return code is received, check to make sure that called modules appropriately contain EXIT PROGRAM or GOBACK statements and that use of DYN, needed for dynamically callable modules, is consistent. For a CICS program review thoroughly the flow of control to determine where execution of EXEC CICS RETURN is needed but missing.

1301 AN I/O ERROR FOR A DATA SET AND NO DECLARATIVE WAS CODED

3361 INTERNAL ERROR IN A COBOL PROGRAM NAME AND SYMDMP OPTION

3440 INSUFFICIENT MAIN STORAGE OR INVALID GETMAIN/FREEMAIN

A library subroutine has insufficient work space. This user return code is associated with error message IKF993I. The cure for it is to increase the REGION size parameter on the EXEC statement that executes the program.

3505 FLOW OF CONTROL ERROR IN A MULTILANGUAGE ENVIRONMENT

This error occurs with an assembler program that is CALLing a COBOL program. The assembler program needs to issue a CALL to ILBOSTP0 before CALLing a COBOL program but this has not been done. The assembler program must be corrected. The CALL to ILBOSTP0 is not performed when the assembler program invokes the COBOL program with a LINK or ATTACH.

The effect of the assembler CALL to ILBOSTP0 is to inform all COBOL programs invoked by the assembler program that they are subprograms; ordinarily the first COBOL program invoked assumes that it is the main program, an assumption that conflicts with its CALL by an assembler routine. ILBOSTP0 loads the COBOL subroutine communications area named ILBOCOM. A COBOL program that begins execution and finds this area already initialized "knows" that it is not the first or main program in the run unit; if it does not find ILBOCOM, it initializes it and assumes that it, itself, is the main program. The distinction is important because it determines whether STOP RUN processing is invoked when GOBACK is issued in the COBOL program.

A similar-named module, ILBOSTT0, is also involved in the resolution of this problem. This module releases all storage acquired by a COBOL program when it returns control to the assembler module that invoked it, and is invoked when the COBOL Compiler "ENDJOB" parameter is used. After a CALL to a COBOL program used as a subprogram by an assembler routine and compiled with ENDJOB, the assembler program should issue a DELETE to release the memory in which ILBOSTT0 resides because it does not delete itself.

Problems of this variety are commonly encountered when assembler-based fourth generation languages are interfaced to locally written COBOL modules. The problem can be resolved by creating an intermediate module in assembler that is called by the fourth generation program, issues the call to ILBOSTP0, and calls the COBOL program. It is interesting to note that some otherwise skilled assembler programmers are not aware of COBOL's use of ILBOCOM in the capacity indicated, and it is possible to encounter this problem even in quite sophisticated fourth generation languages that tout the ability to interface readily with COBOL routines.

APPENDIX G

Disk Device Track and Cylinder Capacities and Optimal Block Size Ranges

Figure G.1 provides an overall summary of disk device characteristics spanning the entire time period from the introduction of the first System/360 computer to the present. Figure G.2 homes in on the essential matter of efficient disk block size ranges for the IBM 3350 and 3380, the two disk devices presently in widespread use. Figure G.3 is a table of raw block size and track capacities; its application to JCL composition for disk data sets is automated in the computational aids of Appendix D.

DISK DEVICE TYPES AND CHARACTERISTICS	2314	3330 Mod-1	3330 Mod-11	3350	3380	3380 Mod-E
Year available	1964	1972	1973	1977	1981	1985
Removable media?	yes	yes	yes	no	no	no
Capacity in megabytes	29.1	100	200	317.5	630.2	1,260.4
Number of tracks	4,000	7,676	15,352	16,650	13,275	26,550
Number of cylinders	200	404	808	555	885	1,770
Tracks per cylinder	20	19	19	30	15	15
Bytes per track	7,294	13,030	13,030	19,069	47,476	47,476
Bytes per cylinder	145,880	247,570	247,570	572,070	712,140	712,140
PDS directory blocks per track	17	28	28	36	46	46
VTOC DSCB records per track	25	39	39	47	53	53
Average head movement time, in milliseconds	75	30	30	25	16	16
Media rotation time, in milliseconds	25	16.7	16.7	16.7	16.7	16.7
Data transfer rate, megabytes per second	.312	.806	.806	1.1	3.0/6.0	3.0/6.0

FIGURE G.1. Disk device types and characteristics

BLOCK SIZE RANGES PROVIDING 90% OR GREATER STORAGE EFFICIENCY

Number of blocks[1] per track	3350 disk length range min	max	maximum efficiency	3380 disk length range min	max	maximum efficiency
1	17,163	19,069	100%	42,729	47,476[2]	100%
2	8,582	9,442	99%	21,365	23,476	98.9%
3	5,721	6,233	98%	14,243	15,476	97.8%
4	4,291	4,628	97%	10,683	11,476	96.7%
5	3,433	3,665	96%	8,546	9,076	95.6%
6	2,861	3,024	95%	7,122	7,476	94.5%
7	2,452	2,565	94%	6,105	6,356	93.7%
8	2,146	2,221	93%	5,342	5,492	92.5%
9	1,907	1,954	92%	4,748	4,820	91.4%
10	1,717	1,740	91%	4,273	4,276	90.1%

Copyright 1987 J.Janossy -- Practical MVS JCL, ISBN 0-471-83648-6 (John Wiley & Sons)

FIGURE G.2.   Disk block size ranges providing 90% or greater storage efficiency

RAW DISK TRACK CAPACITY FOR 3330, 3350, AND 3380 DEVICES

Blocks per track[1]	------ 3330 ------		------ 3350 ------		------ 3380 ------	
	Block length	Track capacity	Block length	Track capacity	Block length	Track capacity
1	13,030[3]	13,030	19,069	19,069	47,476[2]	47,476
2	6,447[3]	12,894	9,442[3]	18,884	23,476	46,952
3	4,253	12,759	6,233[3]	18,699	15,476	46,428
4	3,156	12,624	4,628	18,512	11,476	45,904
5	2,498	12,490	3,665	18,325	9,076	45,380
6	2,059	12,354	3,024	18,144	7,476[3]	44,856
7	1,745	12,215	2,565	17,955	6,356[3]	44,492
8	1,510	12,080	2,221	17,763	5,492	43,936
9	1,327	11,943	1,954	17,586	4,820	43,380
10	1,181	11,810	1,740	17,400	4,276	42,760
11	1,061	11,671	1,565	17,215	3,860	42,460
12	962	11,544	1,419	17,028	3,476	41,712
13	877	11,401	1,296	16,848	3,188	41,444
14	805	11,270	1,190	16,660	2,932	41,048
15	742	11,130	1,098	16,470	2,676	40,140
16	687	10,992	1,018	16,288	2,484	39,744
17	639	10,863	947	16,099	2,324	39,508
18	596	10,728	884	15,912	2,164	38,952
19	557	10,583	828	15,732	2,004	38,076
20	523	10,460	777	15,540	1,876	37,520
21	491	10,311	731	15,351	1,780	37,380
22	463	10,186	690	15,180	1,684	37,048
23	437	10,051	652	14,996	1,588	36,524
24	413	9,912	617	14,808	1,492	35,808
25	391	9,775	585	14,625	1,396	34,900
26	371	9,646	555	14,430	1,332	34,632
27	352	9,504	528	14,256	1,268	34,236
28	335	9,380	502	14,056	1,204	33,712
29	318	9,222	478	13,862	1,140	33,060
30	303	9,090	456	13,680	1,076	32,280
31	289	8,959	436	13,516	1,044	32,364
32	276	8,832	416	13,312	980	31,360
33	263	8,679	398	13,134	948	31,284
34	252	8,568	381	12,954	916	31,144
35	241	8,435	365	12,775	852	29,820

FIGURE G.3. Raw disk track capacity for 3330, 3350, and 3380 devices

Blocks per track[1]	3330		3350		3380	
	Block length	Track capacity	Block length	Track capacity	Block length	Track capacity
36	230	8,280	349	12,564	820	29,520
37	220	8,140	335	12,395	788	29,156
38	211	8,018	321	12,198	756	28,728
39	202	7,878	308	12,012	724	28,236
40	194	7,760	296	11,840	692	27,680
41	186	7,626	284	11,644	660	27,060
51	123	6,273	192	9,792	436	22,236
57	95	5,415	152	8,664	340	19,380
62	77	4,774	125	7,750	276	17,112
65	67	4,355	111	7,215	244	15,860
68	58	3,944	98	6,664	212	14,416
71	50	3,550	86	6,106	180	12,780
78	33	2,574	61	4,758	116	9,048
83	23	1,909	46	3,818	84	6,972
93	6	558	22	2,046	20	1,860

Notes:

1. A block can consist of one or more logical records.

2. This value exceeds the MVS I/O block size limit of 32,760 bytes and is not available through normal programming methods. Use 23,476 as the maximum attainable block size for 3380 disk devices, which will place two blocks on each track.

3. A maximum block size of 6,233 on a 3350 establishes the "compromise" target block size for a mixture of 3330, 3350, and 3380 devices. This target provides for housing two blocks on a 3330 track, three blocks on a 3350 track, and seven blocks on a 3380 track. The maximum efficiency of storage for a block of 6,233 bytes is 95.6% on a 3330, 98% on a 3350, and 91.9% on a 3380.

FIGURE G.3. (con't.)

INDEX